THE WORKS OF PINDAR

THE
WORKS OF PINDAR

TRANSLATED, WITH LITERARY AND CRITICAL COMMENTARIES

BY

LEWIS RICHARD FARNELL

HONORARY FELLOW AND FORMERLY RECTOR OF EXETER COLLEGE, OXFORD, FELLOW
OF THE BRITISH ACADEMY, D.LITT. OXFORD, HONORARY DOCTOR OF THE
UNIVERSITIES OF GENEVA, ST. ANDREWS, AND TRINITY COLLEGE, DUBLIN
CORRESPONDING MEMBER OF THE GERMAN ARCHÆOLOGICAL INSTITUTE

★

TRANSLATION IN RHYTHMICAL PROSE WITH LITERARY COMMENTS

MACMILLAN AND CO., LIMITED
ST. MARTIN'S STREET, LONDON
1930

COPYRIGHT

PRINTED IN GREAT BRITAIN
BY R. & R. CLARK, LIMITED, EDINBURGH

COLLEGIO EXONIENSI

HUNC SENECTUTIS MEAE FRUCTUM

DEDICO

PREFACE

WHEN one ventures to bring forth a new edition of a classical author, three reasons may be urged as explanation or apology: first, that his works are of intrinsic importance; secondly, that existing editions are inadequate; thirdly, that one has some special competence for the task.

The importance of Pindar in the realm of poetry has never been contested, but has been always most vividly felt by those who can read him. He is one of the four spiritual reasons for setting ourselves to the toil of mastering the Greek language, Homer, Aeschylus, and Plato being the other three. But of all the great poets Pindar has the fewest readers, even in the ranks of scholars; and the main reason for this is the difficulty, real or supposed, of his style and vocabulary.

But a further contributory cause for this is the inadequacy of our existing editions and commentaries. To depreciate the work of the scholars of the past has always the air of ingratitude. But our philological world has generally agreed that this poet, above all others of our classical inheritance, stands in need of more penetrating interpretation than he has yet received; and that a full edition of his works, with a literary and philological exegesis illuminated by the light of the most recent research and discovery, is the chief desideratum in the field of classical study. To substantiate this, some discussion of previous 'Pindaric' literature would be necessary; but this will be dealt with more appropriately in my second volume.

The third reason, the competence of the new editor, is a blushful subject for the editor himself to handle. But one does not set oneself to so long and heavy a task as this without counting the cost and doing all that is possible to equip oneself for its adequate performance. To interpret a great poet, it is necessary first to love him; and I have loved Pindar for more than fifty years. Also, for many years I was the only one of our classical teachers in Oxford who gave regular lectures on the odes; and my class was always a small group of brilliant young scholars, such as stimulate the ardour of a lecturer. Long continued exposition, accompanied with critical discussion, throws light on many dark places and reveals hidden beauties. And my main life-study in the classical field, the study of Greek religion and mythology, seemed to give me one special advantage in the interpretation of Pindar which the former editors had lacked; for religion and mythology enter deeply into the very texture of Pindar's poetry. His muse was learned in the heroic past and religious background of Hellenic life; and though all his antiquarian lore was transmuted into poetry, his interpreter must be familiar with many a highway and by-way of prehistoric Greece. But no one can finally judge his own work: τεκμαίρει χρῆμ᾿ ἕκαστον.

The editor of such a classic may appeal to one or both of two different groups of readers, on the one hand to the wider cultivated public, lovers of high literature but unable to read the author in the original, and on the other to the small fraternity of expert scholars who demand severe exposition and minute critical accuracy. I have planned this work with a twofold ambition and have assayed a double task hitherto unattempted, so that I might satisfy both demands, the popular and the scholarly. For there is a call on the Pindar-specialist to propagate Pindar, the older attempts having obviously failed. Our more cultivated public needs him and deserves him; and as they will never learn enough Greek for immediate communion with him, the propagandist must try through the medium of translation to bring them into indirect contact with the poet's light-rays. For he warmed and thrilled his own world, and his radio-activity was so powerful that a portion of it—one might hope—may be transmitted to our people through the medium of an alien language, if only the transmitter has the skill.

Therefore, I offer this first volume to the lovers of literature who are Greekless, as well as to the student struggling with the difficulties of the Greek. It contains a translation of all the preserved and newly discovered works of Pindar, including all the fragments that are preserved sufficiently for literary effect; also a general literary comment on each ode, with an attempted appreciation of its poetic value, and with such exposition of the circumstances, allusions, and the nexus of the parts as seemed necessary to the understanding of the poem as an organic whole. At the same time I have tried to avoid all parade of learning and—as far as possible—controversial argument, so as not to blur the reader's literary impression. Therefore, many of my statements and a few of my renderings, where I have taken my own line, must appear dogmatic and unproved, the more detailed argumentation and discussion of difficulties of text and subject-matter being reserved for my second volume; which will, I hope, appear next year.

The first question was the mode of the translation, the frame in which it should be cast, a question for long and anxious thought. Having two essential aims, to produce a version that should have the quality of literature and at the same time to keep so close to the words of Pindar as to satisfy the demands of the earnest scholar wrestling with the text, I had to choose a medium in which it might be possible to fulfil both these. Any rhyming metre was therefore impossible for my purpose, even if I had the skill to use one. The brilliant rhyming translation of Pindar's four books of the odes by my friend Charles Billson, who had already won laurels by his translation of Virgil, shows us how much can be done in this line; he gives us a beautiful paraphrase of Pindar, in English form, the most charming that has yet been produced. But when a translator has to rhyme, he has to make digressions from his author's track—as Gawain Douglas says: "The ryme causis me to mak digressioun sum tyme", and to say what otherwise he would not have said: he cannot follow his master's lead step by step, and he cannot grapple. One may also doubt whether a rhyming metre is suitable for the unrhymed poetry of Greece, and more especially for Pindar's. For in his metric system there is found nothing that corresponds to the regular recurring 'hammer-tap' of rhyme; his verses have the varied freedom, the undulating rise and fall of a bird's flight. For the same reason blank verse is unsuitable as a vehicle of translation, as being too uniform and monotonous, however one may vary the pause. But fortunately we have another art-mode of speech, that is neither rhyme nor measured verse, yet capable in a high degree of conveying poetic beauty, namely, the rhythmic prose-period—such as abounds in our Bible and still more in the Apocrypha. The appreciative ear is haunted by the musical cadence of many of these, and we feel in them the charm of word-rhythm untrammelled by rhyme or metre. I have therefore adopted this as the English art-speech that gives the nearest rendering of the uncapturable movements of the Greek lyric. But in the composition of rhythmic prose there is always the risk of falling inadvertently into metre, especially into 'blank verse'; and I fear I have not always avoided this. Also, though one cannot always be sure where Pindar intended his musical-metric phrase to end, I have arranged the sentences like the verses in our Bible, so as to give to the reader the impression of a poetic word-system in the original.

Having Biblical cadences in his head, a translator will naturally fall into the use of their archaic language. And in rendering Pindar one has this special justification for archaic for his contemporaries. And our great Poet-Laureate, doing so, that he composed in a language that was already whom we have recently lost, has pointed out in the preface to his last inspired work how much the poetic sentence gains in euphony and 'eurhythmy' by preserving some of the archaic endings of verb and participle.

As I shall probably incur some censure for my tran-
scription of Greek personal and place-names, I must make
clear my principle and defend it. All such names should
now be transcribed directly into our corresponding English
letters, and they should not be deformed by Latinisation
before presenting them to a Greekless or to a Greek-in-
structed public. We are well past the folly of miscalling
Athena Minerva, and Ares Mars; it is time we shook off
the weakness of not daring to write Greek names as the
Greeks wrote and spoke them, but only as the Latins chose
to transform them: for to change 'os' into 'us', 'k' into 'c',
'ai' into 'ae', 'u' into 'y' does not make the name come
easier to our lips or seem more natural to our eyes:
'Alalkomenai', which is Greek, is not more difficult for us
than 'Alalcomenae', which is Latin, both names being
equally unfamiliar to the ordinary reader. It is worth re-
forming our practice for the sake of euphony and eurhythmy:
we are thus saved from the barbaric discordance of 'Ajax',
and we can take pleasure in the music of 'Aias'; and we
need no longer be guilty of such a terrifying plural as
'Ajaxes', having at hand the melodious Greek 'Aiantes'.
And in making the reform we should be thorough and not
compromise, as the committee of the Hellenic Society
proposes. Or, to avoid pedantry, our only compromise
should be that we preserve the English or Anglo-Latin
forms of those Greek names that have become naturalised
and part of our modern nomenclature, Alexander, Aeschylus,
Aristotle, Athens, Olympia, Crete, etc. The haters of change
will complain that we are obscuring the record of the fact
that we came to our knowledge of Greek originally through
a Latin source. The fact was important in the history of
culture, but detrimental to our true knowledge of Greek;
and it can be sufficiently preserved in a record in a library
or museum.

I have concluded the volume with a general account of
Pindar's life and work and the influences that shaped it.
Such a disquisition can only have value if the poet's own
message, as expressed in his poems, has been able to get

through to the reader. I shall be anxious and curious to know from fair-minded critics if I have helped to transmit it. It is a sign of some good augury for me that I have taken great pleasure in the work myself. But that pleasure may have been only a mirage of the climate of Morocco, where I began this volume sitting within view of Atlas, in a sunny radiance that seemed appropriate and congenial to the Muse of Pindar. My reserve of hope is that if this volume fails as literature, still, combined with the second, it may contribute something to Pindaric scholarship.

L. R. FARNELL.

PARKSTONE,
 May 1930.

LIST OF ILLUSTRATIONS

THE OLYMPIAN ODES

THE golden melodies are locked within the poet's Greek and cannot be delivered in another tongue. Only those who have the key can enter the inner chamber of the song.

> Ἐμοὶ δ ὁποίαν ἀρετὰν ἔδωκε Πότμος ἄναξ,
> εὖ οἶδ᾽ ὅτι χρόνος ἔρπων πεπρωμέναν τελέσει.

Nem. iv. 66.

OLYMPIAN I

To Hieron of Syracuse

"BEST of all things is water,
And gold as the peerless pride of wealth gleameth through
    the darkness like blazing fire.
But if, oh heart of mine,
Thou art fain to speak of contests,
Then look for no other star
Shining in daylight through the desert of the sky blither
    than the sun;   5
Nor let us tell of any strife more noble than the Olympian.
'Tis thence the many-voiced hymn ariseth that enfoldeth
    the thoughts of the craftsmen of song,
To raise the loud chant in praise of the son of Kronos,
When they have come to the rich and blessed home of 10
    Hieron,
Who wieldeth the sceptre of judgment in fair-fruited Sicily,
Culling the flower of all excellence,
And delighteth himself in the choicest bloom of poesy,   15
Even in such strains as we are playing in unison around
    his friendly board.
But (oh, Pindar!), take from its peg the Dorian lyre,
If the fair renown of Pisa and of his horse Pherenikos
    chargèd thy mind with the burden of sweetest thoughts,
When he sped in the course by Alpheus' stream,   20
Setting to the task his limbs untouchèd of the lash,
And brought his lord to the arms of Victory,
The King of Syracuse who delighteth in the steed.
And his fame shineth bright in that settlement of goodly
    men that Lydian Pelops founded;

25 Pelops whom Poseidon loved, the mighty girder of the earth,
   From that hour when the fateful goddess of childbirth
       drew him forth from the purifying bath,
   One gleaming shoulder fitted with a plate of ivory.
   Verily many things are marvellous,
   And, I ween, the tradition of men beguileth oft,
   Legends fair-fashioned with the embroidery of lies,
   Surpassing the measure of true speech.
30 But the spirit of Beauty, which fashioneth for mortal man
       all his delights,
   Shedding honour (where it listeth) hath found a means for
       the unbelievable to be oftentimes believed.
   Natheless the days to come are the wisest witnesses of truth.
35 But 'tis seemly for a man to speak fair words about the
       powers divine,
   For lesser is then his reproach.
   Oh, thou son of Tantalos!
   I will tell of thee a tale counter to the tale of old,
   How that when thy father bade thee to a most righteous
       feast and to Mount Sipulos beloved,
   Furnishing a banquet to the gods in requital for theirs,
40 Then the Lord of the gleaming trident, smitten with yearn-
       ing love for thee,
   Bore thee away, and with golden horses wafted thee to the
       high-placed hall of wide-ruling Zeus:
   Whither in the next generation
45 Came also Ganymedes to pay the same debt of love to Zeus.
   But when thou hadst gone from their sight,
   And men searching far and wide never restored thee to thy
       mother,
   Then some one of the jealous neighbours forthwith whispered
       a despiteful tale;
   How that with a knife they shred thy limbs into water
       kindled to the boiling pitch,
50 And distributed thy flesh round the tables as a dainty
       second course, and all ate of it.
   But 'tis hard for me to charge foul gluttony to one of the
       Blessed Ones.

I abhor the thought.
'Tis often seen that little gain befalleth evil-speakers.
If the watchers of Olympos ever honourèd any mortal man,
That man was Tantalos.   55
But he had not the power to stomach his mighty portion
   of bliss:
And in surfeit of wantonness he brought upon himself
   exceeding measure of woe,
To wit, a heavy stone that the All-Father hung above him,
Which ever deeming will smite him on the head,
His mind wandereth far from the paths of pleasantness.
This life that he hath is yoked with desperate pain,
The fourth among three other torments,   60
For that he stole the nectar and ambrosia of the Immortals,
Wherewith they made him deathless,
And gave them to his boon-companions.
But if any man thinketh when he doeth some sin to escape
   God's eye, he erreth.
Wherefore the Immortals thrust forth his son from heaven, 65
To fare once more among the swift-fated tribes of men.
And now when he was nearing the full flower of his growth,
And the fringe of down was darkening his cheek,
He bethought him of a marriage open to all comers,
Namely, to win the glorious bride Hippodameia from her 70
   father, King of Pisa.
And going alone in the dusky twilight to the edge of the
   grey sea,
He called upon the loud-thundering God of the fair trident;
And forthwith He appeared close to his hand,
And Pelops spake to Him—   75
'If, oh Poseidon, the sweet gifts of love inure to any grati-
   tude,
Cumber the brazen spear of Oinomaos,
Waft me on the swiftest of chariots to Elis,
And bring me to the goal of victory.
For thirteen men, suitors of his daughter, hath he slain,
   and ever putteth off her marriage-day.   80
Dire peril calleth not for a faint-hearted man.

But of us men who are doomed to die,
Why should any sit at home in darkness
And nurse his old age in sodden ease, without renown, in
    vain,
Having no part in aught fair and noble?
Nay, but for me, I will abide the hazard of this contest;
85 But do Thou grant achievement according to heart's
    desire.'
So spake he, nor did he deal in speech of no fulfilment,
But for his pride and glory the God gave him a golden
    chariot and winged steeds of tireless flight.
And he laid low the might of Oinomaos, and won the
    maiden, as partner of his bed:
Who bore him six sons, leaders of the host, with souls
    aflame for deeds of valour.
And now as he lieth in rest by the ford of Alpheus,
90 He hath fellowship in the fair blood-offerings,
His tomb being in near neighbourhood by the altar of the
    High God, whereunto men from all lands come:
And the glory of the Olympian contests in the running-
    courses of Pelops
Sendeth a gleam throughout the world:
95 'Tis there that swiftness of foot is tried in strife,
And the highest pitch of strength, bold to brook all toil.
But the man who conquereth there
Hath the sweet calm of repose, at least as touching contests,
    shed around his latter days.
And the blessing that ever befalleth day by day,
100 Cometh as the highest bliss for each mortal man.
'Tis meet for me to crown Hieron with a hymn of praise
    for his horse-victory in strains of Aeolic music.
And I am sure at heart that I shall never glorify in the
    far-famed pages of my songs any guest-friend of all
    men now living a greater master of all noble lore than
105   Hieron,
And withal a lord more supreme in power.
Some God is thy warder, Hieron,
And taketh special heed and thought for thy noble projects.

And if he fail thee not too soon,
I have hope one day to sing the glorious fulfilment of a
    still sweeter thought with the aid of a certain swift 110
    chariot,
Having devisèd a helpful path of poesy, when I have come
    to the far-seen hill of Kronos.'
So be it, then; for me the Muse is rearing to full strength
    the mightiest thunder-bolt of song.
Divers men are great in divers ways,
But the topmost fortune is the crowning boon for kings.
Gaze not too keenly into the far beyond:
May it be thine to tread the heights during this span of 115
    life,
And mine, pre-eminent in the poet's craft in every land of
    Hellas,
To consort again and yet again with men victorious in the
    strife!" (Fig. 1.)

    This ode, which the artificial arrangement of ancient
scholarship has placed first in the 'epinician' collection,
was composed in honour of the Olympian victory won
with the famous horse Pherenikos by Hieron, King of
Syracuse, probably in 476 B.C., when Pindar was at the
zenith of his powers. It may have been thought to claim
this precedence because it was regarded as Pindar's
masterpiece, and because it was dedicated to the greatest
dynast of western Hellas. And in later antiquity Lucian,
whose literary judgment was of the best, speaks of it as
"the most beautiful of all lyrics". Certainly, the modern
reader who begins his study of Pindar with this poem must
feel that he has come into the presence of a great poet of
singular power and individuality, expressing himself in a
style that is entirely original; and that this poet has already
mastered his own poetic method and vocabulary and has
perfected his own ideal of construction for these epinician
themes. Later on, we shall find Pindar proclaiming as one
of his principles of composition that the proem of an ode
should "shine from afar"; and this famous proem of the first
Olympian is radiant with light. He passes immediately to

the praise of Hieron and his mighty horse "The Victory-bringer", and the lines are warm and glowing with the true festal spirit. He then proceeds to mythic narrative; for this had become an almost essential feature of the epinician style; and the myth that he chooses, though it has nothing to do with the foundation of the Olympian games, is relevant to Elis and Olympia; for it gives the origin of the supremacy of Pelops, whose spirit presides over the contests and adds lustre to the sacred enclosure. It contains an account of Tantalos, his sin and his punishment, the translation of Pelops to heaven (the traditional version of which he thinks to amend by substituting the motive of a divine amour for a cannibalistic sacrifice), the dangerous adventure of Pelops for the bride in which the divine lover Poseidon aids him to win the victory over Oinomaos, finally the marriage of Pelops from which issues the great family of the Pelopidai. He returns then to further encomium of Hieron, in noble and satisfying phrase, and he ventures on a prophecy, which was fulfilled, of a still greater triumph awaiting the king at Olympia, and he expresses the hope that he will be commissioned to celebrate it—a hope not fulfilled: for Hieron had the bad taste to prefer Bacchulides. The poem closes with some solemn reflections, and with a prayer for the continuance of Hieron's prosperity and of his own pre-eminence—of which he is fully conscious—in the poetic field.

The poem is a living organic unity with skilful and natural interlinking of the parts: and Pindar's characteristic excellencies are impressively displayed in it. He is a great master of the epic-lyric; and here the narrative of Pelops has the thrill and the tingling warmth of emotion that he knows how to evoke. We discern also that he can create myths, and the later ages sometimes accepted his creations. He has the rare power of fusing his moralising reflections with high poetry; and the sententious passages of this poem have great beauty and uplift.

Yet the modern lover of Pindar will hardly endorse the judgment of Lucian; a greater religious imagination inspires the second Olympian; and the seventh Olympian and the fourth Pythian are even greater masterpieces of epic-lyric. Nor does Pindar's attempt in this poem to reform the religious mythology of his people strike the modern reader as happy: in his eagerness to clear the Gods from the imputa-

Fig. 1. Vase from Ruvo in British Museum, 4th century B.C. Pelops (left),
Oinomaos (right), ratifying terms of the contest: each on one side of
pillar inscribed ΔΙΟΣ. On right, Aphrodite: on left, Hippodameia:
above, two heads of slain suitors.

tion of cannibalism, he invents a myth still more repulsive to our taste. But, to redeem this flaw, we shall find other religious poetry in Pindar of the highest quality; and this ode remains one of the masterpieces of ancient song. Scarcely any phrase of Pindar's was quoted more frequently than its proem.

OLYMPIAN II

To Theron of Akragas

"YE songs that lord it o'er the lyre,
What God, what hero, and what man shall we acclaim?
Verily Pisa is the land of Zeus:
And 'twas Herakles who stablished the Olympian contest,
    as trophy of victorious war:
And Theron is the man whose name must be on our lips,
5   for the sake of his victorious four-horsed chariot;
A man full-righteous in his reverence for the hospitable
    law,
Bulwark of Akragas,
Flower of a fair-named line of ancestors and saviour of
    his city:
Who verily suffered much heart-affliction,
Ere they won the hallowed dwelling on the river,
And were the eye and light of Sicily;
10 And a fateful life-span ever waited on them, bringing
    wealth and all delight, to crown their inborn excellence.
But, oh, Zeus, thou son of Kronos and Rhea, Lord of
    Olympos' seat,
Lord of the chief place of contests and Alpheus' ford,
Soothed by our lays safeguard their fatherland for them
    and for all their unborn children.
Of deeds done in time past, whether lawfully or against
15   law, not even Time the All-Father hath power to annul
    the issue.
But forgetfulness of troubles may come to us with prosper-
    ing fortune;
For the malignancy of woe is quelled and perisheth be-
20   neath the joy of goodly triumphs,

When the destiny of God sendeth a man soaring happiness
    from on high.
This law of life holds good of the fair-throned daughters
    of Kadmos,
Who indeed bore great sufferings,
But deep sorrow passeth away before overmastering bless-
    ings.
Semele of the long tresses, having died by the thunder-blast,
Liveth now among the Olympians,   25
Ever beloved by Pallas, much loved by Father Zeus and
    her son the ivy-bearer.
And men say that immortal life throughout all the ages
    hath been allotted Ino 'neath the sea-waves,   30
In company with Nereus' sea-born daughters.
Verily, the final ending of our days in death is never fore-
    judged for a man,
Nor whether we shall bring to an end any single day,
The offspring of the rising sun,
In tranquillity and with untiring bliss.
At various times varying tides of fortune come upon men
    bearing both joy of heart and sorrows.
Even so High Fate, holding in her hands the benignant   35
    fortune that is the heritage of this house,
Together with heaven-ordainèd prosperity
Bringeth on them at another time the thwarting stroke of
    calamity;
Ever since the fateful son of Laios slew his sire when he
    met him on the way,
And fulfilled the oracle uttered long before in the shrine
    of Putho.   40
But the goddess of Vengeance, keen-eyed (for the wrong-
    doer),
Slew for him his valiant offspring with fratricidal slaughter;
And the fallen Polyneikes left behind him a son Thers-
    andros,
A youth honoured in the young men's contests and in the
    battle-play of war,
A helpful scion to the households of Adrastos' line: 45

From whom Ainesidamos' son draweth the well-head of
    his blood;
And it fitteth this lineage of his that he should win
The praises of the poet's strain and the lyre's voice.
For he himself won glory in the Olympian strife,
And at Putho and on the Isthmos to his brother, the sharer
    of his fortunes,
50 The Graces who love them both brought the flowery gar-
    lands
To crown his chariot of four horses victorious in the twelve
    courses of the race.
But to adventure and to win in the hard strife unbindeth the
    soul from carking care.
Verily, wealth, adorned with all excellence,
Bringeth a man happy opportunity of this and that,
And, prompting deep ambition that chaseth honour,
55 Shineth as a star in heaven, the truest lustre for a man;
If indeed a man possessing it knoweth of the life to
    come,
How that the souls of the wicked, when they have died on
    this earth,
Forthwith pay the penalty;
For the sins enacted in this realm of God there is one below
    the earth that judgeth,
60 Delivering the strict account in bitter terms of Doom:
But the souls of the good win a happy life free from hard
    toil,
Having an equal measure of the sun by night and day,
No longer ploughing up the earth with might of hand,
Nor ploughing the face of the salt sea in the barren fashion
    of the mariner;
65 But, by the side of the most revered of deities,
All men soever who rejoicèd in keeping their oaths' pledge
Enjoy a tearless age:
While those others endure an agony from which the eye
    turneth away.
But all those who, throughout the probation of three lives
    on either side the grave,

Have had the hardihood to stand firm and keep their soul
  wholly from unrighteousness,
These, then, fare along the road of God to the fencèd holy 70
  place of Kronos,
Where airs born of Ocean are wafted round the Island of
  the Blest,
And flowers of gold are gleaming there,
Some, earth's children, born from radiant trees,
Others the water's nurslings;
With clusters whereof they enwreath their hands and twine
  garlands for their brows,
Abiding under the righteous laws of Rhadamanthos; 75
Whom the great Father of the Gods, Kronos, the husband
  of Rhea, the goddess enthronèd in the highest place,
Cherishèd as his trusty peer in judgment.
And among these Peleus and Kadmos are of high account:
And his mother, when with her prayers she had won over
  the heart of Zeus, brought thither Achilles, him who 80
  layed Hector low,
Troy's peerless and steadfast bulwark,
And who brought Kuknos to his death,
And Memnon the Aethiop, son of the Dawn-Goddess.
I have many a winged song-shaft in the quiver beneath
  my arm,
Fraught with speech that hath meaning for the wise, 85
But for the general they need interpreters.
Wise is he who hath rich lore by the light of nature:
But those two men who have only learned by rote,
Violent-mouthed with reckless speech, waste their breath
  in chattering,
Like crows screaming against the holy bird of Zeus.
Now rouse thyself, my Soul, and level the bow at the mark:
Whom shall we smite with our far-famed shafts of song,
Launching them from loving heart? 90
Shooting at Akragas for my mark,
I will utter a word under oath in all truthfulness of thought,
That never from a hundred years agone hath any city
  brought forth a man,

More kindly at heart in his dealings with his friends,
Or more generous of hand than Theron.
95 But his praise hath met envy in its path,
A fellow-traveller heeding no righteousness, but stirred up
    by madmen,
Fain to veil in a cloud of clamorous babbling the fair deeds
    of the noble.
For the sand of the sea-shore escapeth numbering,
And the tale of the delights that Theron hath won for
    others,
Who could ever fully tell?"

    The second Olympian was addressed to another great
Sicilian dynast, Theron, ruler of Akragas, whose prosperity
is still attested in the wonderful ruins of Girgenti, and who
was connected with the powerful Hieron by blood and by
marriage, being sometimes at feud with him. The ode is in
some respects the greatest of Pindar's works, and nowhere
else does his religious imagination clothe itself in words so
beautiful and deep: nor has any other man ever received
such a personal poem from so great a poet, except the unknown recipient of Shakespeare's sonnets. This Olympian
is a marvel of song on the mysteries of life and death; and
the astonishing fact is that it should have been inspired by
a horse-race, a victory with a four-horse chariot won by
Theron in 476 B.C. to which a brief and passing allusion is
made, so as to preserve the form of an 'epinician' ode. But
much of the ode is a high-pitched encomium on Theron,
who may have deserved it or whom Pindar sincerely believed to deserve it: much of it is consolation for a sorrowful
time that has just passed—probably the danger of Hieron's
hostility, and for the shadow of the end that was approaching. The consolation takes the characteristic mythologic
form; the vicissitudes of storm and sunshine that had
marked Theron's career are illustrated by the chequered
fortunes of Kadmos and his descendants, his daughters
Semele and Ino, who became goddesses after death, and the
house of Laios. And this illustration is most relevant and
appealing; for the house of the Emmenidai, to which
Theron belonged, traced their descent to the son of Poluneikes, the grandson of Laios. But Pindar's other source

of consolation is from a deeper spring. He comforts Theron with the glad tidings of a happy life reserved for the righteous beyond the grave; and he develops an eschatologic theory unfamiliar to his contemporaries. Adding to the account of it given in this ode the evidence from some of Pindar's other works,[1] we may state it thus: immediately after death we are judged by a tribunal in the lower world; the guilty souls are punished, the righteous are rewarded with a happy life; but both these states are only of temporary probation; after nine years both classes of souls are sent back to the earth for reincarnation; and this process continues till each soul has passed through a cycle of three lives on each side of the grave: those who have stood the test of these six lives, and have abstained wholly from unrighteousness, pass into an eternal paradise; on the other side, while Pindar gives us a glimpse of the intolerable pains of Purgatory, he is not clear about eternal damnation. By comparing this passage with a page of Plato's Phaedrus and with the most ancient Orphic hymn found in South Italy and Crete, we may pronounce with certainty that Pindar is here expounding a doctrine taught in Orphic circles: the doctrine of a posthumous moral judgment of all souls, of Purgatory whereby the impure stains contracted by the soul while in the flesh might be removed, and of the cycle of a triple incarnation. At the close of the eschatologic part of the Ode, Pindar makes it clear that he is speaking of mysteries, intelligible only to the initiated. We know that the Orphic doctrine was powerful at this time in the western world of Magna Graecia; we may suppose that Theron was a convert and that Pindar was aware of it, and therefore he set himself to expound these comforting doctrines—comforting at least to Theron, whose righteousness is proved—with all the force of his lyrical genius. Working on a hint from Homer, Pindar thus becomes the first original poet of Paradise, the theme that has inspired some of our greatest European poetry. We may feel the Hellenic limitations of the Pindaric paradise, where flowers, odours, games, music are the sufficient rewards of the blessed; at the same time we feel the matchless charm of the golden poetry. The poem is also a landmark in the history of religion; it gives us an eschatology more advanced than any that could be found in any contemporary

[1] Vide *infra*, p. 327, Frag. 133.

people, and a theory of Judgment at least as moral as the Christian, while it indicates the source of the Christian doctrine of Purgatory.

The high style is maintained to the end; but the tone is somewhat marred by the poet's egoistic outburst, in which he defends himself against two rivals who had been railing against him and whom he compares to two jays screaming against the eagle: he is the eagle, the man of genius, the others are dull mechanics of the craft. Some ancient commentators declared that the two rivals were Bacchulides and Simonides. Fortunately we have evidence against the probability of this. We should not like to believe that Pindar could speak thus of Simonides, "the nightingale of Keos".

He recovers himself quickly from this egoistic lapse and ends with a glowing tribute to Theron. The closing words are cryptic, and can be best interpreted if we suppose that on a recent occasion when Theron's praise was being sung, perhaps on the delivery of the third Olympian, a rude crowd interrupted.

OLYMPIAN III

To Theron of Akragas

"THE divine sons of Tundareus, the hospitable Lords,
And fair-tressèd Helen, I may boast, delight in me, glori-
    fying far-famed Akragas,
When I have raised on high Theron's loud hymn of praise—
Fair harvest won by his tireless-footed steeds—in honour
    of an Olympian victory.
In such wise, methinks, was I aided by the Muse,
When I found a mode, bright with the sheen of newness,
    for linking up the voices of my gladsome chorus to the 5
    measure of the Dorian sandal.
For the garlands interwoven on his locks exact from me
    this task of God's appointment,
To mingle full meetly for Ainesidamos' son the manifold
    voices of the lyre and the shrill calls of the flute with
    the framework of sweet speech;
And Pisa bids me speak aloud.
'Tis from that place fateful songs fare forth over the world 10
    of men in honour of him on whosesoever's locks
The glory of the pale-dark olive-crown is cast above his
    brows
By the Aetolian man, the unswerving judge of all the
    Hellenes,
Fulfilling the behests given in a former age by Herakles.
This olive-tree had been brought by the son of Amphitruon
    from the shady sources of the Danube,
To serve as the fairest badge of the Olympian contests, 15
When he had persuaded by gentle speech the Hyperborean
    folk, Apollo's ministers.

In all loyalty of heart he craveth of them,
As a tribute to the all-hospitable sacred plot of Zeus,
The shadow-giving growth, to be a common boon to all
    men, and to furnish the crown of valorous deeds.
For already, after consecration of his father's altars,
The mid-month moon in her golden car had kindled her
20   full-rounded orb, the eye of evening,
And he had set in order the holy trial of mighty contests,
    with the ritual of the fifth-yearly festival, on the steep
    god-haunted banks of Alpheus;
But in the glens of Pelops of Kronos' line no spot was
    verdant with fair trees;
And it seemed to him that the tyranny of the sun was
    bitter over his holy garth being treeless.
25 Then at last his spirit moved him to fare to the land of
    Ister;
Where he had been welcomed by Leto's daughter; the
    swift charioteer,
As he came there from the ridges and the mazy hollows
    of Arcadia's mountains,
What time on the mission of Eurustheus his father's doom
    set him to bring home the hind with the golden horns,
That once the Nymph Taugeta had dedicated and marked
30   as hallowed to the Goddess of Right Measure.
As he followed the quest of her, he came to behold even
    that far land that lieth behind the blast of the cold
    North;
Then he halted and gazed with wonder on the trees,
And sweet desire possessed him to plant shoots of them
    around the twelve-times-circled goal of his horse-
    course.
And now in kindly mood he fareth to this our festival
35 In fellowship with the twin sons of deep-girdled Leda, the
    peers of Gods.
For to them, when he ascended into heaven, he entrusted
    the stewardship of the all-admirèd contest
That trieth the prowess of men and the skill of the driver in
    hurling his chariot down the course.

So then my heart arouseth me to say that this glory hath
 come to the House of the Emmenidai and to Theron,
As the gift of the sons of Tundareus, the lords of fair steeds,
Because that house more than all mortal men doth keep
 fellowship with them at tables of hospitable feasting, 40
Safeguarding with pious hearts the ritual of the Blessed
 Ones.
But if it be true that water is the best of things,
And gold the most reverèd of all possessions,
Even so we may say now that Theron hath attained the
 farthest bourne,
And that the fame of his noble deeds
Reacheth from home to the pillars of Herakles.
Into the world beyond, neither the wise nor the unwise may
 fare.
I will not strive to penetrate there: I should be one of the 45
 witless, did I so."

 This third Olympian celebrates the same victory as the
second, and may be dated 476 B.C. There are various
reasons for regarding it as the prior ode of the two, but
as composed soon after Olympian I, for it repeats at the
close an echo of the brilliant prelude of that poem. And
whereas Olympian II was doubtless intended for a private
recitation, this is more of a processional hymn intended for
the festival called "the Feast of the Gods", at which the
Twin-Brethren were supposed to entertain the other deities
and the people of Akragas—at Theron's expense. Therefore it begins with a great invocation in sonorous cadence,
of the Twin-Brethren, the sons of God—Dioskouroi—or sons
of Tundareus as they were indifferently called, and of their
sister Helen, who in some parts of Greece had become a
goddess and of whose divinity in Sicily the name of the city
Tundaris is some evidence. But the poem is still more concerned with Herakles, Pindar's favourite hero, the founder
of the Olympic games, about whom Pindar narrates at
some length a story relevant enough to the occasion but
possibly wholly a new fiction: when Herakles was pursuing the hind with golden horns, the chase led him from

Arcadia to the sources of the Danube, the land of the Hyperboreans, where he was struck with the beauty of the trees. He remembered them on a later occasion when he was laying out the sacred ground of Olympia; and noting its treeless state he made another journey to the Hyperboreans and persuaded them to give him slips of the wild olive and other trees to plant at Olympia; and therefore the victor's crown of wild olive was originally a gift from the Hyperboreans.

It is a remarkable story and was almost certainly invented by Pindar, who is our sole authority for it; for the later writers who allude to it are only following Pindar. It is not at all *ben trovato*; for most Greeks must have known that the wild olive did not grow in the far North, where Pindar puts these Hyperboreans; and if the victor's olive-crown was Hyperborean, it was Apolline; and yet it was never associated with any other deity than Zeus. He is often wayward and reckless in fashioning mythology; but here we may suggest certain motives that may have inspired him: Pindar must have known of the 'Hyperborean' maidens that were buried in Delos and that above the grave of one of them an olive-tree was growing; and he may have had the idea that she may have brought it with her from the 'Hyperborean' land. Again, there was a local legend at Olympia, which Pindar may have known, that Herakles had fetched the white poplar-tree, the only tree whose wood could be used in the Olympian sacrifice to Zeus, from the territory in North Western Greece called Thesprotis; and this land might be called 'Hyperborean', as it included the 'Hyperborean' Dodona. These two separate sources may have suggested to him this fictitious origin of the Olympian olive.

The dubious value of the myth need not affect our appreciation of the ode as a poem: it is one of his best and brightest, a striking example of his vivid power of description, of his golden style and mellow richness of phrase: the prelude allows us to hear the melodious thunder of the Dorian music.

These two Olympian odes on Theron's victory should be linked with the 'encomium' or eulogy that Pindar composed on him while he was in Sicily,[1] in which he seems to have given more details concerning the earlier history of his family, giving Rhodes as their original seat, whence they migrated to Sicily. Herodotus corroborates this and adds some interesting details to the chronicle.

---

[1] *Vide* fragment, p. 345.

OLYMPIAN IV

To Psaumis of Kamarina

"OH God most High, Thou driver of the tireless-footed
    Thunder,
Thy seasons in their revolving march have sped me forth,
With the many-voicèd lyre accompanying my song,
To bear witness to contests proudest in place of all.
When our friends of other lands win prosperous fortune,
The hearts of the good leap up caressing the sweet tidings. 5
But, oh, Zeus, Son of Kronos, Lord of Aitna,
The wind-swept prison of grim hundred-headed Tuphon,
Give kindly welcome, for the Graces' sake,
To this choral dance that honoureth the Olympian victory
And sheddeth a light to abide for ever on far-prevailing 10
    deeds of prowess.
For it cometh to thy shrine in honour of Psaumis' chariot,
Who crownèd with Olympian olive is fain to awaken glory
    for Kamarina.
May God be kindly disposed towards his prayers for the
    future!
For verily I commend him as one most zealous in the
    rearing of steeds,
As one rejoicing in the hospitable board where all men 15
    gather,
And with his face turned in all singleness of heart towards
    the Goddess of Tranquillity, who loveth the city well.
I will not stain my speech with falsehood:
The test of action is the touchstone of men;
Even such as redeemed the son of Klumenos from the
    scorn of the Lemnian women, 20

When, conqueror in the race in brazen armour,
He spake to Queen Hupsipulé, as he went to take the
    crown—
'Lo such a man am I for swiftness;
25 And my hands and my heart are even as my running.
Verily, even on young men grey hairs may ofttimes grow,
    belying the apparent season of their prime.' "

OLYMPIAN V

To the same

"OH, Nymph of Kamarina, Daughter of Ocean,
With smiling heart receive this sweet flower of lofty deeds
    of valour,
The bloom of Olympian garlands,
The gifts of the tireless-footed chariot, the gifts of
    Psaumis:
Who doing honour to thy city, the nurturer of men,
Hallowed the six twin-altars at the highest feast-tide of 5
    the Gods
With sacrifice of oxen and with strife on the fifth day of
    the contest,
Strife with the chariots of horses and of mules and with
    the single rider's horse.
And having conquered he laid up a treasure of goodly
    fame for thee,
And proclaimed by the herald's voice his sire Akron, and
    his home in the new-built city.
And having come from the lovely abodes of Oinomaos and
    Pelops,
He raiseth the song in honour of thy sacred grove, oh, Pallas,
    Warder of the City,   10
Of thy river Oanis and thy native lake,
And of the hallowed channels wherewith Hipparis watereth
    the host,
And weldeth together swiftly the lofty-membered avenue of
    firm-set dwellings,
Bringing this town-folk from dire distress into the light of
    safety.

15 But ever, in the matter of noble action, the thought of the
   toil and the cost contendeth against the deed that
   danger darkeneth:
But when men have prospered in their venture, even their
   fellow-citizens deem their daring wise.
Oh, Zeus, the Saviour, thronèd on the high clouds,
Haunting the crest of the hill of Kronos,
And honouring broad-flooded Alpheus and the hallowed
   Idaean cave,
I come as thy suppliant addressing thee in strains of Lydian
   flutes,
20 To proffer prayer to thee that thou wouldest glorify this
   city with far-famed flower of men;
And that thou, oh Psaumis, thou Olympian conqueror, may
   carry on to the end a mellow-hearted age,
Rejoicing in Poseidon's gift of horses, with thy sons ever
   by thy side:
But if one watereth the wholesome plant of happiness,
Content with one's worldly goods and adding thereto the
   praise of men,
Let him not aspire to the rank of Godhead."

The two odes, Olympian IV and V, are a double commemoration of the same event, a victory with the mule-
chariot won not long after 460 B.C. by a citizen of Kamarina
called Psaumis. We may suppose that the first was sung at
a private festival immediately after the return of the victor
to his city, the second in a festal procession to the temple of
Pallas, to whom Psaumis may be bringing gifts in his mule-
chariot. The authenticity of the second ode has been much
doubted, but the arguments are strongly in favour of its
genuineness. For no one at this age could have imitated
Pindar so closely except Pindar himself; and it has the
peculiar twisted strength of his style. Neither poem shows
him at his greatest and best, except in the astonishing force
and beauty of the invocation at the opening of Olympian
IV; but both are attractive from their brightness of tone and
tactful appropriateness of sentiment and allusion. The only

mythical narrative illustrates the old Greek proverb "the grey hairs of Erginos": narrating how Erginos the Minyan, one of Jason's crew, competed with the other Argonauts in the games, held by the Lemnian Queen, and having won in the hoplite-race silenced the taunts of the Lemnian women who mocked at his grey hair. The proverb was used of those who when grey retained the vigour of youth; and we may suppose that this was true of Psaumis. In the second poem Pindar shows himself strikingly familiar with the geography and the local cults of Kamarina; and the beautiful coinage of this city abundantly illustrates his ode (Figs. 2, 3, 4).

OLYMPIAN VI

To Hagesias of Syracuse

"As when we have stayed the well-walled forecourt of our
    dwelling on golden pillars,
So will we base deep our stately fabric of song:
'Tis needful to give to the beginning of our work a coun-
    tenance that shineth from afar.
But if a man were Olympian victor,
5 And the steward of Zeus in Pisa for the prophetic altar,
And linkèd with the founder of far-famed Syracuse,
What is the hymn of praise that man could miss when sweet
    singing ariseth,
If he found his fellow-citizens envy-free?
For let this son of Sostratos know that this mantle of pro-
    sperity fitteth him wondrous well.
Barren virtues that confront no peril are not held in honour
10   either 'mong men on land or in hollow ships:
But if a fair deed is wrought with toil, it is long remembered
    of many a man.
Hagesias, to thee is that praise open, which Adrastos right-
    fully spake forth with his tongue,
Concerning the seer Amphiaraos, Oikles' son,
After that he and his shining steeds were swallowed up in
    the earth:
15 And when the seven pyres with the seven dead heroes were
    hallowed in Theban land,
Adrastos of Talaos' line spake such a word as this—
'I yearn sorely for the man who was the eye of my host,
Both a goodly prophet and a goodly warrior with the
    spear.'

Even such praise is ready to hand for the man of Syracuse,
    the patron-lord of our choral band.
To this at least I will bear clear witness,
As one not given to contention
Nor a lover of debate,
But binding myself by a mighty oath: 20
And the honey-voicèd Muses will concede it to me.
Oh, Phintis, now up and yoke with all speed the mighty
    mules,
That we may fare in the mule-chariot along a shining track,
And that I may win even to the cradle of the heroic line.
For they of all other steeds know well how to lead us along 25
    this track,
Now that they have won garlands at Olympia.
It behoveth us then to roll back for them the gates of song.
And 'tis to Pitana along the way of the Eurotas that we
    must this day come betimes.
For verily 'tis said of the Nymph of Pitana that having
    mingled in love with Poseidon, son of Kronos,
She bore the girl Euadne of the violet tresses,   30
And beneath the folds of her garments she hid the travail
    of unwedded love.
Then in the appointed month she sent her handmaidens
And bade them fit forth the babe and give her to Aiputos
    the hero-son of Eilatos,
Who at Phaisana ruled o'er Arcadian men, and the
    valley of Alpheus was allotted for his home.
Having there been reared, she first tasted of the sweet gifts
    of love beneath Apollo's embrace;   35
Nor did the stolen fruits of the God's love escape the know-
    ledge of Aiputos through all her period;
But he, burying in his breast his wrath unspeakable,
In anxious care went from his home and fared to Putho,
To question God's will concerning this intolerable mis-
    chance.
And Euadne, having laid aside her girdle of purple and
    saffron hues
And her silver pitcher 'neath a thicket's gloomy shade, 40

Brought forth a god-inspirèd boy.
Verily to her the God of the golden hair sent the Birth-
    Goddess in kindly mood,
And the Fates to stand by as gentle ministers.
And there came forthwith from her body to the light of
    day, with gladsome birth-pang, Iamos.
45 Him she left on the ground in her sore distress.
But by the counsels of the divine ones two gleaming-eyed
    snakes nurtured him with harmless poison, even the
    honey of bees.
But when the king came driving back from rocky Putho,
He questionèd all his household about the boy whom
    Euadne had brought forth;
For he averrèd that he was born of Phoibos for his sire,
50 And that he would be pre-eminent among mortals as a
    prophet for all men of the earth, nor would his lineage
    ever fail.
Thus he revealed God's answer. But they averred that they
    had heard nought nor seen aught of the child, though
    now four days born.
For indeed he had been hidden in a brake, a pathless
    thicket,
55 His tender body showered with the yellow and the purple
    rays of violets.
Wherefore his mother named him after the violets, 'Iamos',
To be called throughout all time by this immortal name.
And he, when he had won the blessing of sweet Hebe of
    the golden crown,
Went down into the bed of Alpheus' stream,
And called on his ancestor Poseidon, the lord of far-reaching
    might,
And on the Archer-God, the Warder of the God-built isle
    of Delos,
60 Craving that honour might befall his head, to rear a stock
    of men,
Praying beneath the sky of the night.
In clear speech rang out in response his father's voice and
    answered him—

'Arise, my son, and go thitherward to the place of gather-
    ing of all peoples, following my voice.'
And they came to the sun-scorched rock of the high hill
    of Kronos.
And there the God furnished him with a double store of 65
    divination,
At times to hearken the significance of mystic sounds that
    cannot lie;
But afterwards, when Herakles, deviser of daring deeds,
The hallowed scion of the stock of Alkeus,
Had come and founded in his father's honour the festival
    of all resort and the greatest ritual of contests,
Then the God bade Iamos to set up his divination on the 70
    highest altar of Zeus.
And therefrom the fame of the Iamidai spread far through-
    out the Hellenes;
Prosperity withal attended them:
As they honour all excellence, the sunlight is about their path.
Verily each man is provèd in the hour of need.
Carping envy from others hangeth o'er the head of those
On whom, as they drive their chariot before the rest down
    the last course, the stately Goddess of all grace shed- 75
    deth the halo of renown.
But if in very truth the men of thy mother's line, dwelling
    'neath the boundaries of Kullene,
Piously gave many a gift with prayerful sacrifices
To the Herald of the Gods, Hermes, Lord of contests, who
    hath dispensation of the games,
And who honoureth Arcadia, the land of stalwart men;
Then 'tis that God, oh son of Sostratos,   80
Who in unison with his loud-thundering sire bringeth thy
    fair fortune to pass.
Methinks I have, as it were, a shrill whetstone on my tongue,
Which draweth me on full fain with gusts of harmonious
    breath.
My own mother's mother is the nymph of Stumphalos, the
    fair-flowering Metopa, who bore the maiden Thebe,
    driver of the steed,

85 From whose fair fount I drink,
As I weave the manifold song for warriors.
Rouse now thy comrades, Aineas, first with loud acclaim
    to praise Hera, Goddess of Maidenhood,
And then to give judgment whether on a true account
90 We shake off the ancient taunt, 'Boeotian swine'.
For thou art a trusty messenger,
A courier posting in the service of the fair-haired Muses,
A sweet vessel charged with my loud-voicèd songs.
And I bid thee remember Syracuse and Ortugia,
Which Hieron administereth with unstained sceptre and
    with counsels of righteousness,
While he cherisheth the worship of Demeter of the ruddy
    feet,
95 And the feast-tide of her daughter (returning) with white
    horses,
And the majesty of Zeus of Etna.
Indeed the sweet-voiced lyre and the poets' strains are
    familiar with his name;
May no new tide of time shipwreck his happiness.
But with all gladsome cheer of heart
May he welcome this triumph-choir of thine, Hagesias,
Returning homeward from their old home within Stum-
    phalos' walls.
100 Two anchors are good wherewith to stay the swift ship on
    a stormy night.
To the men of both cities may God in loving-kindness
    award a glorious destiny:
Oh, Lord that ruleth the sea,
Husband of gold-spindled Amphitrite,
Grant them a straight voyage free from trouble,
105 And cause the gladdening flower of my melodies still to
    bloom.''

    This ode commemorates a victory with the mule-chariot
won by a certain Hagesias, a citizen of Syracuse, and friend
of Hieron, connected also on his mother's side with the

Arcadian town of Stumphalos, where the ode is being sung
by a chorus under the leadership of Aineas, probably an
Arcadian, whom Pindar calls "his courier of the Muses",
his "charger of loud-voiced songs". No ancient authority
assigns any date; for as the mule-races were abolished about
or near the middle of the fifth century, we must suppose
that no authentic records survived. But internal evidence
makes the date 468 B.C. the most probable. The mule-
victories may have been comparatively unimpressive, but
this one inspired Pindar to compose one of his most beautiful odes, pervaded throughout with a sunny brightness and
warmth and with the flush of happy excitement. And few
passages in all his works can be quoted more beautiful than
the proem, which certainly "shines from afar", or the description of the new-born babe in the thicket with "his tender
body showered with the violets' yellow and purple rays".
The epic-legendary narrative is in his best lyric style. The
metres combine a grave and sweet dignity with a tremulous
swiftness: there is no touch of over-strain, obscurity, or
harshness. And towards the close of the poem we may well
allow him his proud personal outburst; where he asks the
chorus now to decide whether the poet's land of Boeotia
deserves the taunt of the proverb—"the Boeotian pig". In
fact, Hagesias' ancestry and family tradition afforded rich
material, of the sort that Pindar loved to handle. For the
victor had not only fought bravely in Hieron's wars, but
enjoyed the religious prestige of belonging to the family of
the Iamidai, who for many centuries maintained a centre
of divination at Olympia associated with the cult of Zeus,
prophesying by sounds in the air and by marks in the sacrificed victims, and whose individual members played the
rôle of state-prophets in Arcadia and Sparta, as we may
suppose Hagesias did at Syracuse. Therefore he at once suggests to Pindar the figure of the warrior-prophet Amphiaraos,
the most august personality of Greek legend, who fired the
imagination of Pindar here and elsewhere and of Aeschylus
in the *Seven against Thebes*.

To any general survey of Pindar's religious temperament
this ode gives some important evidence. We are struck by
the naive and graceful anthropomorphism, unclouded by
any morality, in his lyric narrative of the amours of the
Gods. These divine loves, that soured Euripides, seem to
have brightened Pindar; he is able to represent them as

happy boons to mankind; for they gave us Herakles and the 'violet-babe' who is to grow into the mighty prophet and counsellor of States. Pindar had some poetic advantage in being untouched by the age of enlightenment that was beginning before he died.

The ode also amply illustrates Pindar's religious antiquarianism: he tells us carefully the details of the Olympian divination; he is interested in that rare cult, found only in Arcadia and one other place, of Hera 'the maid'; but his antiquarian facts are always transmuted into poetry.

It also helps us to appreciate the hold that such local personifications as Pitana, Metopa, Thebe, had upon the popular imagination and upon Pindar in particular; they were by no means barren fictions, but were given life and made to work.

How much of the varied web of mythology that invests this ode is of Pindar's own work, how many threads or skeins he borrowed from older literature and folk-lore, we cannot certainly decide. We discern him borrowing an interesting motive from the old epic poem *Thebais*, which narrated the expedition and the fall of the Seven against Thebes. But we know of no earlier source of the story of Iamos. The great critic Aristarchos confirms our own impression that Pindar freely invented myths on his own account; he is often content to be his own authority. But it is hard to believe that he invented this fascinating story of the origin of the Iamidai; he may well have gathered it as a family tradition at Olympia; and his account of the birth has nothing of the style of folklore, but much that suggests an epic original.

The ode, while maintaining the grand style throughout, is remarkable for its rich luxuriance.

OLYMPIAN VII

To Diagoras of Rhodes

"As when a man taketh in his wealth-dowered hand a cup
    all bubbling with the dew of the grape within,
And, pledging him therein,
Giveth it to the young bridegroom of his daughter,
As a gift from her old home to the new,
A cup all golden, the crown of all his treasure,
To gladden the fellowship of the marriage-feast
And honouring his union with the bridegroom's house,   5
And amidst the gathering of the friends maketh him envied
    for his loving bride;
Even so, by sending round a draught of nectar,
The Muses' gift, my mind's sweet fruit,
To the men who bear the athletes' toil, the conquerors at
    Olympia and Putho,   10
I win their hearts' good-will.
Happy is he who is possessed of good report.
Now upon this man and now that the Goddess of Grace,
    that causeth life to blossom,
Looketh down favouringly, tuning for him at once the
    sweet strains of the lyre and the manifold stops of the
    flute:
And now with music of both kinds I have come into haven
    with Diagoras,
Fashioning the hymn in honour of the sea-born daughter
    of Aphrodite,
The bride of Helios, the nymph of Rhodes,
That I may swell the praises of the man of mighty stature, 15
    the man that turneth not aside from the battle,

For the crowns that he hath won, the guerdon of his box-
    ing, by Alpheus' stream and by Kastalia;
And the praise of his father Damagetas, whom the Goddess
    of Justice loveth,
Both dwelling with warriors of the Argive race,
In the island of three cities near the headland of spacious
    Asia.

20 I were fain, in my message to those whose lineage draweth
    from Tlapolemos,
The far-ruling stock of Herakles,
To fashion aright a story that concerneth all.
For on their father's side they vaunt their origin from
    Zeus:
But from their mother Astudameia they are of Amuntor's
    clan.
Endless are the errors that beset the hearts of men:

25 And there is no device whereby to discover what in the
    present moment and in the final end is best to happen
    to a man.
For erst Tlapolemos, the founder of this land,
In his wrath smote and slew with a staff of hard olivewood
Alkmena's bastard brother, Likumnios, having come (to
    Argos) from his mother's home in Midea.

30 But bewilderment of mind has led astray even the wisest.
And he went and took counsel of the oracle of God.
To him then the God of the golden hair gave voice from out
    the hidden chamber of his shrine—
Bidding him sail away from the cliffs of Lerna straight on
    to the sea-washed pasture-land,
Where once the mighty monarch of the Gods
Rained down on the city with golden flakes of snow,

35 When through Hephaistos' craft, freed by the blow of the
    bronze-forgèd axe,
Athena sprang up and ran down her father's crest,
Shouting with a far-ringing cry,
And all Heaven and Mother Earth shuddered before her.
It was at that time the God, Hyperion's son, who giveth
    light to mortals,

Enjoined on his dear sons to heed well a coming service,   40
To wit, that they should be the first to set up a far-seen
     altar to the Goddess,
And by establishing the holy ritual of a sacrifice
Should gladden the heart of her sire and of the Maid of
     the clanging spear.
Due Observance, born of Forethought, bringeth to mortals
     Virtue and the joys of Victory.
Yet often by ways mysterious there cometh upon men a   45
     cloud of forgetfulness,
And causeth them to swerve from the straight path of
     action.
For those men went up the hill not having with them the
     seed of gleaming fire,
And they established her holy grove on their Akropolis
     with fireless rites.
On them then, gathering a golden cloud,
God sent a rain (of gold) for a long space of time: 50
But the Goddess of the gleaming eyes herself dowered
     them with all art,
So as to surpass all men on the earth in excellence of handi-
     craft.
And their ways teemèd with sculptured forms like to beings
     that live and walk:
And high waxèd their renown.
But in the man who has the craft-lore even the greater
     skill putteth itself forth without the guile of magic.
Now 'tis said in ancient human story
That, when Zeus and the Immortals were allotting the   55
     lands between themselves,
Rhodes was not yet manifest on the sea-plain,
But that the island was hidden in the salt depths.
But the Sun-God was not present at the lot-drawing, and
     no one marked his share.
Therefore the holy God was left portionless of land.
And when he made them mindful of it, Zeus was fain to   60
     draw the lots again.
But he suffered him not: for he said

That he himself discernèd a land rising up from its foundation within the hoary sea,
A land of rich pasture, kindly to men and flocks.
And he bade the Fate-Goddess of the golden frontlet forth-
65   with to hold up her hands and not transgress the
mighty oath of the Gods, but with the son of Kronos
to pledge
That the land now brought forth into the bright light of
day
Should be for ever in the future as a glory for his head.
And the sum of all his speech fell true at last.
An island blossomèd from the wet sea,
70 And the Father who begetteth the rays of light,
The Lord of fire-breathing steeds, hath her for his own:
Where erst he mingled in love with the nymph Rhodos,
And brought to birth seven sons gifted with the wisest
counsels of all the men of old:
Of whom one begat Kameiros and Ialusos his eldest-born
and Lindos.
75 And they, having divided threefold their fatherland,
Held separately each his own city for his share, and their
habitations have been callèd after them.
Then as a sweet repayment for his piteous mischance there
was ordainèd for Tlapolemos, the leader of the Tiryn-
thian settlers, as for a very God,
80 Procession of sheep for burnt-sacrifice and the judgment
of the athletes' strife:
At whose games Diagoras has twice won the flowery garland.
And four times on the far-famed Isthmos prospering,
And garland upon garland at Nemea and in rocky
Athens.
The bronze shield at Argos hath known his name,
The fair-wrought tripods in Arcadia and Thebes;
85 The recurring cycles of Boeotian contests know him,
Pellene and Aigina withal six times a conqueror.
Nor doth the verdict of the stone tablet at Megara tell a
different tale.

But, oh, father Zeus, that hauntest the slopes of the moun-
tain Ataburion,
Receive with honour this our songful service for the Olym-
pian victory
And the man that hath found glory by his boxing.
And grant him reverence and favour alike from citizens 90
and strangers.
For he walketh along the straight path that hateth
wrong,
Having learnèd full well the teaching wherewith his up-
right heart hath inspired him from goodly ancestors.
Suffer no cloud to gather over the stock sown by Kallianax.
Verily with the glad fortunes of the Eratidai the whole
city holdeth solemn festival.
But in one short span of time the various-flickering breezes
speed on diverse ways."   95

This ode was composed in 464 B.C. in honour of the boxer
Diagoras, of Rhodes, who might claim to be the greatest
athlete of the fifth century, and who was the head of a
family of athletes that played some part in history. Never
was a boxing-match so commemorated before or since as in
this ode, perhaps the greatest of the epinicians. When we
have received the full impression that it can produce on us,
we do not wonder that the grateful Rhodians dedicated it
later engraved in letters of gold in the temple of Athena at
Lindos. The record of this athlete and his sons belongs to
the history of Greek Athletics and was enough to kindle
Pindar's enthusiasm. They were members of the great
family of the Eratidai, and one of their ancestors had held
kingly power at Ialusos; therefore they would doubtless
claim to be Herakleids, and the story of Tlepolemos the son
of Herakles, which Pindar draws from Homer, is entirely
relevant at a festal celebration in honour of Diagoras' victory. Pindar deals quite adequately with the athletic facts
and the athlete's marvellous list of triumphs in a few lines
near the close, and manages to avoid the dryness and monotony of a long recital. Earlier in the poem he had given the
personal touch by describing him as "a straight fighter"

and as 'gigantic', an appropriate epithet, for his statue at Olympia represented him as in height about 6 feet 6 inches.

It was natural in Hellas for legends to arise about a man of this type; and according to one his birth was due to a miraculous conception, Hermes the God of athletics taking the place of the supposed mortal father. It was very easy, therefore, for Pindar, in dealing with such a man, to pass into the realms of mythology; and he was sure to delight both the family of the Eratidai and the whole assembled company of Rhodians by narrating the story of Tlepolemos, the legends of the choice of Helios, the fireless sacrifice to Athena whereby the Rhodians in the far past had won the favour of the Goddess and her father Zeus, and of the birth and endowments of the sons of Helios the Sun-God, the autochthones of the island. Hence the great body of the poem is lyrical-epic, interspersed with sententious poetic reflections, serious but hopeful, on the lot of man. The general purport or effect of the poem is the glorifying of the island of Rhodes, and no Greek community except Athens has ever received from any poet so magnificent a tribute of verse. But the glorification deals wholly with the prehistoric and remote past. The story of the Heliadai and the wondrous craftsmen who filled all the ways with the forms of all living things reflects probably the faintly remembered splendour of a Minoan art-period. Rhodes' period of historic glory was yet to come, and its present condition was inglorious; but the mythology that Pindar gives us is more fascinating than any history and perhaps equally real to the ordinary Greek of this period.

Although the ode sets forth three separate myths, the nexus of the whole is well preserved, and the flow of the narrative is unbroken; Pindar in his pleasant wayward fashion reverses the time-order of the events in his mythic world, and thus avoids the stiffness of chronologic consecutiveness, giving us first the story of Tlepolemos, then the birth of Athena for which the Rhodians were watching, then the rise of the island from the depths of the sea and its appropriation by the Sun-God. We would like to know how much of the mythology in this poem is real folklore, how much might have been drawn from earlier literature, how much—if any—was Pindar's invention. The Tlepolemos story was given him by the *Iliad*, and was connected in all probability with the Argive-Dorian settlement of the island,

as I have shown elsewhere.[1] Pindar adds only two points to
the Homeric narrative, namely that Tlepolemos consulted
the Delphic oracle before leaving home, a rule generally
observed by the colonisers of the seventh and sixth century,
and that after his death a ritual of contests and sacrificial
procession was maintained in his honour by the Rhodians.
The other two myths are more pregnant of high poetry.
The thrilling legend of the springing forth of Athena all-
armed from the head of Zeus had already been treated by
the unknown author of a short Homeric Hymn, whose description resembles Pindar's at many points, and by the
gifted Stesichoros. It haunted the imagination of the people,
for it is a common theme of the sixth century vases. Pindar
has handled it so masterfully that the passage is the most
memorable example of the strength and the splendour of
his style: his lines resound as a thunder-echo of the great
cosmic event.

His further narrative of the sacrifice of the Rhodians
is not wholly intelligible without some knowledge of Greek
ritual and the facts of Athena-worship; and Pindar's account
of it is also characteristically incomplete and allusive.
The full statement would be this: the prophecy had gone
forth before her birth that whoever should be the first after
her birth to sacrifice to the goddess should win her immortal favour: the Rhodians, warned by the Sun-God, were
on the watch, but the Athenians were watching as well: the
Rhodians were actually the first, but in their hurry forgot to
bring fire with them when they climbed the high place for
the momentous sacrifice: the Athenians were second in the
race but had the foresight to take fire with them, so that
they could offer a burnt-sacrifice with animal victims: the
prophecy then was not rigidly fulfilled, for the goddess,
being warlike and athletic, preferred the meat-diet—'fireless' offerings being always vegetarian: therefore she made
Athens her primary city and home; but she amply rewarded the Rhodians and frequently resided at Lindos.
The story is mainly 'aitiologic', arising from the fact that
the Athena-sacrifice on the hill at Lindos was always 'fireless', a ritual-law observed in many Hellenic sacrifices; this
combined with the other fact, which no Hellene could gain-
say, that, after all, Athens was the supreme city of Athena,
explains the complex legend. Pindar was the first, as far as

---

[1] Vide *Hero-cults*, pp. 119-124.

we know or can surmise, who gave it literary form; but we cannot suppose that he invented it. He must have embodied some of the folklore of the island, gathered perhaps by a personal visit or from conversation with Rhodians. He does not give us the whole story and nowhere mentions the triumph of Athens; but this must have been at the back of his mind when he gently censures the Rhodians for missing their great chance through momentary oversight. He was too devoted to Athens, now at the height of her power and brilliance, to falsify the facts; and he is tactfully frank with the Rhodians, who, receiving from him the noblest panegyric that they ever received in their history, were not offended by his freedom.

The interesting story of the birth of Rhodes, that it rose from the depths of the sea—a known phenomenon in the Mediterranean—and of its aboriginal allotment to the Sun-God, had not appeared in any previous literature, but must have been drawn from the same source as the former—the folklore of the island; we may trust the assurance of the scholiasts for this. The passionate devotion of the Rhodians to Helios is a unique fact in the history of Greek religion, descending doubtless as a tradition from pre-Hellenic days. The Sun-God counted but little for the other Greek communities; but he so dominated the Rhodian imagination that—as a later writer humorously records—one could not buy a cake in Rhodes that had not the image of Helios stamped upon it. How they imagined him is revealed to us by a gold stater struck by the city of Rhodes in the fourth century, a wonder-work of Greek art (Fig. 5).

This antiquarian lore is interesting, but the dominating feature of the ode is its sustained beauty and strength working with a mellow richness of language, free from excess or overstrain, and with stately metrical flow. The poetic phrase that forms the proem is a master-piece that neither Pindar nor any other Greek lyric poet ever surpassed: the diction is like pure gold glittering in the sun. The triumphant gladness of the opening is answered by the grave, half-melancholy, closing words showing the shadow on human glory and Pindar's normal view of life.

OLYMPIAN VIII

To Alkimedon of Aigina

"HAIL, Olympia, mother of contests for the peerless crowns,
Mistress of the shrine of Truth, where soothsayers make
    trial of the will of Zeus of the gleaming thunderbolt,
    seeking for a sign in the burnt-sacrifice,
Whether he hath ought to say concerning men whose hearts
    are hot to win high renown and solace for their toils 5
    and pains.
Fulfilment (of hopes) is achieved by prayers in reward for
    piety.
But, oh! grove of Pisa beauteous with trees on Alpheus'
    bank,
Welcome this choral band and this solemn carrying of the 10
    garland.
Verily great is his fame,
Upon whom thy bright honour waiteth.
Diverse are the blessings that fall on diverse men.
And with divine aid there are many paths of prosperity.
Timosthenes, Fate hath allotted thee and thy brother to 15
    the charge of Zeus, thy kindred's God;
Who brought thee to be proclaimed at Nemea,
And Alkimedon to be an Olympian victor by the slope of
    Kronos' hill.
Fair to the eye was he on that day;
And, his prowess in the contest in no way belying his fair
    form,
By his victory in the wrestling he blazoned the name of
    Aigina as his fatherland, the land of the long oar,   20
Where the Saviour-Law of Righteousness, sharer of the

judgment-seat of Zeus who guardeth the stranger's
right, is well maintained, more than of all men in the
world.

For in a matter that is manifold and swayeth in manifold
wise in the balance,

To decide with right judgment according to the occasion
is a task hard to wrestle with.

25 But 'tis some ordinance of the Immortals—and may the
ages yet to be born weary never in fulfilling this—
that hath established this sea-girt land to be (no less
than Olympia) a wondrous pillar of defence for strangers
from all parts,

30 A land held in trust for the Dorian folk from the days of
Aiakos.

Him the son of Leto and far-swaying Poseidon,

When they were minded to fashion for Ilion its coronal of
towers,

Summoned to be their fellow-worker at the wall;

Because it was fated that one day when wars arose against it,

35 In battles that ravage cities,

It should breathe forth a column of fell smoke.

But when the tower was newly built,

Three dark-gleaming serpents sprang up against it,

Of whom two fell down

And gasping there cast away their lives,

40 But one of them leaped onward with a loud cry.

And forthwith Apollo, brooding on this portent suddenly
confronting them,

Gave utterance thus—

'Oh, hero, Pergamos is doomed to be captured one day
in the place where thy hands have wrought—

For thus this prodigy sent from loud-thundering Zeus, the
son of Kronos, telleth me—

Not without the might of sons of thine, but it will be brought

45 low both in the first generation of them and the fourth'.

The God then, having given this clear prophecy,

Drave his steeds in hot haste to Xanthos and to the well-
horsed Amazons and to the lands of Ister.

But the God that brandisheth the trident turned his swift
    chariot towards sea-washed Isthmos,
Escorting Aiakos thitherward above his golden steeds,   50
And wishful to visit the ridge of Corinth far-famed for its
    festival.
Nothing among men will ever give equal measure of
    delight to all.
And if I in my verse had exalted the fame of Melesias from
    the striplings he hath trained—
Nay, but let not the hand of envy smite me with sharp 55
    stones.
For I will speak of the same glad victory won by him at
    Nemea (as by Alkimedon),
And later on his glory arising from men's battles in the
    pankration.
Verily 'tis easier to teach others having learned the lesson
    well oneself.   60
'Tis foolish not to have knowledge before one teacheth:
And the wisdom of the untried man is of lighter account.
The well-trained teacher will speak with further insight
    than others on those doings,
What manner of training will bring a man best forward
If he is minded to win all-coveted glory from the sacred
    games.
And now Alkimedon bringeth him honour,   65
Having won this the thirtieth victory (gained by his pupils),
This boy who by the grace of Heaven and failing no whit
    in manliness
Hath thrust off upon the limbs of four other boys the
    burden of the bitter homecoming, the mocking speech
    and entrance by a covert path.
And he hath breathed into his grandsire new life and 70
    vigour, the foe of eld.
Verily when a man hath fared full prosperously, he for-
    getteth coming death.
But 'tis meet that I should awaken memory and tell to the
    Blepsiadai of this bloom of victory won by might of 75
    hand,

Upon whose heads this is now laid as the sixth crown won
    in the contests for the leafy garland.
Even the dead have their own share in the sacrificial
    offerings ordained by law,
80 And the dust of the grave doth not darken the goodly glory
    won by kinsmen.
Iphion[1] might hear the tidings from Hermes' daughter,
    Rumour,
And might tell to Kallimachos[1] of the shining lustre of
    the Olympian victory,
That Zeus hath brought to their kindred:
And may the God be fain to grant them to add noble deeds
    to noble,
85 And may He keep fell sickness from them!
I pray too that He may not set the jealous goddess with
    thwarting purpose about the path of their fair pros-
    perity,
But may foster them and their city, bringing a tearless life
    to both.''

    This ode, composed in the year 460 B.C. in honour of a
young Aeginetan who had won in the boys' wrestling-
match, is one of the interesting group of odes in which
Pindar sings the fame of Aigina, the city to which after his
own he was most devoted. It should be read in conjunction
with the many others that commemorate Aeginetan victors.
The glorious traditions of the Aiakidai, who as leaders of
the Myrmidons, according to the legend, had arisen in the
island in the pre-historic period, whose eponymous ancestor
Aiakos was a semi-religious figure, the apostle-priest of
"Zeus of the Hellenes", and the friend of Gods, while his
descendants Telamon and Peleus, Achilles Aias and Neoptolemos were the outstanding heroic figures of Greek saga,
offered ample material to Pindar's lyric and kindled his
warmest enthusiasm. It was also quickened by his admiration for their stable Doric institutions, their aristocratic
society, their high reputation for commercial justice and

---

[1] One of his buried kinsmen.

kindliness to the stranger, and by their recent prowess in the naval contest with Persia. Their overthrow by Athens, which occurred within a very few years of the composition of this ode, was one of the tragedies of Greek history; and Pindar must have deeply felt that the lustre of the old Hellas that he loved was dimmed by the suppression of this noble city.

The myth that he here selects for the glorifying of Aigina was a strange one and probably unfamiliar to his audience, the co-operation of Aiakos with the Gods Poseidon and Apollo in building the walls of Troy, which is combined with the prophecy that the city would one day be taken at that part of the wall where Aiakos had worked; for so Apollo interprets the portent of the miraculous attack of the serpents, two of whom die on the wall and the third springs forward triumphantly towards the Akropolis. The two who fall are obviously Achilles and Aias, the third is Neoptolemos. We can follow the logic of the omen in other points, but it contains nothing to justify Apollo's interpretation of it as pointing to a double capture of Troy, once by Telamon in the first generation after Aiakos and again by Neoptolemos in the third. The story then is not wholly *ben trovato*; and the scholiasts evidently regard Pindar as the original author of it. If this was so, we may congratulate Pindar on the happiness of his imagination, whereby he could present to the Aeginetans the story of a single thrilling incident that foreshadowed as in a glass darkly the whole of the heroic achievements of the Aiakidai against Troy. But we may doubt if Pindar was in this case springing upon the assembled Aeginetans a brand-new fiction about their ancient heroes. We may believe the scholiasts' assertion that it had not appeared in earlier literature. But we must reckon also with the suggestions of folklore. An interesting passage in the *Iliad* (VI., 435-439) makes it almost certain that Homer was aware of a tradition of a weak spot in the walls of Troy, and of a prophecy that there the city would one day be successfully assailed. Then, as the tradition was early rife that the walls had been built by Gods, it would be natural for folklore to explain the weakness as due to the handiwork of a mortal working with them: this mortal must have been a friend of Gods, someone such as Aiakos. This is how folk-fancy could work. The fact of a weak spot on the wall, "by the wild fig-tree", as Andromache tells us—"where thrice the bravest of the Achaeans have made assay . . . whether

that some one well-versed in divine lore bade them or that
their own spirit urged them on", was handed down in a living memory. The "wild fig-tree" was a remembered local
feature, marking the fatal place, as was the wild apple-tree
on the hill of Senlac in the popular memory of our great
battle.

Another point of interest that we find in the ode is at the
close, where he affords us a glimpse of his speculation concerning the continuance of life after death: the dead kinsmen have some knowledge of, and some interest in, the
fortunes of their living kindred: they can feel with our gladness and our sorrow. This faith is vaguely delivered but
with some conviction. It falls far short of the fervent and
dogmatically articulated scheme of Heaven and Hell in the
Orphic doctrine which he had proclaimed in an earlier ode
to the despot of Akragas.

Though not on the highest plane of his poetry, the ode has
much merit and poetic appeal. The diction is strong, clear,
and flowing; there is pathos and stateliness in the verse at
the close; and we mark his usual skill in turning moralising reflections into song-speech; except in his sententious
remarks about the trainer Melesias, which are not far from
platitudes. There are signs of haste and carelessness, intelligible if the ode was composed in a hurry, to be sung at
Olympia, as the opening lines give us reasons for supposing. But the chief blemish of the poem is the ugly passage about the shameful return of the defeated athletes.
What is still more astonishing is that Pindar should have
repeated this in another ode in honour of an Aeginetan
(*Pyth.* 8). Were the Aeginetans such bad sportsmen or were
the Hellenes generally? Perhaps he was remembering how
the defeated citizen was usually received by the Thebans,
who were an unpleasant people; and he attributed their
malicious temper to other Hellenic communities.

OLYMPIAN IX

To Epharmostos of Opous

"THE strain of Archilochos, giving voice at Olympia,
The triple strain of triumph, rising with loud swell,
Sufficèd to lead Epharmostos' steps
In choral revel with his friends and fellows to the hill of
    Kronos:
But now with such shafts of song as these, launched from 5
    the Muses' far-speeding bow,
Draw near to Zeus, the Lord of the ruddy lightning,
And the holy hill, the crown of Elis,
The hill that the Lydian hero Pelops chose as Hippo- 10
    dameia's goodliest dower.
But let fly withal a wingèd arrow of sweet song towards
    Putho:
Verily thou shall not deal in words that fall idly to the
    ground,
Trilling thy lyre's strings in honour of the wrestling of a
    man from far-famed Opous,
Having fashioned the praise both of her son and her
    the mother,
Opous the allotted home of Themis and her daughter of
    high renown, Law-Reverence, the saviour of the lives 15
    of men.
And she teemeth with glorious deeds done (by her sons)
    on the banks of thy stream, Kastalia, and the stream
    of Alpheus:
The blossoms of whose garlands exalt the famed Mother
    of the Locrians, the city of beauteous trees.   20
Lo, I then, lighting up the dear city with my fiery songs,

47

Swifter than a high-mettled steed or a ship wingèd with
    all her sail,
25 Will waft these tidings through all Hellas,
If with any god-given skill of hand
I work this choice garden of the Graces.
For 'tis they that endow us with all the fair things of life;
    and valour and wisdom come to men in accordance
    with heaven's will.
30 For how could it be true that Herakles brandishèd the
    club against the trident,
When Poseidon took his stand against him to guard Pulos,
And the God smote him hard, and Phoebus in the fray
    smote him with his silver bow,
Nor did Hades hold his rod unswung,
Wherewith he shepherdeth the forms of mortal men down
    the hollow highway of the dead?
35 Let my lips reject in scorn such a tale as this:
For to blaspheme the Gods is an evil play of wit,
And loud-mouthèd unseasonable speech is the accompani-
    ment of madness.
40 Babble not now of such things:
Leave all war and strife far apart from the region of the
    Immortals.
Bring rather the tribute of thy speech to the city of
    Protogeneia,
Where by the providence of the God of the gleaming
    lightning
Purrha and Deukalion, having come down from Parnassos,
First set up their home, and, without the embrace of the
    marriage-bed,
45 Raised up offspring from the stones, to form one folk;
And the stones gave them their earliest name.
Awaken for them the shrill measures of heroic lays,
And ever praise old wine, but the bloom of newer verse.
50 They say indeed that the dark earth was deluged by the
    water's might,
But that through the working of Zeus a mighty ebb drew
    off the water suddenly.

From the beginning your brazen-shielded ancestors were
  of that early folk, of the stock of Iapetos,   55
Sons sprung from their daughters and from the greatest
  of the kin of Kronos,
Native kings in line unbroken:
Until that day when the Lord of Olympos snatched the
  daughter of Opous from the land of the Epeioi,
And in untroubled union mingled with her on the slopes
  of Mainalos,
Then brought her as a gift to Lokros,   60
Lest age should come upon him bearing the doom of
  childlessness.
His spouse had within her the seed of the mightiest,
And the hero was glad of heart when he saw his adopted son,
And he named him by the same name as his mother's
  father,
The child destined to be a man surpassing all in form and 65
  mighty deeds;
And he gave to him a city and a folk to rule.
But stranger-guests from other lands came to him—
From Argos and from Thebes, men of Arcady and Pisa;
But above all the settlers he gave chief honour to Menoitios,
  son of Aktor and Aigina;   70
Whose son Patroklos, having fared with the Atreidai to
  the plain-land of Teuthras,
Stood firm by Achilles' side alone
When Telephos charged in and routed the valiant Danaoi
  right up to their sea-beachèd ships:
So that he gave proof to the discerning to know that the
  soul of Patroklos was a warrior's: 75
From which time the son of Thetis won him over that he
  should never range himself in the deadly battle far
  from his man-quelling spear.
May I be a master-finder of saga-story, meet to soar in the 80
  Muses' chariot,
And may daring and overmastering might be my ministers!
Because he is the guest-friend of our state and for his
  prowess' sake

I went to do honour to the crowning of Lampromachos
    at the Isthmian games, when both brothers were
85   victorious in the trial on the self-same day:
Then came two other triumphs in the gates of Corinth;
And those others that Epharmostos won in the bay of
    Nemea.
At Argos he won glory from among the men, and as a boy
    in Athens.
And at Marathon, when wrongfully barred from the strip-
    lings' contest,
How he held his own in the strife of the older athletes for
90   the silver goblets!
And having overthrown his men with sleight that is quick
    to throw but stumbleth not itself,
With what a shout of acclamation he passed through the
    ring of people,
In youthful bloom and fair to see,
And having wrought deeds most fair!
95 And there, too, to the host on Mount Parrhasios at the
    holy gathering of Zeus the Light-God, he proved his
    wondrous might;
And when at Pellene he bore away the prize, the well-
    woven remedy against cold winds.[1]
The tomb of Iolaos also and sea-washed Eleusis plead the
    cause of his renown.
Best of all endowments is that which cometh to us by
100   Nature's gift:
But many men start to win glory by excellence learnèd by
    rote from others.
Verily everything in which God hath no part is none the
    worse if we pass it by in silence.
105 Certain paths (of life) lead farther on than others;
And one occupation will not nourish us all.
Hard to scale are the heights of wisdom.
But while bringing this prize (to the altar) be bold to roar
    it out[2] to the welkin

---

[1] Pindaric synonym for a cloak, which was given as a prize.
[2] He strangely uses the word for a wild beast's cry.

That this man has been born with more than mortal
    prowess of hand and suppleness of limb, and hath the
    battle-spirit in his eyes:
And he laid his victorious crown on the altar of Aias Oileus
    in the high festival."

This ode was composed to commemorate the victory of
a Locrian athlete won in 468 B.C. It is one—and not the
earliest—of a small group of three, which give him the
opportunity of eulogising and probably also visiting the
people of Lokris: to these we may now add another, a
fragment found in a recently discovered papyrus from
Oxyrhynchos. He eulogises them with great warmth and
with a tone of sincerity as a people pre-eminent in war and
the arts and of a high reputation for truthfulness and
justice. And there is no reason here to suspect Pindar of the
insincerity of the hireling: for the achievements of the
Locrians in Magna Graecia, where one of the earliest legis-
lators of Europe arose, might justify his praises. And this
enthusiasm pervades the whole ode: the diction is striking
and arresting, the tone is excited and high-pitched. The
poem reveals an audacity more than is normal with him,
especially in his treatment of myth, and in his personal,
self-revealing outburst, where he claims to be an original
framer of saga and prays for the spirit of daring and for
immeasurable power. He makes good his claim and his
prayer was answered.

    The contents of the ode are very varied, and at first
sight difficult to bring into any organic unity; but
we are so carried away by the swift flow of the rhythms
and the forceful current of the diction that the movement of thought and feeling seems unbroken to the end.
The proem is comparatively simple, merely a reference
to a three-lined verse attributed to Archilochos invoking
Herakles with cries of exultation, which was habitually
sung by the successful victor and his friends at Olympia on
the last night of the festival in a triumph-procession, unless
they had a more elaborate poem composed in time for that
occasion. This ode Pindar sent to the victor or brought with
him to Opous, where it may have been sung round or near

the altar of Aias Oileus, the leading Locrian hero, who is mentioned at the close. The first mythic digression in the ode, the reference to the combat of Herakles with the three divinities, has no relevance to the main subject and could have no special interest for the Locrians; it is merely introduced as bearing on the moral-religious aphorism, "all our valour and inspiration come to us by divine favour" (or "in accordance with divine ruling"). But how does the myth that he then introduces bear on this excellent principle? My translation expresses a new interpretation that I will try to justify in my critical commentary: namely, that after expounding his dictum of the dependence of our virtues on heaven he remembers a myth that seems flagrantly to contradict it —that so far from being dependent on heaven, the mortal Herakles joined battle with three most powerful deities and came off successfully. Pindar deals summarily with this awkward myth by contemptuously, almost fiercely, rejecting it as blasphemous and untrue; and hereby anticipates Plato, who in his *Republic* would ban all stories about strife among the gods, perfect peacefulness being part of the divine character. Pindar's dictum has a certain importance in the history of theology: but in regard to the myth that he rejects, he might incur the charge of inventing a phantom in order to abolish it; for there never was such a myth as he states—no story of a battle in which Herakles met all these three deities at once. But there were certain mythic elements that could be combined into such a story. Pindar takes from Homer the well-known saga of Herakles' attack on the Pylians, when Hades came to their aid and was wounded by the hero: the poet on his own authority may have drawn Poseidon into this conflict, for the Pylians were Minyans, and Poseidon was the great God of the Minyans and ought to aid them.   As for Apollo, there was a legend well known in the sixth century that Herakles had tried to carry off the Delphic tripod and had thereby come into conflict with Apollo. Pindar with his usual audacity chooses to contaminate these stories; and his carelessness is the more natural because he disbelieves and despises them.

He is more serious and happy about the flood-story, and the myth of the origin of the Locrians from the stones which Deukalion and Purrha flung behind them as they descended from Parnassos after the flood and which were transformed into living men and women. Here at any rate Pindar was not inventing; he could find the main outlines of the flood-myth and of the genealogy of the Locrians in general Hellenic folklore and at least one literary predecessor. But though he tells the tale with some force and charm, he does not care to be minutely accurate, and he somewhat blurs the account of the Locrian genealogy by his vagueness as to the position in it of Protogeneia: she ought to be from her name "the First-Born" woman after the flood, the ancestress of the Locrians; but it is not clear whether Pindar so imagined her. Then, at the close of this story of the foundations of Opous, he takes a sudden new departure, linking it with the name and legend of Patroklos; he was able to do this without violence because Menoitios of Aigina, the father of Patroklos, was one of the earliest immigrant settlers of Opous. This may have been Locrian tradition; for it is confirmed by Homer, who makes Achilles, in his lament over his dead friend, recall pathetically the promise which he gave to the hero Menoitios that he would bring back his son Patroklos safe to Opous after Troy fell. Through Patroklos and Achilles Pindar could now in a few strong and swift touches present to us another and independent myth, the battle of the Achaeans against Telephos on the Mysian coast, where they were saved from disaster by Achilles, as was told in the old epic the *Kupria*, which was familiar to Pindar. It may be on his own authority that he here chooses to make that scene and the conspicuous valour of Patroklos there displayed the first occasion of the intimate companionship that arose between this hero and Achilles. If we take this interpretation of the short passage—which is quite possible and even natural—Pindar boldly departs from the Homeric account of the early history of their friendship. And this might then explain his sudden personal outburst, praying that he may ever be an inventor of new saga. He would hardly have broken out like this at this moment, unless he felt that he had been just giving forth something new and original in epic legend. But in the preceding epic narrative we can discern nothing new or original, except possibly this account of the origin of the famous friendship of the two heroes according to the interpretation here suggested.

He then passes swiftly to the more immediately relevant eulogy of Epharmostos, giving a picturesque record of his many victories, and closes with the moralising reflection, expressed in striking phrase, that such a man must be divinely inspired, just as the poet is divinely inspired, and that this is the source of all great achievement.

As the ode closes with the briefest reference to the hero-cult of Aias Oiliades, we might wonder why Pindar has not chosen some story of his prowess for the epic material of his lyric; for the Locrians through all their history were devoted to him, placing his figure on their coins and, when in battle-array, leaving in their ranks a place for his ghost. But the reputation of this warrior, ever since the taking of Troy, had been under a cloud; and the Locrians throughout all the ages were heavily punished for his sin against Kassandra: so at least they and everyone believed.[1] Pindar may well have thought that his own dictum applied here, "It is best to keep silent about that which is without God."

The ode is strikingly characteristic both of the poet's strength and of his faults. Some of the phrases are twisted and bizarre; and it is hard to justify all the motives. But, though he appears to be composing in a kind of ecstasy and the storm of poetry seems to be hurrying him tempestuously along regardless of his path, on the whole he keeps his head and we can discern his main purpose. We are grateful to him for turning the little-known traditions of the Locrians into ringing verse; and this ode takes high rank also among the products of Greek religious poetry.

[1] *Vide* my *Hero-Cults*, pp. 293-305.

OLYMPIAN X [XI]

To Hagesidamos of the Locrians in Italy

"THERE are times when men's greatest need is favouring
winds,
Times when they need most the sky-waters, the rain-
daughters of the Cloud:
But when with hard toil a man fareth gloriously,
Then honey-voicèd songs become to him the prelude of 5
a long-abiding record and a trusty pledge for the
remembrance of his greatest deeds of valour.
Such praise is dedicate to the Olympian victors in abundant
measure;
And such themes indeed my tongue is fain to shepherd:
But it is only by God's help that a man blossometh with the 10
poet's thoughts according to his heart's desire.
Be assured now, Agesidamos, son of Archestratos,
That for the sake of thy battle with the boxers
I will raise sweet strains on high that will add lustre to
thy crown of golden olive,
Having a care to thy lineage from among the Locrians of 15
the West.
Ye Muses, join with them there in the triumphant dance:
I will go bail to you
Ye will not come to a guest-repelling host of men, untried
in aught fair and noble,
But to a folk masters of all lore, a warrior-folk:
For neither the tawny fox nor the ravening lion could 20
change his inborn mood."

55

The tenth Olympian, in the old tradition reckoned as the eleventh, is obviously the earlier of the two odes composed in honour of the boy Agesidamos of the Locrians of Magna Graecia, whose victory in the boxing contest can be now dated with certainty at 476 B.C. The shorter ode was evidently composed to be sung at Olympia on the last night of the feast, devoted to festive celebration of the triumphs. Therefore Pindar had no time for length or elaboration; yet on the spur of the moment he has thrown off a short master-piece; so happily are blended the praises of the boy-victor, the eulogy on his gifted people, and the exaltation of the poet's craft; the style is pure and strong, there is high imagination in more than one phrase, and the short proem is full of charm. The pithy and forceful condensation of phrase is specially striking at the close.

OLYMPIAN XI [X]

To the same

"READ ye where in my heart is written the name of the
    son of Archestratos, the Olympian victor;
For I had forgotten I was his debtor for a sweet song.
But do thou, O Muse, and thou, O Goddess of Truth,
    daughter of God,
With righteous hand shield me from the liar's reproach of 5
    sinning against my friend.
For the time of my tarrying, falling on me from long ago,[1]
    hath shamèd me for my heavy debt.
But still payment with interest can wipe out bitter
    blame;
And see then now how the rushing stream whelmeth down 10
    its course the rolling stone,
And how for a dear friend's sake we will pay the reckon-
    ing agreed!
For the city of the Locrians of the West is the home of the
    Goddess of Good Faith,
And dear to them are the Muse Kalliope and the brazen
    God of War.
(But Kuknos' onset turned back even Herakles the over- 15
    strong.)
Let Agesidamos, as conqueror of the boxers in the Olym-
    pian contest, render such thanks to (his trainer) Ilas,
    as Patroklos to Achilles.
And verily a man may be a whetstone to another whom 20
    Nature hath shaped for nobleness,

---

[1] Or, the thought of the covenanted time, coming into my mind from
long ago.

57

And spur him on to achieve fame more than mortal in
    accordance with God's planning.
Only a very few have won without hard toil such a triumph
    as sheddeth a lustre o'er their life beyond all other deeds.
Now the ordinances of God have rousèd me to sing of that
25   peerless contest, of trials six in number,
Which Herakles establishèd by the ancient tomb of Pelops,
After that he slew stalwart Kteatos, Poseidon's son,
And slew Eurutos withal, so that he might exact his due
    wage for service done from haughty Augeas, as lord
    from grudging debtor;
And he quellèd those foemen also on his march, having
30   ambushed them in a brake hard by Kleonai,
For that formerly these overmastering Moliones
Had ravagèd his host when camped in Elis' hollow vales.
35 And indeed the Epeian king, the guest-betrayer,
Saw no long time afterwards his all-rich fatherland caught
    in the ruthless flame of war,
And his city sinking beneath the sword-stroke into the
    deep pit of doom.
40 'Tis hard to put aside from one the feud of the stronger.
And he also, Augeas, the last to fall into captivity, did not
    escape sheer death.
He then, the warrior-son of Zeus, gathering his whole host
    and all the spoil into the narrow place of Pisa,
45 Measured out a fencèd garth hallowed to his mightiest
    Sire,
And having pegged the Altis all about, he cleared it fair
    and free,
And consecrated all the level plain around to solace and
    festivity,
Having honoured the stream of Alpheus in company with
    the twelve sovereign deities.
50 And he called the hill by Kronos' name; for of aforetime,
    while Oinomaos ruled, it was nameless, drenched with
    many a snow-shower.
In this first birthday of the solemn ritual the Fates stood
    hard by as witnesses,

And Father Time who alone testeth the very truth of things.
In his onward course He hath recorded the plain tale,   55
How the hero portionèd the war-gift, the first-fruits of the
    spoil,
And establishèd the fifth-yearly festival with the first hold-
    ing of Olympian games and the winning of victories.
Who was it then who won the fresh-woven crown   60
By might of hand or swiftness of foot or chariot,
Having set up in his heart the prayerful hope of triumph
    in the contest and having in actual deed achievèd it?
Best in the foot-race, running the straight course,   65
Was Oionos, son of Likumnios,
And he came from Midea, leading a host of men:
But Echemos it was who by his wrestling won glory for his
    city Tegea.
Doruklos, dweller in Tiruns city, was triumphant in the
    issue of the boxing:
Victor with the four-horsed chariot was Samos from Man-   70
    tinea, son of the God of the Sea-foam;
But with the javelin it was Phrastor hit the mark.
Nikeus, encircling a huge stone in his hand, threw the
    quoit to a distance beyond all others;
And the whole fellowship of warriors blazèd forth into a
    mighty shout.
The lovely light of the sweet-faced moon kindled the   75
    evening sky;
And with the delightful feastings the whole holy place was
    full of song, tunèd to the fashion of the victor's hymn
    of praise.
But we, following the lead of ancient poets at the beginning
    of their lays,
Now, also, in honour of a joyance whereto proud victory
    lendeth its name,
We will sing of the thunder and the fire-forgèd shaft of   80
    Zeus, the awakener of the uproar in the heavens,
The gleaming levin-bolt, welded to Omnipotence.
But the notes of the flute shall meet the delicious warbling
    of these strains

85 That have come to their birth by Dirke's stream late,
         indeed, in time:
   But (they are) even as a child long desired, that the wife
         bringeth to the sire who has turnèd his back on youth;
   And verily it warmeth his heart with love full deep:
90 For wealth that getteth an alien shepherd from without
         the house is most bitter to a dying man;
   And when a man, Agesidamos, having done fair deeds
         with no poet to sing of them, hath come to the hall of
         Death,
   All his high hopes are barren,
   And with all his toil he hath won but a scanty measure of
         delight.
   But on thy head the sweet-voiced lyre and the delightful
         flute scatter grace as dew :
95 And the Pierian Muses, the daughters of Zeus, swell thy
         fame throughout the world.
   And I, harnessing myself to speed,
   Clasp in my embrace the far-famed nation of the Locrians,
   Shedding the honey of my verse on the city of goodly men.
   And I have belauded the sweet son of Archestratos,
100 Whom I saw on that day by the Olympian altar,
   Conquering with might of hand, fair of shape, and tinged
         with that lovely bloom
   That once saved Ganymede from pitiless death with the
         aid of the goddess born of Cyprus."

   The longer poem on the same victory (usually numbered
as Olympian X) evidently followed upon the shorter after
some indefinite interval. All that Pindar indicates is that
the promised date for its delivery was long past. We can
hardly suppose that many years had elapsed: there is nothing to suggest that Agesidamos is now a mature man; and
Pindar's vivid recollection of the circumstances and details
of the contest rather implies that the victory was still recent.
The longer odes were usually intended to be sung at some
religious festival commemorating the triumph, immediately
after the home-coming of the athlete; but the commemora-

tion was frequently repeated on the same festival day in succeeding years, and this ode may have been sent for one of those days, perhaps a year after the event.

Pindar's apology rings true and carries us away; he does indeed pay the debt with interest; and he is composing at the height of his powers, both of imagination and expression. Language and feeling are at white heat; the phrases are often arresting and strained, but never unnatural; the invocation of the thunderbolt of Zeus resounds with the crash of the elements; but the tense energy that animates most of the poem leaves room for grace and sweetness. He seems to have cherished a tender and romantic recollection of the boy-athlete.

There is only one difficulty in the ode which hinders our full understanding and appreciation of it—the cryptic sentence near the beginning about Herakles and Kuknos. It is hard to find an explanation that might satisfy the Locrians or Agesidamos or the modern reader. The phrase comes between his eulogy of the Locrians, closing with praise of their martial valour, and his injunction to Agesidamos gratefully to remember his trainer Ilas, to whom in great measure he owed his victory. The phrase has a proverbial tone, and seems to serve as a transition-link between the praise of the people and the praise of the boy. The proverb ought to apply to one or the other or to both. But Kuknos was an evil giant, the son of the War-God, who murdered Apollo's pilgrims and adorned his father's shrine with their skulls: it would be no compliment to be compared to Kuknos. The earliest version of his story is given in the poem, attributed to Hesiod, called the "Shield of Herakles": there Herakles is represented as, with the aid of Athena, boldly confronting Kuknos and Ares, slaying the one and defying the other: there is no hint of his shrinking or retiring from their onset. But Pindar followed a later version, better known probably to the Locrians, a poem of Stesichoros, in which the hero, seeing the giant supported by the War-God, prudently retired, and only returned to the fray when Athena came to his support; hence arose a proverbial expression in vogue among the later Greeks: "Even Herakles cannot face two at once". If Pindar's phrase has that proverbial meaning here, we cannot imagine how it could apply either to the Locrians or the boy-boxer. But it might as naturally have a simpler meaning: "Even Herakles had to retire sometimes", or, "Even Herakles did not always win at once". This might apply to the Locrians; for just about this date the threatened attack of Anaxilas, tyrant of Rhegium, alluded to in the second Pythian, had been seriously alarming them, until Hieron had come to their rescue. We know nothing precise about this campaign. Anaxilas might well stand for Kuknos, but the mythological parallel is unhappy, for the Locrians and Hieron were two to one against Anaxilas; also it would be unnecessary and tactless for Pindar at this point to be alluding to the Locrians' war reverses. The old interpreters of Pindar were probably right in regarding the proverbial phrase as referring to the boy-boxer and the circumstances of his contest. The whole context indicates that Agesidamos had a very hard struggle to win. If we may suppose that in the first few rounds he was getting the worst of it and seemed to be yielding, and then with a great effort, and perhaps through the encouragement of his trainer Ilas, recovered ground and finally conquered, we could regard the mythic aphorism "Even Herakles did not win at once against Kuknos" as a suitable consolation. Probably this is the best explanation we are likely to find.

As the Locrians of Magna Graecia had no special mythology of their own, Pindar entertains them with a long mythic narrative concerning the origin of the Olympic games, and he gives the first list of victors in a rather dry chronicle form, as if he were copying it from an old record. We may be sure that Pindar did not invent either the legend or the list. But how far he is giving us an authentic and prevalent tradition, and from what sources he derived it, are questions that may be discussed in the critical commentary.

The chronicle itself may be regarded as a flaw in the poetry of the ode; but it is enlivened towards the close with a tingling phrase and a gleam of nature-magic. When it is finished, he seems to draw a deep breath so as to deliver himself of that astonishing outburst about the thunder, perhaps the most daring and stormy verse that he ever forged.

The last part of the ode is conspicuous for a certain graceful sweetness and warmth of feeling.

OLYMPIAN XII

To Ergoteles of Himera

"OH, fair Fortune, Saviour-Goddess, child of Zeus the
    Guardian of our freedom,
I pray thee ward well Himera, the mistress of wide lands.
For 'tis thy power that governeth swift ships on the main,
    and on land ravening wars and the gatherings of the
    wise in counsel.
Verily the hopes of men welter aimlessly, cutting through 5
    many a rising, many a falling wave, in the barren sea
    of falsehood.
Nor hath any of the dwellers on the earth ever gatherèd
    from heaven any trusty token concerning his faring
    in the future.
Blind and dark are our counsels concerning things to come.
Many things fall out for mortals counter to their judgment, 10
Turning men back from joy, while others having confronted
    the storms of bitter trouble
In a short space of time gain high prosperity in exchange
    for woe.
Even so, thou son of Philanor, hadst thou abided by thy
    ancestral hearth, like a cock that fights at home,
The glory of thy running would have lost renown and shed 15
    its leaves;
But that civic strife, setting man against man, amercèd thee
    of thy Knossian fatherland.
But now, Ergoteles, having won the crown at Olympia,
And twice again from Putho and on the Isthmos,
Thou exaltest the fame of the warm baths of the Nymphs
    dwelling on lands of thy own lordship."

The twelfth Olympian, celebrating the victory of an exiled Cretan from Knossos who had now settled at Himera on the north coast of Sicily, and had won an Olympian victory in the long race in 472 B.C., shows us in as striking a manner as the tenth what Pindar could achieve in the short poem. The style of phrasing is perfect throughout: the invocation is melodiously solemn, the moralising musings go deep, and the weightiness of expression reminds us of the best of Aeschylus: one could hardly find in the whole of Greek literature a sentence more masterly for its perfect union of thought and musical speech than his utterance concerning the weltering hopes of man: at the close the style is lighter but most graceful, and he has invented a beautiful phrase for the leaves falling from the chaplet of glory—more striking than Walter Scott's parallel "Randolph, thy wreath has lost a rose".

We may be disappointed that, as this is his only 'epinikion' in honour of a Cretan, he did not weave into it some of the great myths of the island's prehistoric past; but he may have thought that neither the banished exile nor the Himeraeans cared much for Crete. From the fifth century onwards, Crete was out of the main history of Greece; the earliest civilised state of Europe, she was still contributing to Greek culture in the sixth century B.C.; after this she contributed nothing till recently in the Great War. Pindar here lifts the veil for a moment and shows us civic strife raging in the island, which remained a chronic evil until it passed into the Roman Empire.

The opening words of the ode give us a glimpse into the recent history of Himera, which had just escaped the tyranny of the son of Theron: hence the invocation includes a special cult-name of Zeus "the Guardian of Freedom" or "the Freeman's God". (Fig.6.) I have commented elsewhere[1] on the significance of this title, which expressed the highest political aspiration of the Hellenes and is unique in the history of religion. It may seem strange that Pindar should have made the High God, thus specialised, the father of 'Fortune', and Fortune the governing principle of the activities of man. At first sight this might appear the same view as that which appealed to Greek scepticism of the fourth century, and in particular to Demosthenes, namely, that all things are really determined by blind chance, an irreligious

---

[1] *Vide* my *Attributes of God*, pp. 154-155.

view that Pindar would disclaim. His 'Tuche' is here not blind chance, but rather "Happy Achievement"; this is what all our actions aim at, and this is more easy to obtain in a free State than in one unfree.

The ode closes with a reference to the famous warm springs near Himera, that gave its name to the new city of 'Thermai', which arose after Himera was destroyed by the Carthaginians in 408 B.C. (*vide* Fig. 7).

OLYMPIAN XIII

To Xenophon of Corinth

"As I praise the House three times triumphant at Olympia,
The House that is kindly to the citizens and ministereth to
    the needs of guests,
I will become familiar with blessed Corinth,
5 The forecourt of the home of Poseidon of the Isthmos, the
    city of radiant youth.
For therein dwelleth Law-Reverence
And her Sister-Goddesses, the sure foundation-stones of
    cities,
Justice and her fellow-nursling Peace, warders of wealth
    for men,
The golden daughters of Themis the wise of counsel.
10 And they are fain to hold Insolence aloof, the brawling
    mother of Satiety.
I have many fair things to say, and unswerving boldness
    rouseth my tongue to speak.
Truly, man's inborn temper fighteth its way to light.
To you, ye sons of Aletas,[1] the rich-flowering Hours have
    ofttimes granted the victor's delight
15 Of those who have excelled in the hallowed contests by
    height of prowess;
They too have inspired the hearts of your men with many
    a device of ancient wisdom.
Every art is the achievement of the founder.
Whence (save from Corinth) were revealèd the fair fashions
    of Dionusos' service linked with the Dithyramb that
    leadeth on the sacred ox?

[1] The Corinthians.

For who added the controlling bridle to the equipment of 20
    the horse,
Or who set on the temples of the Gods the twain forms of
    the royal bird?
And among you the Goddess of Song is sweet of voice,
And among you the War-God blossometh with the fell
    spear-points of your young warriors.
Oh, Supreme Father Zeus, wide ruler of Olympia,
Grant me all my life abundance of poetic speech,   25
And, shepherding this people of Xenophon's from all harm,
    waft them down a prospering course of destiny.
And receive at his hands this ritual-service of the garlands'
    hymn of praise, which he leadeth to thee from the
    field of Pisa,
Victor at once in the foot-race and the strife of the five 30
    contests:
And he met with such fortune as hath hitherto befallen no
    mortal man.
Nay, but two woven parsley-garlands crownèd him, having
    provèd his prowess in the Isthmian Games.
Nemea withstandeth him not.
The glory of the running of his father Thessalos on the
    banks of Alpheus is recorded there.   35
And at Putho he hath the honour of victory in the single
    and the double foot-race won on the self-same day;
And within the same month in rocky Athens, a day of swift
    running set three tokens of the craftsman's skill most
    fairly on his locks.
And the games Hellotia have crownèd him seven times: 40
While in the service of Poseidon on the double shore a
    still longer song of praise will wait on (his kinsmen)
    Terpsias and Eritimos with their father Ptoiodoros.
But as for all your house's deeds of prowess at Delphoi and
    in the lion's hunting-ground at Nemea—
I am (as one) struggling with a crowd for the multitude
    of your honours;   45
As indeed I should not know how to give a clear account
    of the pebbles of the sea.

A law of measure waiteth on all things;
And it is ever best to discern the rightful moment.
But I, a private venturer in a public theme,
Shall tell no false tale about Corinth when I tell of the
50   wise counsels of her sons of old,
And their warfaring in heroic fields of valour:
Of Sisuphos most like a god for subtlety of device,
And of Medea who won for herself a marriage against her
      father's will,
Verily the saviour of Argo and its fellowship.
And as for their deeds of prowess on the battlefield before
55   the walls of Dardanos,
They seemed on both sides to cleave out the issue of the
      contests,
Some of them aiding the well-loved race of Atreus to
      win back Helen,
The others keeping them utterly at bay.
60 When Glaukos came from Lycia the Danaoi cowered before
      him;
And to them he averred that in the city of Peirene's spring,
      his father[1] had rule and a rich demesne and hall:
(Even Bellerophon) who verily suffered many things near
      the holy fount (Peirene) in his craving to yoke Pegasos,
      the son of the snake-haired Gorgon:
Until the Maiden-Goddess Pallas brought him a bridle
65   with golden frontlet;
And straightway his dream turned to waking truth:
But the Goddess spake thus to him—
'Sleepest thou, oh king of the race of Aiolos?
Arise, take this horse-charm in thy hands,
And consecrate in sacrifice a white-gleaming bull to thy
      Father, the Horse-tamer.'
Such things to him sleeping in the night-tide the Virgin
70   of the dark-blue aigis seemed to speak:
And he sprang up on his feet upright;
And having clutched the wondrous thing lying by him
He joyously found Koiranides, the prophet of his country,

---

[1] Glaukos in the *Iliad* is the grandson of Bellerophon, here the son.

And shewed him the whole matter to the end;   75
Even how in accord with his prophetic word he had slept
    the night through on the altar of the Goddess,
And how the very daughter of Zeus, who wieldeth the
    thunder for his spear, brought him the golden thing
    to quell the steed's pride.
But the seer urged him full swiftly to obey the bidding of
    the dream,
And when he had lifted up for sacrifice the stubborn-
    footed beast to the wide-ruling Girder of the Earth,   80
Then speedily to array an altar to Athena the Horse-Goddess.
The power of the Gods fulfilleth and maketh light the
    accomplishment of the thing that passeth all our vows
    and all our hopes:
Even so verily the strong Bellerophon put forth his might
    and capturèd the winged horse,
Stretching about his jaws the soothing magic of the bit.
And having mounted in brazen armour he forthwith 85
    danced the warrior's measure.
Then with the help of Pegasos on a day he smote the
    women-host of archers, the Amazons, from the cold
    hollows of the desolate climes,
And he slew the fire-breathing Chimaira and the Solumoi.
About his fate I will keep silent;   90
But the ancient horse-stalls of Zeus in Heaven welcome
    the steed.
As I launch the straight-whirring darts of song, I must
    speed my quiver-full strongly from my hands, not 95
    missing the mark.
For I fared full fain to the aid of the gay-thronèd Muses
    and the house of the Oligaithidai.
In a brief word, I will make manifest the full tale of their
    triumphs on the Isthmos and those in Nemea:
The loud proclamation of the goodly herald, giving sweet
    voice from both places sixty times, shall be withal the 100
    sworn voucher of my truth.
Their triumphs in Olympia have been, methinks, erewhile
    recounted:

As for those that are to come, I might proclaim them
    clearly at a later day.
At this moment I am full of hopes, but verily in God's
    hands is the future issue.
105 But if the inborn fortune of this house fareth on free,
We will leave this in the hands of Zeus and the War-God
    to accomplish.
Six are those victories of yours on Parnassos' brow;
How many in Argos and in Thebes!
And to how many will the Arcadian altar of King Zeus
    Lukaios testify as it towereth on high.
Yea, and Pellana beareth witness and Sikuon and Megara
110   and the well-fenced grove of the Aiakidai, Eleusis
    and the rich land of Marathon:
The wealth-crowned cities beneath the high ridge of
    Aitna, and all Euboea.
Search in fine throughout all Hellas and thou wilt find the
    tale too long for a single glance.
But now let me swim to shore with lightened stroke of feet.
115 Oh God, the All-fulfiller, grant us the high regard of men
    and the sweet portion of all delights!''

This ode was composed in 464 B.C., when a certain
Xenophon, a Corinthian, of the noble house of the Oligaithidai, performed the unique feat of winning two Olympian
victories in the same celebration, the foot-race and the contest known as the 'pentathlon', namely, the competition in
five events—running, the long jump, throwing the quoit,
throwing the javelin, and wrestling. He also had won in
many other athletic contests elsewhere: so also had his
father and his nearest kinsmen, and the full tale of victories
won by his house is more than Pindar can sum. Here indeed was ample material for the panegyrist of games. Also
this commission afforded Pindar the only public opportunity that came to him in his career of celebrating Corinth, a
city great in commerce, famous for its wealth and luxury,
stable in its politics, and offering copious themes to the
mythological poet in its traditions of the past. And Pindar

is at the height of his powers, master of all his methods.
Yet, except in the metrical structure which is perfect in its
severe beauty, he has failed to produce a masterpiece. Evidently the victor-patron insisted on full measure for his
money and claimed that the ode should enumerate in detail the astonishing record of family victories. Pindar evidently found it a weary task, and broke down under the
effort—in which he is usually most successful—of finding a
striking and picturesque phrase for each one of them, there
being at least sixty. And he adopts the device of breaking
up the long record into two sections, one dealing with the
victories of Xenophon and his nearest of kin, father, grandfather, uncle, and another with those of the whole family
of the Oligaithidai, and the two records are separated by
the long mythic digression concerning Bellerophon. The
device does not work happily. His object was to avoid
the monotony of carrying on the same theme too long: but
he has not avoided it, for the second section becomes almost
a mere catalogue, and—what rarely happens to Pindar—
fatigue shows itself in forgetfulness of syntax; and he seems
glad to hurry to a rather breathless close.

Yet in much of the ode there is charm and characteristic
force: there is warmth and glow in his eulogy of Corinth:
his prayer to Zeus has a noteworthy religious quality: his
poetic aphorisms have pith and originality; and he shows
his usual power in the epic-lyric passage, the mythologic
narrative. We may feel disappointment that he did not develop the legend of Medea, which was rooted in Corinth;
and we may regret that in so slight an account of her he
should make the 'banal' observation that she married without her father's consent. But the shining part of the poem
is the story of Bellerophon, his 'incubation' by the altar of
Athena, of her vision and stirring speech to the hero, the
gift of the bridle, with which he captures and tames Pegasos, the hint of the Bellerophon's sad end after his many
triumphs, and—by way of contrast—the mention of the
happy reception of Pegasos into the stalls of Zeus. Pindar
is here giving us genuine folklore, based on facts of cult.
Bellerophon was a native-born Corinthian hero, and his
adventures in Lycia were connected with the earliest Hellenic penetration of that country. Also, we have independent record of the worship of Athena "the Bridler" in Corinth, associated with the story of Pegasos.

OLYMPIAN XIV

To Asopichos of Orchomenos

"YE Goddesses of Grace, Queens of rich Erchomenos and
   themes of many a song,
Ye whose portion are the waters of Kephisos and your
   home the fair-horsed plain,
Ye guardians of the Minuai of ancient birth—Hearken,
5   for I pray!
For 'tis only with your aid that all delightful, all sweet
   things are brought to bloom for mortals,
Whatever gifts a man hath, wisdom or beauty or radiant
   life.
For not even the Gods can order their dances or their feasts
   without the Graces :
But they, the ministers of all things done in heaven,
10 Have set up their thrones by the side of the Pythian Apollo,
   the God of the golden bow,
And there they hallow the everlasting majesty of the Father
   of Olympos.
Oh, Lady Aglaia! and thou Euphrosune! friend of all
15   music, Daughters of the Supreme God, give your
   ear unto my song,
And thou, too, Thalia, lover of melody, cast thine eye upon
   this choral band for their blessed fortune,
As they tread the light measure of the dance.
Singing the praise of Asopichos I have come, in the Lydian
   mood of music and with studied verse,
For that owing to thy blessing the land of the Minyans
   hath won an Olympian victory.
20 Fare now, O Echo, to the dark-walled home of Persephone,

Bearing the ringing tidings to his father,
That when thou seest Kleodamos thou mayst tell him of
    his son,
How that in the folded plains of far-renowned Pisa,
He hath crowned his youthful locks with the winged
    wreaths of the glorious contests."

    This ode, that might pass as the most brilliant among his
short poems, was perhaps composed in the year 488 B.C.
It commemorated a victory in the foot-race of the boy
Asopichos, a citizen of the Boeotian Orchomenos on Lake
Kopais. The ode was sung in a procession that moved from
the city through a fertile plain to the temple of the Graces.
Here was rich opportunity for Pindar. The city of Orchomenos cherished memories of pre-historic greatness, having
been one of the most brilliant centres of Mycenaean culture
and art. Also, its earliest days were associated with the
heroic stock of the Minuai, and it remained the last surviving home of that people in historic times. But Pindar
might have felt himself precluded from dwelling at length
on the mythical glories of Orchomenos, as the Minyan city
had been through all the ages the bitter enemy of Thebes.
But Orchomenos was in the literal sense the home of the
Graces: not that she had done anything in the historic
period for the arts of Greece: her only glory in this period
is that Pindar wrote this ode on her. There is little doubt
that the strange cult of the 'Charites' or Graces had its
birth in this Minyan city and was thence diffused over the
Greek world. Originally—we may believe—deities or half-
deities of nature, powers of fruitfulness and growth—they
had become in the pre-Homeric age the personifications of
the charm and glory of human life, in all its varied forms
of beauty and delight. They, like the Muses, are unique
creations of the Hellenic imagination, and in no other religion do we find a true parallel.[1] Though Pindar has done
them passing homage elsewhere, this ode is the greatest
tribute that Greek poetry has paid them. It is a brief hymn,
but perfect in its technique, especially in its rhythms, and
the diction is radiant. And the athlete is sufficiently re-

---

[1] *Vide* my *Cults of the Greek States*, vol. v. pp. 427-431.

membered and rewarded with the sweet words at the close, where Echo is bidden to waft the great tidings of his renown down to the halls of the Queen of the dead, where his father dwells.

We may detect a faint echo of this ode in Theocritus' lines on the Charites in his sixteenth Idyl. But Pindar is their only poet. What has become mere common stuff of our literary language was real divinity for him and his people.

THE PYTHIAN ODES

PYTHIAN I

To Hieron of Aitna—King of Syracuse

"HAIL, golden lyre, rightful heirloom of Apollo and the
    Muses of the violet crown,
Thou that rulest the dancer's step, the precursor of delight,
Thou whose calls the singers follow, when with thy quiver-
    ing strings thou fashionest the opening strains of the
    preludes that lead on the chorus:
Thou lullest the spikèd thunderbolt of everlasting fire;   5
And the eagle sleepeth on the top of Zeus's sceptre,
Letting his keen wings droop on either side,
He, the king of birds; and thou hast shed upon him, over
    his curved head, the dark-faced dream-cloud, sweet
    closer of his eyelids;
In slumber he heaveth his languid back, spell-bound by
    thy tides of music:
For even the violent War-God, leaving the fell spear-point 10
    far aside, solaceth his heart with slumber.
Yea, verily, thy magic sootheth the souls of the Gods,
As they gather round the song-craft of the son of Leto and
    the deep-girdled Muses.
But the voice of these maidens of Pieria confoundeth utterly
    all things that Zeus hath hated throughout the earth
    and ravening sea,
And that foe of the gods that lieth in grim Hell,   15
Even Tuphōs of the hundred heads, that once was nurtured
    in the far-famed Cilician cave,
But now the ridges above Kumai that fence back the sea
And the whole land of Sicily press down his shaggy
    bosom:

And a pillar that reacheth unto Heaven holds him fast
     down,
20 Even snowy Etna, foster-nurse of biting snow all the year
     through:
From the hollow depths whereof virgin fountains of fire
     unapproachable are belchèd forth;
And in day-time hidden rivers pour forth a lurid torrent
     of smoke,
But in the darkness of the night, the ruddy flame hurls
     rocks into the deep plain of the sea with a thunder-roar.
25 'Tis that worm below that sendeth up these most fearful
     streams of the Fire-God;
A portent marvellous to gaze upon and a wonder even to
     hearken to as men go by.
Such a monster is in bondage beneath the dark-leaved
     spurs of Etna and 'neath the plain;
And his hard bed rendeth and goadeth all his back that
     is stayed thereon.
May it be vouchsafèd to us, O Zeus, vouchsafèd to be
     pleasing to thee,
30 Who dost fill this mountain with thy presence, this forehead
     of a fair-fruited land;
Whose neighbouring city, named after it, the far-famed
     founder glorified,
When in the racing-course of the Pythian festival the herald
     lifted up his voice and proclaimèd its name, for the sake
     of Hieron winning fair triumph with his chariot.
To men who are borne o'er the sea in ship the first boon at
     the start of their voyaging is the coming of a favourable
     breeze;
For 'tis the greater likelihood then that they in the end will
35   win to a fair home-coming.
Looking then to the happy thing that hath chancèd, the
     law of the fair beginning bringeth to us expectation
That this land will throughout the time to come be famed
     for garlands of victory and for its steeds,
That its name will be raised on high midst the music and
     singing of the feast—

Oh, Phoibos, Lord of Lycia and Delos, Lover of Parnassos'
    fount, Kastalia,

Incline thine heart to this my prayer—and will be blessèd 40
    with fair breed of men.

From the Gods come all the means for the achievement of
    every excellence;

'Tis they who dower us with wisdom, might of hand, and
    skill of speech.

Purposing to sing the praises of that man, I have sure trust

That I shall not be as one who whirling the bronze-cheeked
    javelin casteth it (blindly) outside the course,

But that with a mighty cast I shall surpass my rivals.   45

Would that the whole of his life-days may, with no less
    certitude, waft his bark to (the shores of) wealth and
    the gift of all abundance,

And at the same time bring him forgetfulness of pain!

Verily they might bring to his mind in what manner of
    battles he bided firm on his war-farings;

When by the Gods' devising he and his brother achievèd
    such renown as no Hellene culleth to-day,

To crown their wealth with pride.

But of late he hath wagèd war following the fashion of 50
    Philoktetes:

And in the grip of necessity one of haughty heart had to
    fawn on him for his friendship.

Even so they say the godlike heroes journeyed to bring
    [to Troy] from Lemnos the mighty archer, the son of
    Poias,[1] albeit afflicted with an ulcerous wound:

Who sacked Priam's city and ended their war-toil for the
    Danaoi,

Faring afield with weakened body, but 'twas fate that led 55
    him on.

Even so may God prove Hieron's saviour through the time
    that is drawing near, giving him the fair harvest of all
    his heart's desire!

Oh Goddess Muse! Hearken to my prayer, and in the
    presence of his son, even Deinomenes,

[1] Philoktetes.

Raise the loud song in guerdon for the four-horsed chariot's
    speed.
60 A joy not alien to the son's heart is his father's victory.
Up then and let us fashion a hymn that shall be dear to
    the heart of the King of Etna;
For whom his father Hieron founded that city framed with
    God's freedom on laws of the Spartan rule.
And the descendants of Pamphulos, aye, and of the Hera-
    kleidai, dwelling 'neath the ridges of Taügetos are fain
    to abide ever steadfast to the ordinances of Aigimios,
65   Dorians true.
Issuing from Pindos they held Amuklai in happy estate,
    the high-renownèd neighbours of the twin sons of
    Tundareus, those drivers of white steeds, and on their
    spears the garland of fame hath bloomed.
Oh God that bringest all things to pass, grant that a true
    report of men may ever arede that such is the destiny
    of citizens and kings alike by the waters of Amenas!
70 Surely with thy aid and giving (wise) mandates to his son,
    the ruler paying due honour to the people may turn
    them down the path of harmonious peace;
Grant, I pray thee, son of Kronos, that the battle-shout of the
    Carthaginian and the Etrurian may bide quietly at home,
Having witnessed their ships bewailing their insolence before
    Kumai!
Such sufferings were theirs when they were quellèd by the
    ruler of Syracuse,
Who flung into the sea the prime of their youth from their
    swift-faring ships,
75 Freeing Hellas thus from the heavy yoke of slavery.
From Salamis I win the singer's guerdon, as a grace to the
    men of Athens—
In Sparta I will tell the tale of the battle of Kithairon—
The battles wherein the Medes of the curving bow were
    sorely distressed:
But by the well-watered heights of Himera I win by
    fashioning the hymn of praise, in honour of the sons
    of Deinomenes,

The praise that they have reaped by the overthrow of 80
    foemen.
If thou speakest a word in season, in brief utterance
    straitening out a tangled skein, lesser carping followeth
    from the hearers;
For weary satiety soon blunteth the short-lived eagerness of
    men.
And the heart of the citizens is oppressed in secret (by too
    much said) on the prosperity of others.
Nevertheless, since to be envied is better far than to be 85
    pitied,
Hold on thy course towards noble things.
Govern the host with the rudder of righteousness,
Shape thy speech on the anvil of truth.
If some light chance-word flasheth forth from thee, it
    gathereth mighty import coming from such an one.
Thou art the warder of many a destiny; and many watchers
    stand by, faithful witnesses of good and ill.
Abiding ever in the flowering-tide of soul, be not distressèd
    too much by the expenditure of wealth, if thou lovest 90
    to hear men speaking ever sweet things of thee:
But like a ship's pilot set full sail to the wind.
Be not deceived, dear friend, by the lure of cunning
    gains.
'Tis the loud acclaim of posthumous renown that alone
    maketh manifest to masters of prose and song the life
    of departed men.
The loving-hearted excellence of Croesus fadeth not from
    our memory;
                                                95
But to Phalaris of the savage soul, who burnt men in the
    brazen bull, a hateful report clingeth everywhere;
Nor do the lyres that ring out beneath the festal roof
    receive his name as sweet fellow for the song-speech
    of the boys.
To achieve prosperity is the first of boons:
To gather good fame is next in the scale of blessings:
If a man findeth and winneth both, he hath gained the 100
    highest crown of life." (Fig. 8.)

The first Pythian gives the highwater-mark of Pindar's inspiration and is one of the masterpieces of the world's lyrics. To understand all the allusions, and fully to appreciate the poetic content, some knowledge of the historic situation is necessary. The great Syracusan dynast, Hieron, with whom Pindar since 476 B.C. had become intimate, had achieved a victory in the chariot-race in a Pythian contest that can now be safely dated at 470 B.C.; and Pindar was commissioned to celebrate it. But the commission was evidently intended to deal with a theme far dearer to the heart of the monarch, namely, the glorifying of his newly founded city of Aitna, on the site of the former city of Katana and at the foot of the great mountain. We may date this foundation near the year 474 B.C.: doubtless it would take some time to settle and mature. And it must have been shortly before the composition of this ode that Hieron had installed his son Deinomenes as king of the new city; and there is much to be said for Wilamowitz's view that the dynast desired an ode to be sung at the installation of Deinomenes in his palace at Aitna where Hieron would be present: so that the Pythian victory is only a happy coincidence, only slightly mentioned as of good augury for the new state, and the ode is not strictly an 'epinikion'. Hieron's policy in the foundation of Aitna was an original experiment; it is likely, as Wilamowitz supposes, that his primary intention was to provide for his discharged veterans, and thus to have a reserve force near at hand on which he could rely. He may also have desired to provide a secure position for his son Deinomenes, arranging the city on the basis of a constitutional monarchy for him, a form of government which at that day existed only in shadow at Sparta, and in reality perhaps only in Epeiros: and as the new settlers were mainly Dorians, Hieron may have amused himself by giving them some form of the Spartan constitution. Pindar therefore found the opportunity pregnant of great effects for him. He was able to glorify the great achievements of Hieron both as a warrior and a statesman; he could also with relevance describe the general traits of the Dorian state and the early incidents of the Dorian conquest; and what he tells us is not without value for history. But it is of still more value for poetry; for Pindar has the rare gift of raising history—even constitutional—up to the plane of poetry. And, as Aeschylus and Simonides were the in-

spired singers of the triumphs of Hellenism over Persia in
the eastern waters, so Pindar was of the achievements of
Hellenism against the barbarian in the west.

He is justified in exalting the great victory of Himera,
in which Gelon, Hieron, and Theron defeated the Carthaginian host (480 B.C.), as no less momentous than the victories of Salamis and Plataea. And in telling phrase he
commemorates the battle of Kumai (about 474), in which
Hieron's fleet rescued the Greek city from Etruscan attack
and destroyed the Etruscan thalassocracy. The unexpected
and daring phrase, "the Punic and the Tuscan war-shout
may henceforth bide quietly at home", is characteristic of
Pindar's poetry.

The historical interest is so strong for him here that he
does not feel the usual call to stray into the field of mythology. We have only one passing reference to a myth and
a very apt one. He says that Hieron took the "field after
the fashion of Philoktetes", who was summoned from
Lemnos to the battlefield of Troy by the haughty Achaean
chiefs, and who, though limping from his wound, came as
their destined saviour. The parallel would be exact if
Hieron, at the abject entreaty of the haughty city of Kumai,
took the field when crippled by gout or stone, borne perhaps on a litter like Surrey at Flodden. But it is very doubtful if Hieron went with his fleet, and we hear of no land-
service. At any rate the analogy between the hero and the
king was close; and we have evidence that Philoktetes was
popular in Magna Graecia.

The central portion of this ode deals with great real facts,
transmuted into poetry, and with a slight mythic halo
attaching to them at one or two points.

The close of the ode is also practical, being emphatic-
ally didactic; and Pindar, whom we have come to admire
as one of the few masters in didactic poetry, never shows
his mastery more brilliantly than here. After first addressing himself, warning himself against prolixity—for a pro-
longed encomium soon satiates the audience—he delivers
an address to the ruler, expounding some of the golden precepts of righteous rule. There is a happy boldness in the
expression he invents for the moral law of truthfulness
("shape thy speech on the anvil of truth"), and a solemn
gravity in his reminder of the king's responsibility and of
the many watchers that eye his actions (he may be thinking

of Hesiod's unseen divine watchers). At the close of the
song he dwells on the value of posthumous renown in a
clause echoing with musical thunder; and he contrasts the
fair fame of the benign phil-Hellene Croesus with the hateful report of the cruel tyrant Phalaris. When he says, in a
phrase of characteristic charm, that this abhorred name is
for ever excluded from "the song-speech of the boys", he
is thinking of some such beautiful custom as we are told
prevailed in Arcadia, of choral singing by troops of boys
after the evening meal, commemorating the famous deeds
of the men of old.

A question may well arise—to whom is this impressive
poetical preaching which closes the greatest of Pindar's
odes addressed, to the old Hieron or the young Deinomenes, both kings being present in the palace of the latter
at Etna? The scholiasts and nearly all modern commentators have regarded Hieron as the person addressed: it is
only Wilamowitz in his recent *Pindaros* who maintains
that it must be Deinomenes, chiefly on the ground that
Pindar would not be so tactless or so bold as to address
Hieron thus. Certain general considerations, as well as the
nexus of the sentences, may convince us that Wilamowitz
is wrong. Pindar knows how to address the great ones of
the earth; as a free aristocrat, he would have borne himself
towards even the Persian king with perfect equality. We
need not be surprised at his greeting Hieron as "his friend";
so he greets a dynast no less great, Arkesilas of Cyrene; and
to both of them he gives frank and noble advice that may
well have conveyed an innuendo of blame; for he was probably aware of some of Hieron's misdeeds. And his frankness may well have been the reason why Hieron commissioned Bacchulides, not Pindar, to celebrate his Olympian
victory in 468 B.C., thereby bequeathing to us a second-
rate poem by a minor poet and depriving us of a second
masterpiece by a great one.[1]

It was to avoid a possible anti-climax that the consideration of the prelude of this ode has been reserved for the end.
Pindar has here been more than usually faithful to his own
formula: "the prelude of the song must shine from afar":
for this shines all through the ages as the highest outburst
of Greek lyrical genius: so marvellously inspired is it
with elemental force, primal beauty, severe sublimity; it is

---

[1] *Vide* Wilamowitz, *Pindaros*, p. 304.

as if a flowing lava-stream could be chiselled into a perfect form of sculpture. Ancient and modern poets and writers have been equally moved by it. Aeschylus, his compeer and contemporary, has borrowed something from it in his *Prometheus Vinctus*, where he describes the phenomena of the volcanic eruption. The great poet is the cause of poetry in others, and Pindar is the ultimate begetter of two striking choral odes in Matthew Arnold's "Empedocles on Etna". And our modern poet and critic in his original essay on the "grand style" takes this prelude as the most masterly illustration of it. Apart from stylistic criticism, we may maintain on a comparative survey of literature that the spiritual power of music has never been set forth with such inspiration. First, its functions in the human sphere in relation to the song and the dance are precisely shown in his golden phrases; then its potency in the divine world is enchantingly conveyed in the picture of the eagle of Zeus, drowsy with the strains of the lyre. Then to show by way of contrast the other world, the world of chaos and destruction, hateful to the world of fair order which the Apolline lyre dominates and evokes, there follows the picture of Tuphōs and the rolling torrent of words describing the terrible eruption of Etna, which had been raging for some years since 477 B.C.; and mythology and physical realism are here combined with strange power.

Finally, we can perceive that in Pindar's imagination, and for the minds of his audience and readers as it worked and works upon them, the two themes of the prelude, the praise of the lyre and the picture of the volcano, are perfectly relevant to the theme of the whole. Pindar speaks as if he were there in person, the poet of Apollo, the god of the lyre: Hieron has just won an Apolline victory and has founded a city on a basis of good laws, and it is Apollo's music that gives the law-abiding temper.[1] But behind this vision of fair forms of order arises the dark elemental background of the volcano: and it is well to pray for the grace of God. Never were the parts of a great and complex ode more organically welded together.

[1] *Vide* my *Cults of the Greek States*, vol. iv. p. 249.

PYTHIAN II

To Hieron of Syracuse

"Oh, Syracuse, mighty among cities, the holy place of high-
    battled Ares, wondrous nurse of men and horses that
    delight in their iron array,
To you I come bearing from fair Thebes this song that
    spreadeth the tidings of the earth-shaking four-horsed
    team,
5 Wherein Hieron, the goodly charioteer, won his victory,
And bedecked Ortugia with garlands radiant from afar,
The island-shrine of Artemis, goddess of the river, not
    without whose aid he tamed with light gentle hand
    those colts of fretted bridle.
For the Maiden-Goddess that scattereth the shafts
10 And Hermes, God of contests, with both hands array the
    glittering harness,
When Hieron fitteth on the polished car and yoketh the
    mighty steeds to the rein-obeying chariot,
Calling on the God of far-ruling might, the wielder of the
    trident.
Diverse men have wrought for diverse kings the ringing
    hymn of praise in requital for their goodliness.
15 Ofttimes the voices of the Cyprians swell high in praise of
    Kinuras, the priestly fosterling of Aphrodite,
Him whom the golden-haired Apollo loved with all his
    heart:
They are moved by the gratitude of friends, having due
    regard for good deeds done.
And thy name, oh, son of Deinomenes, the Locrian maiden
    of the West proclaimeth before the portals of her house,

Having, thanks to thy might, beheld the light of safety 20
    after desperate straits of war.
This is the lesson that, it is said, Ixion by divine behest
    proclaimeth to all men, as he rolleth on his wingèd
    wheel full-circle:
'To honour the benefactor, meeting him with kind requital',
But he learned the truth full well: for, having won sweet 25
    life in company with the kindly children of Kronos,
He could not stomach his high happiness, but in phrenzy
    of heart set his love on Hera, the allotted partner of
    the glad marriage-bed of Zeus.
But sinful insolence plungèd him into monstrous madness.
Soon the man suffered his due, winning strange tribulation. 30
And those two sins of his were pregnant of trouble,
The one that the hero was the first to bring into the world
    the stain of shedding kindred blood, not without guile:
His other that in the high-vaulted bridal bowers of Zeus
    he attempted his spouse.
Verily one must take measure of all things looking to one's
    own strength:
Lawless love flingeth the guilty wooer into plenteous woe; 35
For he lay with a cloud, chasing a sweet illusion, like a
    witless mortal man;
As in form she was fashioned like to the daughter of
    Kronos, the all-surpassing Queen of the Heavenly
    Goddesses.
The devices of Zeus set her there as a snare for him, a 40
    beauteous bane.
Bound on the wheel he made the four-shanked love-knot,
    but he at least to his own undoing;
And thrown into fetters that grip his limbs for ever he
    receivèd the mission of this message to all mankind.
But the Cloud bore a monstrous offspring, in whom the
    Graces had no part,
Strange mother and strange son, having no place of honour
    among men or Gods.
Him she reared and named Kentauros, who mingled with
    the Magnesian mares on the spurs of Pelion: 45

And there was born from them a marvellous wild host,
Horse-shaped below from their mother's side, but above
    bearing their father's form.
All things are brought to their destined end by God accord-
    ing as he planned,
50 He whose swiftness passeth the winged eagle in flight and
    the dolphin of the sea,
He who hath ofttimes bent the neck of the high-minded,
And to others hath given undying fame.
'Tis meet for me to shun the ravening tooth of slander:
55 For from afar I have seen that Archilochos, while battening
    on feuds for his evil speech, was for the most part in
    dire distress.
But to be rich in wisdom and to have the fair gifts of
    fortune withal, is the best lot.
Such wealth, Hieron, thou hast full manifestly, to bring
    forth with ungrudging spirit,
Thou Lord and ruler of fair-battlemented ways and
    hosts.
60 Verily if any sayeth that another in the past has been born
    in Hellas surpassing thee in wealth or honour,
He is as one who striveth with a vain heart barrenly.
And I will mount the flower-crownèd prow, raising my
    voice for thy virtue's sake.
Youth is aided by bold spirit in the fell battlefield;
65 Whence I aver that thou also hast won endless renown,
    warring among horsemen and men on foot:
Withal the wise counsels of thy elder years make my speech
    fearless to praise thee on every ground.
Hail and farewell.
This song is sent over the dark sea like a bale of Phoenician
    merchandise:
But the other song, named after the horse-hero Kastor,
    framèd in Aeolic measures, give willing heed to when
70   it draweth nigh thee for the sake of the seven-voiced
    lyre.
Having learned thy true self, be true to thyself (in act).
A pretty thing for children is the ape of flattery.

But Rhadamanthos hath been blest, because he gainèd the
    unblemished fruit of wisdom,
Nor in his inmost soul doth he delight in cozening.
Mark what things ever befall through the craft of whisper- 75
    ing traitors.
A deadly evil, both to themselves and those who listen are
    the secret púrveyors of slander,
Altogether like unto foxes in their moods.
But what profit to the crafty Renard is all this craft?
'For as the cork above the net, while the rest of the tackle 80
    laboureth in the depths of the salt sea, I am free from
    the sousing of the brine.'[1]
But 'tis impossible for the guileful citizens to utter a word
    of mastery among the noble: [2]
Yet by ever fawning upon all, he weaveth the toils of his
    web full cunningly.
'I do not share his boldness. Be it mine to love my friend:
But in dealing with a foe, in foeman's guise, I will spring
    upon him like a wolf from under his guard,
Circling round him by devious tracks, now here, now there.'[3] 85
But under every form of rule the man of straightforward
    speech hath the advantage,[4]
Under one man's lordship, or when the violent host or when
    a few wise men are shepherding the city.
One must not struggle against God, who at one moment
    exalteth the power of these, at another bringeth others
    to great honour.
But not even these things soothe the mind of the envious; 90
But they, measuring for themselves by an unfair measuring-
    line, stab their own heart with bitter pang ere they
    win their desire.
To take and wear lightly on one's neck the yoke of circum-
    stance availeth much.
'Tis a perilous course to kick against the pricks.
May it be mine to please the good and to win their fellow-
    ship."

[1] The slanderer speaks.   [2] Pindar speaks.
[3] The slanderer.   [4] Pindar.

This is a strange and difficult poem, unique among the
productions of Greek lyric. It is not so much an 'epinikion'
ode, a song to commemorate a chariot-victory—though
there is an allusion to this triumph, won we know not
where—as a general encomium on Hieron and a personal appeal from Pindar to him. The myth that is characteristically interwoven, the myth of Ixion (Fig. 7), to illustrate and enforce the duty of gratitude, is presented with all
his strength of style and moral imagination. It is relevant,
since he wishes to enlarge on the theme of Gratitude—for
the Locrians will never and ought never to forget their
debt of gratitude to Hieron, who has recently delivered
them (about 477 B.C.) from the attack of Anaxilas, tyrant
of Rhegium—and it may be that Pindar also wished to re-
assure Hieron of the permanence of his own gratitude; and,
failing a positive myth concerning gratitude, a tale of
heinous ingratitude and its evil consequence points the
moral just as well. But Pindar does not always know where
to stop in his myth-narrative; and the superadded account
of the birth of the Centaurs is irrelevant to any purpose.

After the myth comes a meditative reflection on the power
of God, which reaches a high level of religious poetry.

The chief interest and difficulty of the poem are found in
the latter part, which is like the postscript to a letter. We
must suppose that Pindar was aware that certain envious
people were slandering him to Hieron; and that he wished
to warn Hieron against the danger of trusting too much to
the whisperings of the informer and the spy. Part of Pindar's
greatness lies in his ethical poetry; and the closing part of
this poem gives us the greatest and the deepest of his poetic
sentential phrases: "learn thy true self and live in it" is
not adequate—perhaps no English phrase is adequate—to
the matchless Greek. It reminds us of Polonius' words to
Laertes:

> "To thine own self be true,
> And it must follow, as the night the day,
> Thou canst not then be false to any man."

And it suggested to Goethe his own striking aphorism,
"Werde was du bist". But most of the latter part of the ode is
poetically unsatisfying. It seems to be mainly a dialogue between Pindar and certain malicious people who were poison-
ing Hieron's mind against him, and whom he likens to the

FIG. 9. Vase from Cumae, 4th century B.C. (Berlin). Ixion bound on fiery (?) wheel: below, winged Fury with torch: on right, Hephaistos: on left, Hermes: above, on each side, winged figures, ? moral personifications or clouds.

ape, the fox, and the wolf. Nowhere else in his lyrics, so far as we can detect, does Pindar employ the device of the dramatic dialogue; but the suggestion[1] that he has employed it here is the only one that throws light on the nexus of the phrases. There is little poetry in this, and still less charm; but the power of the weighty aphorism and the telling phrase are maintained throughout.

This ode more than most of the others has the character of a personal letter, and therefore many passages were likely to be obscure to others that were clear to the recipient.

The proem is a warm and genial encomium with originality and radiance of phrase; the rest of the ode is markedly didactic, and the myth of Ixion is almost wholly moralised, with a touch of grim humour, as a warning against adultery and ingratitude.[2] It is indeed strange that Pindar should allow himself the licence of preaching at such length to Hieron of all people: in this as in other ways he is unique and a law to himself. We discern the situation more clearly when he comes to his own affair, his defence before Hieron against the envious slanderer and would-be supplanter. He is lordly in his egoism, and his 'Olympian' or imperial bearing and temper emerge vividly here.

The poem ends in a solemn religious tone and with a profound reflection: that as our fortunes, whether high or low, are in the hands of God, those who envy the prosperity of others are kicking against the divine dispensation. This view of Providence always commends itself to the prosperous. (Fig. 9.)

[1] Put forth in Gildersleeve's edition.
[2] To ask who Ixion is exactly meant to be in this context is an example of the old-fashioned way of misunderstanding Pindar.

PYTHIAN III

To Hieron of Syracuse

"WOULD that Cheiron, son of Phillura,—
If from my lips 'tis meet to utter a prayer that concerneth
    all—
Were now alive, he that hath gone from the earth,
The mighty son of Kronos the Heaven-born,
And that he, the kindly creature of the wild, were ruling
    in the dells of Pelion,
5 Having a heart friendly unto man;
Even such as he was when he reared Asklepios in days of
    old,
That craftsman of limb-restoring, pain-quelling remedies,
The hero that warded off all manner of disease.
His mother, daughter of Phleguas the horseman,
Before she could bring him ripe to birth with the help of
    the Birth-Goddess who tendeth mothers,
10 Was smitten by the golden shafts of Artemis,
And in her bower departed to the house of Death through
    the devising of Apollo.
The anger of the sons of God is never turnèd aside.
But she in sinfulness of heart despisèd the God and con-
    sented to another union, her father being unwitting,
Having first mingled in love with Phoebus of the flowing
    locks,
15 And bearing in her body the pure seed of the God.
She could not expect that to her would come the bridal
    feast, the joyful sound of voices singing in unison the
    hymeneal refrain,
Such words of mocking blandishment as maidens, com-

panions of the bride's age, are wont to utter in evening
    songs:
But verily she yearnèd for what was not, a folly common 20
    among men.
And there is a tribe among us most ineffectual,
Who despising their own native gains strain their eyes on
    that which is afar,
Chasing profitless dreams with barren hopes.
Even such great infatuation possessèd the passionate heart 25
    of fair-robed Koronis,
For she slept in the bed of the stranger-guest that came
    from Arcadia;
Nor did she escape the eye of the watchful God:
But Loxias, the temple-Lord, chancing to be in sacrificial
    Putho, had knowledge of it, having persuaded his own
    judgment,
At the bidding of his most trusty counseller, his all-
    knowing mind.   30
Falsehood never toucheth him, nor can either God or man
    by act or counsel hoodwink him.
He at the instant knew of her couching with the stranger,
    Ischus son of Eilatos, and the lawless treachery,
And he sent his goddess-sister fired with unquenchable
    wrath to Lakereia:
For the girl was dwelling on the rocky banks of Lake Boibias.
But an untoward fate brought her to evil and quelled her life; 35
And many of the neighbours were caught in her doom and
    perished with her:
Even as a fire on a mountain wasteth a wide tract of
    woodland, having sprung on it from a single spark.
But when her kinsfolk had set the girl's limbs on the pyre-
    wall, and the fierce blast of the Fire-God had leaped
    up around it—
Then spake Apollo: 'My heart can no longer brook that 40
    my own child should perish in a most piteous death,
    sharing his mother's deep affliction'.
So spake he; and in one stride, he reached the child and
    snatched it from his dead mother's side;

And the blaze of the burning pyre clave asunder for him.

45 Then he brought him to the Centaur of Magnesia to teach
him the healing of diseases afflicting men in manifold
ways.

Those then who came to him having long fostered self-
generated ulcers, or those whose limbs were wounded
by the grey steel of war or by the far-thrown stone,

50 Or those whose bodies were ravagèd with summer-heat or
winter's cold,

He releasèd and brought out each man free from his
particular ill;

Tending some with soothing stanching-songs,

Others by meet potions, others by tying remedies all about
their limbs;

Others by cutting with the knife he set on their feet
again.

But even wisdom is ofttimes the slave of gain;

55 And the gleam of gold in the hand tempted even him, by a
mighty guerdon, to bring back a man from death who
was already in death's hands.

But Zeus, the son of Kronos, hurled his lightning and
swiftly smote through the gullet of them both;

And the gleaming bolt brought death crashing down.

It behoveth a man with mortal thoughts to crave from
heaven what fits our lots,

60 Knowing the near path we must tread, of what destiny
we are.

Do not, dear heart of mine, press on to win the life of the
Immortals,

But draw deeply on the resources that are in thy power.

Verily if the wise Cheiron were still dwelling in his cave,

And my songs with their honied voices could have cast
some spell over his soul,

65 Then I would have persuaded him even now to send some
healer to save good men from feverish diseases,

Some reputed son of Apollo or of his father Zeus:

And I would have fared on shipboard cleaving the Ionian
sea to the fount of Arethusa and my host of Etna,

Who dwelleth at Syracuse as king, mild to the citizens, free 70
 from envy of the good, and a marvellous kind father
 to all guests.
If I came to harbour bringing a double boon to him,
The golden gift of health and a choral hymn in honour of
 his Pythian contests, adding lustre to his crowns,
That his horse Pherenikos through his prowess won at
 Kirrha in times gone by,
Then verily I may say I would have come, faring over the
 deep sea,
As a light (of hope) to him more resplendent than a star 75
 of heaven.
But now I am fain to pray to the mother of the Gods,
To whom in fellowship with Pan troops of maidens by my
 forecourt sing in nightly service, the Holy Goddess.
But if, Hieron, thou knowest how to lay to heart the true 80
 crowning-word of wise speech,
Thou bearest in mind the lesson of the men of old—
'For every single blessing two woes are meted out to men
 by the Immortals'—
This dispensation, then, fools cannot meetly bear,
But the good can, turning to view the fairer side of things.
Surely a fated portion of happiness waiteth upon thee;
For upon the sole ruler, the leader of the people, if upon 85
 any man, the great Lord of Chance keepeth watch.
A life wholly unruffled was not found either by Peleus, son
 of Aiakos, nor by Kadmos, the peer of Gods:
Yet of all men they are said to have had the highest bliss,
Who heard on the mountain and in seven-gated Thebes
 the Muses of the golden frontlet singing, 90
When the one married large-eyed Harmonia,
And the other, Thetis, the far-famed daughter of wise
 Nereus;
And Gods feasted at both their bridals,
And they saw the kingly sons of Kronos on golden thrones;
 and they receivèd bridal gifts from them.
Then through God's favour, having passed away from 95
 former sorrows, they raised their drooping hearts.

But a change came in time: his three daughters by their
    sharp sufferings wasted Kadmos of a portion of his joy:
Albeit Zeus, the Father, visited the longed-for marriage-bed
    of white-armed Thuonë:
100 And the son of Peleus, the only child that the immortal
    Thetis bore in Phthia, lost his life beneath the arrow
    in the Trojan war;
And, as he was burning on the pyre, he awakenèd lamenta-
    tion from the host of Danaoi.
If a man's mind hath sense of the true course of life,
He must be well content with the good things he chanceth
    to win from the gods.
The winds that come down from heaven blow diversely at
    diverse times;
105 And a man's bliss remaineth no long time hale and whole,
    when it waiteth on a man in overfull measure.
In lowly fortune I will be lowly: in great fortune I will
    bear me greatly.
The fortune that accompanyeth my path from day to day,
    I will ever cherish, tending it according to the measure
    of my skill.
110 But if God were to put into my hand luxuriant wealth,
I have great hopes that I could win to high renown in
    time to come.
Nestor and Sarpedon, the themes of human story,
We know well because of the ringing verse that the crafts-
    men of song have forged.
115 Virtue winneth a long life through far-famed poesy: but to
    few is it an easy task to accomplish that."

    This ode is one of the series addressed to Hieron and
like the former is no true 'epinikion'; for it does not commemorate any special victory, but contains only a general
reference to victories won long ago in the Pythian games
by the famous horse Pherenikos. It was written to console
Hieron in his serious illness to which the first Pythian also
contains allusions. But probably no monarch has ever re-

ceived such a letter of condolence from any poet. It bears the deepest imprint of Pindar's genius in its flowering-time of perfection. The mythic ingredients of the ode, the story of Asklepios' birth and death, of the weddings and subsequent fortunes of Peleus and Kadmos, are all relevant. At least, the story of Asklepios is relevantly introduced; once introduced, it is told at great length as a romantic and fascinating tale, to solace the sick man. It may well have solaced him; for we may be almost sure that Hieron was not familiar with it, unless he was a devoted reader of Hesiod; nor is it likely that he had ever heard before an ancient folk-tale transfigured with such lyric and dramatic pathos and force and rendered in such mellifluous and golden style as marks out Pindar at his best.

In his treatment of the Koronis-legend, Pindar reveals himself a champion of the Delphic Apollo; he excises any detail derogatory to the dignity of the high God; and he does not consider it derogatory that Apollo should have pursued an amour with a mortal maiden. Here Pindar is at the opposite pole as a critic of the polytheism to Euripides.

Pindar was born and flourished before the age of modernism, which scarcely touched him. Hence this account of the Asclepian cures includes the old magic cure by incantation.

The poem is also a landmark in the diffusion over the Greek world of the Asklepios-legend and cult. He had not yet achieved godhead, and few communities had received him or knew much about him; and there is no hint in Pindar of his coming greatness. He knows him only as a mortal physician of the old world, of surpassing skill, but in the end punished deservedly by Zeus for taking a heavy fee to perform an illegal operation, namely the raising of the dead.

The whole ode well illustrates how in Pindar's age, at least in the circles for whom he worked, the faith of the Hellene in his own mythology was still fresh, vital, and naïve.

The poem also testifies strongly how Pindar is possessed through and through with the moralising spirit: he cannot speak of the mythic past or the real present without moralising; and he is never more a poet than when he moralises. He almost justifies Matthew Arnold's amazing definition of poetry as "a criticism of life". Pindar owes much to one of his spiritual ancestors, the old Boeotian Hesiod, who was more a teacher and preacher than a poet. Some of the sententious passages in the ode have ethical value, all have poetical. The close is slightly marred by the suspicion of self-praise that underlies the rich and stately verse.

PYTHIAN IV

To Arkesilas of Cyrene

"To-day, indeed, oh Muse, thou must take thy stand by
the side of a man beloved,
Even the King of Kurana, the city of fair steeds;
So that, in fellowship with Arkesilas in his festal band,
Thou mayest swell the breeze of the hymn owed to the
children of Leto and to Putho;
Where once, at a time when Apollo chanced to be at home 5
among his people,
The priestess, who hath her seat by the golden eagles of
Zeus,
Prophesied of Battos as one who should settle corn-bearing
Libya,
How that, leaving his holy island, he should found a city
rich in chariots on the white chalk hill:
And that now in the seventeenth generation he should 10
reap the prophecy
Which Medeia, the wild daughter of Aietes, mistress of the
Kolchians, breathèd forth from her immortal lips near
Thera.
Thus she spake to the godlike mariners of the spearman
Jason:
'Hearken, ye sons of high-hearted men and Gods!
I say that from this sea-washed shore the daughter of 15
Libya shall one day bring to birth the seed of many
cities, high-placed in men's record, in the precincts
of Zeus Ammon's home.
In place of light-finnèd dolphins, they shall deal with swift
steeds,

In place of oars their hands shall handle reins and storm-
swift chariots:

20 Thera is destined to be the mother of mighty cities:

This is the issue to be fulfilled by that wondrous sign that
in the outlet of lake Tritonis Euphamos, leaping from
Argo's prow, receivèd at the hands of a god in form
like unto a man,

Offering him as a guest-gift a clod of earth.

And above his head Father Zeus, the son of Kronos,
clangèd in thunder fatefully.

It was when he found them hanging on the ship the bronze-
25   cheeked anchor, the bridle of swift Argo.

For twelve days ere this we had been carrying the wooden
ship from Ocean over the desert ridges of the
land,

Having by my counsels dragged her up to shore;

At that time a lonely-faring god approachèd us,

Having taken to himself the shining aspect of a revered
man:

And he began in friendly speech, even as well-doers proffer
30   hospitality at the first greeting to strangers newly
come:

But in vain, for our dear home-faring was a plea that
forbade delay.

And he said that he was Eurupulos, the son of the immortal
Girder of the Earth, the Shaker of the land.

But he perceivèd that we were hurrying.

35 Then snatching a handful of earth, he was fain to give it
as a guest-gift, the first that came to hand.

Nor did the hero Euphamos refuse his proffer,

But leaping on the shore pressed his hand in his and
received the fateful clod.

And I hear that it hath been washed forth from the ship
and plunged into the sea at eventide, following the
watery wave.

40 Verily I urged him to guard it well, with his henchmen
saving him the toil.

But their minds were forgetful of the task.

And now this immortal seed of spacious Libya has been
    washed up untimely on this island:
For if the King Euphamos, son of Poseidon, Lord of steeds, 45
    whom Europa, Tituos' daughter, brought forth by
    Kephissos' banks aforetime,
Had thrown it out at home near the nether mouth of Hades,
    when he came to the holy mount of Tainaros,
Then, when the fourth generation of his children were
    being born,
His stock in fellowship with the Danaoi would have won
    that broad continent:
For then they shall go forth from their homes in mighty
    Lakedaimon, the gulf of Argos and in Mycenae.
But, as it is, he shall fashion in the couches of alien women 50
    a choice breed of men:
Who by favour divine shall come to this island and beget
    a man to be the lord of rich plains watered by the
    dark rain-cloud.
Him one day Phoibos in his golden shrine shall by his
    oracles make mindful of his task, when in the time to
    come he hath entered the Pythian shrine, 55
How that he must lead a host in ships to the rich holy
    ground of Zeus the Nile-God.'
Such were the measured verses of Medeia's utterance: *? serried ranks*
And the heroes, the peers of Gods, brooded speechless and
    still,
Hearkening the counsel of deep wisdom.
Oh, blessed son of Polumnastos, in fulfilment of this word
    of prophecy,
The voice oracular of the Delphic priestess gave thee thy 60
    high task in unpremeditated utterance,
Who, having thrice bade thee hail, revealèd thee as destined
    King of Kurana,
When thou wert asking (only) what remedy the gods might
    grant for thy stammering voice.
Verily, even now late in time, in the generations of his
    blood, there flourisheth this eighth branch, 65
Arkesilas, as in the full flush of his purple-flowering spring.

To him Apollo and the vale of Putho have brought the
glorious crown for his chariot-racing awarded by the
dwellers round the temple.

But I will dedicate him as a theme to the Muses, yea, and
the story of the Fleece of God.

For 'tis since the Minuai sailed on that quest that the seed
was planted of Heaven-sent honours for him and for
his house.

70 What, then, was the first beginning that ushered them on
that voyage?

What was the peril that bound them to it with rivets of
adamant?

God's voice had prophesied that from the kingly sons of
Aiolos should come the death of Pelias either by
violent hand or by counsels not to be turned aside:

Also there came to him an oracle that chilled his wary
soul,

Spoken at the centre of the tree-clad Mother Earth,

75 Bidding him to beware above all of the one-sandalled man,

Whensoever from the high mountain-halls he should
descend into the sunny plain of far-famed Iolkos,

Whether stranger or citizen. And he came at last,

Wielding two spears, a man of wondrous form;

80 A twofold garb enwrapt him, the native dress of the Mag-
nesians, clinging close to his lordly limbs,

And a leopard-skin round his shoulders kept off the
shivering rains.

Nor were his long bright tresses shorn away, but they
flamed down all his back.

85 Swiftly faring right on he took his stand in the gathering-
place of the throning folk, and put his unblenching
spirit to the proof.

Him they knew not: yet one of the pondering crowd spake
even thus (to his neighbour):

'I ween this cannot be the God Apollo, nor Aphrodite's
husband of the brazen car:

And men say that Iphimedeia's children, Otos and thou
King Ephialtes the bold, died in fair Naxos:

And indeed Tituos was brought down by the keen shaft 90
    of Artemis, sped from her unconquerable quiver,
In order that men may learn to be fain to grasp at such
    love only as is within their reach.'
Such words they spake in interchange one with another.
And devouring the way came Pelias in all haste, erect in
    his well-polished car of mules.
At once he stood amazed, glaring at the well-known sign, 95
    the single sandal on his right foot.
And, cloaking his fear in a show of wrath, he thus addressed
    him:
'What land, oh stranger, dost thou vaunt to be thy home?
What drab of the outcast folk brought thee forth from her
    aged womb?
Tell me thy birth, and do not stain the story with hateful 100
    lies.'
Boldly then with gentle words thus answerèd him Jason:
'Verily I shall deliver the tokens of Cheiron's teaching.
For from his cave I come back again, from Charikles and
    Philura, where these holy daughters of the Centaur
    nurturèd me;
And having fulfillèd my twentieth year, I having never 105
    done a wrongful deed nor spoken wrongful word to
    them,
I have come back to my home to gather to my hands the
    ancient lordship, held now by a king unrighteously,
That Zeus in old times bequeathèd to Aiolos the Leader
    and his sons.
For I hear that unrighteous Pelias, at the bidding of an
    evil heart,
Wrested it by violence from the hands of our parents, by 110
    ancient right the rulers.
They, when first I saw the light of day,
Fearing tyrannous wrong from the overmastering lord,
Made show in their halls of a darkling funeral as over one
    dead;
And accompanied with women's loud lamenting
They sent me secretly forth in purple swaddling-clothes,

115 Making night the partner of their deed, and gave me to
    the fostering of Cheiron, son of Kronos.
But ye know well the main story of these things.
Trusty citizens, tell me clearly where is the home of my
    fathers, drivers of white steeds.
For being the son of Aison, native-born, I would not come
    hither as to a stranger-land of aliens.
The godlike Beast[1] was wont to call and address me by the
    name of Jason.'
120 So spake he. And as he entered his home he was known to
    his father's eyes.
But from his withered eyelids the tears gushèd forth,
As he rejoicèd in his soul when he saw his son as the fairest
    flower of men.
125 And, as the rumour of the hero spread, a pair of brothers
    came to them from near at hand, Pheres leaving the
    fount of Hupereida,
And from Messene Amuthan. Swiftly also Admetos and
    Melampous in right good will came to aid their cousin.
Jason received them with sweet words at a duly apportioned
    banquet,
And furnishing fit provision for his guests he held festival
    long and high,
130 Having through five unbroken nights and days culled the
    hallowed flower of goodly living.
But on the sixth the hero, turning to earnest speech, im-
    parted to his kinsfolk the whole tale from the begin-
    ning:
And they followed it heedfully.
Then suddenly he arose and went forth with them from
    the banquet-seats;
135 And they came to the hall of Pelias, where surging in they
    took their stand.
When he heard of their presence, he himself, the son of
    fair-tressed Turo, came to meet them face to face.
Then Jason in honeyed voice shed gentle speech like dew,
And laid the foundation of wise words.

---

[1] Another name for the good Centaur, Cheiron.

'Son of Poseidon, the God that rent the rock,

The minds of mortal men are overswift to give the prefer-
　　ence of praise to treacherous gain in place of justice,　140

While nevertheless they fare on to a bitter morrow of the
　　feast;

But it behoveth thee and me to weave our future happiness
　　by bringing our passions under the law of righteous-
　　ness—

Verily, I will speak to one who knoweth.　Kretheus and
　　Salmoneus of daring counsel were calved by the self-
　　same mother.

And in the third generation thou and I, sprung from their
　　seed, are looking on the golden sunlight.　　145

But the divine Powers of Law depart from us,

If hateful feud riseth up among kinsmen,

So as to banish all pitiful regard.

It beseemeth us not to divide the mighty heritage of our
　　ancestors, the honour of our house, with bronze-
　　forgèd sword or spear-point.

For I hereby freely give up to thee the flocks of sheep and
　　the herds of ruddy oxen and all the lands that thou　150
　　has reft from our parents and holdest, swelling thy
　　store of wealth;

Nor does it irk me that these should furnish thy house
　　abundantly.

But the monarch's sceptre and the throne,

Whereon the son of Kretheus sat in old times and meted
　　out straight judgment to his horse-loving folk,

Let them pass from thy hands to me without the woe that
　　may fall to both,

Lest some new unknown evil should arise therefrom.'　155

Softly then Pelias answered him—

'Verily such a man will I be:

Only, the season of old age is upon me now,

But for thee, the flower of thy youthful bloom is swelling
　　to the full:

And thou canst save our house from the wrath of the
　　underworld;

160 For Phrixos biddeth us go to the halls of Aietes and convoy
    home his spirit,
And to bring back the deep-tufted fleece of the ram, which
    in old days savèd him from the sea,
And from his stepmother's godless shafts of hate.
A wondrous dream haunteth me and giveth me this
    message.
And I have asked the oracle by Kastalia's stream, if we
    must seek further into this.
And the God doth egg me on with all speed to fashion for
    the dead man a homecoming in a ship.
165 Do thou, then, be fain to fulfil this venture for me.
And I swear I will give up to thee the right to rule and to
    be king alone.
And, as a mighty oath, let Zeus the God of both our kins
    stand as a witness to us.'
Having then assented to this covenant they parted.
170 Then Jason himself now stirred up heralds to blaze the
    tidings all around of the voyage determined.
Soon there came to him three sons of Zeus the son of
    Kronos, warriors tireless in the fight,
Sprung from glancing-eyed Alkmena and from Leda:
Next came a pair of heroes with high-bound tresses,
Offspring of the Earth-shaker, stirred by high thoughts of
    prowess,
One from Pulos, one from the far limits of Tainaros:
Whose fair fame was established far and wide, of Euphamos
175   and thine Periklumenos, the mighty in many lands.
Then came well-praisèd Orpheus, the lyre-player,
    inspired by Apollo to be the father of all song.
But Hermes of the golden rod sent to this quest of endless
    labour twin sons, Echion and Erutos, bursting with
    the bloom of youthfulness.
180 Then came swiftly heroes dwelling about the roots of
    Mount Pangaios:
For with heart full fain and kindly, the king of the winds,
    their father Boreas, wafted speedily Zetas and Kalaïs,
    warriors with purple wings quivering on their backs.

And the Goddess Hera kindled in the heroes the sweet all-
    persuasive yearning for the good ship Argo,
That none might be left behind to lead the soft, sleek life 185
    of inglorious ease by his mother's side:
But in the fellowship of his peers might find in his renown
    the fairest solace-charm even in the face of death.
And when the flower of all mariners came down to
    Iolkos,
Jason musterèd them all with words of praise:
Then the prophet Mopsos, declaring to him God's will by
    the flight of birds and by the drawing of consecrated 190
    lots,
Gladly embarked the host.
And when they had hung the gangway above the anchors,
The captain of the ship, standing in the stern with a golden
    goblet in his hand,
Called on the father of the Heavenly Ones, Zeus, who
    wieldeth the thunder for his spear,
And called for swift-speeding tides and courses of the winds, 195
    days of calm voyaging, and (in the end) the sweet
    fortune of the home-faring.
But from the clouds there answerèd him the fateful voice
    of thunder,
And breaking forth from them came flashing gleams of
    lightning.
And the heroes held their breath, submissive to the wonder-
    signs of God.
Then the soothsayer gave them the word to dash their oars 200
    into the sea, speaking to them words of sweet hopeful-
    ness;
The oars untiringly sped back from under their swift hands;
And helped by the breezes of the south they farèd, bring-
    ing their ship to the mouth of Euxine,
Where they set up a holy shrine to Poseidon of the sea,
    furnished forth with a drove of tawny Thracian bulls, 205
And with an altar new-wrought of stones, with sockets for
    libations.
But, fain as they were to confront deep peril, they prayed

the lord of the ship to avoid the overmastering shock
of the clashing rocks;

For they were twain and alive, and they rolled together
210   swifter than the gusts of loud-roaring winds.

But now those heroes, faring through them, brought their
clashing to an end.

Then they came to the river Phasis, where they joined battle
with the dark-visaged Kolchoi in the very presence of
Aietes, their king.

But the Goddess born in Cyprus, the mistress of the bitter
pangs of love,

Then for the first time brought down to mortals as a gift
from Heaven, even the spotted wryneck,[1]

215   Having bound it on a wheel in a fast knot four-spoke-wise;
She also taught the wise son of Aison prayerful spells,

So that he might remove from Medeia all reverence for her
parents;

And that the yearning for Hellas might beat down her
burning soul with the lash of Love's Persuasion.

220   And full soon she taught him the accomplishment of the
toils her sire devisèd for him.

Withal she gave him oil to anoint himself, having mingled
it with magic against bitter pangs.

And they pledged one with the other to join in mutual
bonds of married love.

But when Aietes had thrown down in the midst of them a
plough of adamant

225   And the bulls who were breathing blasts of burning fire
from their tawny muzzles,

And rending the ground with their brazen hoofs as they
stamped alternately,

Having led them up unaided he brought them beneath the
yoke;

Then he drove them o'er the field, pressing upon the soil
a long line of upright furrows,

And he rent the back of the clodded earth full fathom deep.

---

[1] *I.e.* she taught Jason to work love-magic on Medeia: the wryneck
bound on a wheel was an ancient love-charm.

Then he cried aloud, 'Let the king who ruleth the ship
   carry off the deathless fleece, the woolly hide gleaming 230
   with tassel of gold,
When he hath wrought this deed for me.'
When he had spoken thus, Jason, trusting in God's help,
Threw off his saffron robe and set his hand to the task.
And because of the behests of the strange maiden, the
   mistress of all magic,
The fire harmèd him not, but snatching up the plough
By main force he bound the bulls' necks to the harness,
And smiting their monstrous bulk with an unceasing goad, 235
The masterful man worked to the end the measure of earth
   assigned.
Then Aietes, albeit in unspoken anguish, acclaimèd him
   with a cry of wonder at his might.
And his comrades stretchèd out loving hands towards the
   strong hero,
Crowned him with garlands of grass, and caressèd him 240
   with sweet speech.
But the Sun-God's wondrous son [1] gave tidings forthwith
   of the bright fleece,
Where the flaying-knives of Phrixos had stretched it out.
And he trusted that this task at least would be never
   achievèd by him;
For it lay in a brake and was guarded by a dragon of
   ravening jaws,
In length and bulk surpassing a ship of fifty oars that the 245
   strokes of the iron tools have finished off.
'Tis long for me to return by the beaten way; and the hour
   of return is nigh.
And I know of a certain short track for my song to fare
   along.
(I am a master in song-craft to many another man.)
By magic arts, O Arkesilas, he slew the blue-faced dragon
   of mottled back,
And with her own consent stole away Medeia, the bringer 250
   of death to Pelias.

----

[1] Aietes.

Then they came to know the waters of the Ocean and the
    Red Sea,
And the tribe of Lemnian women, who did to death their
    husbands;
Among whom they set up a trial for the might of their
    limbs in contests for a prize of raiment;
And they couchèd with them.
There then, O Cyrenaeans, some fated day or night re-
255   ceived the seed of your bright-rayed prosperity sown
    in alien fields.
For then Euphamos' race was planted, and ever waxèd
    stronger in the later days.
But, having joined themselves to the haunts of the men
    of Lakedaimon, at some later time they changed their
    habitation for the isle Kallisto:
Whence Apollo, son of Leto, gave to you in possession the
    plain of Libya,
To cherish it with the honouring of the Gods,
When ye had devisèd wise-planned counsel for setting in
260   order the holy city of golden-throned Kurana.

Be wise now, oh, King, in the wisdom of Oidipous;
If with sharp-edgèd axe one were to lop the branches from
265   a mighty oak and mar its stately aspect,
Even so, albeit barren of its fruitage, it giveth true verdict
    of itself,
Whether it cometh, last in the woodstack, to feed the
    winter-fire,
Or with the upright pillars of the lordly palace, bearing
    the roof's weight,
It sustaineth a hapless burden of toil among alien walls,
Having left its ancient habitation desolate.
270 But thou art a surgeon most quick to know the need,
And the God of healing honoureth thy star.
'Tis meet to bring a gentle hand to tend the ulcerous
    wound,
For 'tis easy even for feebler folk to shake a city to its
    foundations;

But again to set it upright in its place—this is a toil hard
    to wrestle with,
Unless some God come suddenly to aid the rulers at the
    helm.
For thee the fair grace of this task is being woven on the 275
    loom of destiny.
Be strong and patient to take all heed in behalf of blessed
    Kurana.
And ponder in thy heart and bring to bear this word of
    Homer:
He sayeth that a good messenger enhanceth greatly every
    matter in hand.
The Muse itself gaineth much through a true interpreter.
Verily Kurana and the far-famèd hall of Battos have made 280
    trial of Damophilos' righteous heart;
For he, bearing himself among children as a youth,
And in the Council-chamber as an elder who hath fallen
    upon the hundredth year of life,
Bereaveth calumny of its loud speech:
He hath also learnt to hate the man of insolence,
In no way setting himself up against good men,   285
Nor hindering the accomplishment of ought:
For opportunity hath but a short-lived span for men's
    handling.
He is well aware of it, and followeth it as a free helper, not
    as a hireling-drudge:
This is the bitterest thing of all that a man with noble
    thoughts should have no hand in any deed.
Verily, he like a second Atlas doth wrestle with the Heaven's 290
    burden on his shoulders, far from his fatherland and
    household-goods.
Zeus, the deathless God, at last released the Titans.
There comes a time when the gales cease and the sails are
    changed.
But he himself, having drained the cup of affliction to the
    dregs, prayeth that he may one day see his home,
And, revelling with his fellow-feasters by Apollo's fountain,
He may surrender his soul full oft to the joys of youth,   295

And handling the carved lyre in the company of the wise
    he may touch tranquillity;
Bringing no bane to any of the citizens, and unvexèd him-
    self of them.
And he might tell the tale, what a fount of deathless verse
    he discovered for Arkesilas, having been of late at
    Thebes my guest-friend.''

    This ode, composed about 462 B.C., is not only the long-
est of Pindar's surviving works, but it must also be esteemed as one of the greatest, if not actually the greatest,
of his masterpieces. And apart from its poetic appeal, it
throws some light on the early history and much more on
the early legend of Cyrene. It contains two separate themes,
united more by Pindar's inner purpose than by any organic
connection. The main theme, occupying by far the greater
part of the ode, is the glorification of King Arkesilas and
of his noble city of Cyrene; and this is well timed, for the
king had recently won a Pythian victory in the chariot-
race, to which, however, the poet makes only the slightest
passing allusion: so that the ode has nothing of the epinician character, except the joyousness and elation proper
to such an occasion.
    But the poet's imagination seizes instantly on the great
foundation-story of the city, and with all the greater ardour
because gods, heroes, and prophets, especially his beloved
Delphi, play a striking part in it: it has also the still stronger
attraction for him because it was associated with the heroic
adventure of the Argonauts, which had never before—we
may surmise—been recounted to the Greek world in verse
worthy of it. That association was grounded on the descent
of Battos, the historical founder of Cyrene, from the mythical Argonaut Euphemos; a tradition that could not have
been invented by Pindar, for it is in the main attested by
Herodotus.
    The poet was again following old tradition in linking the
foundation of the city with the Lemnian Minyans, who
migrated to South Laconia and thence to Thera, the island
which could rightfully claim to be the motherland of
Cyrene. The interesting story in the ode of the manner in

which Euphemos "took seisin" of Libya for his descendants—a story somewhat undramatically woven into the
over-prolix prophecy of Medea—is probably a bold venture
of Pindar's own fancy; at least it cannot be traced to any
older source; but the other main details in his foundation-
legend reappear in the independent narrative of Herodotus.
And we may believe that the Cyrenaeans maintained and
were proud of their claim to Minyan descent, for among the
names of their magistrates that appear on their coins of the
earlier period the heroic name of Jason is not infrequent.
Therefore, the poet could have found no more acceptable
theme for Arkesilas and his people than the story of the
Golden Fleece, which had never been presented continuously and in full detail, so far as we know, by any earlier
authority—though the main separate incidents had been
recounted—and was never to be treated again with such
fervour and inspiration by any later poet of Greece. And
Pindar himself, aware that the lyric poem has not the licence
and spaciousness for a long-continued epic narrative, does
not give us the whole of the story. He omits, for instance, the
sowing of the dragon's teeth, the springing up of the armed
warriors from them and their speedy destruction by Jason,
the incident which naturally would follow on the ploughing
of the fire-breathing bulls. We are sorry for the omission,
for no story in the whole range of folklore is so thrilling as
this, and no poet was so fitted as Pindar to treat it. It could
not have been omitted for mere economy of time; for he
finds time for less interesting incidents. It is more likely
that he omitted it deliberately, refusing to sanction its
transplantation to Kolchis; for at Thebes it was a real
ancestor-story with a meaning, but transplanted to the land
of Aietes it had no meaning at all, only thrill.

Pindar's story of the Argonauts contains a passing allusion to the death of Pelias, but he does not pursue the
events consecutively beyond the point where the heroes
land at Lemnos and Euphemos there begets the line of
which Arkesilas is the late descendant. And this brings him
back to Cyrene and to an entirely new subject. He is gener-
ously anxious to do a service to an exiled Cyrenaean noble,
Damophilos, who had recently been his guest at Thebes;
and giving him the highest testimonial of character, he
pleads with Arkesilas to restore him to peace and happiness in his beloved city. He prefaces this petition by a

parable which is easy to read, though commentators have misread it, the parable of the oak felled and shorn of its verdure and dragged from its ancient home but always proving its virtue as the best of wood. Damophilos is as the transplanted oak. The petition is put forth with that admixture of delicate tact and frankness which mark Pindar at his best in his dealing with potentates; and he skilfully adopts that rhetorical device—which we need not call flattery—of declaring that Arkesilas is just that sort of ruler that he urges him to be—considerate and merciful, a physician of gentle hand in dealing with the wounds of the State; but we discern a grave warning in the lines of deep and beautiful wisdom that convey the political counsel. The closing words of the ode cause us to believe that it was not commissioned by Arkesilas at all, but was inspired by Pindar's generous desire to serve his friend, that the pith of it was really in the postscript and that the story of the Golden Fleece was merely a splendid preface to ingratiate Pindar with the king before he ventured on his request, that in fact Damophilos may himself have suggested this mode of approach and for that reason is said to have discovered at Thebes this "deathless fount of song". The ode then is unique in character, lacks real organic unity, and may be called 'occasional' poetry: but Pindar knows how to turn the passing occasion to eternal value.

We have learned how great was his power in sententious and moralising verse, and in this as in other ways he reminds us of Shakespeare; and he was never greater than in the last part of this ode. The moral verse thrills us with poetic mesmerism. The parable of the oak—strong, noble, and true, with a plaintive pathos at the close—has inspired other great poets. We find the daring phrase, without overstrain, and the closing passage of the poem has the characteristic mellowness and richness. Not the least memorable feature in this latter part of the ode is the enforcement of the lesson of mercy by the myth that Zeus himself forgave his enemies, the Titans: a myth which Pindar may have derived from a statement in Hesiod's poems, though he is the first to make a moral use of it.

But it is the longer theme, the story of the Argonauts, that makes the strongest appeal to most readers. And certainly this is the most brilliant example of the epic-lyric, a branch of poetry which blossomed in the early part of the

sixth century, that Greek literature has preserved for us.
The narrative is tense, tingling, and at times "fiery-hot
with speed". The story is epic, but the atmosphere is lyrical,
and the action is compressed and concentrated as in a
drama. And few Greek masters could equal and none surpass Pindar's power of clear and imaginative realisation of
a scene or a situation. The image of Jason striding into
Iolchos to claim his own is that of a well-chiselled statue
set in a golden light. He is described at first with intense
vividness in realistic phrase; then no less vividly in the awe-
stricken speech of the citizens who talk in Pindar's strange
mythologic manner, comparing him with gods and heroes
who, as they know, cannot be the man at whom they are
gazing. The yoking of the fire-breathing bulls and the
ploughing with them are recounted in words that are
fraught with the same strong magic as was the feat itself.
No less masterly is his character-drawing of Pelias and
Jason: Pelias the terrified tyrant, who tries bluster and in-
sult at first but who can change his tone swiftly at need into
gentle and guilefully alluring speech: Jason, the ideal of the
best fifth-century type realised in a living personality, one
who "brings with him the teaching of Cheiron", one, that
is, who has been perfectly bred to play the part of the gentleman and the hero, one who combines the most daring boldness with a noble courtesy and self-restraint—we note the
delicate irony with which he confronts the gross brutality
of Pelias in their first encounter by pretending to ignore his
presence—and finally one who knows how to reveal the
iron claw under the velvet covering. Such a character
would have attracted Shakespeare, who framed his high-
bred and daring Orlando on somewhat the same lines. In
fact, the lyric-dramatic dialogue between the two protago-
nists, Pelias and Jason, in both their encounters, is in its
own style a masterpiece unrivalled in Greek literature.

The mellow golden diction of the ode shows Pindar at
his height as a master-artist of speech: it is wholly free from
his characteristic faults: it is forceful without violence or
overstrain, it is genial and sunny without lusciousness. And
the rhythm of the musical phrases is of the noblest Doric
quality, at times grave and sonorous like a roll of thunder,
at times undulating and rippling like falling water. He could
do even higher things than this work; but he was never more
characteristically Hellenic in the best sense than in this.

PYTHIAN V

To Arkesilas of Cyrene

"THE might of wealth extendeth far,
When from the hands of Fate a mortal man receiveth it
    linkèd with unsullied virtue,
And exalteth it only as a friendly handmaid.
5 Oh, Arkesilas of the godlike destiny! thou from the first
    threshold of a glorious life dost pursue it with renown,
Through the boon of Kastor, Lord of the golden chariot;
Who after wintry storms hath shed on thy blessed hearth
10   the gleam of the fair sky.
The wise among men are able more fairly and nobly to
    sustain even the sovereign power bequeathed by God.
As for thee, as thou farest in the paths of righteousness,
    manifold prosperity foldeth thee round:
15 First because thou art king of many cities,
Inasmuch as this reverèd privilege of kingship, going
    hand-in-hand with thy nobility of soul,
Is as an ancestral light and glory for thy house;
Also, thou art most blessèd even at this time, for that thy
20   horses have won for thee thy heart's desire from the
    far-famed Pythian trial;
And therefore thou hast welcomed this festal band of men,
    Apollo's playfellows.
Wherefore, when thy name is being sung in Kurana round
    about the sweet flowery shrine of Aphrodite,
25 Forget not to assign all things to the working of God's
    hand.
And love Karrhotos more than all thy comrades,
Who came back to the dwelling-place of the sons of Battos,
    the rightful rulers of the land,

Not bringing with him Excuse, the daughter of late-
   minded After-thought;
But having been the guest-friend of Kastalia's waters,
He hath crowned thy locks with the garland due to the 30
   mightiest chariot,
Keeping his harness all unscathèd throughout the holy
   place of the twelve courses of swift running.
For he broke no portion of his horses' strong equipment,
But it hangs dedicated there, all the carvèd work of cunning- 35
   handed craftsmen,
All that he brought up with him as he passed by the
   Crissaean mount on to the hollow glen of the God.
The treasure-house of cypress-wood containeth it hard by
   the statue that the Cretan bowmen dedicated under 40
   the Delphic roof,
The form of a man carvèd from a single tree-trunk.
'Tis seemly to go to greet our benefactor with heart full fain;
And verily, oh, son of Alexibias,[1] the fair-haired Graces 45
   shed rays of glory on thee.
Blessed art thou who after heavy strife hast won for thy
   memorial words of noblest poesy;
For that thou hast come back from the illustrious contest
   to the plain of Libya and the city of thy fathers,
Having among forty charioteers who fell   50
Convoyed thy chariot hale and whole with unblenching
   heart.
But no one ever is or will be outside all share in trouble:
Even so the prosperity of the house of Battos, the bulwark 55
   of the city, and a radiant beacon of hope to stranger-
   guests, from of old followeth (each generation), albeit
   dispensing fortune, now this, now that.
That Battos even the loud-roaring lions fled from in
   exceeding fear,
When his strange voice fell upon their ears from across the
   sea;
And Apollo, the leader of the colony, planted fearful terror 60
   in the hearts of the beasts,

[1] Karrhotos the driver.

Lest he might fail to fulfil his prophecies to the Warder of
    Kurana.

This is the God who dispenseth to men and women the
    healing of fell diseases,

65 Who brought us the gift of music and giveth the Muses'
    inspiration to whomsoever he will,

Having led into our hearts the spirit of peace and obedience
    to Law.

And he is Master of the prophetic sanctuary, by the power
    whereof he settled the descendants of Herakles and

70   Aigimios in Lakedaimon, in Argos, and holy Pulos.

From Sparta, too, resoundeth the glad tale of my fame,

Whence were sprung my fathers, the Aigeidai, who came

75   thence to Thera, not without the guidance of God:
    but some high destiny led them on:

It was from them we have inherited thy festival Karneia,

80 ˙   oh, Apollo, the many-victimed feast,

And now honour in the banquet the well-founded city of
    Kurana,

The stronghold of the war-loving strangers from Troy,
    Antenor's sons:

For they came hither with Helen, when they had seen their

85   fatherland whelmed in the smoke of war.

And this race of drivers of the steed are sedulously tended
    by men faring oft to their tombs with gifts,

The men whom Aristoteles[1] brought hither, opening the
    deep path of the sea in his swift ships.

He founded sanctuaries of the Gods greater than of old;

And laid down the straight-hewn way well paved with
    stones,

90 To be level and smooth for the horses' tramplings in the
    processions of warriors that guard the land;

And by the side of this in the rearward of the market-
    place he lieth apart in death.

Blessèd was he when he dwelt among men,

95 And after death a hero worshippèd by the people.

Others of his house, when the doom of death fell on them,

---

[1] The real name of Battos.

lie buried as kings reverèd, each aloof before their
  portals:
And, I deem, with the dim mind of the dead, they hear of
  this high renown,[1]
Bedewèd with the soft spray of song and the gentle streams 100
  of festal hymn—
Wherein is their happiness and a joint and well-earned
  grace to them and to their son Arkesilas:
Whom it behoveth, having won from Putho this sweet
  triumphal melody, a fair quittance for all his spending, 105
To proclaim the name of Phoibos of the Golden Bow in
  the song the young men sing.
That man Arkesilas is praisèd by the wise:
I shall speak as all men speak:
The mind he nurtureth within him and his words are riper 110
  than his years:
And for his daring he is as a broad-wingèd eagle among
  birds.
What a bulwark of the strife is his strength!
And in the Muses' art he is full-fledgèd from his dear
  mother's teaching.
He hath proved himself withal a skilful charioteer.   115
And where'er his landsfolk enter the lists for honour,
He hath dared the issue.
Even as a kindly God is now perfecting his power for
  him,
Even so in the time to come, oh blessed sons of Kronos,
  may ye grant no lesser blessing on his deeds and
  counsels,
Lest haply some withering blast of winter storms may 120
  quell his bloom.
The great mind of God piloteth the course of the guardian
  spirit of the men he loves.
I pray that God may grant withal the same glory at
  Olympia to the house of Battos."

[1] The victory of Arkesilas.

The fifth Pythian is concerned with the same victory as the fourth; but it must have been composed and delivered nearly a year after the event, about 461 B.C.; for it was intended to be sung at the Karneia, the Apolline festival in Cyrene. It differs in kind from the former, for it deals very slightly with epic legend, and much more with the actual victory in the chariot-race and the high deserts of the charioteer Karrhotos, a kinsman of the king, who by his skilful driving saved his chariot when forty others crashed and fell, an incident which proves the great peril of the race.

But the ode contributes something also to the legendary prehistory of Cyrene in the interesting narrative—derived from the indigenous folklore—of the migration to these shores of the sons of Antenor in company with Helen after the capture of Troy, a story which may have some ethnographic value. It contains also some material for Pindar's biography; for it appears to prove that he was himself an 'Aegeid', one of the noble Theban houses that had links with Sparta and Thera; and he might feel himself thus to possess some personal interest in Cyrene. The minute knowledge of Cyrenaic topography and legends, shown here and in Pythians IV and IX, together with his known devotion to the cult of Zeus Ammon and his knowledge of its origins, make strongly for the belief that he had travelled to Cyrene and about its vicinity. But the ode is of far more than antiquarian interest: although not on the same level with the fourth Pythian, it must be ranked among Pindar's greater works, if only for its lyrical expression of high religious feeling and intuition: he speaks almost as a missionary of the Apolline religion. His poetry is seen here in the flower of its growth: the grand style is mellowed, and though high-pitched is not overdaring, while it shows sufficiently his love of the far-fetched phrase. The whole poem is ardent with tense feeling; the various motives are happily blent; and the rhythms, though hard to analyse, capture us with the grace of undulating movement.

PYTHIAN VI

To Xenokrates of Akragas

"HARKEN, ye people; for we are tending the garden of
the Love-Goddess of the quick-glancing eyes, or of the
Graces,
As we draw near to the sacred shrine-stone, the holy thing
of this region of thunder-voices,
Where a treasure-house of triumph-song, born of their 5
Pythian victory, has been strongly founded in Apollo's
golden glen for the Emmenidai,
For river-washed Akragas and verily for Xenokrates;
A house that no onrush of wintry rain, the pitiless host 10
born of the roaring cloud,
Nor any blast of wind shall bear down to the engulfing
sea, smitten with confused mass of shale.
But a countenance lit with radiant light[1] shall proclaim
the tidings of the chariot-victory in the folded vale 15
of Krissa, a common glory to thy father and thy race,
Thrasuboulos, a theme of renown on the lips of men.
Thou verily, holding him ever in the place of honour,
keepest upright the behest— 20
Even the counsels that Cheiron, as they say, the son of
Philura, gave to the mighty son of Peleus, when he
left his father's side—
First and above all to reverence Zeus, Lord of the deep- 25
voiced levin-bolt and thunder:
Then never to amerce his parents throughout their destined
life of the honour that was their due.

[1] The countenance of the Messenger.

Even in time of old, Antilochos the mighty proved himself fraught with this disposition,

30 Who died for his father, having abided the onset of
Memnon, the man-slaying leader of the Aethiopian
host.

For Nestor's horse, smitten by the dart of Paris, hindered
his chariot's flight;

And Memnon with his mighty spear was pressing hard
upon him.

35 Then the old man of Messene with heart adread called
loudly on his son;

And he did not cast forth into the air a word that fell to
the ground;

But the god-like youth stood fast there in the path,

And purchasèd at the price of his own death his father's
safe return:

Wherefore, having wrought an exceeding great deed, he
40 won repute of being peerless among all the younger
men of the olden race in duty touching parents.

Those things are past and over.

But of all men of the present day Thrasuboulos also hath
45 followed most closely his father's rule of life,[1]

And walking in his uncle's footsteps hath shown lustre of
renown.

He maketh Wisdom the captain of his wealth,

Culling the flowers of youth without wrong or insolence,

And the lore of poesy in the secret haunts of the Pierian
maidens.[2]

Also to thee, oh, Poseidon, Shaker of the land, who yearnest
50 ever for the contests of the steeds,

He cleaveth with heart full pleasing to thee—

Withal in converse with fellow-revellers

The sweetness of his mood surpasseth the honey in the
fretted work of the bees."

---

[1] Or "has walked most closely in the path of duty towards his father".
[2] The Muses.

As this ode was composed about 490 B.C., when Pindar was probably twenty-eight, commentators have tried to detect signs of youthful immaturity. But a poet has generally passed his immaturity by twenty-eight; and the ode shows considerable advance beyond the really youthful tenth Pythian. He does not indeed rise to his highest in this short poem; but the passage concerning the treasure-house of song, which inspired the well-known passage of Horace— *exegi monumentum*—is masterly enough; and the sixth Pythian reveals Pindar's salient characteristics, his daring venturesomeness in phrase, his aptitude for the lyric-epic narrative and for ethical poetry. The myth of Antilochos is quite relevant enough, more than some that he inserts; we are not asked to find it applicable in all its details; it is enough that the mythic Antilochos and the real Thrasuboulos were models of filial piety.

The proem of his ode has the usual force; showing Pindar's power to capture his hearers at once by some phrase that thrills and arrests: the Love-Goddess is here taken as the incarnation of all lovely things, including poetry; and she is again linked with the Graces at the beginning of the sixth Paean addressed to Delphi.

Here, as in the fourth Pythian, we have an interesting allusion to a collection of moral precepts attributed to the good Centaur Cheiron, the tutor of heroes. The ode also illustrates Pindar's familiarity with the post-Homeric epic poetry, whence he derives the story of Memnon, Nestor, and the death of Antilochos. The figure of Memnon seems to have interested him, for he introduces it several times into these odes.

The circumstances in which this ode was composed and the relations between the poet and Thrasuboulos are touched upon in the criticism of the second Isthmian ode.

PYTHIAN VII

To Megakles of Athens

"THE name of Athens, great among cities, is the noblest
prelude whereon to rear a structure of song in honour
of the Alkmaionidai, the mighty in many lands, for
their horse-victory:

5 Since whom shall I ever proclaim as of a father-land or
house more illustrious in the ears of Hellas?

For in all cities the story is familiar of those citizens of

10 Erechtheus who wrought thy house, Apollo, a marvel
to behold in holy Putho.

And five victories, oh Megakles, of thy house and ancestors

15 won at Isthmos, one surpassing triumph at Olympia
from Zeus, and two from (the plain of) Kirrha lure me
on to sing.

In thy new good fortune I have some measure of joy.

But this is a grief to me that envy should be the requital of
noble deeds.

20 Even so, verily, they say that happiness, even when
flourishing for a man full steadfastly, bringeth him now
this, now that."

This short ode was composed in honour of Megakles the
Athenian, of the great house of the Alkmaionidai, who had
been ostracised from Athens in 487–486 B.C. and who had
just won a Pythian victory in the chariot-race, which may
be dated with probability at 486 B.C. The treatment of the
theme is reserved and the expression is chastened, though
it shows power and grace. The prelude contains a high-

pitched panegyric of Athens, the earliest literary encomium of the great city. But he cannot dwell on its Pan-
hellenic achievements; for he was commissioned by the
ostracised Megakles, and the Alkmaionidai had played a
questionable part on the day of Marathon. He is content
therefore to refer to the fame that this family had won by
their generosity in rebuilding the temple of Delphi on a
magnificent scale. He then consoles Megakles for the envy
that has assailed him and driven him forth by the reflection
that such passing mischances are a test and a condition of
permanent prosperity.

The ode has a special interest as being one of the few
that bear on the important question of Pindar's relations
to Athens, which will press more insistently when we try to
understand certain parts of the ninth Pythian.

PYTHIAN VIII

To Aristomenes of Aigina

"OH, loving-hearted Peace, daughter of Justice, sovereign-
power of cities, holding in thy hands the master-keys
of counsels and of wars,

5 Welcome this rite of honour for Aristomenes on his
Pythian victory:

For thou knowest with unerring timeliness how to do the
deeds of gentleness and to gather her fruits withal;

But at other times, when a man provoketh his heart to
pitiless rage,

10 Sternly thou dost confront the might of the evil-minded,
and whelmest wrong in the deep sea.

Indeed Porphurion knew thee not, when he challenged
thee recklessly.

(Only that gain is kindly that one fetcheth from the homes
of willing givers.)

15 The spirit of Insolence trippeth the loud boaster at a later
day:

She ensnarèd the Cilician hundred-headed monster
Tuphos, and the King of the Giants withal;

They were quelled by the thunderbolt of Zeus and the
arrows of Apollo:

Who with kindly heart welcomèd Xenarkes' son coming
20   from the plain of Kirrha, garlanded with leafage of
Parnassos and girt with dancers of the Dorian
measure.

Truly the lot of the isle Aigina, that holdeth the city of
justice and is linkèd with the renownèd glories of the
Aiakidai,

Hath fallen not far from the Graces' seat:
And she hath full-grown fame from of old;   25
For she is besung by many a bard as the nurse of ancient
    heroes, peerless in the contests that bring triumph and
    in the swift tides of battle;
And withal she is illustrious for her living breed of men.
I have no leisure to dedicate to the lyre and to the soft
    speech of poesy the long full tale of her glory, lest 30
    satiety come and vex us.
But let thy affair, dear youth, that toucheth me now, the
    story of thy newest honour, speed full swiftly,
Mounting on the wings my song deviseth.
For by thy wrestling-feats thou followest on their track
    and dost not shame thy mother's brethren,   35
Nor thy kinsman Theognotos at Olympia,
Nay, nor the bold-limbed victory of Kleitomachos at
    Isthmos.
Exalting thy fathers' house of the Midulidai, thou reapest
    the word of praise that the prophetic son of Oïkles
    spake darkly,
Seeing the children of the Seven standing steadfast with 40
    the spear-point in seven-gated Thebes,
What time the sons of the heroes came from Argos on the
    second war-faring:
Thus spake he as they fought:
'By thy birth-right from thy sires the generous flame of 45
    courage gleameth around thee, boy!
I see full clearly Alkmaion foremost in the gates of Kadmos,
Brandishing the speckled dragon on a burning shield.
The hero Adrastos, he who was smitten with a former
    overthrow,
Is now destined to tidings of happier augury: 50
But as touching his own house his fortune shall be contrary;
For he alone of the Danaan host shall gather the bones of
    his dead son, by the Gods' dispensation, e'er he shall
    reach his home with unscathed folk, even the broad-
    spaced ways of Abas.'[1]   55

[1] The city of Argos.

Such was the speech of Amphiaraos; and I myself with
    joyful heart shed garlands on Alkmaion, and sprinkle
    him with the dew of song,

For that, being my neighbour and warder of my goods,
    he met me in a vision on my way to the far-famed
    centre of the earth,[1]

60 And with mantic lore, the heirloom of his kindred, he
    dealt in prophecy for me.

But thou, oh, Apollo the Far-darter, lord of the all-
    welcoming glorious shrine in the hollow vales of
    Putho, didst then grant (to Aristomenes) the greatest
    of all boons,

65 And aforetime in his island-home thou didst bring to him
    the coveted gift of the victory in the fivefold contest
    linkèd to thine and thy sister's festival.

Oh, King, with heart full fain I pray that I may see eye
    to eye with thee in every task I take in hand.

70 Verily, the Spirit of Justice is present with this choral ritual
    of sweet song:

But I pray that for the future fortunes of thee and thy
    house, oh, Xenarkes, the Gods' heedful care may
    never pass away.

For if a man hath won many blessings without exceeding
    toil,

He seemeth to many as a wise man among fools,

75 In crowning his life with counsels of prosperous policy.

But such things lie not in man's hands: a divine power
    meteth out our fortunes, casting up on high now one
    man, now another, and hurling down another to the
    ground.

(?) Set some measure in thy challenging of contests.

Thou hast won pre-eminence in Megara and in the hollow
    plain of Marathon, and (at Argos) having by main
80   force triumphed over the native contest of Hera in
    three victories.

And (at Putho) thou didst fling thyself from above with
    fell intent on the limbs of four striplings,

[1] Delphi.

To whom the Pythian judgment awarded a home-faring
   no whit so blithe as thine,
Nor did sweet laughter shed grace around them when they 85
   came back to their mothers:
But they slink home by a side-path, shrinking from the
   taunts of enemies, heart-broken by defeat.
But he who has won some fair new thing, with his path
   full soft before his feet,
In his hope is lifted up with soaring cravings of renown,   90
Having a thought of honour overmastering (greed of)
   gain.
Yet the time is brief wherein the joy of mortals blossometh,
And even so falleth to the earth again, shatterèd by some
   baffling will.
We are creatures of a day: what thing is man, or what 95
   thing is he not?
Man is but the shadow of a dream.
But when there cometh a heaven-born gleam, men are
   crownèd with bright glory and sweet life.
Oh, Aigina, Mother belovèd, pilot this city on the path
   of freedom
With the help of Zeus, of mighty Aiakos, Peleus, goodly
   Telamon and Achilles."

   This ode is dedicated to an Aeginetan victor of the noble
family of the Midulidai, and, like the other odes in honour
of Aigina, testifies to Pindar's warm admiration for this
Hellenic state, which attracted him specially on account of
its heroic traditions, its glorious recent history, its Doric
constitution, its immemorial worship of the Pan-hellenic
Zeus, and its deserved reputation for commercial justice.
But the eighth Pythian has a marked individuality and
offers much difficulty to the interpreter. We might understand it better in places if we could be sure of the date. The
ancient authorities place it at 446 B.C.; but at this time
Aigina was wholly subject to Athens, while the closing
words of the ode seem to imply that she was free. Again,
there is a difficulty in understanding the remarkable invo-

cation and the whole of the proem concerning the Peace-Goddess and her enemies. The personification is original and bold. This Goddess is not "Peace at any price"; but an armed peace, a warrior-maid, guarding law and order, inspiring wise counsels, whom the powers of evil will attack to their shame and loss. But who in this case and at this time is the evil power symbolised by the giants and the monster Tuphos, the foes of the Gods? We cannot date the ode early enough to suppose an allusion to the Persian struggle. Could it be Athens that is thus symbolised, the inveterate foe of Boeotia and the destroyer of the Aeginetan navy and independence? But it is not likely that Pindar's feelings towards Athens were ever such as to allow him or to provoke him to speak of her as a power of darkness. We may imagine it thus—-that Pindar is yearning for peace and that to a great extent it seems secured; that though Aigina is under the power of Athens, she enjoys local autonomy; that Boeotia is free, that Athens has made the five years' truce with Sparta, and that the Greek world is secured as against Persia by the Peace of Kallias; and that Pindar allows himself the reflection that it is only the evil powers that would attack peace, but does not wish to fit the cap of darkness on the head of any Hellenic state.

In spite of obscurities and a few flaws, the ode shows Pindar at his highest and best. The epic digression and the prophecy of Amphiaraos have the tingling strength of his inspired style; and the closing passage concerning the transitoriness of mortal joy is of unsurpassable beauty, reflecting "the light of setting suns". If this is his last poetic work, his genius remained strong and radiant to the end; and he is able to strike a deeper and brighter note than the Preacher who said "All is vanity". He reminds us that all things pass, but he discerns more profoundly than Plato that the glory of the transitory has worth and value. Ancient critics condemned this passage as irrelevant to the joyous occasion. But we are often deeply indebted to Pindar for his seeming irrelevancies.

The chief flaw in the ode are the lines dwelling on the shame and insults that the defeated competitor must expect from his own city when he returns home; and it is strange that Pindar should have twice been guilty—both here and in the eighth Olympian—of this slur on Greek kindliness and chivalry.

Another noticeable feature of the ode is that it is the only 'epinician' in honour of an Aeginetan containing no reference to any myth of the Aeacid family: the myth that he dwells on, the warfare of the Epigonoi or Sons of the Seven against Thebes, was wholly irrelevant to Aigina: it seems suggested to him merely by the reflection that the young Aeginetan is showing the high spirit of his family just as young Alkmaion did; but it is possible that Pindar is haunted by the remembrance of the vision that he recently had of Alkmaion when he was journeying to Delphi, and that therefore he cannot refrain from telling his story, attaching it to the context as well as he can. For his silence here about the achievements of the Aiakidai he makes amends by closing his prayer at the end of his ode by the impressive roll of their great names.

PYTHIAN IX

To Telesikrates of Cyrene

"I AM fain, with the aid of the deep-girdled Graces,
To proclaim with herald's voice the name of Telesikrates,
The Pythian victor (in the race) of the brazen shield,
5 The crowning glory of Kurana, the city of swift chariots.
Her the long-locked son of Leto snatched from the wind-
echoing vales of Pelion, and bore away the maiden-
huntress in his golden car,
And made her mistress of a land fertile in pasture and
richest of all lands in fruits,
In blessèd estate to inhabit the lovely third branch of the
continent of earth.
But silver-footed Aphrodite welcomèd the stranger God of
10 Delos, touching with gentle hand his God-built car;
And shed upon her winsome bashfulness on the sweet
bridal-couch,
Linking in the accord of wedlock the God and the maiden-
daughter of far-ruling Hupseus:
Who at that time was king of the overweening Lapithai,
A hero of the second generation of the stock of Okeanos:
15 Whom erst in the storied dells of Pindos Kreoisa bare, the
Lady of the Waters,
Having known the joy of the love-couch of the river
Peneus,
She the daughter of the Earth-Goddess.
And Hupseus reared the fair-armed child Kurana.
She never loved to pace to and fro before the loom,
Nor the joys of banquets with home-keeping comrades;
20 Rather she was fain to slaughter the beasts of the wild,

Doing battle against them with bronze-pointed spears and   20
    sword,
Bringing of a truth deep peace and tranquil to her father's
    herds,
But rarely wasting (on herself) the gift of sleep, sweet fellow
    of her couch, falling on her eyelids towards break of   25
    day.
Apollo, the God of the broad quiver, the Far-darter, found
    her once wrestling alone and weaponless with a raven-
    ing lion;
And forthwith he summoned Cheiron from his halls and
    addressed him thus—
'Leave thy holy cave, oh, son of Philura, and come and   30
    marvel at a woman's courage and mighty force:
What a contest she upholdeth with unblenching front,
A girl bearing a heart within her that mocketh at toil!
Nor hath any storm of fear ruffled her soul.
Who of mankind were her parents? From what stock was
    she reft away that she dwelleth in the secret hollows
    of the shadowy mountains?
She putteth to the proof her boundless valour.   35
Is it <u>lawful and meet</u> to lay upon her my hand of
    renown,
Or to pluck the flower of honeyed sweetness from the couch
    of love?'
To him at once the mighty Centaur, laughing gaily with
    bright glance,
Answering told the thought in his mind.
'Secret are the keys of wise Persuasion (to unlock the
    chambers) of sacred loves, oh Phoibos;
And both Gods and men alike blush to win openly the   40
    sweet couch of virginity.
For, indeed, a merry mood drave even thee, for whom it is
    not lawful to handle falsehood, to utter this glosing
    speech.
Askest thou, oh King, the girl's stock, whence it is sprung?
Thou who knowest the destined end of all things and all
    the world-ways: 45

All the spring-leafage that the earth doth send forth,
And the number of the grains of sand in sea and rivers
    that are buffeted by the waves and blasts?
And thou discernest well what is to come to pass and whence
    it will come.
50 But if one must even strive in wisdom with the wise,
I will tell thee (what shall be).
Thou hast come to this glen as the maiden's spouse,
And thou art minded to bear her across the sea to the
    choice garden of God:
Where thou shalt make her a City-Queen, when thou hast
55   gathered an island-host to settle on the ridge that
    fringeth the plain.
But at the present time the Goddess of broad-meadowed
    Libya shall welcome with loving-kindness the glorious
    bride in her golden halls:
Where she shall give her forthwith a destined portion of
    land, to flourish with her as her lawful heritage,
Not without its tribute of all fruits that grow, and not
    unknown of the beasts of the wild.
Then she shall bring forth a man-child, whom far-famed
60   Hermes shall bear in his arms from his dear mother
    to the fair-throned Season-Goddesses and Mother
    Earth to nourish:
And they having set the nursling on their knees, shall drop
    nectar and ambrosia into his lips,
And shall make him thereby immortal, another Zeus or
    holy Apollo,
A heart's joy to the men he loves,
65 To be named the Flock-follower, the Lord of the wild, the
    Pasture-God, and by some men Aristaios.'
Having spoken thus, he set him on to work the sweet
    consummation of the union.
When Gods are now hot on the quest, swift is the accom-
    plishment and short the journeyings:
That day determinèd the thing in hand.
And they mingled in love in Libya's all-golden bridal-
    chamber,

Where she cherisheth a city most fair to see and famous
    (for victories) in contests.   70
And now in holy Putho the son of Karneiadas hath joined
    hands with fair-flowering Fortune,
Where by his triumph he proclaimed Kurana's name,
Who will welcome him in all good-will
When he hath brought back from Delphoi a lovely report 75
    to his father-land, the home of beauteous women.
Great deeds of prowess are ever a prodigal fount of words:
But to fashion a short tale fairly on a lengthy theme is
    good hearing for the wise.
And the fitting season is ever the crown of all things what-
    soever.
Nor of aforetime did Iolaos despise it, as seven-gated 80
    Thebes knew well;
Whom, when he had severed Eurustheus' head with the
    edge of his sword,
They buried beneath the earth in the grave of Amphitruo
    the charioteer,
His father's father, where he lay the stranger of the Spartan-
    folk,
Having changèd his home for the Kadmeian streets gay
    with white horses.
Wise-hearted Alkmena, having mingled in love with him
    and Zeus, bore in one and the same travail-pang a 85
    mighty pair of sons, unconquered in the battle.
Dull and insensate is that man who linketh not his speech
    to the name of Herakles,
Who hath not Dirke's waters in ever-green memory, that
    nurturèd him and his brother Iphikles:
To them will I fashion a triumph-song when I have gained
    a satisfying boon in fulfilment of my prayer.
May the bright glory of the shrill-voicèd Graces never 90
    leave me!
For I aver that thrice already, in Aigina and on the hill of
    Nisos, I have glorified this city of Thebes,
Having escapèd the reproach of silent helplessness by song's
    achievement.

Wherefore let no one, whether friend or foe among the
    citizens,
Darken (with envy) the fair deed wrought nobly and in
    fellowship,
And thus dishonour the counsel of the old man of the sea:
For he bade us praise with full justice and with all one's
    heart
95 Even the foeman when he doeth high deeds of worth.
I have seen thee crownèd with many a victory in the
    seasonable rites of Pallas—
And I marked how each maiden prayed in silence that her
    spouse or son might, oh Telesikrates, be such as thou—
100 And in the games of Zeus Olympios and of the deep-
    girdled Earth-Goddess and in all thy native contests.
Even then as I was fain to slake the thirst of my [tired]
    song, someone exacts a debt (as due from me),
Even to awaken the glory of thy forefathers of old;
105 How that for a Libyan woman they fared to the city Irasa,
Suitors in quest of the fair-haired, far-famed daughter of
    Antaios,
Who was wooed by many a noble man both of the kindred
    and from stranger-stock.
For wondrous was the maid to behold;
110 And they were fain to pluck the fruit of golden-crownèd
    youth in its bloom.
But the father, trying to bring to birth for his daughter a
    marriage of greater renown,
Heard of the fashion of a speedy bridal that Danaos
    devisèd erst in Argos
For his forty and eight maiden daughters, e'er the noontide
    (of life?) fell on them:
For he ranged the whole band of them at the ends of a
    running-course,
115 And with the strife of the foot-race he bade decide
Which bride should fall to any of the heroes who came as
    wooers for them.
Even so the Libyan chief sorted out and gave a bridegroom
    to his girl:

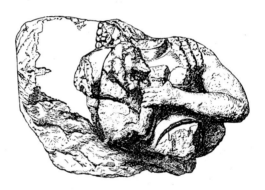

FIG. 10. Limestone relief, sixth century B.C., from Treasury of Cyrene at Olympia, Cyrene gripping paw of lion.

Having adornèd her in fair raiment, he placed her on the
   line to be the goal for the runners,
And he proclaimèd among the throng of wooers that he
   should lead her away
Who having outstripped all in the race for her should first 120
   touch her garments.
Then Alexidamos, when he had sped in swift flight down
   the course,
And had clasped his hand in the hand of the true maid,
Led her away through the press of the horse-loving Nomad
   folk.
They cast upon him many a leafy garland, many a crown;
Even as in former days he had won many a winged trophy 125
   of victory."

   The ninth Pythian celebrates a victory in the 'hoplite-
race'—the race run in full armour—won by Telesikrates of
Cyrene in 474 B.C. The ode is evidently sung at Thebes.
What I wrote on this ode in 1915[1] appears still to me to be
true. "The ninth Pythian is one of Pindar's masterpieces.
It contains the romantic story of the love of Apollo for the
heroic nymph Kurana, which is the foundation-legend of
the great city of Cyrene, and he attaches to the end of the
ode another graceful love-tale which was a family tradition
of the athlete's ancestors. The style of the ode is suitable
to the subject, and the rhythm is partly Dorian, partly
Lydian. Therefore the grand style which is maintained
throughout, the style in which Pindar always excels, is
richly mellowed and tempered with a certain lusciousness,
a rarer quality of his work, but appropriate here to the
romantic theme. And Pindar combines here the energy
which is his birthright with a certain dignified ease and
clearness; and his occasional faults of harshness, over-
pungency, or overstrain are absent altogether. 'Out of the
strong hath come forth sweetness.'"
   It is rarely that Pindar succeeds in being arch; but a certain archness, delicate and refined, appears in the badinage
between the Centaur with his smiling mockery and the God

---

[1] See *Classical Quarterly*, 1915, p. 193.

The amour is more delicately treated than in the somewhat similar narrative of the love-affair of Aphrodite and Ares in the Odyssey; but the tone is scarcely up to the level of the high seriousness with which Pindar usually treats the actions and characters of divinities. Apollo here strikes us rather as the delightful young man than as the God; and Cheiron has to remind him gaily of his divine omniscience. We may feel that the scene reveals a certain weakness in the anthropomorphic imagination of Greek religion. On the other hand, the girl-huntress Kurana is presented with impressive force and vigour, and the lyrical drama has all the thrill and glow that his best workmanship always imparts to such passages. For Kurana had captured his imagination. She is no fictitious incarnation of the city of Cyrene. She was a real flesh-and-blood figure of Thessalian folklore, whom their Minyan-Thessalian tradition preserved in the memories of the first founders of the Libyan city. She was probably an aboriginal Thessalian Goddess, akin to Artemis, a "mistress of wild-beasts", who gave her name to the city as Athena gave hers to Athens. Pindar could have heard sufficiently about her from his Cyrenaean friends, and he could have been stimulated by the archaic sculpture which he had seen at Olympia on the treasure-house of the Cyrenaeans, where she was carved in relief, in the act of strangling the lion (*vide* Fig. 10).

When his epic narrative is finished, he breaks out into a personal appeal to his fellow-citizens of Thebes, which gives us the most interesting personal poetry that is to be found in the odes. He begins with the praise of 'Opportunity'; and illustrates it by the story of Iolaos, who knew the right moment to come to the help of the Athenians when they were waging battle with Eurustheus to save the children of Herakles. According to one story Iolaos rose from the dead to come to their aid, like Theseus at Marathon; according to another, he prayed for and obtained from the Gods the boon of a brief rejuvenescence, during which he showed his prowess and slew Eurustheus. This gives Pindar the cue for an eloquent outburst in praise of the heroes and the land of Thebes. And he uses this opportunity to shield himself against two connected charges: (*a*) lack of patriotism in never praising Thebes, (*b*) disloyalty in his warm eulogies on Athens, the immemorial enemy of Thebes, recently uttered on some public occasion. He defends him-

FIG. 11. Relief in British Museum, second century A.D., from temple of Aphrodite in Cyrene: Goddess Libya with native headdress crowning Cyrene strangling lion.

self by vehemently denying the first charge and declaring that he has thrice glorified Thebes in epinician odes and that he will rejoice always to glorify her when some good chance befalls her. He meets the second charge by a stirring appeal to their magnanimity, and by reminding them of the high counsel of an ancient sage, that we should praise even an enemy when he does noble things for the common weal. At this juncture and in this context the only enemy of whom this could be said was Athens. And we may find value in the story that for the splendid dithyramb which he wrote in praise of Athens the Thebans fined him and the grateful Athenians paid the fine. He tactfully avoids mentioning the name of Athens, but the story of Iolaos and Eurustheus must have brought it into the minds of his Theban audience. Otherwise Pindar speaks out boldly and nobly and proclaims the generous sentiment, rarely heard in Greek literature, in a passage of great ethical beauty.[1]

The episode which ends the ode, the love-story of one of the victor's ancestors and the race for the bride, is composed as a postscript, as an after-thought suggested by Telesikrates or one of his relatives. The ode, therefore, altogether lacks unity; but Pindar never cares too much for that principle of composition: hence the varied interest of his Epinicians.

The whole ode, both in its main narrative and in its epilogue, gives more prominence to the love-motive than is found in any of his other poems of this collection. The Pindaric Muse is not specially attracted to erotic poetry, but occasionally, as in this ode and in the eighth Nemean, utters some bright and striking phrases that are contributions to it.[2]

We may discern the influence of this poem on some later Greek art dealing with the story of Cyrene (Figs. 11 and 12).

---

[1] I have developed this view of the passage in the paper referred to above.
[2] *Vide infra*, pp. 325-326.

FIG. 12. Gem in Hermitage collection in Petrograd, showing Apollo bearing Cyrene over the sea in chariot drawn by swans, Graeco-Roman period.

PYTHIAN X

To Hippokleas of Thessaly

"BLESSED is the land of Lakedaimon:
Happy, too, is Thessaly; and both are ruled by a stock
    descended from the self-same sire, even Herakles,
    lord of the battle-field.
Why do I thus blate unseasonably?
Nay, but Putho and the township of Pelinna and the
5   children of Aleuas call to me, fain as they are to lead
    on the far-famed singing-band of men in honour of
    Hippokleas.
For he is handselling the athlete's labour:
And the hollow dell of Parnassos proclaimèd him to the
    host of the dwellers round the shrine as surpassing all
    other boys in the double running—
'Tis by impulse divine, oh Apollo, that man's achievement
10   from its beginning to its close waxeth sweet.
He, I trow, has wrought this deed by thy fore-ordering;
But his own native spirit hath followed in the footsteps of
    his sire,
Who twice conquered at Olympia, clad in the War-God's
    battle-staying arms.
And the strife in the deep meadow beneath the rocks of
15   Kirrha brought victory to the feet of Phrikias.
May such fair destiny follow them in days to come, so that
    their wealth may ever proudly blossom for them!
As they have been allotted no small portion of those
    things that Hellas deemeth delightful,
20 So may no shiftings of envious fortune befall them from
    the Gods.

(Only) a God could be for ever free from sorrow of
    heart:

But a man achieveth happiness and the singer's praise in
    the estimation of the wise,

Who having triumphèd by strength of hand or the prowess
    of his running,

Hath won the greatest prizes in the contests through his
    daring and might;

And who while still alive seeth his young son achieving 25
    Pythian crowns by the ruling of Fate.

Verily the brazen vault of Heaven he cannot scale:

But so far as we mortals can reach to glorious things,

He saileth furthest on that course.

Yet neither on shipboard nor by land-faring couldst thou
    find the wondrous road to the gathering of the 30
    Hyperborean folk:

Into whose homes Perseus, the leader of the people, entered
    and joined their feasts,

Having found them offering goodly hekatombs of asses to
    the God:

In whose revels and holy speech Apollo taketh great 35
    delight, and laugheth to see the lustful wantonness of
    the strange beasts.

The Muse is no stranger there in their rule of life,

And everywhere the singing - bands of maidens, the
    voices of the lyres, the trills of flutes throb in their
    ears;

And having bound their locks in golden laurel they hold
    festival in gladness of soul. 40

Neither age nor wasting sickness is the portion of that holy
    race;

But they live far aloof from toil and battle,

Freed from the o'erstrict judgment-court of Nemesis.

Of old came the son of Danaë, kindled with boldness of
    spirit,

And Athena led him on to the fellowship of these happy 45
    men.

He slew the Gorgon, and farèd back, bearing to the

islanders the head with its speckled snake-locks, the
Terror that froze to stone.

When the Gods have been at work, nothing appeareth to
50   be past belief, too wondrous in my eyes.

Back water! swiftly cast from the prow thy anchor to the
firm bottom, a safeguard 'gainst the rocky reef:

For the pride of these songs of praise speedeth from tale
to tale as bee from flower to flower.

55 But I hope that, when my utterance welleth forth sweet
from the lips of the men of Ephura by the banks of
Peneus,

I shall make this youth, Hippokleas, even more than now
the object of all eyes, with the accompaniment of
songs for the crowns he hath won, both among his
young comrades and the elders,

And the young maidens' heart's desire.

60 For Love's sting is diverse in different souls.

And, when one winneth that which he craveth, he may
hold in his hands the longing of his heart for the
present moment;

But that which awaiteth at the year's end is baffling to
foresee.

I trust in the kindly hospitality of Thorax, who in hot zeal
65   for my sake yokèd this four-horsed chariot of the
Muses,

Friend helping friend, leader and follower in willing turn.

Gold and righteousness of mind are provèd for one who
testeth on the touch-stone.

We will greatly praise the goodly brothers,

70 For that they exalt and foster the Thessalian land:

The rule of states in noble hands by ancestral right is
trusty and sure."

This ode has the interest of being undoubtedly the earliest
of Pindar's surviving works; for the boy Hippokleas, a
Thessalian of the noble family of the Aleuadai, won the
Pythian double foot-race in 498 B.C., when Pindar was

some twenty years old. It is interesting therefore to compare
it with his more perfected and matured style.

We certainly recognise marks of the tyro's hand. He
begins with what might have been a brilliant and effective
proem; but almost at once he pulls himself up and apologises as if he had been too bold at the start. And here and
there we may note the doubtful phrase, a mixed metaphor,
a moralising platitude; and his mode of introducing his
myth is hardly dexterous. The myth itself, the story of the
happy society of the Hyperboreans, has appeared both to
the commentators and the modern reader as irrelevant.
In fact, the ancient scholars of Alexandria declared the
latter part of the ode to be a failure, partly because he
introduced the irrelevant Hyperboreans, partly because he
made Perseus visit them, an unvouched-for and unnatural
fiction, only repeated by one later writer who borrowed it
from Pindar; for they were in the far North, and the
Gorgons against whom Perseus went lived in the far West
or South-East.

But irrelevance was not specially a youthful vice in
Pindar; he seems still more guilty of it in the eleventh
Pythian, a much later work; in fact he was always capable
of it according to our ideas of relevance, and some of his
'irrelevances' are great inspirations.

But from Pindar's point of view, and possibly from the
Thessalians', the Hyperborean story may not have appeared so inappropriate; for, as I have tried to show elsewhere, the Thessalian country was full of Hyperborean
associations.[1] And our poet was interested in 'Paradise-
poetry', which he here attempts for the first time in a
manner that foreshadows his triumph in the second
Olympian. As regards the intrusion of Perseus there is no
defence, for he had no traditional connection with the
Hyperboreans or with contests or with the Thessalians.
We may say that Pindar in his youth was bold enough to
be his own mythologist, as he occasionally was in his
maturer years. And we may imagine the train of thought
that prompted this audacious irrelevance. "You have
attained the highest happiness possible for mortals: ab-
solute and lasting happiness is impossible. We cannot scale
Heaven or find Paradise. If a man ever got there, it must
have been under divine, miraculous guidance, such guid-

[1] *Cults of the Greek States*, iv. p. 104.

ance as Perseus had who travelled very far. Perhaps he got to the Hyperborean Paradise, as he got to the Garden of the Hesperides. Let us say that he did."

What is most noticeable is that in this, his first work, most of Pindar's leading style-marks and his method of handling the epinician theme are presented—if in somewhat crude form. Those who had ears to hear might have felt that here was a new poet arisen who would go far.

PYTHIAN XI

To Thrasudaios of Thebes

"YE daughters of Kadmos, Semele that art neighbour to
    the Heavenly Goddesses,
And Ino Leukothea, sharer of the sea-nymphs' chambers,
Fare ye with the mother of Herakles, the noblest child e'er
    born,
To the presence of Melia into the secret treasure-house 5
    of the golden tripods,
The house that Apollo honoured above all others and
    called Ismenion, true seat of divination;
Where even now, oh, daughters of Harmonia, he sum-
    moneth into one company the host of the heroines of
    our land,
In order that, with the fall of eventide, ye may sing the
    praises of the Goddess Themis, of holy Putho, and
    earth's centre, whence God's judgments come,   10
As a gracious joy to seven-gated Thebes and to Kirrha's
    contest;
Wherein Thrasudaios hath made memorable his father's
    house,
Bringing to it the third crown through his victory in the
    fertile fields of Pulades, guest-friend of Orestes of 15
    Laconia.
Him, at the time of his father's murder, his nurse Arsinoe
    deliverèd out of the woeful treachery from the violent
    hands of Klutaimnestra,
When, with the cold grey steel, she sent Kassandra,
    daughter of Dardan Priam, to join the soul of Aga- 20
    memnon along the shadowy bank of Acheron—

A woman without pity.
Was it indeed that the thought of Iphigeneia, sacrificèd
     on Euripos' bank far from her fatherland,
Stung her so as to awaken heavy-plotting wrath,
Or was it that, won to another's bed,
25 The adulterous embraces of the night beguilèd her?
But for young wives this is the most hateful trespass, and
     hopeless to hide from the tongues of others.
Citizens are prone to evil speech, and great prosperity hath
     envy no less great.
30 But he who draweth humble breath muttereth in secret.
Howbeit, the hero-son of Atreus, having come back after
     long time,
Perishèd himself in far-famed Amuklai,
And brought to her death the prophetic maid,
After that in Helen's quarrel he had brought down the
     Trojan homes from their luxurious estate and had
     kindled the fire above the Trojan folk.
35 But he, the young child, came to the home of his aged
     guest-friend Strophios, dwelling at Parnassos' foot;
And, waxen in years, with the War-God's might he slew
     his mother and laid Aigisthos low in blood.
Oh, friends, have I verily swerved down a false track at
     the parting of the ways,
Faring along the straight path hitherto?
Or has some gale driven me from my course like a sea-
     bark?
40 Oh, Muse of mine, if thou hast covenanted to furnish song-
     speech at the price of silver,
It behoveth thee at other-times in diverse ways wildly to
     riot,
But now at least to give thy voice to Puthonikos or to
     Thrasudaios:
45 Who shine in the glow of festal delight and renown.
From of old, crownèd with fair triumph in their chariots,
From Olympia's much-vaunted contests,
They won the swift-glancing light of victory with their
     steeds.

And at Putho, having entered for the bare-limbed foot-race,
They put to shame the whole host of the Hellenes by their 50
    swift-running.
May I yearn for the fair things of God's giving,
Striving only after that which the time of my life may win!
For finding that the middle estate flowereth with fuller
    prosperity than all others in the city,
I praise not the tyrant's lot.
Only for praise and honour open to all do I strive;
And if a man having won full measure of these and
    dwelling in tranquillity shunneth fell insolence,
The envious are kept at bay.   55
He will find in the end the dark hour of death the fairer,
Having left to the dear ones of his race the grace of
    auspicious fame, noblest inheritance of all.[1]
'Tis this that spreadeth the glory of Iolaos, son of Iphiklos,
    in our songs,
Of mighty Kastor, and thee King Poludeukes, ye sons of
    Zeus,
Abiding one day in your homes at Therapnai,
The next day within the courts of Heaven."

    This ode is certainly unique among Pindar's works; for
while it is marked by vigour and other characteristics of
our poet, it is quite unpardonable; so wilful and amazing
is the irrelevance of the greater part of it, an irrelevance
which no commentator's learning or penetration can explain or excuse. The proem is stirring and promises well:
he calls upon the divine daughters of Kadmos, the heroine
Alkmena the mother of Herakles, and the other heroines
of the land, to gather in the Ismenion, the famous shrine
of Apollo in Thebes, and there to sing the praises of Putho
and Themis (a Delphian-Theban Goddess) in honour of the
victory of the Theban Thrasudaios, which is the immediate
occasion of this ode. But immediately he staggers off the
natural track and falls upon the story of Agamemnon,
and deals at some length with his death and Kassandra's

---

[1] The text is too uncertain for an exact translation.

at Amuklai in Laconia, with the motives of "the pitiless woman" Klutaimnestra and with the later vengeance of Orestes. The transition to this alien and to our eyes wholly inappropriate myth is forced and clumsy. Having naturally mentioned Putho (Delphi) in the proem, he chooses to call it the territory of Pulades. No one else ever called it so; and Pindar's sole motive for this improper description of the place was that the name Pulades could suggest the name Orestes; and having mentioned this latter he breaks loose, and gives us the outlines of the famous story down to the death of Aigisthos. Then he recovers himself, blames himself, and remembers his duty to the victor and his family. In a few lines of forcible poetry that rings true he praises their achievements at Delphi and Olympia. But soon he leaves them again and indulges in moralising about himself, and some of his sententious phrases here belong to his higher poetry. At the close of the ode he returns to mythology, with a word in praise of Iolaos, but more about the Dioskouroi, the Laconian Twin-Brethren and their miraculous double life, half in heaven and half on earth. In fact, another mystery of the ode is its preoccupation with Laconia; Orestes is given as a Laconian and the whole of the great tragedy is transferred to Laconia. We know that Pindar had some authority for this and that the Spartans tried to annex the great legends of the ancient royalty of the Argolid. But what was all this and what were the Laconian Twins to Thebes, and why does Pindar force such subjects upon them at this time?

We might suppose there was more chance of explaining the riddle if we knew certainly what the time was. The scholiasts gives Thrasudaios two Pythian victories, one in 474 (according to the later dating of the Pythiads) and another in 454, and they and most of the moderns assign the ode to the earlier date. There is nothing in the poem itself which gives conclusive evidence. But our difficulties, though heavy enough, are slightly less if we connect it with the later victory. For Sparta was much more popular at Thebes in 454 B.C., and by this time Pindar could have heard or possibly read the *Agamemnon* of Aeschylus. For in Pindar's story of Orestes we are reminded again and again of the great Athenian drama; and it is far easier to believe that Pindar had seen or read the work of Aeschylus than that Aeschylus had borrowed from this bizarre production of Pindar's. Can we imagine that our poet was so possessed by the mighty creation of the Athenian that on his next public opportunity he was bound to expatiate on the same theme, however irrelevant? Even if this supposition explained, it does not justify.

Can we justify him by imagining certain events that may have been happening at Thebes or in the family circle of Thrasudaios, to which the Orestes-Klutaimnestra saga afforded a parallel conveying a warning? To invent fiction, so as to explain Pindar, is of dubious value; and such fiction, if it might absolve him on the charge of irrelevance, would affix a slur on his good taste and sense of propriety. When one is paid for a joyful epinician ode, it is better to be irrelevant than inexcusably insulting. The ancient critics blamed the greater part of this poem. We can discover no way of defending him, nor can we detect in it any constructive unity, though it is something to have Pindar's account of the great tragedy told with some lyrical and dramatic thrill. He must have been very sure of his position to have indulged himself with such a literary freak. He composes like a privileged public favourite who can say what he pleases.

PYTHIAN XII

To Midas of Akragas

"THEE I entreat, oh, Goddess, thou the fairest of all cities
 of men,
Thou lover of delight, home of Persephone,
Thou that on the hilltops dost inhabit the fair-built crest
 of sheep-pasturing Akragas,
Oh, Queen, propitiously and with all kindliness of Im-
 mortals and of men,
5 Receive this crown from Putho in well-famèd Midas'
 honour,
And welcome the man himself fresh from the triumph o'er
 all Hellas,
Won by the art that Pallas Athena fashionèd
When she wove into a varied strain (on the flute) the fierce
 Gorgon's deathful dirge;
10 The dirge that she heard welling forth from beneath the
 maidens' lips and the serpents' fearful heads,
In sorrow and heaviness of heart;
In the hour when Perseus ended the life of the third one
 of the sisters,
Thereby bringing doom to the isle Seriphos and its folk.
Verily he bereft of light the weird progeny of Phorkos,
And made Poludektes rue the bridal-gift,
15 His mōther's hard slavery and enforcèd couch,
When that son of Danae, who we aver was begotten of the
 free-flowing shower of gold,
Reft the fair-cheeked Medusa of her head.
But when Athena had redeemèd the man she loved from
 all these toils,

The Maiden-Goddess fashioned the many-voicèd melody of
  the flutes,
In order that with instruments of music she might render
  the loud-resounding lamentation reaching her from 20
  the ravening jaws of Eurualë.
The Goddess did devise it, and having devisèd it as a
  possession for mortal men,
She named it the many-headed strain,
The noble summoner to folk-arousing contests,
Issuing from the thin lips of bronze and the reeds withal, 25
Faithful witnesses of the dancers' steps,
That grow by the city[1] of the Graces gay with the dance,
In the holy precincts of the Goddess of Kephisos.
But if any bliss is to be found among men, it showeth not
  itself without hard toil.
Verily even to-day (perchance) God's power will accom-
  plish it to the full.
That which is destined cannot be avoided.
But there will come that hour which, though it may have 30
  smitten a man with mere despair,
Will, counter to his expectation, grant him one boon
While keeping back another."

This ode is of the lesser order and shows immaturity.
It was composed about 490 B.C., when Pindar would be
just past his first youth, in honour of a certain Midas of
Akragas, who was victor in the musical contest of the flute.
As Pindar has accepted the principle that in the normal
construction of an epinician ode a myth is necessary, he
finds himself here limited in his choice; for Akragas had
no myth, and probably Midas' ancestry provided none. It
must then be a myth about the invention of the flute or of
this particular kind of flute-music. Pindar is our first
voucher for the strange story that he gives us; he may have
invented it or found it current at Delphi: a similar story
was there in vogue concerning the "Pythian strain", which

[1] Orchomenos in Boeoiia.

was said to commemorate the victory of Apollo over Python.

The ode is not without an austere charm in the diction and the grave and regular rhythm; but there is occasionally a vagueness and lack of precision in the phrasing, and the aphoristic poetry is not at his usual level. In the proem his confusion of the Goddess Akragas and the city is not happy, and in the moralising that closes the ode he seems slightly to lose his head. But much of it shows the true Pindar with his characteristic sweep and brightness.

THE NEMEAN ODES

NEMEAN I

To Chromios of Etna

"Hail, Ortugia,
Holy place where Alpheus breathed again,
Flowering-branch of famèd Syracuse,
The couch of Artemis, Delos' sister-isle,
From thee speedeth forth the sweet-voiced hymn, to 5
    establish the high renown of storm-footed steeds, to
    the glory of Zeus, the God of Etna's city:
The chariot of Chromios and (the fame of) Nemea urge me
    on to yoke a strain of praise to victory-bearing deeds.
I have set the names of divinities in the fore-front of my
    song in keeping with that man's deeds of more than
    mortal prowess.
In fair success is the crowning-point of full renown;
And mighty contests the Muse loveth to bear in memory. 10
Shed now some flowers of brightness upon the island that
    Zeus the Lord of Olympos gave to Persephone:
And nodded with his waving locks upon the pledge, that
    he would exalt Sicily to excel in all earth's abundance,
    and cause her to teem with the wealth of high-crested 15
    cities.
And the son of Kronos furnished her with a folk whose
    heart was set on bronze-clad war,
Full oft withal familiar with the lustrous olive-crowns of
    the Olympian games.
Here have I touched the very heart of a manifold theme,
    casting forth words unmixed with falsehood.
I stood singing a fair song by the court-door of a guest- 20
    fain man,

Where a banquet had been meetly set in order for me.
And oft-times are these halls familiar with the guest from
other lands.
Verily the cavillers at good men are in the plight of those
who would quench smoke with water.
Diverse are the arts of different men.
It is meet for a man to fare along the straight path, and
25   to wage the strife with all his native power.
When deeds are doing, strength is of all avail,
But, in the giving of counsel, wisdom, so that those on whom
this inborn gift attendeth may foresee the future.
Oh, son of Agesidamos, in thy disposition are uses manifold
30   (for thy friends):
I do not love to keep wealth buried in my chamber,
But to enjoy the present store and to win a good name as
one who helpeth his friends.
For the hopes of care-worn men come [to all of us] in
fellowship.
But for myself, I cleave with heart full fain to Herakles,
Awakening an ancient story among the high places of his
deeds of prowess—
How, when from his mother's womb, he, with his twin-
brother came suddenly into the radiant light of God,
35   safe from the travail pangs,
He in no way escapèd the eye of Hera of the golden throne,
when he lay wrapped in saffron swaddling-clothes:
But she, Heaven's Queen, spurred on by wrath, sent (two)
40   serpents suddenly.
And they, the gates being open, fared on to the chamber's
broad recess, with fell desire to enfold the children in
their swift-ravening jaws:
But he raised his head erect, and for the first time made
assay of battle,
45 Seizing the twain serpents by the necks in the grip of his
twain hands invincible:
And as they strangled, their fated span[1] (?) breathed forth
their souls from their monstrous limbs.

[1] The Greek word is doubtful and scarcely intelligible.

Then fear intolerable struck the women who chancèd to
    be tending the child-bed of Alkmena:

Yea, and she herself, albeit unclad, sped on her feet from 50
    her couch and tried to ward off the violence of the
    monsters.

But swiftly the Cadmeian chiefs, armed with brazen
    weapons, ran up in a band;

And Amphitruon came, brandishing his unsheathèd sword
    and smitten with sharp pangs.

For the evil in one's own house presseth on each man alike,

But alien trouble passeth straightaway from the heart
    without afflicting it.

Then he stood confusèd with troubled and delighted 55
    amaze.

For he saw his son's courage and strength surpassing the
    measure of man:

And the will of the Immortal Gods had belied the dread
    tale of his messengers.

Then he summoned his neighbour, a peerless prophet of
    high God, the unerring soothsayer Teiresias;   60

And he foretold to him and all the warriors of Thebes,

What strange fortunes the hero will encounter,

How many he shall slay on land,

How many wild and outlawed creatures in the deep sea:

And one, the fellest foe of all, one who walkèd with deceit 65
    and the loathing of men,

He averred that he should bring to his doom.

For he foretold withal that when the Gods shall join battle
    with the giants on the plain of Phlegra,

Beneath the storm-rush of his arrows their fair locks shall
    lie bedabbled with the soil of earth.

Verily the hero himself in peace for all time hereafter un-
    endingly shall have a priceless reward for his mighty 70
    toils,

In halls of happiness; and having won blooming Hebé for
    his bride,

And having held the bridal-feast, he shall praise that holy
    realm by the side of Zeus, the son of Kronos."

The first Nemean ode was composed about 473 B.C., and belongs therefore to Pindar's period of mature style, displaying his characteristic excellencies, yet not being wholly flawless or rising to the highest pitch of his inspiration. It celebrates the Nemean chariot-victory of a certain Syracusan called Chromios, about whom the ninth Nemean, which should be read in conjunction with this, tells us more. We gather that he was a rich Syracusan noble, a friend of Hieron, who gave him a responsible office in his newly founded city of Etna and that he had distinguished himself in his youth in Gelon's and Hieron's campaigns.

We find in this poem all the elements that are usually employed in the construction of Pindar's greater epinicians; the solemn invocation of divine powers in the prelude, the glorifying of his patron's achievement and the proclamation of his virtues, the moralising on human life and its varied aspects, the lyrical narrative of some myth more or less appropriate to the occasion or suggested by something in the poem. But in every ode these elements are differently mingled.

In Pindar's preludes we usually are confronted at once with the daring and arresting phrase, but never more strikingly than here. The phrases in the invocation of the island Ortugia, the original site of Syracuse, halt between personification and natural description. The opening words, literally meaning "the holy exhalation of Alpheus", that is, "the place where Alpheus breathed up when he came to the surface" are only intelligible as applied to Ortugia, in so far as Pindar can identify Ortugia with Arethousa, the fountain that has through all the ages supplied the best fresh water to the settlement, and can suppose in his hearers familiarity with the romantic story of Alpheus' amorous pursuit of Arethousa from Elis under the sea, which continued until he "bubbled up" in Ortugia, mingling his waters with hers. The story may already have been well known to the Western Greeks from a poem on the theme by their own poet Ibukos. It was supported by actual cult, the cult of the nymph Arethousa and of "Artemis of Alpheus" or "Artemis of the river" in Ortugia itself. Therefore Pindar can speak of it as "the couch of Artemis"—her shrine in the island may have contained an actual couch—and as the "twin-sister of Delos" in the affections of the Goddess. And in the roll of divine powers he tactfully remembers

Zeus of Etna, a deity of special interest for Hieron and Chromios.

Then he expands the praise of Chromios into a glowing eulogy of Sicily, Persephone's cherished island, and his warm and rich phrases of praise ring true to those who know its ancient history and even to the modern traveller familiar with the region. Then he returns to Chromios, speaking charmingly of himself as a welcome guest singing in the forecourt of a hospitable house. And he moralises in his characteristic way on the advantages of natural endowments, and on the true value of wealth for joyous living and for helping our friends in their need, and relieving the hardships of life. The ideal type of the Helper, who after many hardships won peace and felicity at last, was Herakles, and the rest of the ode—more than half of it—is devoted to that hero, and there is no further reference or discoverable allusion to Chromios or the present occasion. What is more remarkable is that the only incident in the life of Herakles which is dealt with in great detail is the story of him as a wonder-baby strangling the snakes: a portent that awakens the prophecy of the great Theban prophet Teiresias, whom the astonished Amphitruon, the reputed father, calls to the scene, and who forthwith predicts the life of heroic achievement that awaits the babe. There is no allusion in clear terms to any other single exploit except his participation in the great battle between the Gods and the giants, which brought victory to the Gods and won for the hero admission to Olympus and Hebe for his bride.

The scholars of Alexandria, the later scholiasts, and the modern commentators have been puzzled to discover the relevance of all this. Many absurd theories have been put forward and fictions invented. It might be agreeable to believe that Chromios had done something remarkable as a baby, so that the relevance of the myth might be perfect. But as Pindar does not mention it, it is not for us. We know that Chromios distinguished himself as a youth in the battle of Heloros, but that brings us no nearer to the baby and the snakes. When Pindar wants to tell us something definite about Chromios, he does so in the ninth Nemean quite clearly. The belief that Pindar is prone to cryptic allusion has led to much misinterpretation of him; and we will not believe, because he tells us that the baby had two fists, that therefore Chromios had two calumniators. In point of fact, the modern commentator is often more concerned about Pindar's relevance than Pindar was himself. We are dealing with a poet astonishingly wayward, whom a single phrase is often enough to send off the track, spinning down a long by-path of myth. The mere mention of gratitude in the second Pythian plunges him at once into the legend of the ungrateful Ixion, which he narrates to the bitter end before he returns to Hieron. In fact, there are other odes in which the question of relevance is far more hopeless than in this one. The following considerations may be helpful :

Herakles had already become in the Greek imagination an ideal personality, the archetype of the warrior and athlete, the Helper and Warder-off of evil. Therefore in celebrating any exploit in war or the games, it was not far-fetched to mention the name of Herakles as a parallel, especially for a poet of Thebes, the city of all others most devoted to him. And the surviving odes of Pindar attest the truth of his own statement by which he prefaces the Herakles-episode in this poem—"I cleave with heart full-fain to Herakles"; even so in the ninth Pythian he had burst forth even more fervently, "dull and senseless is the man who does not crown his speech with the name of Herakles". We may remember also that on the last night of the Olympian games the victorious athlete, if he and his friends had nothing better to sing, chanted the refrain in honour of "the victorious Herakles". Therefore his name and even his story was appropriate to the song at any epinician feast, especially when, as in the case of Chromios, neither the victor's family nor his state had any traditional or local myth that could be naturally interwoven with the ode. Finally, we may be sure that his audience expected and desired a mythic story from Pindar. He could here find nothing more appropriate than an outline-sketch of the life-career of Herakles, leaving it to his hearers to apply it to Chromios as far as they liked or could.

These are general reasons that suffice to justify him in introducing the personality of Herakles; but we have still to explain why the long roll of the hero's other achievements should be passed over with vague general terms or in one case with very slight definite mention, and why the poet should single out for long, detailed and enthusiastic narrative the feat of the babe with the snakes. Two reasons may commend themselves as sufficient and as artistically plausible. Pindar would have no time, and, as a great artist in lyric narrative, would have no desire, to give them a summary catalogue of all the deeds and 'labours' of Herakles: and they had nearly all been treated in detail by at least one earlier poet. And Pindar, as he specially informs us elsewhere, loves a new song. Now we have every reason for supposing that this remarkable story of the amazing infant had never been recorded, at least in high poetry, before. We may be sure that he did not himself invent it; otherwise it would hardly have spread broadcast round the whole Greek world, as we know it did; also we find it on two Attic vase-paintings, contemporary with Pindar, but certainly not influenced by his ode. We may believe it to be genuine Theban folklore; and in general motive it has some affinity with the Edda-story in the *Volsunga* saga how the bravery of the one child—Sinfiotli —and the cowardice of the other child are tested by the terror of the snake. And as it is most probable that the Syracusans had never heard it before, at least not in any literary form, Pindar might be sure that his audience would receive his brilliant narration of it with delight

Another reason is one based on poetic economy: it occurred to Pindar, and it has occurred to other masters of saga, that it is an excellent poetic device to put into the mouth of a prophet some foreboding sketch of a hero's future career, delivered at his birth or in his infancy, or before the events develop. And if the hero did something miraculous in his infancy, it would be natural at once to call in the prophet. It was just this wonderful feat of the infant Herakles that gave Pindar his opportunity, as no other of his feats could have given him. Therefore he only details this legend of infancy and then brings in Teiresias to adumbrate the marvellous story of the coming years through which the hero passes on to final bliss. Instead of a mere chronicle of events we have a thrilling and inspired utterance

This is enough to justify the choice of this theme; but it is just possible that it may have evoked in the mind of Pindar and his audience something more. It is a curious fact that near the beginning of the fourth century B.C. certain Greek states, including Thebes, who banded themselves together to resist the tyranny of Sparta, adopted as a coin-badge the type of the infant Herakles with the snakes.[1] It possessed then a symbolic significance, typifying the conflict of light with darkness, right with wrong. It could not well have acquired this secondary value until literature and art had familiarised the public with it. It is hazardous therefore to assume that it had acquired it by the time that Pindar composed this ode. If it had, there would be this further justification for its insertion here, that it might remind the Syracusans of the recent overthrow of Carthage and Etruria, the enemies of Hellenism and light, against whom Chromios may have done valiant service. At least, we may bear this possibility in mind; and it may be a mere coincidence or a further hint of the same underlying thought that the only other exploit of Herakles to which clear reference is made is his warfare with the giants; and certainly in the later periods, probably already in the fifth century, the battle of the Gods and giants was the mythic counterpart of the struggles of Hellas with barbarism.

Whatever may be said of its relevance, there is no doubt but that the narrative is one of Pindar's masterpieces in the sphere of heroic lyric; the whole drama is swiftly presented in terse and thrilling phrase: at the first moment of peril the babe is transfigured and "raises his head erect" —the last impossibility for a new-born babe. The only serious flaw with which the poet may be reproached is that he pauses, in the midst of Amphitruon's rush to his infant's aid, to moralise on the obvious truth that we care more for our own children than for other people's!—the nearest approach to a platitude that we can find in Pindar's works, however well concealed its triteness may be by the poetic expression of it. The poem closes with the solemn harmonies of the prophecy of Teiresias and ends with a golden glow shed around the immortal happiness in heaven. The poet leaves us there and makes no return to earth, as we might have expected: nor is there any hint of the hero's agony on Mount Oita, a late legend of which Pindar was either unaware or incredulous.[2]

[1] *Vide* Fig. 14.
[2] *Vide* my *Greek Hero-cults*, p. 171.

NEMEAN II

To Timodemos of Acharnai

"IN the far-famed holy grove of Zeus of Nemea—
That God whom the minstrel-sons of Homer, that weave
    the web of heroic verse, invoke most often in their
    preludes—
This man hath received the first earnest-pledge of victories
    to come in the sacred contests.   5
And the debt is yet due from him, if the fair-speeding
    breeze of his destiny, wafting him down his ancestral
    track, hath brought him as a glory to mighty Athens,
That the son of Timonoos should oft-times cull the fairest
    flower of the Isthmian triumphs and conquer in the
    Pythian games.
It may well be looked for that Orion (the hunter of the 10
    mountains) should fare along not far from the
    mountain-maids, the Pleiades:
And indeed the land of Salamis availeth to breed a warrior:
I ween that in Troy-land Hektor heard of Aias:
And, O Timodemos, the soul-straining prowess in the 15
    pankration exalteth thee.
Acharnai, too, was faméd in days of old for its breed of
    men:
But in all that toucheth manly contests, the house of
    Timodemos are, before all others, proclaimed surpass-
    ing.
Four triumphs from the strife on high-throned Parnassos
    have they brought home:
But by the hands of men of Corinth,   20
In the folded vales of the realm of goodly Pelops,

They have been encircled with eight crowns already;
And seven at Nemea (crowns at home past number)
In the gathering-feast of Zeus.
Wherefore, oh, citizens (of Athens), celebrate that God in
     your choral song in honour of Timodemos, together
     with his glorious home-faring;
25 And raise the prelude of the hymn with melodious voices."

We cannot date this ode by any external or internal
evidence. Only the passing mention of Salamis and its
mythic association with Aias, without any allusion to the
great naval victory, may incline us to suppose that it was
composed before 480 B.C. At any rate, the style shows the
mellow maturity of Pindar's prime; the phrasing is strong
and bold, but with a certain simplicity and freedom from
overstrain. The only elaborateness is in the prelude, and
we may regard it as a happy thought that suggests to
Pindar the parallel between the young athlete, whose victory at Nemea has associated him with Zeus, giving him an
earnest of many more to come, and the Homeric rhapsodists
who invoked Zeus to aid them before they began their
recitation of the Homeric poems. The thought may have
seemed to him the more natural here, as the victor was an
Athenian, and Pindar was aware that the rhapsodical
recitation of Homeric poetry had been an established part
of the Panathenaic festival since Peisistratos. The gem in
the poem is the Orion-passage; "The athlete's family, the
Timodamidai, pursue athletic glory as naturally as Orion
pursues the Pleiades"; Pindar throws this into the form that
he loves, not the form of a simile, but of the abrupt aphorism, trusting to his hearers to apply it easily; it is so easy of
application and so transparently simple that it has puzzled
commentators, who strain to find some resemblance between the athletes and the Pleiades ladies.

What is most noteworthy is that this ode and the seventh
Pythian are the only odes in the four groups of the epinicians
that commemorate victories by Athenians; and both these,
though in excellent style and not without charm, are short
and slight poems not showing the labour and effort that he
devoted to most of these compositions. And all that he tells
us of the land of Attica, so rich in mythic and religious

tradition, is that Acharnai produced a fine breed of men. This was not mere flattery; Aristophanes' play *The Acharnians* suggests the same, and still more Thucydides' statement that the Acharnians contributed three thousand hoplites to the Athenian army. But this detail hardly satisfies our poetic expectations of Pindar. An Athenian's victory would have been a relevant occasion for him to tell us the great legend of Eleusis or any of the great cluster of myths that hung round the rock of the Akropolis. He chose not to do so, and we are the losers, and it is not easy to say why. Pindar may have cut down his poem to suit the narrow means of Timodemos, but if Timodemos was poor, certainly the Alkmaionid Megakles was not, yet the seventh Pythian in honour of the latter is even shorter and slighter than this. We cannot explain it as due to a certain dislike of Athens, which may have arisen in his mind much later after she had destroyed Aigina. For we have many references in his earlier works to the great city, warm and generous in their appreciation, and among his greatest poems was the magnificent dithyramb which he composed on Athens, of which the beauty still survives in fragments.[1] We must remember that we are dealing with a wayward poet, who did not always care to put himself fully forth; he may have also been held back by the discovery that any praise of Athens excited enmity at Thebes.

The paucity of odes on Athenian victors suggests that Athenians were rarely successful in the great contests, although the Athenian trainers were regarded as the best of their profession. Certainly, the family of the Timo-demidai to whom the hero of this ode belongs could vie with any in Greece in the number of their victories; but these may have been gained before Pindar's poetic position was established.

---

[1] *Vide infra*, p. 321.

NEMEAN III

To Aristokleidas of Aigina

"Oh, Muse, Goddess revered, oh, Mother of our craft,
I pray thee, come in the holy tide of the Nemean festival,
To the Dorian isle Aigina, open to all guests.
For young men are waiting by the banks of Asopos,
5   framers of sweet-worded triumph-songs, yearning for
    thy voice.
As our business changeth, so doth our craving.
The athlete's victory loveth nought so much as song,
The most auspicious minister that waiteth on garlands
    and deeds of worth;
Whereof (oh, Goddess) dispense an abundant spring, well-
    ing from my thought.
10 Begin, oh, daughter of God, a seemly hymn, consecrate to
    the Lord of cloudy heaven.
I will share it with the song-speech of those young men
    and with the lyre.
And it shall have a pleasant burden, the glory of the land,
    where the Myrmidons of old days dwelt:
Whose gathering-place, famous of yore, Aristokleidas
15   hath not shamed, thanks to thy dispensation,
Through any weakness in the stubborn host of pankratiast-
    combatants.[1]
But the voice of triumph, at least in the deep plain of
    Nemea,
Bringeth a healthful salve for crushing blows.
If, then, being fair of form and doing deeds consonant
    therewith,

---

[1] Or "in the stubborn journey of the pankration".

166

The son of Aristophanes hath set himself to ventures of 20
    high prowess,
(Let him remember) it is not easy to pass beyond the pillars
    of Herakles into the untrodden sea beyond:
Those pillars fixed by the hero-God, as glorious witnesses
    of his farthest voyaging.
And he quellèd the overmastering monsters in the seas,
And by himself searchèd out the tides of the shallows,
Where he landed at the goal that sent him back homeward;
And he planned out the region there.   25
But, oh my soul, why dost thou suffer my bark to swerve
    away along alien coasts?
I bid thee waft the Muse to the service of Aiakos and his
    race.
The fulness of justice cleaveth to the story that is the praise
    of noble men.
Nor is the love for alien things a better freight for a man 30
    to carry.
Search nearer home: (in the Aiakidai) thou hast won a
    theme of honour meet for sweet utterance.
Among the tales of the brave deeds of old (is the tale of)
    King Peleus, how he rejoicèd when he cut (from the
    wood) his all-surpassing spear,
And how he capturèd Iolkos single-handed without a host
    of men,
And caught the Sea-Goddess Thetis in swift pursuit.   35
Also Telamon of the mighty girth, war-comrade of Iolas,
    sackèd the city of Laomedon,[1]
And followed Iolas at another time to meet the brazen-
    bowed array of the Amazons,
Nor ever did Fear that quelleth men dull in him the keen
    edge of his soul.
A man renowned by nature's gift weigheth down the scale: 40
But he who only hath what he hath learned from others,
    fareth in the shadow unstable of purpose, and never
    entereth the fight unswervingly;

---

[1] He refers to the first expedition against Troy, when the city was taken
by Herakles and Telamon.

But dabbleth in countless brave adventures with ineffective
    will.

The golden-haired Achilles in his childhood, abiding under
    the roof of Philura, made great deeds his play;

45 And oft-times brandishing a short-tipped dart, in wind-
    swift onset he was able to bring death to the lions of
    the wild,

And to slay wild boars, and bring in their bodies panting
    to the Centaur, son of Kronos, he at first a child of
    six years only;

And afterwards, all through the span of his time spent
    there;

50 Artemis and bold Athena gazed at him with wonder,

Slaying deer without hounds or the meshes of snares:

For by running he overcame them.

I have this story handed down from the lips of men of
    old—

Cheiron of the deep counsel rearèd Jason within his house
    of stone,

55 And after him Asklepios, to whom he taught the whole
    law of healing and the art of the light hand.

Withal, he held the marriage-feast for Thetis, Nereus'
    radiant-bosomed daughter,

And he reared her offspring for her, the noblest child,

Nourishing his soul on all fitting food;

So that later, when wafted by the gusts of the sea-breezes
    up to the walls of Troy,

60 He might abide the spear-clashing war-shout of the Lycians,
    Phrygians, and Dardanoi;

And mingling in the grip of battle with the Aethiopian
    spearmen,

He might set this resolve deeply in his soul,

That their leader Memnon, the wild cousin of Helenos,
    should never fare back home.

The beacon-glory of the Aiakidai is fixed for ever, sending
    a far-gleam from Troy.

65 Oh, Zeus, their blood is thine, and thine is the contest,

Whereat our hymn levelled a shaft when with the young

men's voices it pealèd forth in honour of our native triumph.

The loud acclaim chimeth well with the victory-bearing Aristokleidas,

Who linkèd this island with a tale of renown, and the holy hall of the ministers of the Pythian God with bright 70 hopes of honour.

The trial of danger proveth the perfecting of that wherein a man hath been fashionèd surpassing others,

Whether as a boy among the young or as a man among men,

Or—in the third stage—among elders;

According to the apportioned time of life we mortals have.

Yea, and four virtues are yokèd to the car of our mortal life; and it biddeth us think the thought proper to each 75 present age.

And from all these Aristokleidas liveth not afar.

Hail, my friend! verily I send thee this draught of honey commingled with pure milk, crested with curdling foam,

A draught of song in the Aeolian breathings of the flutes—

Albeit late in the sending. But lo! the eagle is swift among 80 wingèd things:

And he seizeth suddenly the torn prey in his talons, swooping down from afar:

The croaking daws have pasture on lower grounds.

At least for thee, fair-thronèd Kleio so willing it, and because of thy high victorious spirit,

From Nemea, Epidauros, and Megara the light of fame hath gleamed."

This is one of the large and fascinating group of poems dedicated to Aeginetan victors. We gather from the ode that it was composed in honour of a certain Aristokleidas, son of Aristophanes, who had conquered in the pankration —the most trying of all contests—in the Nemean festival: he had won victories elsewhere—at Epidauros and Megara

—and was evidently of noble family. This is all that we
know of the circumstances, and ancient learning contributes
nothing to our knowledge of them; and evidently the date
of the victory was unknown to the commentators of Alexandria. All that we can be sure of is that the victory was
won and the ode composed before the downfall of Aigina,
before 458 B.C.; for the ode reflects a bright and peaceful
local atmosphere, and there is no hint of trouble in the
prosperous island-state. How long before that date this
poem was written we have no means of determining, except
that the language, the thought, and the technique belong
to Pindar's perfected period. So far modern critics are
agreed; but some have been misled by certain passages into
believing that the poem was composed very long after the
victory was won, and that the victor was at this time a man
of advanced years commemorating the anniversary of a far-
distant triumph. This belief has arisen from an unnatural
view of two passages in the closing part, one containing a
word of apology for lateness, the other mentioning the four
virtues and the three periods of human life, childhood,
manhood, and age. As regards the first, Pindar closes a
glowing commendation of his own poem with the simple
words "albeit late": this is the least that a gentleman would
say who had kept someone waiting two or three days for
his letter or manuscript: and he informs us at the beginning
of the ode that certain young men were waiting impatiently
on the banks of the Asopos, yearning for his ode: they surely
did not wait there several years. The other passage, which
has been misunderstood as indicating that Aristokleidas is
now an elderly man and therefore many years removed
from his victory—for no one past his prime could win the
pankration,—needs more consideration; for in any case it
is one of the impressive examples of Pindar's power in
ethical poetry. The passage begins, and for the most part
carries on, with general aphorisms, applicable to every one:
our respective excellencies, whether of boy or man or elder,
are only proved by experience and the test of action, according to the period of life we happen to be in. And our mortal
life is conducted with the help of four virtues (the aphorism
is brilliantly expressed by a term borrowed from the metaphor of the car of life). Now the poet certainly does not
mean that these four virtues are severally attached to four
separate periods of life; for he has not allowed four separate

periods, but only three. These general reflections close with
a poetic aphorism of value as a life-maxim: "Life bids us
be minded in accord with our present (period of life)", that
is to be youthful-minded in youth, to be mature-minded in
maturer years. The four cardinal virtues are obviously those
familiar to the popular morality of early Greece, Courage,
Temperance, Justice, and Wisdom: and none of these is
the single virtue of a single age. He then returns to Aristokleidas and declares that he has a share in all of them.
From this it has been concluded that as Aristokleidas has
wisdom he must now be in advanced years, and therefore
his victory must have been won long ago; a necessary conclusion only if Pindar had ever said that wisdom was the
exclusive prerogative of advanced life; but fortunately he
nowhere says anything so foolish.

We may be sure that the interval between the victory and
the ode was very brief: there is the tone of excitement and
thrill, as evoked by a recent triumph. Aristokleidas has still
the beauty of youth upon him and may still, as it seems to
be suggested, be suffering from the bruises of the contest.
Therefore he may be compared with Herakles—a moral
warning being obscurely attached—but still better with the
heroes of the line of Aiakos; and Pindar joyfully seizes the
relevant opportunity for the lyric-epic narrative in which he
delights.

The Aeginetan saga was pre-eminent in Greece for the
rich material that it offered to this type of poetry. And the
Aiakidai "rejoicing in battle as in a banquet" were for the
Hellenic hero-world what the Volsungs were for the Teu-
tonic. In the many odes on Aeginetan victors, except the
eighth Pythian, Pindar narrates, embellishes or moralises
on some portion of their complex story; and there is no
episode in it known to us that he has omitted. He has taken
over by far the greater part of it from the older epic poetry,
Homeric and post-Homeric; some portion he may have
derived from the island folklore, with which his frequent
visits must have made him familiar; some little he may have
ventured to invent himself. But he never touches on that
which is the central theme of the *Iliad*, the wrath of Achilles:
doubtless it did not belong to Aeginetan saga, and was not
such as it would try to claim.

In this ode, after briefly and with some striking phrase
narrating the exploits of Peleus and Telamon, he con-

centrates on Achilles; but he is too practised an artist in lyric to give us his full biography *seriatim* or in historical sequence. He gives us a brilliant picture of the wonderful childhood of Achilles brought up in Cheiron's cave, the home of Philura his daughter, where the good Centaur trained him in all the exercises suitable to the heroic part he was to play in the Trojan war: his maturer exploits are thus glanced at prospectively. He interrupts the narrative for a moment to tell us that Cheiron also trained Jason and Asklepios, the father of medicine: this is not irrelevant, for it deepens the impression of Cheiron's skill as a trainer of heroes. Pindar is perhaps too hurried to consider how this is consistent with the aphoristic phrases that precede the mythic description, putting the view that heredity and natural gifts outweigh everything else and that mere learning counts for very little, a theory expressed with more haughty self-confidence in the second Olympian ode. But it is characteristic of him that he should not trouble about possible or latent inconsistencies.

On the whole, a genial unity knits the various parts together without constraint, and the mythical-ideal elements combine naturally with the real and the personal. The moralising is relevant and always raised to the poetic pitch. One saw is certainly impressive and original: "Life bids us be like-minded with the present time" is worthy of Shakespeare, who gives us what almost sound as echoes of it— "The spirit of the time shall teach me speed" and "Be a child of the time. Possess it, I'll make answer."

Another masterly phrase, that shines out in a poem that is not altogether one of his masterpieces, are the lines describing his song as a draught of milk and honey, in a rich luscious style that he does not often allow himself.

There is no obscurity that matters, and nowhere any call for far-fetched explanations. We may be content to leave it unexplained why he should call Memnon "the cousin of Helenos": we know that he was, but it does not seem important. Some doubt has been felt as to the meaning of the figure of the eagle towards the close. Looking carefully at the context, and at other contexts in the odes where the holy bird appears, we may be sure that primarily the eagle typifies Pindar, who may be late, but when he once starts, has the high-soaring eagle's swiftness, and like the eagle swoops unerringly on what he desires. In contrasting him

with the inferior birds who feed at lower levels, he need not
be intending a malicious hit at his rival poets, as the ancient
commentators supposed. He softens the egoistic effect by
the closing phrase of the ode which assures Aristokleidas
that he at least is not one of the birds that fly low, as the
light of glory has beamed on him from three athletic
festivals, where he was victorious.

NEMEAN IV

To Timasarchos of Aigina

"The best physician for (the pains of) toils well ended is
    festal cheer:
Songs withal, the skilled daughters of the Muses, soothe
    them as with the light touch (of the healer).
Nor doth warm water so soften and relax the limbs of the
5   weary, as words of praise wedded to the lyre.
And speech hath a longer life than deeds,
Such speech as with the blessing of the Graces the tongue
    may cull from the deep places of the soul.
Even such speech may it be mine to set forth, as a prelude
    to the hymn and dance,
In honour of Zeus, the son of Kronos, of Nemea, and of
10   Timasarchos' prowess in the wrestling;
And may it be welcome to the fair-towered city-home of
    the sons of Aiakos,
That sheddeth on all men the light of Justice defending the
    stranger's right!
But if Timokritos, thy father, were still warmed by the
    sun's strong rays,
15 Bowed by the spell of my verse he would oft-times awaken
    the changeful music of his lyre, acclaiming his
    triumphant son,
For that he sent back home a festoon of garlands from
    Kleonai's place of contests and from the radiant
    Athens of happy auspices;
20 Because, also, in seven-gated Thebes by Amphitruon's
    fair tomb
The Kadmeians ungrudgingly smothered him with flowers,

For the love they bear Aigina.
For his eyes beheld a hospitable city, when he had come
as friend to friend
To the rich court of Herakles—
In whose companionship the mighty Telamon in days of 25
old
Quellèd Troy and the Meropes,
And the great giant-warrior Alkuoneus;
But not before he with hurlèd rock had brought to earth
twelve chariots and twice as many horse-taming heroes
mounted therein.
Unskillèd of warfare would he be proven who under- 30
standeth not my tale:
For 'tis very like that he who doeth ought should suffer
also.
But from telling the long story (of the Aiakidai) the law
(of poesy) restraineth me, and the urgency of the
flying hours.
Yea and my heart is drawn on potently, as by a love- 35
charm, to keep touch with the festival of the new-
moon.
Nathless (oh, Pindar!) albeit the deep sea hemmeth thee
around,
Hold front against thy rivals' plottings:
Verily we shall seem to challenge the contest in the light
of day,
Triumphant o'er our foemen.
But there is another man, with envy looking from his eyes,
lurking in the dark, who tosseth barren maxims 40
about that fall idly to the ground.
As for me, I am well assurèd that whatever excellence
Destiny, the Lord of life, hath given me,
Time in its onward march will bring to its fore-ordainèd
harvest.
Yea, even at this very moment, oh, sweet lyre!
Interweave with Lydian harmony this song dear to the 45
heart of Oinone[1] and of Cyprus,

[1] The old name for Aigina.

Where Teukros, the son of Telamon, beareth rule far-
    removed:
But Aias holdeth his ancestral land of Salamis,
Achilles the gleaming island in the Euxine sea;
50 Thetis holdeth sway in Phthia,
And Neoptolemos in far-flung Epeiros,
Where the out-jutting spurs of the mountains, the pastures
    of the kine,
Rising from Dodona fall down to the Ionian sea.
But by the foot of Pelion, Peleus turned with foeman's
55   hand against Iolkos,
And gave it over in bondage to the men of Haimonia.
For Akastos, son of Pelias, availing himself of the guileful
    craft of his wife Hippoluta, and of the cunningly
    carved weapon (of Hephaistos),
Sowed for him the seeds of death from ambush;
60 But Cheiron fended off the peril,
And carried through to an end the fateful design of God.
But Peleus wedded one of the high-throned daughters of
    Nereus,
Having baffled the all-mastering flame, the sharpest claws
65   of wild-willed lions, and the edges of their dread teeth.
And he saw the fair-circled congress wherein the Kings of
    heaven and ocean seated (at the bridal)
Revealèd their gifts and the promise of victory as the birth-
    right of his stock.
But 'tis not possible to pass beyond Cadiz towards the
    darkness of the West.
70 Set thy sails back again (oh, Pindar!) to the mainland of
    Europe:
For 'tis a hopeless task to tell at length the whole tale of
    the sons of Aiakos.
Having pledged my word to the house of the Theandridai,
I went a ready herald of the limb-quickening contests at
75   Olympia, Isthmos, and Nemea,
Where biding the trial, not without the glorious harvest of
    the victors' crowns,
They come back to their home,

Wherein we hear, Timasarchos, that thy clan is a ready
    minister to furnish forth the choral odes of victory.
But if indeed thou further biddest me raise in honour of 80
    thy mother's brother
A monument of verse brighter than Parian marble,
Know then that as gold refinèd in the fire showeth all its
    (hidden) rays,
So the song in praise of the goodly deeds of prowess
Fashioneth a man the peer of kings in fortune.
As for him, dwelling on the banks of Acheron,   85
Let him mark my ringing voice proclaiming where in the
    contest of the loud-thundering Shaker of the trident[1]
His glory bloomed with the Corinthian parsley-crowns:
Whose praise Euphanes, thy aged kinsman of the past,
    will be fain to chant, oh, boy!   90
Each man hath his own generation for his comrades,
And every man aspireth to speak best of that which he him-
    self may have confronted with his own eyes.
Were he now praising Melesias, how he would turn and
    twist in the strife of speech,
With grappling phrase, hard to trip or stagger in the word-
    play,
A man gently minded towards the good,   95
But a stern foeman for malignants to reckon with at the
    end!"

The fourth Nemean is a fascinating product of Pindar's
maturest art, showing his mastery in phrase, in the technique
of rhythm and melody, and in the happy blending of the
elements drawn from mythology and from contemporary
life: there is not much moralising, but in the sententious
passages he kindles our imagination no less than in the
epic and descriptive parts. But the perfection of the poem
is certainly impaired by the obscurity and comparative
flatness of the close.

The ode was composed before, but probably not long
before, 460 B.C., in honour of the Aeginetan boy Timas-

---

[1] Poseidon, the patron of the Isthmian games.

archos, who had conquered in the boys' wrestling match
at Nemea and who belonged to the distinguished family of
the Theandridai, distinguished not only by athletic achievement but by the poetic and musical skill of some of its
members and by the liberal provision it afforded to the
choral performances of the state. It was intended to be sung
in procession through the streets at some festival of the
new moon, for which Pindar is thrilled with anxiety to
be ready.

His unflagging originality reveals itself nowhere more
impressively than in his prologues. And this one has its
peculiar charm: it is merely an imaginative development of
the simple thought that music and good cheer are the best
"poultice for aching bones"—we may suppose the boy has
not yet recovered from his bruises—and of the simple fact
that a warm bath restores tired limbs. As Swift was said to
be able "to write poetically about a broom-stick", so Pindar
can raise a warm bath into poetry. The phraseology also
avails itself of the association in the popular religion and
speech between song or music and the art of healing; and
these verses of Pindar's have something of the mesmerising
effect of Tennyson's

> "Music that gentlier on the spirit lies
> Than tired eyelids upon tired eyes."

After consecrating the prelude with proper piety to Zeus,
the God of Nemea, he bestows a few words of deserved
praise on Aigina, here, as elsewhere, specially commending
her for her kindness and justice to strangers; then easily
and gracefully he introduces the boy athlete and his victories at Nemea, Athens, and Thebes. And the long-standing
friendship between Thebes and Aigina gives him a natural
opportunity for straying into the field of mythology.

For that friendship was mythically foreshadowed by the
comradeship of Herakles with Telamon, who for Pindar
is unquestionably a son of Aiakos. After describing certain
of their common exploits, he reminds himself that the
urgency of the present time debars him from pursuing
further that mythic theme. But it does not debar him from
digressing into a personal statement. He calls upon himself
to hold his own against some calumniator who was plotting
against him. His words, though some of them have been
misunderstood, reveal his drift sufficiently. Some enemy,

possibly some local rival poet, envious and working in the dark, has been trying to discredit Pindar with the Aeginetans, spreading around "barren maxims" concerning art, so as to disparage Pindar's proficiency and deprive him of his employment. In self-defence, Pindar merely rides over his enemies' heads in his crushing and lordly style. What is really astonishing is that he should be able to raise an expression of arrogant egoism to the level of high poetry, as he does here by his master-sentence—

"I am well assurèd that whatever excellence Destiny, the
    Lord of Life, hath given me
Time in its onward march will bring to its fore-ordained
    fruit":

a phrase of which, I fear, no English rendering can convey the music, the pride, and the quiet majesty.

We must indeed excuse Pindar's egoism, even when it seems most intrusive and irrelevant, if it can deposit for us golden ore like this.

He then calls to his lyre, in another striking phrase, to approve his poetic claim; and he gives a lyrical roll of the famous names of the Aeacid stock, merely mentioning the places where they had lived and held rule. He is here dealing with genuine local saga: he dwells lovingly, and with warm feeling for the landscape, on Neoptolemos' association with Epeiros, and the long survival of it in the popular tradition is proved by the adoption of the names Pyrrhos and Neoptolemos by the later Epeirote kings:[1] he knows that Salamis was the home and realm of Aias, a tradition carefully maintained by the Athenians after they had conquered it: he touches on the legend, embodied in the post-Homeric epic, that after his death Achilles was translated to the "White Island" off the mouth of the Danube; and long after Pindar Achilles survived there in the popular belief, a very dangerous ghost; but in his earlier poem, the second Olympian, he had given the hero a happier posthumous settlement in Elysium. But now Pindar is more interested in Peleus, and he gives a rapid narrative of some leading events in his career. We cannot say that he is altogether happy in his arrangement and choice of incident. We can discern no credible reason why he should have mentioned

---

[1] *Vide* my *Hero-Cults*, p. 313.

at all the capture of Iolkos by Peleus,[1] and the style of the narrative is here unusually flat. Nor does he show its connection with the next legend which is of greater interest, the story of the wife of Akastos and the magic knife given to Peleus by Hephaistos. The first part of this is told at greater length and more impressively in the fifth Nemean. Pindar sets it down here in a kind of lyrical shorthand, assuming that it was well known to his hearers, for it had been told in detail by Hesiod, from whom he also borrows the motive of the magic knife; his allusion to it here is too obscure to be intelligible to those who were not previously acquainted with it. From various sources we can thus piece together the details that Pindar condenses or slurs over here: the Gods present Peleus with a magic knife or sword, forged by Hephaistos: a well-known motive of heroic saga that appears also in the *Volsunga* saga and Arthurian legend: when the faithless wife of Akastos, his friend and host, tempts him in vain and falsely accuses him to her husband, Akastos will not or dare not murder him himself; he lures Peleus to hunt with him, waits till Peleus is asleep, then steals the magic weapon and hides it, knowing that Peleus when he misses it will go searching far and wide for it through the wilds till he is slain by wild beasts; and slain he would have been, only that the good Cheiron restored the weapon to him in the nick of time. Finally in revenge Peleus captures Iolkos, the city of Akastos, as Pindar says in the preceding ode "without an army".

We cannot praise Pindar here for lucidity in the arrangement of the facts or in their presentation. But the style and the tone rise in pitch towards the close where he connects this adventure of Peleus with the fateful dispensation of divine Providence; namely, Peleus must be saved in order to carry out the will of Zeus concerning Thetis: then follow fragments of the Thetis story, mainly of the folklore version, combined with a hint of the higher theologic or epic account which is developed in the eighth Isthmian. In the folktale, Peleus seizes Thetis, as any hero would seize a dangerous fairy-bride, and holds her fast through all her fairy-transformations into fire, lion, and serpent. Pindar is the first literary handler of the story, so far as we

---

[1] It would only harmonise with the context if Peleus was believed to have lived at Iolkos or was worshipped there in later times. We have no legend that he did or evidence that he was; in fact we can assert that he was not.

know; but it appears also as an art-theme on early vases and
doubtless is good folklore of old Thessaly: for such a story
no God and no Providence was needed. But to understand
why, after dealing summarily with this fairy-tale, Pindar
passes on to describe the gathering of all the Olympians at
the wedding of Peleus and Thetis, why they should be so
interested in that wedding that they bring lavish gifts and
promise glory and power to the race of Peleus, we must
read another version in the eighth Isthmian which belongs
to the higher theology.

The question of the relevance of all this mythic digression
presents no difficulty to those familiar with Pindar's manner
and Greek contemporary feeling. And we should not waste
time by trying to discover any parallelism between the
individual Aiakidai and members of the athlete's house.
Pindar's myths have rarely any special connection with the
athlete, but concern usually his community. On any public
occasion in old Aigina it was relevant to speak about the
Aiakidai; just as the sculptors who carved the Aeginetan
marbles found it relevant to represent the deeds of the
Aiakidai in the gables of the temple of the Goddess
Aphaia.

The most vexing problem of the ode arises in connection
with the last two strophai.

Having turned back from mythology by a skilful and
graceful transition, he eulogises the family of the Theandridai in strong and tingling verse. Then he gives us to
understand that the young athlete had begged him to compose an epinician ode in honour of his deceased uncle
Kallikles, who had won an Isthmian victory in his life-time.
Pindar's answer is somewhat confusing and perhaps in-
tentionally evasive; and at one point his meaning is obscured
by an undoubted corruption in the MS. The following
paraphrase may express what his lyrical sentences are
intended to convey. "You ask me to compose a hymn in
honour of your deceased uncle. Song certainly adds lustre
to deeds, as the refiner's fire to gold; and I hope my song
might penetrate even the lower world where he now resides.
But probably your grandfather, Euphanes, who was himself a poet and who saw his victory—as I did not—will
compose a poem for him in the world below; for everyone
best describes what he has seen himself." This might be
a polite way of intimating that as Pindar had not seen his

uncle's victory, he would rather not compose an ode in its honour.

The last phrase of the ode is the most puzzling; and many solutions of the riddle have been attempted. But looked at in the light of the context the passage lends itself to this interpretation: Pindar desires to praise the Athenian trainer Melesias, as we find him praised in two other odes; but he feels, as he showed that he felt on the occasion of the eighth Olympian, that such praise was invidious in Aigina, where Athens was naturally unpopular: therefore he adopts the rhetorical device of putting the praise into some other person's mouth, and that other person is the grandfather Euphanes, who has only recently died and who is still vividly remembered as a man of striking personality and very forcible style: so that the closing words of the ode amount to this: "if only Euphanes were alive and would undertake the eulogy of Melesias, what a striking and characteristic speech we should hear from him, who was always a genial friend and a formidable foe".

At any rate this ode and the sixth Nemean end with the praises of Melesias; and in each case we feel, though the style is forcible, something of the flatness of an anticlimax.

The fourth Nemean has some elements of greatness that claim for it a place in the higher realm of poetic literature; but as it ends abruptly with the praises of a trainer, queerly and obliquely conveyed, we cannot regard it as a perfect work of art. It suggests here, as Pindar's epinicians occasionally suggest, something of the careless and irresponsible style of a friendly letter. What disturbs us is that such temporary passages should be tacked on to others that are meant for eternity.

NEMEAN V

To Putheas of Aigina

"I AM no sculptor, one that should carve statues to abide
    idle for ever on the self-same base:
Nay, sweet song, fare forth from Aigina on every hull and
    every pinnace,
Casting the tale abroad that Putheas, Lampon's son, a
    youth of mighty girth,
At Nemea won the garland of the pankration,   5
Not yet showing on his cheeks the darkening bloom, child
    of life's summer;
And he hath shed lustre on the Aiakidai,
The warrior-heroes sprung from Kronos, Zeus, and the
    golden daughters of the sea;
Also on his mother-city, the land that befriendeth strangers.
On behalf of this land in olden days, that it might be blessèd
    in breed of men and for fame of ships,
They, the far-famed sons of Endais, together with Phokos, 10
    the mighty prince,
Whom his Goddess-mother, Psamatheia, bore by the break
    of the wave,
Offered prayers standing by the altar of their father, Zeus,
    the God of all the Hellenes,
And spread their hands to the sky in common supplication.
I feel shame to speak of a great deed, rashly venturèd, not
    in the way of righteousness,
In what fashion they left at last the renownèd isle,   15
And what power divine banishèd the valiant men from
    Oinone.
I will halt. It is not always increase of gain for Truth to
    lift the veil from her face:

And oft-times silence is a man's wisest device.
Now if the theme decreed be prosperity or might of hand
    or [prowess in] mailèd war,
20 With this House as my starting-point, let them level out a
    long leap indeed for me.
Verily, I have a lightning-spring in my knees:
And the onrush of eagles fareth beyond the Ocean.
Yea, to those heroes also on Mount Pelion
The fairest choir of Muses sang once in gladness,
And in their midst Apollo, with golden quill chasing the
25   notes of the seven-tonguèd lyre,
Led forth all manner of holy strains;
And they, preluding their song with the name of God,
Sang first of reverèd Thetis and of Peleus,
Telling how Hippoluta, Kretheus' dainty daughter, was
    fain to enmesh him in treachery,
Having with counsels of subtlety persuaded her spouse,
The watcher o'er the Magnesian commonweal;
And she patched together a forgèd tale of falsehood;
How that, forsooth, he was making attempt on her marriage-
30   bed in the chamber of Akastos;
But the contrary was true:
For with many a prayer she wooèd him, tempting him in
    her speech with all her soul.
But her rash wanton words stung his heart to anger:
And straightway he repellèd the wedded woman,
Fearing the wrath of the Father, who guards the right of
    guest and host.
35 But Zeus, King of the Immortals, the Gatherer of the
   clouds, marked it and decreed to bring to pass
How that Peleus might swiftly win as his bride one of the
    sea-princesses that ply the golden distaff:
When he had persuaded thereto Poseidon, their sister's
    spouse,
Who oft-times fareth from Aigai to the Dorian Isthmus,
Where with the shrill voice of flutes glad companies of
    worshippers welcome the God,
And vie in the bold contests of mighty limbs.

'Tis hereditary fortune that adjudgeth the issue of all 40
    athletic strife.
And thou, Euthumenes, in Aigina, falling into the arms of
    the Goddess Victory,
Wast crowned with many-voicèd hymns.
Verily also at this present hour he, thy uncle, Putheas,
    speeding on the path (of former triumphs) is shedding
    lustre on the kindred stock of Peleus.
Surely his fame is riveted to Nemea,
And to his island's festal month that is dear to Apollo.
And over his compeers, who came against him both at 45
    home
And in the fair glen of Nisos' hill, he was victorious.
I rejoice that every city joineth in the strife for honour.
Know well that 'tis through the fair fortune of Menandros'
    teaching
That thou hast won a sweet requital from thy hard toils.
Truly the athlete must seek from Athens the craftsman to
    fashion him;
But if thou comest as far as [the house of] Themistios, so 50
    as to sing his praise,
Throw off all coldness, raise thy voice and hoist thy
    topsails,
And proclaim that he won at Epidauros a double meed of
    valour,
Both as boxer and in the pankration.
And bring the grass-inwoven flower-garlands to the fore-
    courts of the shrine of Aiakos
Under the guidance of the fair-haired Graces."

    This ode is one of a series of three; for this Nemean and
the fourth and fifth Isthmian odes celebrate victories won
by members of the same distinguished family of Aigina
called the Psuchalidai, the two young brothers, Putheas
and Phulakidas, the uncle Euthumenes, the grandfather
Themistios. Reading the three together—as is necessary for
full literary appreciation—we discern that the fifth Nemean

is the earliest, and that the fifth Isthmian was composed
before the fourth; and as this last contains a reference to the
battle of Salamis as a recent event, we may give the fifth
Nemean a date not long before 480 B.C.

It is, therefore, a work of Pindar's mature prime, as its
style and composition would attest. The prelude is as usual
striking and impressive. He contrasts his art to its own
advantage with that of the sculptor. The ancient commentators, to explain this original starting-phrase, invented
a biographical fiction about Pindar, not to his credit: he
had demanded as much for his ode as would pay the cost
of two statues! We need not search behind the scenes here
to explain the working of Pindar's imagination. Elsewhere
he had compared his poems with works of architecture.
The reflection may have crossed his mind that statues were
often carved of the victorious athlete; he feels he can do
better than this, because song is mobile and the sculptured
form is immobile, a thought which Lessing will develop
later in the *Laocoon*, but to which Pindar here gives a simple
and literal sense: the statue cannot leave its base; there it
stands "taking holiday", that is, doing nothing: his song
will fly round the world, on every ship that leaves Aigina,
proclaiming the tale of triumph. There is point in the contrast, though Pheidias would have had something to say
on the other side. But what exactly does Pindar mean in the
phrase about his song's flight, which is more than a mere
façon de parler?

We can hardly suppose that Pindar contemplated manuscript reproduction of his ode immediately after its delivery,
and that Aeginetan ships would bear the copies broadcast
through the literary world. Or did he mean that his ode
was so sweet and memorable that every sailor would have
it on his lips henceforth? We can as easily imagine a sailor
whistling a Beethoven's sonata. Pindar had the buoyancy
of supreme self-confidence; but all that perhaps need be
said here is that he dared a happy phrase without intending
to be taken to task about it.

At any rate, his vision has been fulfilled: the song has
travelled down to us through the centuries, proclaiming
the son of Lampon, the boy who has not yet the down on his
cheek; and this is almost all that he says of the young
victor. We note that Pindar often thinks it unnecessary to
dwell long on the individual whose victory evoked the ode;

but he generally dwells longer than he does here. He digresses immediately into the mythic background, and when he returns to real life he has more to say about the victor's uncle Euthumenes, and ends with eulogy of the Athenian trainer Menandros, and of another elder member of the family, Themistios. The same may be observed in the fourteenth Olympian, of which the Graces take the greater part, while the boy-athlete has to be content with a short glowing notice at the close. Pindar may have been influenced by the moral etiquette of the old Greek family that objected to the undue prominence of its youngest members; but he was not always so reserved. In any case, being in Aigina, he would soon have left the athlete for the Aiakidai; for he tells us later in the sixth Isthmian that he makes it a law "to besprinkle the Aiakidai with praises, whenever he sets foot in the island". His first phrase about them here is of religious rather than mythic import, and is rendered in solemn and noble style and stately metre. The three sons of Aiakos—Telamon, Peleus, and Phokos—stand by the altar of Zeus Hellanios and pray for the prosperity of the island. This cult-name is of deep significance and is the central religious fact of Aigina, being originally the name of the tribal God of the small Thessalian stock called Hellenes, closely akin to the Myrmidons, Achilles' people: these plant the cult in Aigina, and gradually the term expands so to include the whole community of kindred tribes and stocks whom we call Hellenes; and Zeus Hellanios becomes Panhellenios, the God who held the Hellenes together—if any God could so far overcome their politics. Aiakos becomes his High Priest, and the cult reflects a pre-historic connection between Thessaly and Aigina.

Then Pindar behaves strangely. The name Phokos suggests to him the story why Peleus and Telamon had to leave Aigina and could never make the island their permanent home; the story, namely, that Peleus and Telamon murdered their half-brother Phokos through jealousy of his athletic prowess, and that the righteous Aiakos banished them for ever in consequence. It belonged to the genuine tradition of the island, and had been recounted at full in an earlier epic, perhaps two centuries before Pindar composed this ode. But it is an ugly tale, and Pindar, after alluding to it and in a veiled way reprobating the deed, shrinks from recounting it. He shrinks, not through fear of hurting the feelings of the Aeginetans, who themselves must have told it and believed in it, but because it was a slur on the fair fame of the two great Aiakidai and would be strangely out of place on a genial and festive occasion. When Pindar dislikes unpleasant stories about the deities, he merely rejects them and proceeds happily: but he cannot deny this tale, for everyone knew and believed in it. (We have here, by the way, one more example showing how seriously Pindar and the Aeginetans took their mythology.) Here, then, he only evades it and says that silence is often best. We agree with him, especially on this occasion. But what we do not understand is why a poet with any control over his invention should bring us up to the very brink of the story and then recoil from it. For he was not called upon to tell the whole legend of the heroic family, and there was nothing in the situation or the circumstances that compelled him to mention the unfortunate Phokos. But we are dealing with the most wayward and capricious of poets, and we cannot hope to account for all the flittings of his fancy. And his *faux pas*—if he regarded it as one—gave him the occasion for two good poetical aphorisms about Truth and Silence. And frequently he may have been too hurried to prune his ode.

He redeems himself by some great phrases, suggesting the flight of the "Theban eagle", before he returns to the Aiakidai. At once he falls upon the myth, which is perhaps the brightest in Greek mythology, of the marriage of Peleus and Thetis; which was handled also with fervour and with interesting differences in motive and effect by Aeschylus in a lost play and by Euripides in his *Iphigeneia in Aulis*. And it so clings to Pindar's imagination that he gives it another expression in the eighth Isthmian in a more grandiose religious setting. But the opening words of the scene presented in this fifth Nemean show Pindar at his best and the perfection of Hellenic style; the rhythm and the diction combine to suggest the golden light in which the Song-God stands. Then follows the song of the Muses, of which the theme is the noble continence of Peleus in rejecting the adulterous advances of the wife of Akastos. (In this part of the ode we have a salient example of Pindar's heedlessness that accompanies some of his happiest work: he takes no trouble to indicate where the song of the Muses ends and his own narrative starts again.)

This moral myth does not so much exemplify the sanctity of our seventh commandment for the earlier Greeks as their conscience concerning the law of hospitality; both Peleus and, in the similar Argive story, Bellerophon are guests of the men against whom they refuse when tempted to commit this wrong: both observe the law of Zeus "the God of hospitality". Something of the same idea is half-expressed in the parallel story in Genesis concerning Joseph. But of all the three this one, as here presented and again in the eighth Pythian, is most infused with religious colouring; for the allocation of Thetis as a bride to the mortal Peleus is explained as a divine reward, bestowed by Zeus upon Peleus for his virtue's sake. This is reconcilable with the version of the story given in the eighth Isthmian which attaches to it the higher motive, congenial to epic 'theology', of the oracle uttered by Themis, namely, that Thetis' son would be greater than his father; hence Zeus and Poseidon were deterred from their thoughts of marriage with her, and Zeus deemed it safer to bestow her upon the "most pious" of mortals: Peleus had proved himself to be that by his recent conduct in regard to the wife of Akastos (the murder of Phokos was ignored apparently, for mythology cannot think of too many things at once). Hence all the deities graced with their presence and their gifts this unique marriage, which was glorified by early Greek art and continuously by Greek literature. And Pindar here shows his independence of the old Boeotian poet, Hesiod, whose authority he usually follows in such matters; who preferred an inferior and more vulgar version of the Thetis legend, equally far removed from the simplicity of folklore, namely, that Zeus bestowed her upon a mortal by way of punishment or degradation, because she had refused his advances. Pindar must have known this story, for it also appeared in a post-Homeric epic that was familiar to him; but he prefers not to degrade his High God and to remain on the higher Homeric plane.

As was said in regard to the former ode, we need not raise any question as to the relevance of all this; nor need we suppose that Peleus is being held up as a moral example to young Putheas. The story of the Aiakidai was always interesting enough in Aigina to justify itself.

The latter part of the ode sufficiently explains itself, in spite of one or two difficulties and uncertainties in the textual tradition. He returns to his immediate theme, the praise of the athletes' family, and of their trainer, again an Athenian. He keeps the high style and the strained phrase almost to the last, and the *finale* maintains the solemnity prevalent in the mythic part of the ode, which is clear, uniform, and free from any obscurity in the choice and arrangement of the subject-matter.

NEMEAN VI

To Alkimidas of Aigina

"Men and Gods are of one race,
And both from the self-same mother we draw our breath.
But measureless difference of power divideth us;
For the one is a thing of nought,
But of the other the adamantine firmament abideth the
    unshaken dwelling-place for ever.
Nathless, albeit we know not what path of fortune Destiny 5
    hath markèd out for us to fare along,
Either in this single day or during the courses of the night,
Yet in some measure we come near at least to the Immortals
Either in respect of mind or our outward form.
And now Alkimidas attesteth that the power of kinship
Is in its visible effects like to the power of fruitful fields,
Which at one season bring forth abundant life from the 10
    earth for men;
At another lie in fallow rest, recapturing their strength.
Behold! from Nemea's lovely field of strife the athlete-boy
    hath come,
Who following this law of God's dispensation
Hath proved himself no empty-handed hunter (of glory)
    in the wrestling-ring,
Treading in the kinsman-footsteps of Praxidamas, his 15
    father's father.
For he, being conqueror at Olympia,
Was the first to bring to the line of Aiakos the garland of
    victory from Alpheus,
And having crownèd himself five times at Isthmos
And thrice at Nemea, 20

He redeemèd from oblivion his sire Sokleidas,
Who thus won the highest place among all the sons of
    Hagesimachos;
25 In that he had three sons who assayed and brooked the
    hard toil of the athlete's life
And won to the heights of fame.
Thanks to Heaven's blessing, no other house in the farthest
    recesses of all Hellas
Hath been proclaimed by the boxing-conquest as the
    warder of more crowns.
Having spoken a strong word, I trust to have cleavèd the
    mark,
As a good archer from a bow.
Oh, Muse, let the breeze of my verse blow towards this
    house, a breeze of renown:
30 For of their men who have passed away, song and tale
    have brought down to us (the memory of) the noble
    deeds,
Wherein the house of the Bassidai have no lack:
A family of ancient fame,
Sea-traffickers in themes of their own praise,
They are able to furnish the tilth-land of the Muses with
    plenteous seed of song
Touching their proud exploits.
For Kallias once, of this clan's blood, his hands bound
35   with the boxer's strap, conquered at holy Putho,
Having found favour with the deities that bloomed from
    Leto, Goddess of the golden distaff;
And in the eventide by Kastalia's fountain, a light was
    shed on him by the Graces' loud acclaim.
40 Also the land that bridgeth the restless sea[1] did honour to
    Kreontidas
In the high-tide held with sacrifice of bulls, in alternate
    years, by the men of the countryside in Poseidon's
    holy place.
Once, too, his victor's brows were shaded with a garland
    culled from the lion's feeding-place,[2]

[1] The Isthmus of Corinth.   [2] Nemea.

'Neath Phleious' forest-clad primeval mountains.   45
Broadly the paths are open from every point to the framers
　　of tales to deck this isle with praise:
For verily a peerless portion (for their chronicle) do the sons
　　of Aiakos furnish them withal,
Putting forth their mighty deeds of prowess;
And over the land and through the sea from afar flieth 50
　　the name of them.
It leaped as far as the Aethiopians, when Memnon came
　　not home again;
And Achilles fell upon them, a heavy wave of onset,
When he sprang from his chariot to the ground,
And slew the son of the radiant Dawn-Goddess with the
　　point of his raging spear.   55
These deeds the poets of old time found a beaten highway
　　of song;
And I follow in their track myself full of stress of thought;
But 'tis said that the wave that rolleth now by the ship's
　　keel shaketh the soul of every man most of all.
With willing heart I sped as a messenger, my back charged
　　with a double burden,
Proclaiming this the twenty-fifth fulfilment of their prayers, 60
That thou, Alkimidas, hast furnished to thy far-famed
　　clan,
From the contests that men call holy.
Verily in the sacred place of the son of Kronos[1] it was
　　only the random throw of chance that bereft thee 65
　　and Polutimidas of two Olympian crowns.
I might say of Melesias (the trainer)
That he matcheth the swiftness of the dolphin in the brine,
In guiding his team to deftness of hand and strength."

　　This ode is remarkable for its originality and boldness of
phrase and for the singular quality of the proem.
　　It commemorates the victory of an Aeginetan boy called
Alkimidas in the boys' wrestling contest at Nemea. We

[1] Olympia.

cannot fix its date precisely, but as the Athenian trainer, Melesias, is praised at the end, we must place it before 460 B.C., but probably not long before.

The boy-victor belonged to the aristocratic class of the Bassidai, whose record of athletic successes in the great games was so remarkable that Pindar felt obliged to devote the greater part of the ode to their chronicle and to the eulogy of their prowess. But his professional preoccupation nevertheless left him free to begin his song with an outburst of such startling originality that it must have evoked the same wonder in the Aeginetans who heard it as it does in the modern reader, this proclamation, heard now for the first time in higher Greek literature, of the general kinship between man and the Gods—"we draw our breath from the same Mother Earth"; then immediately falls the shadow of the inevitable thought of the weakness and transience of man, but only to be brightened by the bold assertion that in our mind or in our physical form we bear some re-semblance to divinity. The whole passage containing this thought, expressed most musically and in perfectly chiselled diction, is a masterpiece of religious lyric, which suggests a comparison with our "Lord, what is man that thou art mindful of him?"; but it contains a nobler and more hopeful thought than is to be found in those verses. This pregnant idea of the divine kinship of man was to have a great future in religious speculation; and special account must be taken of this passage in a general survey of Pindar's religion. For our present purpose, a critical judgment of the ode, it is only necessary to consider what could have prompted and what could justify such an exordium to a poem commemorating an athletic triumph. We know that when Pindar has been deeply stirred or when some thought has been working strongly on his mind, he is not scrupulous in observing the rules of relevance. And here he takes no trouble to reveal the appropriateness of his opening words to the present occasion; for his next clause about the fallow-field introduces a different and independent reflection. Yet some appropri-ateness he must have himself perceived and have imagined that his hearers would feel. To all his epinician odes he gives a religious tincture. Some might be intended for sing-ing in or near a shrine; and if this one were so—there is no hint of its place of delivery—it would be natural to open with a reflection on the relations between man and God, just as there was an ancient tradition for beginning an epic recitation with an invocation. Again, the festival where the boy-athlete triumphed was a religious event: men drew near to the Gods there as at the other great contests, which, as Pindar in this ode strangely emphasises, "men call divine"; and to a poet it would not seem alien on such an occasion to meditate on God and man. But perhaps the more special stimulus to the inspiration of this prelude was the impression made on Pindar at the recent Nemean celebration by the splendour of the athletic forms there displayed, perhaps notably by this boy-athlete. And the reflection could have arisen in his mind—as under similar stimulus it may have arisen in Homer's—that, ephemeral and improvident as we are, we are still the kinsmen of the Gods, and our wisdom and our beauty have in them something divine. He might then determine that this thought could make an acceptable proem for his ode.

His next clause contains the less inspired and more scientific reflection, that the law of heredity in the trans-mission of qualities resembles the law that compels the tilled field to lie fallow every other year. Pindar's dictum that the inherited clan-genius "skips a generation" bears a resemblance to some modern medical theories about certain diseases. And it is worked out with curious accuracy in this athlete's family. Pindar may claim originality for this thought, for there is no trace of it in any earlier literature; and evidently it appealed to him, for he uses it again to-wards the close of the eleventh Nemean ode, which has the air of belonging to his later period. It is expressed in both passages with independent poetic effect, and the one is not a mere echo of the other.

In this poem he is more than usually considerate of the athletic claim, to which he gives ample satisfaction; and in the full review of this remarkable family's triumphs he avoids monotony by the pungency and richness of his phrases, whereby he succeeds here, as so often elsewhere, in the difficult feat of transforming an athletic record into poetry. It is difficult in any English to convey the arresting force of such lines as "lading their ship with themes of their own praises" or the word-magic of the Greek verse on "Phleious' forest-clad primeval mountains", which some bad ancient and modern 'emendation' has sought to destroy.

Nor are the contemporary topics of the ode overlaid too

heavily with the mythology. He feels an obligation to refer to the Aiakidai as the heroic archetypes of all Aiginetan prowess; but he may have bethought him that he had dealt with them variously and at great length in other Aeginetan odes; and he merely allows himself a brief reference to the world-wide diffusion of their renown, which he illustrates by the statement that it had spread as far as the Ethiopians, whose great leader Memnon had been slain by Achilles on the plain of Troy. He is fond of the Memnon legend, as he deals with it or alludes to it no less than five times in the odes; and he must have been well acquainted with the famous post-Homeric epic called the 'Aithiopis', which first brought it into literature. Then he quickly leaves the world of myth to return to the present; and expresses a feeling that he rarely reveals, a preference for treating of the present rather than of the past: for that is the intention of the metaphor of the wave that is nearest to the ship: it is of that type which compares by contrast, and it cannot be called altogether apt. In fact the close of the ode is the least happy part of the whole, and its lack of finish, of clarity and coherence, suggests hurry and carelessness, as is the case also with the conclusions of other odes. We know that Pindar was sometimes composing "against time", and that may have been the case here. His reference to the Olympian victories which the boy-athlete and a young kinsman of his had just missed owing to "an overhasty lot" is abrupt and dislocated in the context and is expressed in such a way that no modern has been able to understand it: if it was intelligible to the Aeginetans, that would be its justification from the point of view of 'occasional' poetry; but happily for us most of Pindar's poetry appeals to a wider audience than that present at the singing.

In fact, the *finale* of the ode strikes the modern critical reader as infelicitous. It has no organic connection with the ode at all, but rather the air of a disconnected post-script to a letter. We know the subtlety of the Greek taste that loved to tranquillise towards the end the violent emotion of a drama or lyric or speech by ending on a minor key; but that does not justify this anti-climax, where the praise of the Athenian trainer is dragged in as an afterthought and strikes us as even less harmonious here than at the close of the fourth Nemean, being less connected with the context. The phrasing in itself is certainly strong and in the re-

verse of common-place style. Pindar wishes to praise the
trainer for the remarkable celerity with which he can turn
out a first-rate wrestler; it might be quick work to effect
this in six months; and to compare that sort of celerity in
a process necessarily long to the swiftness of a dolphin's
leap through the waves does not strike us as natural; it is
also obscurely expressed, so that though the ancient commentators understood it, some of the moderns have quaintly
supposed that the poet is praising the veteran trainer for
being able to run as fast as a dolphin can leap! Again, the
bold and pregnant phrase with which he closes the ode,
calling Melesias "the charioteer of hands and strength",
meaning that he guides his team of pupils to deftness and
strength, has proved too dark for the modern commentator,
though the scholiasts were able to penetrate its meaning.

As Pindar himself says of his own account of certain
religious mysteries, we may say of some of his own characteristic diction—"For the general it needs interpreters";
and some commentators are occasionally found among
"the general".

NEMEAN VII

To Sogenes of Aigina

"O̓H, Goddess of child-birth, thou that art enthronèd with
    the deep-minded Fates,
Daughter of mighty Hera and parent of all child-life,
Hearken to our voice!
Without thy aid our eyes would never open on the light of
    morn or the shade of evening,
Nor should we have won (the boon of) thy sister, Hebe
    the radiant-limbed.

5 But we do not all draw the first breath of life for equal
    fortunes,
And different men are yoked to diverse constraining
    destinies.
Thanks also to thy aid, Sogenes, Thearion's son, elect
    among men for his prowess,
Is glorified by song as of fair renown among combatants
    in the five-fold contest.
For he dwelleth in the music-loving city of the sons of
    Aiakos, the warriors of the clashing spears,

10 And they are right fain to cherish a soul that is wedded
    to the trials of strife.
But if a man winneth ought through strife, he launcheth on
    the current of the Muses a burden of song freighted
    with sweet thoughts.
Yea, for through lack of any hymn of praise, actions of
    great valour are shrouded in deep darkness.
And we know only of one way whereby we may hold a
    mirror up to fair deeds,

15 If by the grace of Memory, Goddess of the radiant frontlet,

A recompense for hard toil hath been found by the far-
    famed songs of bards.
Wise men foresee the tempest coming two days hence,
Nor suffer scathe through greed of gain.
The rich man and the poor fare together to the bourne of
    Death.
But I trow that the fame of Odysseus passeth the measure 20
    of his sufferings because of sweet-voicèd Homer:
For authority crowneth his feignèd tales and his light-
    winged invention;
And craft beguileth us, leading us astray with words,
And the great multitude of men hath ever blindness of
    heart.
For were it possible for it to discern the truth, 25
Then the mighty Aias would never have staked the smooth-
    edged sword through his breast,
Wrathful for [the adjudgment of] the arms:[1]
Aias who save Achilles was the strongest warrior that the
    breezes of speeding Zephyr brought in swift ships to
    Ilion city, 30
To win back his wife for fair-haired Menelaos.
Nay, but death's rolling wave fareth on without favour,
And falleth equally on him that looketh for it and him
    that looketh not.
But honour accrueth to those whose fair-flowering fame a
    God cherisheth after death.
Verily Neoptolemos came to the great centre of the broad-
    bosomed earth with helpful intent[2]—
But he lieth now 'neath the floor of Putho— 35
After he had sacked Priam's city, where the Danaoi also
    had hard stress;
Sailing away he missed the isle of Skuros, and wandering
    from their course they came to Ephura;
And for a brief space he ruled in Molossian land,
Albeit his line hold this prerogative there for ever.

---

[1] The reference is to the arms of Achilles, which after his death were
adjudged by a vote of the Achaeans to Odysseus rather than to Aias.
[2] This translation involves a new interpretation that I propose of the text.

40 But he went on journey to Apollo bringing him tithe of
the consecrated spoils from Troy:
Where, falling in with a fray concerning the flesh-offerings
of the altar, a man smote him with a dagger.
The guest-guardians of the Delphians were bitterly
afflicted;
But he paid the debt predestined:
And Fate had decreed that some one of the lords of the
45 line of Aiakos should abide for ever in the most
ancient holy place hard by Apollo's well-walled
habitation;
And should dwell there as guardian of right order in the
processions that lead the offerings up to the altars of
the heroes.
For the fair name of Justice three words shall avail:
50 Aigina, he watcheth over—and no false witness is he—
the mighty deeds of thine and God's descendants.
I am bold to say this, that from their homeland a highway
stretcheth for the tales of their valour [to travel far]—
Nay, but in all our doings respite is sweet:
Even honey and the delightful flowers of the Love-Goddess
bring satiety.
We are different, each one of us, in gifts of nature,
55 And one man hath this, and others that, having drawn
their lot of life.
It is not possible for one man to have the good luck of
achieving full prosperity,
Nor can I tell you of any to whom Fate has offered this
consummation steadfastly.
But to thee, Thearion, she granteth fair measure of happiness,
And while thou bearest a spirit venturesome for noble things,
60 She marreth not thy mind's quick insight.
I am the guest-friend of this people; and holding all darkening blame aloof
I will bring to the hero[1] beloved a fertilising stream of
praise and glorify his true renown.

---

[1] He is still speaking of Neoptolemos.

For good men this is the due reward.

Nor would any Achaean man, dwelling on the shore above 65
the Ionian Sea,

Blame me if he were with us now;

I am their city's host, and I trust in that;

Also among my folk at home I have a sunny glance for all,

Keeping from all excess and withdrawing all violence from
my path;

And may the coming years draw nigh me in all kindliness!

Any man who hath known me will stand forth and say
whether I am coming to you with censorious speech
untuneful.

Oh, Sogenes, scion of the Euxenidai by lineage, 70

I swear I have not overstepped the line in hurling forth
rash speech, like a bronze-cheeked javelin,

Which (thrown thus) quitteth a man's neck oft-times of
the wrestling-match,

His strength unbathed in sweat, before the sun's burning
heat falleth on the limbs.

If the toil was hard, the sweetness (of victory) cometh
afterwards in greater measure.

Bear with me! If carried beyond myself I brake forth into 75
discordant speech,

I am not sullen in paying the due grace of tribute to the
conqueror at least.

The weaving of crowns is light task for me:

Oh, singer, lift up thy voice and begin!

Verily the Muse is welding gold and white ivory and the
lily-bloom she snatcheth from the sea-ooze for a
diadem.[1]

Mindful of Zeus for Nemea's sake, set stirring in grave 80
cadence the many-voicèd swell of hymns;

It behoveth us to call upon the King of Gods on this holy
ground with solemn utterance;

For here,[2] men say, he set the seed of Aiakos in the store-
house of his mother's womb,

---

[1] This seems to be a paraphrase for coral.
[2] The ode was probably sung in the shrine of Aiakos.

85　That he should grow up to be a warder for his fatherland
　　　　of fair name,

And for thee, oh, Herakles! a right willing guest-friend and
　　　　brother.

But if one man maketh trial of another man in ought,

Then we might say that neighbour to neighbour is the
　　　　worthiest boon of all, if he hath befriended him with
　　　　heart unswerving.

But, if God himself upholdeth this saw, then it lieth with
90　　thee, oh thou that didst vanquish the Giants!

That Sogenes should dwell prosperously by the hallowed
　　　　way where his ancestors lived in wealth,

Cherishing a child's loving heart towards his father:

For, as he goeth forth on either hand, he hath his house
　　　　placed between thy shrines as between the yoke-straps
　　　　of a four-horsed chariot.

95　It beseemeth thee, oh, blessed one, to win for them the
　　　　favour of Hera's consort and of the Maid with the
　　　　flashing eyes;

And thou thyself canst grant to mortals in many a pass
　　　　deliverance from desperate straits.

Would that thou be fain to wed them to a life of perdurable
　　　　strength,

100　And weave it out of happy texture both for their youth
　　　　and gracious old age!

And may their children's children ever keep the honour that
　　　　they have and win still fairer!

My inmost heart will ne'er confess that I mangled the
　　　　fame of Neoptolemos with unseemly speech.

But to say the same thing three or four times again

105　Is poverty of wit, like the senseless-whining refrain in the
　　　　children's game, 'Korinthos, son of God'." [1]

---

[1] The adage in the Greek—"Corinth, the son of Zeus"—refers to the
monotonous and wearisome repetition of the same thing; it means nothing
to English ears, and I am not aware of any English equivalent.

Pindar's originality is so outstanding a feature of all his compositions that nearly every ode appears to possess a certain individuality or a unique quality of its own; but none in so marked a degree as this seventh Nemean. In the first place, it is of all his epinician odes the most personal and—we must even say—egoistic; he uses the victory won at Nemea in the pentathlon by the Aeginetan boy Sogenes, son of Thearion, of the noble clan of the Euxenidai, as an opportunity for making a personal apology to the Aeginetans, and for defending himself against an imputation which was damaging his credit with the community that he esteemed most after his own. Secondly, the ode is more obscure than usual, both in regard to certain passages and to much of the framework and nexus of it; and the first impression of the most intelligent reader is bewilderment, which the explanatory efforts of modern commentators, who have laboured greatly on this poem, have not hitherto sufficed to dispel.

To its elucidation the ancient learning of Alexandria has contributed two items of information, one of small and one of great importance. First, the boy Sogenes was born to Thearion late in life: these biographical details about victors and their families given us by ancient learning are often invented, but this is attested by convincing authority. We accept it then as a valuable fact that may help to dispel the first surprise evoked by this extraordinary ode, namely, that the deity invoked in the proem is the Goddess Eileithuia, the Goddess of child-birth. We may wonder what this deity of the nursery and of women has to do with a vigorous young athlete and an epinician ode. But if we examine the Hellenic cults of her more closely, we find that she was much more than this,[1] and was recognised by many States as a great power in the divine world, and that Pindar was in accord with ancient tradition when in the opening words he styles her "the Consort of the Fates"; for she could be imagined as weaving the destiny of men's lives as she ushered them into the world. And it was specially appropriate to the present occasion, in view of the fact mentioned above, to remind the family and the clan of their debt to the great Goddess that had given them this unexpected boon of the late-born child, who had grown up under her fostering care into such splendid boyhood. The impression,

---

[1] *Vide* my *Cults of the Greek States*, vol. ii. pp. 608-614.

therefore, produced by the deep tones and solemn music of the proem is enhanced by the feeling of its appropriateness.

The second and more important piece of information handed down to us is that at some time previous to the delivery of this ode Pindar had composed a paean for a festival at Delphi in which he had traduced the character of Neoptolemos and that the Aeginetans were offended with him for speaking disrespectfully of one of their beloved Aiakidai; and that, therefore, Pindar throughout this ode is trying to reingratiate himself with them by giving a more favourable account of the relations of Neoptolemos to Delphi and of his end there. Now this statement is mainly confirmed by the fortunate recovery of a substantial part of Pindar's paeans. And the sixth Paean in the papyrus is certainly the offending one,[1] which might well have displeased the Aeginetans, if they were sensitive about the reputation of the young hero who was the last of their great heroic family. In that poem Pindar dwells on Apollo's anger against Neoptolemos for his cruel sacrilege in slaying old Priam at the altar on the night of the sack of Troy: the God swore that for this he should never return happily to his own home or live till he was old, but should perish at Delphi in a quarrel with the temple-servants; and in the paean nothing is said about his honourable burial in the precincts of the temple and later heroic cult. The paean was sung at a spring festival at Delphi, before a large concourse which may have included some Aeginetans. It was probably in the summer of the same year that Pindar's seventh Nemean was delivered in Aigina; and he finds himself not so popular as he was among the Aeginetans, who had heard or knew by report what he had recently said at Delphi. This may astonish those of us moderns who, as they do not take Greek mythology seriously themselves, imagine that the ancient Greeks did not. This is entirely false, and this passage alone is a salient disproof of such imagination; we have other ample evidence that for the average Greek of the fifth century the tales of the old heroes were as real and living as the old Bible records were for the Hebrew. We must always remember that Pindar was the great poet of the age before the sceptical enlightenment. It was then as dangerous for any one in Aigina to have disparaged one

---

[1] *Vide infra*, pp. 308-313.

of the Aeacid heroes on a public occasion in Greece as it might have been for an English poet to have proceeded through Scotland a century ago chanting verses in disparagement of Wallace or Bruce. It made no difference that the Aeginetans of the time of Pindar could claim no blood-relationship with the ancient heroes of the island; for they were Dorians who had dispossessed the Achaeans to whom Aiakos and his family belonged. But like the Dorians in Sparta they had adopted the great epic traditions of the older stock; and in ancient Hellas adoption had the same force as blood-relationship.

Therefore Pindar was justified in feeling anxious about his position in this important community and in adopting a bold and tactful method of maintaining or regaining it. And that he dared to use an epinician ode for which he was paid as an opportunity for a personal apology would not seem to his audience so improper as at a superficial glance it may seem to us. As it was always relevant there on such an occasion to recount something about the Aiakidai, it would be relevant if the recital took the form of a palinode, clearing the reputation of one of them from a slur that the poet himself was supposed to have put on it.

Now a real difficulty arises—what was that slur and how does Pindar apologise? It was thoughtless of some ancient commentators to declare that the passage in the paean which offended the Aeginetans was the statement that Neoptolemos was killed by the temple-ministers in a quarrel about "the duly allotted honours"—whatever that may mean: for that version was certainly not more offensive and—one would think—rather more dignified than what he gives in his 'palinode' (Nem. 7, l. 42) as the cause of the quarrel, the distribution of the sacrificial meats. Of greater importance and verisimilitude is a statement made by an ancient commentator of critical judgment, Aristodemos, a pupil of the great philologist Aristarchos, that Pindar had offended the Aeginetans because "in the paeans he seemed to say that Neoptolemos came to Delphi to sack the temple". This was an ugly story, such as might agree with the character of a northern Berserker, but would shock all Greek sense of piety. We are not sure it was the prevailing Delphic tradition; and it certainly does not seem consistent with the honourable burial allowed to Neoptolemos in the temple-precincts and the subsequent heroic honours maintained by the Delphians. But it was in vogue as a floating tradition of the fifth century; for Euripides in his *Andromache* refers to it more than once; and it survived here and there in later authors. It would offend the feelings of the Aeginetans all the more because it was unproven. But now we have recovered the main part of Pindar's paeans, and though many of them are in a very fragmentary condition we can discern that it was only in the sixth that he dealt at all with the story of Neoptolemos; and all that he had to say of him in that poem is fully and clearly preserved; but he nowhere mentions or alludes to the story of his intended sacrilege. Nevertheless the Aeginetans believed that he had given sanction to the slander in that paean; and we may be more inclined to believe it ourselves if the new view that I have put forth concerning lines 33-35 in this Nemean ode is accepted—"Verily Neoptolemos came to the great centre of the broad-bosomed earth with helpful intent"; for this would be the natural retractation of a previous wrongful statement that the hero had journeyed to Delphi with evil intentions against the God. We should then have to suppose that Pindar for the sake of his own credit re-edited his sixth Paean to please his Aeginetan friends; he could not so far re-edit it as to clear the memory of the young hero from the sin of slaying old Priam at the altar: this was 'broadcast' through Greece by the old epic.[1]

Accepting this, then, as the personal significance of much of the seventh Nemean, we have still to consider the coherence and poetic logic of the ode as a whole. Our interpretation should be, like Pindar, straightforward and, in a sense, simple. We should not look for dark innuendoes and cryptic hints between the lines. We should not pretend to know more of Thearion and the young athlete than Pindar or some other trustworthy ancient authority chooses to tell us. We shall not imagine that when Pindar speaks of "the flowers of Aphrodite" he maliciously or didactically hints that a certain young person was too fond of those flowers.

Ignoring these false lights, we may find it not so difficult to trace the connecting links of this long ode. In the first part of the poem at least the thought is clear and works without dislocation or excessive abruptness. After the

---

[1] I have discussed the Delphic story of Neoptolemos in my *Hero-Cults*, pp. 314-321.

solemn and melodious proem, which links itself naturally
with the next period, he pays a noble and satisfying tribute
to Sogenes and the Aeginetan State: Aigina loves music
and poetry, as much as manly contests, and therefore he
naturally passes to his favourite reflection that the bard
alone can confer immortality on great deeds. Now comes
the first obscurity and—we may say—blemish in the poem:
the aphorism about the wise foreseeing the coming tempest
can only be interpreted thus—"just as the wise merchant
foresees a storm coming and does not put forth to sea
risking his cargo through avaricious hurry to dispose of it,
so Thearion has not hesitated to spend money on hiring
an expensive poet, so as to perpetuate his son's fame, which
otherwise the tempest of Time might overwhelm". This
was certainly obscure even for Thearion, and the simile can
only be applied with great strain; and the mercenary allusion
strikes a lower note than is heard elsewhere in the poem;
but it is so veiled as to be almost delicate.

Then he illustrates the power of the poet by an artfully
chosen example, showing that poetry not only perpetuates
glory but sometimes can immortalise even the less worthy:
thus Odysseus through Homer has been raised to a pin-
nacle above his real merits: this immediately suggests his
wrongful triumph over Aias in the matter of the arms, and
the tragedy of Aias is part of the great Aeacid tradition and
therefore as relevant here as any other part of it. We mark
the same depreciation of Odysseus in the next Nemean ode
and on the Attic stage; this had been prepared for by the
post-Homeric epic, but was probably due also to his quarrel
with Aias, the hero specially dear both to Aigina and
Athens. The story about the arms of Achilles had points
of connection with Neoptolemos, to whom the poet has
been anxious to lead round the legendary narrative: and
he now begins his 'palinode' without at once revealing
himself and his personal concern. The story mainly deals
with the hero's visit to Delphi and his lamentable end there.
After clearing his character of any imputation of sacrilegious
purpose, Pindar is able to represent the death not as a mere
"regrettable incident", nor as due to the anger of Apollo, but
as brought about by a higher dispensation, "in order that
the Scriptures might be fulfilled", namely, the pronounce-
ment of Fate that one of the Aeacid kings should be buried
in the holy precincts, so that his spirit might preside over

the spring-festival of the "Feast of Hospitality", whereto the God invited the souls of the heroes. We may be sure that this "higher theology" was Pindar's own construction. But it may have offered a solemn and beautiful consolation to the Aeginetans, especially as coupled with the impressive declaration that they have at Delphi a semi-divine friend, who watches with the deepest concern the glorious deeds of Aigina and his descendants. He might have been content with this attractive restatement. But the situation, he felt, demanded more personal pleading.

He excuses himself from dwelling any more on the glories of the Aiakidai, because (as Homer said) "of everything there cometh satiety". After a little more not irrelevant moralising he feels the moment has come to make his own personal statement; and we shall only catch the true sense of it if we discern that he is not referring in any phrase of it to Thearion or Sogenes, but merely to himself and Neoptolemos, whom he has censured recently at Delphi. He starts with an appeal to Thearion as a witness for his own good character; for Thearion, he declares, combines honourable boldness with good sense: we may then paraphrase his defence: "I am not likely to speak evil of Aigina, for I am their guest-friend; and I am far from any censorious habit, and I will bring oceans of praise to the hero we all love. None of his own people, no Achaean in Epeiros by the Ionian Sea,[1] will bear me any grudge for what I have said at Delphi; else why did they make me their public host? I have also a good reputation among my citizens as one who never speaks evil but who seeks peace and ensues it. Be sure then that I have never slandered Neoptolemos."

By this time he naturally felt that he had neglected the athlete too long; therefore he addresses to him the closing words of his personal statement, comparing himself to a competitor in the 'pentathlon'. Unfortunately, these words are among the most difficult that Pindar has delivered to us. We must suppose they were intelligible to his audience, but the

---

[1] To understand this we must remember that the Molossoi of Epeiros pretended to have been brought there by Neoptolemos, and the names of Purrhos, Neoptolemos, Aiakides, occur among the names of their rulers in historical times. This is why Pindar had above dwelt on the tradition that Neoptolemos had reigned a short time in Molossia and had handed on the kingship to his descendants. He can thus avail himself afterwards of the argument that the 'Achaeans' of the Ionian Sea bear him no grudge.

learning of commentators has scarcely made them so to the modern reader. To anticipate a more elaborate discussion of them I would offer this interpretation: in the five-fold contest—the contest in which Sogenes was a victor—an athlete must win in three events to win the crown: the last event was the wrestling, which, therefore, usually fell about noon, in the fiercest heat of the summer sun: the last event but one is the spear-throwing: in that, if a competitor over-stepped the line in discharging his spear he was disqualified; and that might virtually relieve him from the wrestling by making it useless for him to enter. Pindar may then say, in a bold figure: "I swear I did not overstep the mark in anything I said at Delphi, like a rash spear-thrower, and thereby get myself disqualified from further employment." Pindar's audience would have to think a good deal; but Pindar, unlike Bacchulides, often demands that.

He then apologises frankly to the athlete—as he well might—and asks to be forgiven for his personal outburst, at the same time declaring that he knows how to pay due tribute to a victor. He proves that he knows by a fascinating outpouring of rich diction, with subtle rhythm, in a high key of emotion. Then with perfect relevance he passes to a solemn strain of religious poetry, first invoking Zeus of Nemea, and then addressing Herakles with an original and impressive prayer, and giving him the full status of a God. He hopes that a God, like man, can be a good neighbour; and he reminds Herakles that he is the nearest neighbour to Sogenes, for the latter's house was built between two shrines of the God. Let him, therefore, help Sogenes and his father to live together in loving concord and happiness down to a mellow old age. There is a certain naïveté, due to the frank feeling of good fellowship in Greek religion, in imputing neighbourliness to a God.

It is unfortunate that the beauty and right-mindedness of this latter part of the poem should be marred in the con-cluding phrase by a returning attack of egoism. We could have tolerated the difficult and strained words if they had been placed earlier in the ode: they are intolerable at the close. They come as the unnecessary postscript to an anxious letter where the writer feels that he can never say enough and so repeats himself at the end. We may note that Pindar is sometimes as careless about the end of his odes as he is always careful of the opening. We cannot call this an anti-climax; he is powerfully wrong, and reveals how much he was perturbed about his own position. The ode, therefore, cannot be pronounced artistically perfect; but it strikingly reveals Pindar's forcefulness, daring, and warmth of imagination.

NEMEAN VIII

To Deinis of Aigina

"HAIL! Spring-time of Beauty, Goddess divine,
Herald of the deathless loves of Aphrodite,
Thou who hast thy seat on the eyes of maiden and boy,
And bearest one man in the gentle arms of Love's bondage,
Another in arms ungentle:
It is a goodly thing to win the nobler loves, not failing of 5
    our mark, whatever we fare to do.
Even of such kind were the loves that waited on the bridal
    bed of Zeus and the nymph Aigina, shepherding the
    Cyprian's[1] gifts:
The bed whence sprung Oinone's king,[2] a man surpassing
    all in strength of hand and wise counsel.
Many prayed fervently to see his countenance (in time of
    need);
For without the threat of battle, of their own accord the
    flower of the heroes that dwelt round his realm were
    fain to obey his behests, 10
Both those who arrayed the host in rocky Athens,
And the sons of Pelops throughout the land of Sparta.
Suppliant of Aiakos, I clasp his holy knees, praying for
    this city belovèd and her citizens,
And bringing this garland of Lydian melody sweetened 15
    with pipings of flutes:
An offering of gladness from Nemea because of Deinis'
    and his father's victory in the twofold running-course.
For prosperity planted with God's fostering care is more
    abiding for mortal men.

[1] Aphrodite the Goddess of Cyprus.
[2] The old name for Aigina, of which Aiakos was king.

It was God who loaded Kinuras with wealth in Cyprus, the
  isle of the sea.[1]
Behold! I stand quivering on light feet,
Drawing in my breath before starting on my tale;
20 For things manifold have been told in manifold wise;
But to devise new matters, offering them to the testing of
  the touchstone, is all-perilous.
And the poet's speech is a morsel for envy to batten on,
Which ever fasteneth on the noble, but hath no quarrel
  with the baser sort.
It was even envy that piercèd the son of Telamon, sheath-
  ing the sword in his flesh.
Verily the man who is valiant of heart, but powerless of
25   tongue, is held by dumb forgetfulness in the bitter
  strife of words.
But the greatest honour is proffered to the shifty liar.
For the Danaoi were servile to Odysseus in the secret
  voting;
And Aias, wrongfully despoilèd of the golden arms,
  wrestled with Death (and fell).
Ah, verily, when they were reeling back 'neath the [Tro-
  jans'] man-subduing spear,
Unequal were the gashes that they rent in the warm flesh
  of the foemen,
30 Whether o'er the new-slain Achilles or on murderous days
  of other battle-toils.
It seemeth then that even in old days there was hateful
  cozening,
Companion of crafty speech, suggester of treachery, a
  baneful reproach among men,
Which quelleth the bright light and setteth on high the
  hollow glory of the men of darkness.
35 Oh! Father Zeus, may my nature be never such as this,
  but may I cleave to the guileless paths of life!
So that after death I may attach to my children a reputation untouchèd by evil word.

---

[1] Kinuras, beloved of Apollo and Aphrodite, had become a proverbial
name for a mortal favoured by the Gods.

Men pray for gold, others for boundless land;
My prayer is that I may give pleasure to my fellow-
    citizens,
Praising what meriteth praise, and on sinners strewing
    blame,
Until I wrap my limbs in earth.
As when a tree, nourished by the fresh dews of heaven, 40
    shooteth aloft,
Even so virtue waxeth, rearèd on high into the liquid
    air, in the judgment of the wise and just of men.
Manifold are the services of friends:
In the hour of toil and trouble their help surpasseth:
But joy also yearneth to set up for itself a sure pledge in
    the eyes (of a friend).
Oh! Megas, to recall thy soul back to the world of life is 45
    impossible for me—
Barren is the harvest of empty hope—
But I can at least plant firmly above the earth a loud-
    sounding monument of the Muses' praise, on behalf
    of two athletes' feet blessed with good fortune in the
    contest, for thy fatherland and thy clan the Chariadai.
And I rejoice uttering loud acclaim, due tribute at the
    time when a fair deed is done;
But also by the soothing spell of song a man oft assuageth 50
    the pains of hard toil.
Nay, but the triumph-hymn of praise was heard in old
    days, even before the strife arose between Adrastos
    and the men of Kadmos' city."

This ode maintains on the whole the higher standard of
Pindar's poetry; there is less in it to puzzle us and to jar
upon our sense of fitness than in the preceding; and in one
passage he reaches the height of inspiration.

Yet an element of obscurity pervades part of it, and we
cannot dispel it by any external evidence that we can bring
to bear concerning the circumstances in which the ode was
composed. The scholiasts, representing the ancient learn-

ing, tell us nothing of any positive value, and some of their statements are foolish. Nor is there any internal evidence that enables us to date it, save that it reveals itself as belonging to Pindar's maturest period, and as composed before Aigina lost its independence and probably not far from the date of Nemean IV.

The proem is certainly original, as usual, glowing with imagination and beauty of diction: it is an invocation of 'Hora', not in the usual personal sense of Goddess of the seasons, but as a mere personification of youthful bloom, not, I think, found elsewhere in Greek literature or art. And in these opening lines Pindar is the first to reveal to us the idea, of which such varied use is made by later poets, of Love or Beauty enthroned in the eyes or on the cheeks of the loved one, though an older contemporary poet, the Athenian tragedian Phrunichos, had already approached it with the phrase that Sophokles admired, "on the purple cheeks the light of love is gleaming".

One might have supposed that this warm lyrical outburst on the power of Beauty was evoked by the striking beauty of the young athlete. But Pindar in the proem of his ode would scarcely allow himself such expression of his own personal feelings, and this Love-stanza is linked by a curious and not here very appropriate moralising reflection with the love of Zeus and Aigina, which brought Aiakos into the world; and then follows a glowing account of him, entirely in place, as this ode, like the other Aeginetan ones, was probably sung in his shrine. What he says of him here is brief but interesting. In his statement that "many prayed to see his face" he is probably alluding to the tradition that the afflicted inhabitants of all Greece implored his aid in a time of a dire drought, and that Aiakos sacrificed in their behalf to "Zeus the Hellenic God", whose priest he was, and the trouble was stayed. Then he intimates here that Aiakos became the voluntarily chosen arbiter for the powerful states on his borders;[1] and in naming them Athens and Sparta, Pindar need not be supposed to be pointedly alluding to troublous contemporary events; he only imagines that the powerful states of the mythic period were those of his own day. We may note in passing that this is one of the passages explaining the growth of the

---

[1] He extends this idea in *Isthm*. viii. l. 25, and makes Aiakos the arbiter of disputes among the Gods.

conception of Aiakos as still continuing after death to occupy the position of judge.

This praise of Aiakos is religious lyric, made more solemn by a prayer proffered by Pindar at the shrine for the abiding prosperity of the island, and he links this prayer skilfully with the athletic occasion by speaking of his song as a suppliant-garland, an offering brought from Nemea to the hero's shrine.

Only in this context, and once again indirectly at the close, does he mention the athlete Deinis, who had commissioned the ode. We are aware that Pindar allowed himself a very free hand in dealing with his athlete-patrons: but in this ode he is more than usually reticent about him as an individual. Having mentioned his and his father's Nemean victories, he moralises appropriately on human happiness; and according to his own convention illustrates his aphorism by a mythic example, in this case Kinuras of Cyprus, the beloved of Apollo and Aphrodite, the ideal type of human happiness secured by divine favour. But we are not here interested in Kinuras, and Pindar wisely drops him at once.

We may detect here, what is very rare in so collected and self-assured a poet, a certain embarrassment, even an uneasiness, as to the selection of further subject-matter for his ode. He seems to speak of himself as a runner straining at the start and drawing in his breath; and this may strike us as scarcely natural, as he is already well advanced in his ode. He seems anxious to deliver some new or original narrative; but he hesitates, reflecting on the dangers to which original composition is always exposed from the malicious criticism of the envious: for envy always attacks the good and the noble. Then, as an appropriate illustration of this aphorism, he gives the story of the death of the great Aeacid hero, Aias, told with deep lyric feeling and even passion. This should be the new thing that he was labouring to bring forth; and, as a version of the well-known story about the judgment of the arms, it is so far new in that it not only carefully ignores the madness of Aias and his onslaught on the cattle, but also represents Odysseus as the villain of the drama, the crafty plotter of the false tongue, who cheated the Achaeans into voting wrong. This defamation of Odysseus in this matter is indeed original, in that it contradicts flagrantly all the older epic and more authoritative account; and he almost gives Homer the lie direct. We cannot call this new edition of the myth a happy one or a contribution to higher literature; and it may be partly responsible for the odious characterisation of the old Homeric hero which Attic tragedy occasionally permits itself. This glorification of Aias would of course please the Aeginetans and would in itself be sufficiently relevant at any of their epinician festivals; but it could have been effected without the bitter calumny on Odysseus, which goes far beyond the disparaging reference to him in the former ode. Modern commentators have supposed that it may have been suggested by the stress of contemporary political circumstances, to which the story of Aias and Odysseus, thus handled, could serve as an analogue. But such interpretation is in this case found to be strained and unnatural. If we grant that Aias might stand for the state of Aigina, there is no Greek state that Odysseus could be supposed to represent or that would be interested or affected by his praise or dispraise. It would also be humorously absurd to suppose that Aias, "the tongueless man", could stand for Pindar or the triumphant athlete.

It is more important, in order to surmise what may be at the back of Pindar's mind, to observe that, both before he introduces this story and after he has concluded it, he speaks anxiously and earnestly about himself. It is he himself who must be the object of the envy and detraction which was in the air, and he may have found himself in the same position in the island as when he composed the fourth Nemean, in which he defends himself against hostile and envious critics. He can illustrate the evil of envy and at the same time gratify Aigina by giving a new version of the great Aeacid tragedy, the judgment of the arms of Achilles and the death of Aias; he narrates it then with great warmth and fervour, and to illuminate the baseness of envy he blackens the character of Odysseus, ignoring Homer, whom elsewhere he praises for doing noble justice to Aias.[1] Apart from any personal temptation to rehandle the story, Pindar would not find the personality of Odysseus sympathetic; he has told us before that he loves "the man of straightforward speech";[2] and the Homeric Odysseus in the *Odyssey*, with all his charm and many virtues, is scarcely that.

The story as told well illustrates the lyric as distinct from

---

[1] *Isthm.* iii. 55.   [2] *Pyth.* ii. 86.

the epic narrative of myth; it is told with personal fervour
and deep moralising on life.

When the tale is finished, he allows himself another personal digression, but in such great style and with such
spiritual nobility that it would win lustre and high distinction for a less beautiful ode than this. The prayer to
the Father-God, that he may walk in the guileless paths of
simplicity,[1] is of religious value in itself and throws light
on the soul of Pindar, and helps the question concerning
his religion. It concerns us here chiefly for the perfection
of its form. The austere and simple phrasing, maintaining
the satisfying mean between the too much and the too little,
with every word rightly placed, is lit up with a golden light
and tinged with a slight melancholy as if Pindar's sun was
turning to the west. It is such passages as these which
inform us what the true Hellenic spirit was, which we
sometimes call 'pagan'. And Pindar seems here to be content if he realises the aspiration expressed by Keats of

> "Bards who died content on pleasant sward,
> Leaving great verse unto a little clan."

After this, he returns to the athlete and his deceased father,
but still retains a touch of the more solemn mood up to
the close, which itself is more impressive and more interesting than in some other odes: for the closing words have a
back-reference to something said earlier; namely, if in
ancient times there was already cozening and envy obscuring merit, so also there were true hymns of praise exalting
the noble: and such, he implies, will continue for ever.

The ode has scarcely any of his characteristic defects;
and the obscurity that half-veils a part of it is not Pindar's
fault and may be penetrated. The personal digressions are
of the highest value, and reveal how far the epinician ode
could be used for the lyric expression of the poet's soul.

---

[1] Compare the prayer in the rhyming Latin of Gottschalk of Fulda in
the ninth century:

> Da mihi mentem
> fraude carentem
> prava caventem.

NEMEAN IX

To Chromios of Aitna

"WE will lead the triumph-dance, oh Muses, from Apollo's
    shrine in Sikuon
To Etna's new-founded city, where the festal doors flung
    wide are overpowered of guests,
Thronging into Chromios' abundant home.
But do ye fashion sweet music of the heroic lay!
For he now, mounting his victory-controlling car, gives the
    word to cry aloud on the Mother-Goddess and her
    twin children,
5 The watchers of Putho's steep in equal sovereignty.
There is a saying among men, not to hide beneath a
    bushel the light of a noble deed accomplished:
Right meet for it is a wondrous song with the proud words
    of ancient story.
But raise ye up on high the ringing voice of the lyre,
The voice of the flute to greet the very crown of the strife
    of horses,
Which Adrastos 'stablished by Asopos' streams in honour
    of Apollo.
Having made mention whereof, I will bedeck the memory
10   of that hero with glorious words of praise.
He, being there at that time king, made the city (of Sikuon)
    famous and known unto men with new-founded
    festivals, with trials of the strength of men and the
    swiftness of hollow chariots.
For fleeing from bold-hearted Amphiaraos and a bitter
    faction-feud,
He was an exile from Argos and his father's home:

And the sons of Talaos were no longer rulers there, being hard pressed by civic discord.

The stronger man maketh to cease the ancient right.   15

Then, having given in marriage to Amphiaraos, son of Oikles, Eriphule—her husband's bane[1]—as a faithful pledge of amity,

They were greatest in power of the fair-haired Danaoi.

Thence (from Argos) at some later day they led against seven-gated Thebes a host of men, unblessèd by the flight of fair-boding birds.

Nor in their wild yearning to leave their homes did Zeus, the son of Kronos, speed their departure by hurling down his thunder—nay, he bade them withhold from 20 that war-path.

But the host of warriors in brazen armour, with horses in their harness of war, sped on to manifest doom;

And having fought the fight for sweet return[2] on the banks of the Ismenos,

They fed the funeral-flames as pale-cold corpses.

For the young limbs were the banquet of seven pyres;

But for Amphiaraos, Zeus clave the deep-bosomed earth with an almighty thunderbolt,

And concealed him with his horses, before he was smitten 25 in his back by the spear of Periklumenos and the heart of the warrior put to shame.

For in the hour of God-sent terror even the sons of Gods will flee.

Oh, son of Kronos, I would fain put off to the farthest point of time this trial for life or death (that threateneth us),

The fierce hazard of the embattled Punic spear:

And I pray to thee, oh, Father Zeus, to grant to the sons of the men of Etna the destiny of long life under the 30 fair rule of law,

And that its folk may mingle in all the glad delights of the city-dweller.

---

[1] According to the story that Eriphule was bribed to persuade her husband Amphiaraos to go to his death on the expedition against Thebes.

[2] The reading is doubtful.

Verily in this place are men, lovers of the horse, and
  possessèd of souls too noble for the lure of wealth.
I have said a thing hard to be believed:
For Honour is stealthily beguilèd by [thought of] gain.
Wert thou shield-bearer to Chromios in the battle of foot
  or horse or on ship-board
35 Thou would'st have some judgment of the peril of the fell
  battle-shout;
For that the Goddess of Honour fashionèd his soul of
  warrior's mettle in the work of war, to ward off the
  havoc of the War-God.
There are but few men who have the might in hand and
  heart
To devise the turning of the blood-cloud rolling close
  upon them back on the foemen's ranks.
'Tis said indeed that for Hektor bloomèd the flower of
  fame by Skamandros' flowing streams:
40 And on the beetling crags of Heloros' banks, at the place
  where men speak of Rhea's ford,
This light of glory beamèd on the son of Agesidamos in
  the first days of his prime.
And I will tell of those deeds of his, wrought on other days,
Many on the dry mainland, some on the neighbouring
  sea.
But from toils that are conjoinèd with youthful strength
  and with Righteousness,
45 There ariseth a gentle span of life towards old age.
Let him know that God hath allotted him marvellous
  measure of bliss.
For, if with abundant wealth one winneth high renown
  among men,
There is no further higher peak whereto a mortal's feet
  may climb.
But peace loveth indeed the festal board,
And the new bloom of victory is fosterèd by the fellowship
  of soft-voiced song.
And voices wax bold over the wine-bowl.
50 Now let one mingle it, sweet harbinger of dance and song,

And portion out the masterful son of the grape in the
   silver goblets,
Which his horses won for Chromios aforetime and sent
   from holy Sikuon together with the garlands of Apollo,
   woven in due rite.
Oh, father Zeus, I pray that with the Graces' aid I may
   swell the fame of this deed of honour,
And above many a bard may worship the Goddess of
   Victory in my verse,
Ever shooting my shaft of song nearest to the Muses'   55
   mark."

This ode and the two that follow, though not dealing
with Nemean victories, have been included among the
Nemeans, because they were found as stray compositions
by the ancient editors and added for the sake of convenience
to the end of their manuscript, which had ended with the
Nemean collection. It is fortunate that they were so added,
for we should have been the poorer for their loss, as they
belong to Pindar's best work.

This ode was composed, as was the first Nemean, for
Chromios, the minister and kinsman of Hieron, who had
appointed him, according to the scholiast, governor of the
newly founded city of Etna, perhaps under Hieron's own
son Deinomenes, who is addressed in the first Pythian as
king of that city. We cannot date the present ode to a precise year; it is evidently later than the first Nemean, for it
describes Chromios as verging on old age. But it cannot
be many years later, for he is able to speak of the city of
Etna as "newly founded", and the date of its foundation
was 476 B.C.

It commemorates a chariot-victory won by Chromios in
the Pythian festival of Apollo held at Sikuon, where the
prizes were of value, "silver goblets", as at Marathon and
our 'Henley', though crowns of a sacred character were
awarded also.

As Pindar chooses to maintain, in defiance apparently
of a better attested historical account, that these games
were founded by Adrastos, the mythical King of Sikuon,

who was the leader of the unfortunate Argive expedition
against Thebes, known as the "Seven against Thebes", he
is able to weave that great myth into the body of his poem.
It is worked in quite naturally and with sufficient relevance
for Pindar. An 'epinician' ought to contain a myth: this
victory has been won at a festival instituted by Adrastos;
therefore the audience will certainly approve of the poet
dwelling on the great epic story, of the "Seven against
Thebes", just as in any 'Olympian' ode Pindar would feel
free to tell Olympian stories about Pelops and Herakles,
if it suited him. It is likely to lead us seriously wrong, if we
try to find a deeper, more inward relevance, some mystic
significance attaching to the myth, some cryptic allusion
to contemporary events, or some moral warning against
an unrighteous war: Adrastos and Amphiaraos do not stand
for Carthage or Chromios; they are sufficiently interesting
in themselves. In fact in this ode Pindar naïvely reveals his
own principles in the matter of mythic digressions. It is
nothing more than this—to turn a rich Pindaric phrase into
simple language, "Having mentioned Adrastos, I will now
tell you something interesting about him".[1] What may surprise is that Pindar never uses this story for any of his
~~Isthmian~~ _Nemean_ odes, to which it was really more relevant; for it
was the foundation-story of the ~~Isthmian~~ _Nemean_ games, as according to the accepted tradition they were instituted by the
army of Adrastos on its march against Thebes. But no one
can control or account for Pindar's waywardness. At any
rate the story was more relevant here than was that of the
baby Herakles in the first Nemean; and the poet's former
audacity must have pleased Chromios, or he would not have
commissioned him again. It speaks well both for Pindar
and his patrons that they allowed such a free hand to this
inspired hireling.

The myth of the seven heroes, which has been the fertilising stream of much European literature, was doubtless well
received by the audience; and we may be grateful to Pindar
for giving us a very noble example of epic-lyric verse. The
long series of events that built up the great drama of Thebes
had inspired a striking post-Homeric epic of unknown
authorship, called the _Thebais_, from which Pindar freely
draws here and elsewhere: but he has to tell the tale lyrically,
with rapidity, fervour, and thrill, lighting up a few salient

---

[1] L. 10.

points, with moralising reflections that illustrate his faculty
for a poetical "criticism of life".

Having ended the mythic narrative with the mysterious
fate of the great Amphiaraos, who becomes a buried hero-
prophet of Boeotian territory, he turns suddenly to a theme
of more burning present interest, the danger to Sicily from
the Carthaginian power, "the embattled Punic spear".

He prays strangely, not that the danger may never arise
again, but that it may be postponed as long as possible.
Had he the prescience to see that at one time or other it
was inevitable, and did he determine to leave in this great
poem a warning to the joyous revellers not to be too regardless of the future? And he knows it is a struggle for life or
death. These are strange words for a 'komos', a jubilant
dance-song. And there is no doubt as to his meaning, although his striking and original phrasing has been mis-
interpreted. This allusion to the Carthaginian peril, couched
in words so serious and memorable, attaches to this ode
something of the same historic significance as attaches more
closely to the first Pythian, composed for Hieron at a date
not far removed from this. Each in a different degree is a
lyrical celebration of the triumph of Hellenism over the
alien powers of the Western Mediterranean. Here, then,
with the victories of Himera and Kumai in his mind, Pindar
goes on to dilate on the martial prowess and military skill
of Chromios, praising him in this sphere as he had never
praised an athlete-patron before, and with singular originality and forcefulness of phrase. The latter part of the poem
has a strange festive brightness, and almost a bacchanalian
ring, if Pindar's stateliness could ever be bacchanalian.

The poem is a masterpiece of the noble style, majestic
in its rhythms, full of fervour and thrill, with bold and
original, but not far-fetched, phrasing, lucid in significance .
and coherent in its parts.

NEMEAN X

To Theaios of Argos

"Ye Muses, sing of the city of Danaos and his fifty fair-
throned daughters,

Argos the home of Hera, meet dwelling-place for a God!

It is lit up with many a glorious story for bold deeds
done.

Long is the tale of Perseus in his dealings with Medoisa:

5 Many were the cities planted in Egypt by the wise counsels
of Epaphos.

Nor did Hupermnestra stray from the right path,

When she kept in its sheath the sword that cast its sole
vote [for a husband's life]:

And of old time the fair-haired Goddess of the flashing
eyes made Diomedes a deathless God.

Theban earth, cleft by the bolt of Zeus, receivèd into its
hollows the prophet-son of Oikles, that thunder-cloud
of war.

Yea and from of old this city of Argos beareth the palm

10 for its fair-haired women.

· And Zeus made clear the truth of this report by drawing
near to Alkmena and to Danae:

And in Talaos Adrastos' father, and in Lunkeus Zeus
linked the mind's fruit, wisdom, with the spirit of
unswerving justice:

He fosterèd, too, the spearman Amphitruon,

Who, surpassing all in happiness, came into the kinship

15 of that God, after that clad in brazen armour he had
smitten down the Teleboai.

Like to him in outward form the King of the Gods came

into his court, bringing with him the fearless seed of
 Herakles;

Whose spouse is Hebe, most beautiful of Goddesses, faring
 throughout Heaven ever by her mother, Hera, Goddess of the marriage-rite.

Straitened are my lips to recount the full tale of the
 portion of the blessings that the holy land of Argos 20
 holdeth:

Yea, and the satiety of men is grievous to encounter.

Nathless, awaken the well-strung lyre and take thought of
 wrestling-matches.

Lo! the strife for the brazen shield urgeth the people on to
 the ox-sacrifice of Hera, and to the judgment of the
 contests;

Wherein Theaios, son of Oulias, having twice conquerèd,
 won forgetfulness of toils nobly borne.

At one time also he vanquishèd at Putho all the host of 25
 Hellenes,

And, faring on auspiciously, he (conquered them again)
 achieving the destined crown at Isthmos and at
 Nemea—

And gave this seed of song to the tillage of the Muses—

Being thrice victorious in the Gates of the Sea and on the
 holy sward in the ritual of Adrastos' ordering.

Oh, Father Zeus, his mouth is silent of that which his heart
 is set upon:

In thy will lieth the full fruit of deeds:

Armèd with daring he prayeth earnestly for this boon with 30
 no weak heart that shrinketh from toil:

The thought in my verse is known to God and to whatso-
 ever athlete striveth for the summit of all honours in
 the highest strife of all.[1]

Herakles gave to Pisa pre-eminence in the ritual of
 games.

At least, by way of prelude sweet voices twice acclaimèd
 him in the triumph-song in the Athenians' holy festival;

---

[1] *I.e.* God knows and every athlete knows that an Olympian victory is the
secret ambition of every athlete's heart.

35 And in earth burned in the fire was brought to Hera's
    stalwart folk the fruit pressed from the olive-tree in
    chargers with variously painted walls.[1]

The honour of the prosperous contest, oh, Theaios, is an
    apanage of the far-famèd stock of thy mother's
    ancestors, with the help of the Graces joined with the
    hero-twins of Tundareus.

40 Verily, were I kinsman of Thrasuklos and Antias, I would
    be too proud in Argos to lower the light of my eyes
    in shame.

For with how many triumphs hath this clan swelled the
    glory of the city of Proitos, nursing land of steeds,
    triumphs won in the hollow land of Corinth and four
    times from the men of Kleonai!

And from Sikuon they came away lustrous with the silver
    goblets,

And from Pellene with their shoulders clad in the soft
    woven cloak.[2]

45 As for the myriad bronze-work prizes, it is not possible to
    count the tale—the numbering would crave a longer
    leisure—

All that Kleitor offered and Tegea, and the Achaeans'
    high-placed cities, and Mount Lukaion by the 'run-
    ning-place of God', to be won by the aid of strength
    of feet and hands.

But since Kastor and his brother Poludeukes came to
50   visit [their kinsman] Pamphaës for hospitable welcome,

It is no wonder that the inborn heritage of their stock is to
    be goodly athletes.

For these heroes, warders of broad-wayed Sparta, hold in
    their hands the festal dispensation of all games with
    Hermes and with Herakles,

Caring first and foremost for righteous men.

Verily the kindred of the Gods keep faith.

55 But the Twins in changeful alternation spend the one day
    in the presence of the dear father Zeus,

---

[1] Olive oil in Attic vases, the prize at the 'Panathenaia' games.
[2] A not unusual prize in Greek games.

The next in the secret chambers of the earth in the hollows
    of Therapne,
Each fulfilling a like destiny:
Since Poludeukes, when Kastor had perishèd in warfaring,
    chose this life rather than to be a God in full measure
    and to dwell in Heaven (alone).
For Idas angered in some strife over [raided] oxen,   60
Wounded Kastor with the point of his bronze-headed lance:
Lunkeus, gazing from Taügetos, had seen the brothers
    sitting in a hollow oak-stem;
For, of all men upon the earth, he was born of keenest sight.
Then speedily those sons of Aphareus with violent running
    covered the ground between,
And swiftly contrived to bring about a heavy deed,
And suffered bitter punishment by the working of God's 65
    will.
For forthwith came in chase of them the son of Leda:[1]
But they took their stand confronting him near their
    father's tomb,
Whence they wrenched away a hewn stone, a monument
    of Death,
And hurled it against the breast of Poludeukes.
Yet him they staggered not nor made give back at all:
But, charging with swift spear, he drove the bronze-point 70
    into the ribs of Lunkeus.
While Zeus smote Idas with a smoky thunder-bolt fraught
    with fire;
And those two were burned to ashes in that lone place.
'Tis hard for men to engage in strife with the stronger.
Swiftly the son of Tundareus sped back to mighty Kastor,
And found him not yet dead, but gasping with rattling
    breath.
Then, shedding warm tears, in loud lamentation, he raised 75
    his voice on high:
'Oh, Father, son of Kronos! What deliverance from sorrow
    can there be at last?
Unto me also award death with this one, oh, King.

             [1] Poludeukes.

Bereft of friends, a man's honour perisheth.
But few of mortals are there faithful in the hour of trouble
    to share the burden with one.'
80 So spake he: but Zeus came to him face to face and spake
    aloud this word—
'Thou art my son: but this man, after thee, her hero-
    husband drawing near thy mother sowed of mortal
    seed.
But lo! I grant thee, nevertheless, thy choice of these two
    things:
If thou art fain for thyself to dwell in Heaven with me,
    with Athena, and Ares of the lowering spear,
Free from death and abhorred old age,
85 This portion is thine to choose:
But if thou strivest to save thy brother, and art minded to
    share equally with him in all things,
Then half of thy time thou mayest draw thy breath living
    below the earth,
And half in the golden halls of Heaven.'
The God having spoken thus, the hero set no double
    counsel in his mind,
90 But at once openèd the dying eye and set free the voice of
    the bronze-belted Kastor."

There is some evidence, but none that is entirely convincing, that this ode was composed at some time between
468 and 461 B.C.; and as it shows the maturest development
of Pindar's powers and style, it may well fall within that
decade. As it was commissioned to commemorate a victory
of an Argive named Theaios, of a family pre-eminent for
its athletic record, it gives Pindar the opportunity, which
he evidently welcomed, of composing an encomium on the
greatness of Argos and a lyrical chronicle of the glories of
her mythological past, a more inspiring theme than her
political present. He selects certain heroic incidents and
names, some of which were genuinely Argive; others had
been usurped by Argos from Mycenae and Tiryns, just as
Sparta usurped the myths and glories of the Pelopidai.

And Pindar shows some intimate local knowledge, the knowledge at least of a visitor; for some of the names that he singles out were not broadcast through the world of Greek mythology, such as Talaos and the Argive Lunkeus, names drawn from the old list of kings of Argos and commemorated by local monuments that Pindar may have seen.

His dwelling on the story of Hupermnestra, the one daughter of Danaos who, in defiance of her father's order, refused to murder her young husband, and his allusion to her trial for that disobedience and her acquittal, may have been suggested by the impression made upon him by Aeschylus' dramatic trilogy dealing with the story of the Danaides that Pindar might have recently seen performed He is still more interested in the legend of Alkmena, Amphitruon, and Herakles, which only concerned Argos in so far as she had absorbed the traditions of those older cities of the Argolid, but it concerned Thebes as well. He does not allude to the achievement of Argos in the sphere of art, which was coming to its zenith in Polukleitos and was her one title to greatness in the fifth century. We may regret that he did not consider it relevant, as he did in his eulogy of Rhodes and Corinth. But on the whole his panegyric on the ancient city is noble and satisfying; his style of lyrical chronicle is swift and vibrant, and he covers much in little space.

He passes then to his immediate theme, the triumphs of the athlete and his family, avoiding monotony in the ample record with his usual skill, and touching the sober facts with poetry and religious feeling. And, doubtless, the family had a special interest for him because it cherished a tradition that an ancestor of theirs called Pamphaës, who may have been a real person, had once hospitably entertained the great Twin-Brethren, the Dioskouroi or "Sons of God", Kastor and Poludeukes. The belief that these glorified Twins, who were now receiving worship in many Hellenic communities and whose true home was Therapnai near Sparta, did occasionally visit favoured mortals was rife in Greece; and this family tradition of the athlete's maternal kin may have been suggested by their maintenance of a yearly ritual where they entertained these Gods. In any case, the tradition was a happy fact for Pindar and for us; for it enabled him with ease and perfect relevance to pass at once into the world of myth, and to compose what is

perhaps the most charming epic-lyric narrative that Greek
poetry has handed down.

He derived the outlines of the story of the combat
between the Twin-Brethren and the Messenian Twins,
Idas and Lunkeus, over the cattle,[1] the slaying of Kastor,
the vengeance of Poludeukes and his recovery of his
brother's fellowship by his own self-sacrifice, from the old
post-Homeric epic called "the Kupria"; but we cannot believe that he was indebted to it for the inspiration that
lights up his own version. The legend as he gives it us has
value for the folklorist and student of old religion, but
still more for the lover of high literature. I have given
elsewhere[2] expression to what appears to me to be the
spiritual quality of this part of the ode—

"The myth of Kastor and Poludeukes expresses and
ennobles the sentiment of friendship, an emotional moral
ideal that was passionately cherished by the Hellene and
that entered as an unique element into the highest ethical
system of Greece. The myth of the self-surrender of Poludeukes, his abandonment of the crown of perfect immortality for the sake of his brother's fellowship, shines
out in the mythology of the world, and for moral sweetness
is comparable to the best of the Buddhist legends. It has
had the advantage also of attracting the genius of Pindar,
who consecrated to it one of his golden moments of
inspiration."

His narrative of the battle, the sorrow, the divine col-
loquy and the choice, exhibits the salient marks of his best
style, being swift, strong, terse, and thrilling. And especially
he reaches the heights in the passage expressing the grief
of Poludeukes. It is of such pathos as a young Spartan
warrior might have allowed himself, severe and noble and
the more deeply moving for that. We can appreciate its
quality best by comparison with any wailful passage in
Euripides: the pathos of the Theban poet being masculine
and terse, that of the Athenian feminine and verbose.
Poludeukes makes his choice instantly without words; and
the ode ends abruptly on that. There is no single law
governing the 'finale' of Pindar's odes. He has now and
then injured his poems by an unworthy close. But he never
ended a great ode more happily than this

[1] There were various versions as to the origin of the quarrel, not all to the
credit of the Dioskouroi. [2] *Greek Hero-Cults*, p. 228.

NEMEAN XI

To Aristagoras of Tenedos

"DAUGHTER of Rhea, oh, Goddess Hestia, whose portion
    is the public hall of cities,
Sister of Zeus most high and Hera the fellow of his throne!
Welcome Aristagoras with blessing to thy bower,
With blessing, too, his comrades near thy radiant sceptre,
Who, paying thee honour, guard Tenedos from falling,   5
Ofttimes with libations and ofttimes with the smoke of
    sacrifice doing thee worship in the first place of
    deities.
And for them the lyre's voice and the song are loud:
And the righteous law of Zeus, the guardian of the guest-
    right, is cherishèd on tables of ever-flowing cheer.
But with glory (oh, Goddess!) bring him through his
    twelve-months' magistracy with heart unscathèd;   10
As for the man himself, I count him happy for his sire
    Hagesilas,
For his goodly form and his unflinching courage, the
    heritage of his race.
But if a man, blessed with abundant wealth, surpass all
    other men in beauty,
And hath shown his might by prowess in contests of
    strength,
Let him remember that the limbs he gaily appareleth are 15
    mortal still,
And that at the end of all he will do on a garment of earth.
Nay, but 'tis meet that he be commended in the fair speech
    of citizens,
And the lyre's music with honey-sweet ringing songs

Should richly fashion his renown.

20 Sixteen bright victories, won from neighbouring townships,
In wrestling and the boastful strife of the pankration,
Have crownèd Aristagoras and his clan of auspicious
name.

'Twas only the faltering of his parents' hopes that held
back their son's might from making trial of the
contests at Putho and Olympia.

For, by the power of the Oath, had he farèd thither and
25   mingled in the strife by Kastalia's stream or by the
well-wooded ridge of Kronos,

He would have returned to his home in fairer fashion to
my deeming than his rivals,

Having joined the band of revellers in the fifth year festival
ordained of Herakles,

And having bound his locks in dark-gleaming blossoms.

30 But some men are cast down from their goodly estate by
vain-hearted vaunts:

Another man, slighting his own strength too much,
Hath been turned aside from his rightful glory,
By the clutch and backward drag of an unadventurous
spirit.

Verily 'twas no hard matter to track in him Peisandros'
blood coming of old from Sparta—

35 For he fared from Amuklai with Orestes bringing to this
isle a bronze-clad host of Aeolian warriors—

Also, from Ismenos' streams, the blended blood of
Melanippos, his mother's ancestor.

The virtues of ages past renew their strength with alterna-
tions [of ebb and flow] in the human generations.

Nor indeed doth the dark earth of the tilth-land yield
continuously its harvest,

Nor in each revolution of the years are the fruit-trees
40   willing to bear fragrant blossom with equal yield of
wealth, but in varying measure.

Even so our destiny guideth the race of mortals.

That which cometh from God to men followeth no clear-
marked track.

Nathless, we put hand to many a proud design,
Yearning for many a deed's fulfilment: 45
For insolent hope enslaveth our limbs, and Wisdom floweth
    down a hidden track.
'Tis well to seek a measure to curb the lust of gain.
From longings unachievable cometh madness passing fell."

    This ode is obviously an 'occasional' poem, and as obviously is not an 'epinician'; it may be called 'inaugural'—the only specimen that Pindar has left us of such a type—for it is written to celebrate the inauguration of a certain Aristagoras into his one year's office at Tenedos. We may suppose that Pindar himself visited the island, perhaps on this occasion, for he appears to have been intimate with the family of Aristagoras; whose father Hagesilas had a younger son called Theoxenos to whom the poet was passionately attached and dedicated a fervent love-poem.[1] The family was noble on both sides, on the father's tracing its descent to a certain Lacedaemonian Peisandros, who came to Tenedos with the early settlers led there by Orestes, on the mother's to the Theban hero Melanippos famous in the epic story of the "Seven against Thebes".
    The ode is preluded by a beautiful and solemn invocation of Hestia the Hearth-Goddess. The lines accord well with other religious records of the worship of this interesting divinity.[2] The chief centre of her cult was always the 'prutaneion', the place where the 'prutaneis' or rulers met, the public hall of the state, where entertainments were held and city-guests invited. Here was the public hearth, on which was often maintained the perpetual fire, the token and guarantee of the continued life of the state. Here Hestia, who was not so much for the popular mind a real personality, but herself the Holy Hearth with the burning fire, presided in unseen presence. Statues of her were very rare; and we need not imagine that Pindar was describing one, when he prays to her to welcome Aristagoras and his colleagues "near her radiant sceptre". For Pindar this is a conventional attribute of any Goddess,

---

[1] *Vide Fragments, infra*, p. 341, Fr. 123.
[2] *Vide* my *Cults*, vol. v. pp. 345-365.

whether visibly represented or imagined. She was not really a prominent or important personage of the Greek polytheism; but by an immemorial ritual law, which, as Pindar here attests, was observed at Tenedos, she has the right to the first offering or libation at any sacrifice where fire was used.

After the prayer he passes to personal compliment, but the eulogy on the wealthy and handsome noble is tinged with grave reflections on "the end of all flesh". Then he strikes a brighter and more festal note and praises his athletic prowess that won him many triumphs in local contests; and he declares that he might have won a Pythian or Olympian victory, had he not been kept back by the unadventurous spirit of his parents; which gives him the cue for some excellent moralising. He then recounts the glorious ancestry of Aristagoras; and he is led to a reflection on the law of heredity, to which he has given a similar expression in the sixth Nemean, comparing it there as here to the law that governs the varying fertility of the cornfield or the orchard. In both passages this pregnant idea is clothed in fitting poetic phrase, and we cannot determine which is the earlier, which is the later, version.

The conclusion of the ode is grave and there seems some hint of the possibility of future trouble. We should have expected that on such an occasion the ending phrases would be bright and auspicious. But the last two lines seem to contain a serious moral warning; and it is possible to suppose that the kinsmen of Aristagoras being aware of his weaknesses had suggested to Pindar to convey this to him.

In fact, though the ode has bright passages of congratulation and festal joyousness, its salient feature is its grave ethical colouring. And he does not allow himself to be led away into mythology, though he had opportunity for this when dealing with his patron's ancestry. The ode belongs mainly to religious and ethical poetry: the tones of the preacher are heard in the midst of the music and festal voices: and Pindar, as we are well aware, can infuse his sententious morality through and through with poetry; the greatest of the Attic tragedians are like him, but do not surpass him, in this. The metrical structure of the poem is stately and fascinating, the style mellow and crystal-clear: the phrases are strong and sometimes penetrate deep: we notice here and there the shadow of melancholy such as

might arise from the feeling of old age approaching. We
may believe the poem to be one of his latest, but we cannot
date it. At any rate, Pindar's genius shows no decline
through the passing years; and no one entering an office
on a city council ever received such a poem of congratulation.

THE ISTHMIAN ODES

ISTHMIAN I

To Herodotos of Thebes

"OH, Thebe, my mother, Goddess of the golden shield, the
task that concerneth thee I will set in the very front
of all occupation.

Let not craggy Delos cherish wrath against me, Delos to
whom my heart goeth out!

What is dearer to the good than parents in whom they 5
trust?

Give place to Thebes, oh, Apolline isle; verily I will bring
round the accomplishment of both these joyous works
full-circle;

Praising in choral verse both Phoibos of the flowing locks—

In sea-washed Keos with its sons of the sea—

And the ridge of Isthmos that fenceth back the waves:

Since from the contests held therein it hath furnishèd six
crowns to the Kadmeian host, a fair-triumphant glory 10
to our fatherland,

The land where Alkmana gave birth to the child that knew
no fear,

Before whom at one time the fierce hounds of Geruon
trembled.

Nay, but 'tis for Herodotos I am working, fashioning first
an honour for his four-horsed chariot,

Then, as he suffered no alien hand to ply the reins,[1] I am 15
fain to fit him with an ode proper to Kastor or
Iolaos:

For they were brought forth in Lakedaimon and in
Thebes, of all heroes the mightiest charioteers.

---

[1] The whole phrase in the original is rough and asymmetric.

239

And in trials of manly prowess they bore their part in
    many a contest,
20 And they decked their home with bronze tripods, cauldrons,
    and beakers of gold,
In their hot quest of victory-bearing crowns.
Undimmèd shineth their excelling worth
In the courses where men ran stript or in armour with
    clanging shields,
And in such deeds (as they wrought) with their hands,
25   hurling with sharp-pointed spears or in the match
    with the diskos of stone.[1]
For there was then no five-fold contest, but each feat had
    its own issue of victory determinèd for itself.
With their locks bound with many a garland from these
    contests they were seen ofttimes by the waters of
    Dirke and Eurotas' stream,
30 Iolaos, son of Iphikles, being fellow-townsman of the race
    sprung from the dragon's teeth,
And Kastor, son of Tundareus, dwelling among Achaeans
    in his home on the hill of Therapne.
Farewell, ye heroes! But, while I now deck my song in
    praise of Poseidon and the holy land of Isthmos, and
    Onchestos' strand,
I will proclaim in the story of this man's honours the
35   famous fortunes of his sire Asopodoros and his
    ancestral fields at Orchomenos,
Which rescued him from the boundless sea in the chill
    hour of misfortune, when bowed beneath the heavy
    blows of shipwreck.
But now again his natal star hath set him on the path of
    his old prosperity.
40 The mind reapeth prudence as the fruit of trouble past.
But if a man, both in expenditure of wealth and bodily toil,
    inclineth with all his heart to Honour,
Then 'tis meet to bring to those that have achievèd it the
    tribute of the proud hymn of praise in no grudging
    spirit.

---

[1] The syntax of the original is again rough and faulty.

For 'tis a light gift for a skilled craftsman of verse to give,   45
Speaking a good word in recompense of toils manifold,
To raise a fair monument of song for all men to delight in.
For divers rewards are sweet for divers doings of men,
For herdsman, tiller of the soil, fowler, and him whom the
    sea nourisheth:
And every man straineth hard to ward off from his maw
    ever-wearying hunger.
But if a man winneth the grace of renown in the athletes'   50
    strife or in the battle-field,
Then words of praise, the flower of speech of citizens and
    strangers, he receiveth as his highest gain.
It beseemeth us well to raise the loud hymn in honour of
    the son of Kronos, the Shaker of the Earth, our
    neighbour (at Onchestos),
Giving him grateful requital as the Helper of our chariots,
    the God of the racing-course of horses,
And to greet thy sons, Amphitruon,[1] and the far-retirèd   55
    home of Minuas,[2] Eleusis, Demeter's famed and
    hallowed ground, and Euboia, when we talk of the
    circling running-places of the horse.
And I throw in with these thy shrine, Protesilaos, at
    Phulake in the land of Achaean men.
But a hymn of short measure debarreth me from telling the
    full tale of the triumphs that Hermes, God of contests,   60
    brought to Herodotos with his steeds.
Verily, often the unuttered thing bringeth greater pleasure
    to the soul.
May it yet be his fortune, borne aloft on the radiant wings
    of the Pierian Maids of melody, to encircle his hand
    with choicest garlands cullèd from Putho, and from   65
    the Olympian contests on Alpheus' banks, fashioning
    honour for Thebes of the Seven Gates!
But if a man shepherdeth his riches in the secrecy of his
    home,
And falling in with men of other minds mocketh at them,

---

[1] Herakles and his nephew Iolaos the charioteer.
[2] Orchomenos in Boeotia, one of the earliest scats of the Minyans.

He regardeth not that he is paying to Death the tribute
of his life ingloriously."

Among the Isthmian odes we shall find many scattered
passages instinct with Pindar's higher poetry, but no ode
as a whole that can be reckoned among his masterpieces

The first is composed in honour of a certain Theban,
Herodotos, who had just won a victory at the Isthmian
games with his four-horsed chariot, driven by himself. We
know nothing about this Herodotos, except what this poem
tells us; and it tells us very little beyond the fact that his
father Asopodoros had at some time in the past suffered
severe losses from shipwreck and that he had retired to a
family estate near Orchomenos, where he had regained his
prosperity. It is safer to regard this shipwreck as real rather
than as symbolical and alluding to political troubles of
Thebes. There are no clear allusions anywhere in the ode
to external history that might enable us to date it. Certainly,
the emphasis laid on Iolaos and Kastor, as if they were
close comrades—which in old legend they never were—
would seem most intelligible, if just at this time Thebes
and Sparta were drawing close together, and this would
suit a date near to the battle of Tanagra, 458 B.C.

But we cannot rely on such an argument; for Pindar
does not need any political cue for his mythologic allusions
and digressions. And without any political significance at
the back of his mind, he would regard it as entirely relevant
here to dwell on the fame of Kastor and Iolaos; and so
would his audience, we may believe. For this was a horse-
victory, and Kastor was the ideal type of the horseman, so
that any ode commemorating such a victory was generically
called a 'Kastoreion'. And the name of Iolaos would naturally occur in a poem in honour of a Theban athlete; for
Iolaos was not only the charioteer and 'squire' of Herakles,
but a hero-athlete beloved by Thebes, in whose honour
annual games, named after him, were held, attracting
athletes from all parts. Therefore a Theban 'winner',
especially a winner in the chariot-race, would enjoy hearing
his praises conjoined with the names of these heroes.

It is to be remarked that the mention of their names does
not prompt Pindar to digress into any mythic story; and

this ode is one of the few longer ones that contain no mythic narrative. He seemed, indeed, on the point of breaking away into the story of Herakles and the giant Geruon; but he contents himself with a brief allusion to the "dogs that trembled before him". Why he should have allowed himself even this casual reference to the not very thrilling or very noble adventure of his favourite hero, it is not easy to give any convincing explanation. If the name of Geruon had the symbolic value of suggesting the farthest limits of the known world, like the name 'Hyperboreans', then the phrase might here be intended to enhance the fame of Thebes as the birth-place of the wonderful child, whose invincible might was proved in the farthest confines of the earth. And this idea may have been in Pindar's mind and satisfied him. There may also have been some 'topical' motive at work. We know that in later times the Thebans were supposed to possess and were proud of showing the bones of Geruon; and there is no evidence when they acquired these interesting relics: if they had been a recent acquisition when Pindar was composing this ode, he might be pardoned for alluding to them.

In the absence of any mythic narrative he gives us merely an outline sketch of the athletic careers of Kastor and Iolaos; and the style, though characteristic and therefore unlike that of any other poet, is comparatively dry, and one or two passages approach perilously near to prose; and scarcely anywhere in the ode does he find a theme that excites his full inspiration: nor is the moralising, in which he usually shows mastery, so striking and pungent as in other odes, though the strophe in which he dilates on the variety of rewards has some nobility and much brightness.

Here and there also the style and composition betray roughness and haste. The reason for this may be found in the circumstances in which the ode was composed, as they are indicated by the proem. This is certainly the most beautiful and charming part of the poem, a melodious and ardent outpouring of Pindar's devotion to his city, as of a son to his mother. He informs us that she makes a claim on him to celebrate the victory of one of her sons, which must suspend the other occupation on which he was engaged, namely, the composition of a paean in honour of the Delian Apollo for the men of Keos. He, therefore, gracefully apologises to Delos and the Ceans, begging them to excuse him for giving Thebes the preference, and promising that in the end he will amply fulfil both commissions. As the paean has been mainly recovered, thanks to the papyri-finds in Egypt, we are almost in a position to judge if he has kept his promise. We may feel that the paean was a higher work than the epinician ode; but the latter would satisfy the Theban audience, being clear, relevant, and patriotic and in melody and structure the work of a practised master.

The closing sentence is cryptic, containing probably an allusion to some Theban who had been disparaging Herodotos.

ISTHMIAN II

To Thrasuboulos of Akragas

"OH, Thrasuboulos! the men of old who mounted the car
    of the Muses of the golden snood,
In fellowship with the ringing lyre,
Lightly launchèd their arrows of sweet-voiced song
In praise of their boy-loves, whosoever was fair of form,
And had the sweetest bloom of loveliness, that prompter 5
    of the fair-throned Love-Goddess.
For in those days the Muse was not yet greedy of gain nor
    a hireling worker;
Nor did silver yet stain the countenances of the sweet,
    soft-speaking songs of honey-tongued Terpsichore,
Nor were they bought and sold.
But nowadays she biddeth us heed the saw of the Argive 10
    man,
That cometh nearest to very truth:
''Tis money, money, maketh the man', as said one bereft
    of goods and friends.
Enough! for thou art wise (to discern my meaning):
Not unknown are the themes of my song,
The Isthmian chariot-victory wherewith Poseidon blessèd
    Xenokrates,
And was sending the man himself for the binding of his 15
    hair a wreath of Dorian parsley,
Honouring thus the lord of famèd chariots, the light of
    the men of Akragas.
And Apollo the God of far-ranging might, looked (favour-
    ably) on him at Krissa and gave him the gladness of
    victory there also:

20 Moreover, in shining Athens, where he was furnished with
    the famed things of delight made by the Erechtheidai,
He had no fault to find with the hand of the man who
    saved his car and goaded on his horses,
The hand that Nikomachos brought to bear on all the
    reins at the nice point of peril.
'Twas he whom the men of Elis knew again, even the
    heralds of the Sacred Seasons who bring round the
    truce of God, the son of Kronos,
For that they had enjoyed some hospitable work of his.
25 And they welcomed him with sweet-breathèd utterance,
    when he clasped the knees of golden victory,
In their own land which men call the holy ground of Zeus
    Olympios:
Where the sons of Ainesidamos[1] were wedded to immortal
    honours.
30 For verily not unfamiliar are your halls, oh, Thrasuboulos!
    with lovely triumph-dances or with the sweetness of
    proud songs of victory.
For the path is not steep or cumbered [against the poet],
If one is bearing the tribute of the Maids of Helikon to
    the homes of high-renownèd men.
35 Having thrown a goodly cast of the quoit, may I hurl the
    javelin as far beyond all rivals,
As Xenokrates was far beyond all men in sweetness of
    mood!
Reverèd was he in converse with the citizens,
And in breeding of horses he upheld the fashion of the
    Pan-Hellenes.
To all holy festivals he openèd his arms:
Nor at his guest-loving board did any breeze blow so
40   strongly as to lower his sail;
But (in his hospitality) he was even as a mariner, that in
    the summer season fareth as far as Phasis,
And in the winter as far as the Nile-banks.
Therefore now let not his son, because envious hopes are
    clustering about the hearts of men,

      [1] Theron and Xenokrates.

Hush the tale of his father's virtue nor silence these hymns
    of mine:
Since verily I did not fashion them to abide in idleness.
Oh, Nikasippos, give these into his hand, when thou
    comest to my all-honoured guest-friend!''

The chief problem of this ode is the proem, with its
description of the mercenary Muse of Pindar's own day,
set in contrast with the disinterested inspiration of earlier
lyric poetry. Ancient and modern commentators have been
puzzled, and have put forth diverse interpretations of the
innuendo implied in it. For our present purpose, the criticism
and appreciation of each ode as a work of literature, the
question cannot be evaded, for the solution of it might
throw light on the guiding purpose of the whole poem.
But we cannot form a probable theory without determining,
if possible, the date of this second Isthmian. And in the
absence of direct attestation there are certain other facts
that bear on the chronology. It is addressed to the noble of
Akragas, called Thrasuboulos, to whom Pindar had dedicated the short but striking panegyric of the sixth Pythian
as early as 490 B.C. He is proved by these two odes to be
the son of Xenokrates, whom—also on Pindar's clear
evidence—we know to have been the brother of Theron,
the great dynast of Akragas, for whom our poet composed
the second and third Olympian odes in honour of Theron's
Olympian victory in 476 B.C. These three are the prominent
members of the great house of the Emmenidai, who were
dispossessed of the royal power in Akragas at some time
in 472 B.C. Now our ode lays special stress on an Isthmian
victory in the chariot-race won by Xenokrates, and this
achievement could not have been later than the early part
of 476 B.C., for it is clearly referred to in the second Olympian
composed later in that year. But our ode must be placed
some years after that Isthmian victory, for it is obvious
that Xenokrates is no longer living, and almost equally
clear that the Emmenidai have fallen; for Pindar is entirely
silent about Theron, but alludes to certain dangers that
may give cause for anxiety to Thrasuboulos, "the envious
expectations of mortal men", probably the malicious hopes
of the demos to confiscate the wealth of the once royal

house, dangers which might recommend Thrasuboulos to keep quiet and not advertise his affluence at present. Therefore Pindar encourages him to be bold and to proclaim his father's virtues; which he could do most effectively by arranging for the public recitation of this hymn, its main subject being a fervent panegyric of Xenokrates. Therefore this hymn must have been composed at the earliest in the later part of 472 B.C., Pindar having now left Sicily and availing himself of a trusty acquaintance called Nikasippos, who was travelling there, for its delivery. Its date was probably not much later, for Thrasuboulos is evidently still living at Akragas, not yet disturbed in his possessions.

It may also help us to consider what we can gather of Pindar's relations with Thrasuboulos. These were evidently very friendly and intimate and perhaps hitherto unmercenary. The sixth Pythian was more preoccupied with the filial son than with the father, though the father's victory was the occasion of it. And it was not Pindar but Simonides whom Xenokrates formally commissioned to celebrate both that Pythian and this later Isthmian triumph. Therefore the sixth Pythian was probably a volunteered effusion of congratulation, composed immediately at Delphi after the victory, to be sung at the celebration on the last night of the festival: we cannot say that it was written on contract or in expectation of pay. Further, we have a surviving fragment of a drinking-song[1] composed by Pindar to be sung at some festal entertainment that Thrasuboulos was giving in Akragas, probably in honour of one of his father's victories, though there is no hint of the occasion in the lines that are preserved. Finally, this second Isthmian addressed to Thrasuboulos after the death of his father, though almost entirely concerned with the eulogy of Xenokrates and the record of his triumphs, shows that the old friendship between the poet and the son was still warm, the closing verse of the ode styling him "my revered guest-friend".

We may also note that there is no hint in the whole of his lyrical correspondence between the two of any warmer, more romantic, feeling of love, which Wilamowitz[2] detects as latent in the sixth Pythian, of which the opening phrase has misled him. Thrasuboulos is praised for his filial piety, his self-restraint, his sweetness of disposition, and his devotion to poetry; there is no hint of his beauty, and if we

---

[1] *Vide infra*, p. 340, Fr. 124.　　　　[2] *Pindaros*, p. 312.

= 109 Bowra

insist on the exact usage of the epithet just referred to in
the last line of this Isthmian, he was an older man than
Pindar. This has a slight bearing on our question, for if
Wilamowitz's *innuendo* hit the truth, we should be slightly
less inclined to believe that Pindar's mysterious proem veils
a somewhat indelicate demand for money.

For, candidly judged, this astonishing proem lends itself
to this interpretation as *prima facie* the most natural. To
save Pindar's reputation for delicacy and high-mindedness,
other explanations have been advanced by modern commentators, some of which are too tortuous or far-fetched or
irrelevant to be worth discussing. The ancient commentators suggested two mutually inconsistent interpretations,
one that Pindar is suggesting that a fee was owing to him
which he would be glad to receive, another that he is girding at Simonides for his well-known avarice. This latter is
the only interpretation that finds favour with Wilamowitz
in his recent life of Pindar,[1] and he maintains that this
alone lends unity to the whole poem. Against this one may
protest that, in the first place, it is hard to discern the unity;
we should rather say that between the unpleasant personal
gibe in the proem and the body of the poem, which is an
eloquent and almost impersonal tribute to Xenokrates,
there is a yawning gulf: in the second place, that the gibe
was singularly clumsy and unblushing. He might have
been safe and justified if he had sneered at Simonides for
charging too much, for 'profiteering' in the field of the
Muses, though this is what some ancient critics whispered
about Pindar himself; but obviously the proem makes no
such reproach against anyone, but simply laments the fact
that, whereas the old lyrists poured forth the songs without
any *gêne* "for love", nowadays poets are compelled to work
for money; "for nobody is anything now without money".
This is very sad, and doubtless it applied to Simonides,
but to nobody more than to Pindar himself. It is likely
enough that he had occasionally written poems *gratis*: but
in regard to his main life-work, and certainly in regard to
his 'epinicians', he was a hireling, and he confesses it openly
enough in the eleventh Pythian. Aeschylus, Sophocles,
or Euripides might have written this proem as a diatribe
against Simonides, Pindar, and Bacchulides, and their own
withers would have been unwrung, for the great Attic

[1] *Pindaros*, p. 312.

tragedians were not hirelings. But Pindar of all people
could not reproach others for making poetry a trade; and
it is the professional 'urge' in him that occasionally prompts
him to exhort his wealthy and lordly patrons not to grudge
expense but to spend freely; just as the court saga poets of
Scandinavia praised the king or the hero for "scattering
the rings of gold". We must then seek some other explanation of the proem.

There may of course be latent in it some cryptic meaning,
which the words do not reveal and to which only Thrasuboulos had the key. In that case it does not concern us, for
it is no longer a literary question, but one of cypher-reading.
But Pindar is not so given to writing cryptograms as some
scholars suppose; and in framing poems intended for public
recitation, as this evidently was, he must have considered
what interpretation the public would put upon a prominent
passage. If now we reduce the elaborately phrased proem
to its simplest dimensions of thought and speech—as thus
"The poets of old days wrote for love: we modern poets,
now that money makes the man, are obliged to sell our
works: you are quick enough to understand me without
my saying more"—surely any audience would be likely to
interpret this as a delicate hint to Thrasuboulos that Pindar
would like to receive a fee which he considered due to him.
We are not called on to defend the poet's character in the
matter of delicacy. But we need not suppose him capable
of the indelicacy of sending unasked a brilliant lyrical
letter of condolence and then asking a fee for it. The fee,
we may suppose, that he would like to receive, may have
been long due to him from Xenokrates or Thrasuboulos
for some literary service rendered. There may be much
more behind, but we are never likely to know it, and it
does not concern us therefore.

On this interpretation, then, we must frame our poetic
judgment of the whole. The afflatus of poetry is not usually
inspiring a man when he is demanding cash. But Pindar is
able to hint at his need most delicately, and is such a master
in the technique of poetry that he is able to wrap up his
meaning in rich and melodious diction. And as it is his
principle that his proems should "shine from afar", we
may say that of this proem also in respect of its phrasing.
We detect, indeed, a false glitter in the "silvered countenances" of his 'Songs'; for the Greeks were not familiar with

any women or Goddesses who silvered their faces; and the term has no meaning except in the allegory, and that is a fault of style. And there are other places in the ode where the style does not strike us as perfect, but as somewhat far-fetched, strained, and unnatural, especially the sentences in which he seems to combine metaphorically the throwing the quoit with the hurling the javelin, and in which Xenokrates in his hospitality is said to have journeyed to Phasis in the summer and to the Nile in the winter: we may wonder how many of the audience would understand that; for certainly the scholiasts did not. Pindar's style is unique and arresting; but he was not always blessed in his ambition to say things otherwise than as other men. Yet there are happy passages and a certain tender beauty in much of the poem. When he is most at fault, he still remains great; and we may feel a touch of his greatness in the verse concerning the path of the poet bringing his tribute of praise to the home of famous men.

ISTHMIAN III AND IV

To Melissos of Thebes

"IF any man is blessèd with fair fortune either in following
    contests that bring renown or through the might of
    wealth,
And in his heart subdueth insatiate insolence,
He is worthy to have his name blent with the fair speech of
    his fellow-citizens.
But all the high excellence that attendeth mortal men hath
    its source in thee, oh, God!
5 And of those who reverence thee the prosperity hath
    longer life;
But it flourisheth not in equal measure for all their span
    of days in the fellowship of the crooked-minded.
In recompense for deeds of renown, it behoveth us to sing
    the praises of the good,
And with festal dance and song to exalt him with the
    lovely gifts of the Graces' giving.
10 Melissos hath had such fortune allotted by two contests
As to turn his heart to the sweetness of festal cheer,
Having won garlands in the dales of the Isthmian land;
And again in the hollow glen of the deep-breasted lion he
    proclaimèd by the herald's voice the name of Thebes
    through his triumph in the running of steeds;
And on the hereditary valour of the men of his house he
    bringeth no reproach.
15 Ye know forsooth the ancient renown of Kleonumos in
    chariots.
And they being the inheritors on their mother's side of
    the Labdakidai,

For the toil of the four-horsed racing-teams wealth lay
    about their path:
But time with its rolling cycle of days bringeth diverse
    changes at diverse seasons.
The Gods indeed abide unscathed."

"By the favour of the Gods I have endless paths of song all
    around about me, oh, Melissos;
For that thou [conqueror] at the Isthmian games, hast re-
    vealed to me an ample theme, so as to track out in my
    singing the famous deeds of thy line;
Wherewith the kin of Kleonumos abounded ever,
As they fared with God's guidance down to the mortal 5
    end of life.
The changeful breeze of fortune, varying with the times,
    with sudden gusts driveth all men before it.
Even so, the men of this house are spoken of as honoured
    in Thebes from their earliest days,
As the city-hosts of the neighbouring towns, as men in
    whom loud-mouthed Insolence is dead.
And as touching all records concerning the dead and the
    living, attesting boundless fame, that have been 10
    bruited among men, these have grasped it in all
    fulness;
And by highest deeds of valour their renown stretcheth
    from home to the Pillars of Herakles,
So that they do not even yearn for any further-reaching
    glory.
They grew to be rearers of the horse and dear to 15
    bronze-clad Ares.
But lo! on a single day the bitter snow-drift of war made
    desolate their happy hearth of four men's lives.[1]
But now once more it is as when, after the wintry gloom
    of the changeful months, the earth hath blossomèd
    with dark-red roses through the will of powers divine.

[1] A reference probably to the battle of Plataea in 479 B.C.

20 And the Earth-Shaker, who hath his dwelling in Onchestos
and on the bridge of land 'twixt the two seas before
the walls of Corinth,
Having brought this wondrous hymn of victory to the clan,
Rouseth from its couch the ancient fame of their renownèd
deeds;
For it had fallen asleep; but now awakenèd, its countenance
shineth like the morning-star well-seen among the
other stars.

25 This fame having heralded their chariot's victory in the
fields of Athens and in Adrastos' games of Sikuon,
Brought them from the poets of that time such wreaths
of poesy as I bring them;
Nor did they refrain their curvèd car from the gatherings
of all the Hellenes,
Vying with whom they rejoicèd in the costly upkeep of
steeds.

30 For of those who venture no trial fame is silent and
knoweth naught,[1]
And even for those who enter the fray, darkling are the
ways of Chance, until the last issue is achievèd.
For she giveth us now of this and now of that, and oft-
35   times the craft of the worser man hath caught and
tripped the stronger.
Verily ye know of the deadly might of Aias, which he
himself rent asunder in the last hour of night, when
he fell upon his sword and is a cause of reproach to
all Hellenes who went to Troy.
But truly Homer hath done him honour among all men,
Who, having established firmly his great prowess, hath
told the story in the measured roll of his immortal
verse, for other poets to disport themselves therewith.

40 For if a man speaketh excellently of anything, this fareth
forth, a deathless voice.
And over the all-fruitful earth and the spaces of the sea
are shed the sun-rays of glorious deeds, unquenched
for ever.

---

[1] Or "For those who dare not face the trial there is silence unrenowned".

May I win the helpful favour of the Muses, so as I may
 kindle such a beacon-fire of song, even for Melissos,
 scion of Telesias, a victory-wreath worthy of his 45
 pankration:
For in the stress of fight he is like in soul to the boldness
 of wild roaring lions,
While he is like to a fox in craft; that throweth itself on its
 back and thus checketh the eagle's swoop:
All things are lawful to do so as to baffle the foe.
For Melissos hath not the goodly stature of Orion;
His outward semblance is a reproach to him.   50
Yet in the shock of spears he is stubborn to confront.
And verily, once on a time, there went from Kadmeian
 Thebes against the house of Antaios,
Even to corn-bearing Libya, a man short of stature, but
 unblenching in spirit, Alkmana's son, fain to wrestle
 a fall with him,
That he might stay him from crowning Poseidon's shrine
 with the skulls of travellers.
He it was who fared to Heaven, having explored all lands 55
 and the hollow cup of the cliff-girt dark-grey sea,
And made the straits kindly to the seafarer.[1]
And now he dwelleth near the God that holdeth the aegis,
Cherishing the fairest happiness,
And he hath honour of the Immortals as their friend,
And he hath Hebe to wife,
The lord of a house of gold and son-in-law to Hera.   60
To him, on the height above the Alektra Gate, we citizens fur-
 nish a sacrificial feast, with circle of new-built altars,
And we offer rich burnt-offerings to his eight dead mail-
 clad sons, whom Megara, daughter of Kreon, bore
 to him.
For their honour in the dusk of daylight, a flame mounting 65
 up flareth unceasingly in all-nightly celebration,
Spurning the upper air with smoke from the fat of victims;
And throughout the second day there falleth the decision
 of the yearly games, where strength is put forth;

---

[1] The Straits of Gibraltar, the Pillars of Herakles.

Whereat this man Melissos, crowning his head with the
70   whitening myrtle-crown, proclaimèd his two victories,
As in former times a third won in the strife with boys,
  having hearkened to the many-counselled wisdom of
  his teacher, the pilot-helmsman of his course.
And in fellowship with Orseas[1] will I now glorify him
  with triumph-song, shedding on them the sweet dew
  of verse."

The compositions that have come down to us as the third
and fourth Isthmians were received by the learned men of
antiquity as two separate odes, while they recognised their
intimate connection; but close examination of them reveals,
as most modern commentators are agreed, that they were
framed to form one complete poem. The circumstances
may be stated thus: a certain Melissos, son of Telesiadas,
of the wealthy family of the Kleonumidai, who claimed
descent from the ancient royal house of the Labdakidai,
had won a victory in the 'pankration' at the Isthmian games;
and in honour of this Pindar composed the ode that appears
in our collection as the fourth Isthmian, a poem evidently
complete in itself; the public recitation of this ode was for
some reason postponed, and before it could be given—
perhaps a few months later—Melissos had won another
victory in the Nemean games with his chariot; and Pindar
was commissioned to commemorate this also. He thereupon
composed what is called the third Isthmian, commemorating both victories, as a preface to the ode already written
which mentioned only the Isthmian; for it is obvious that
the so-called 'third' Isthmian, though of later composition,
could never have been intended to stand as a separate poem;
but it was planned as a preface to the earlier, and it was
therefore naturally composed in the same metre. The juncture, we may mark, has not been effected with perfect skill;
for the thought that appears in the penultimate phrase of
the 'third' is found again with slightly different expression
in the opening 'strophe' of the 'fourth'. Nevertheless, they
fuse together into a fairly consistent whole, and certainly
the older poem was the richer for the addition.

[1] The trainer.

The 'fourth' Isthmian begins abruptly, plunging us into
medias res without the usual brilliance of the Pindaric
proem. But this is amply supplied by the opening phrases
of the 'third', which give expression to deep religious thought
and feeling in stately and solemn rhythm. We are tempted
to believe that Pindar is trying to convey a moral lesson to
his countrymen of which they always stood in need. He
then pays a fitting tribute in happy poetic phraseology to
the double victory of the athlete, and informs us of the
interesting fact that on their mother's side his family
claimed descent from the Labdakidai, we may suppose
through Thersandros, the son of Poluneikes, whom he had
mentioned as the ancestor also of the Emmenidai of
Akragas.[1] It is important to note that there were persons
in the fifth century at Thebes and elsewhere who still could
trace their genealogy to the famous house of Oedipus,
maintaining no doubt that his children were born from
his lawful wedlock, and not allowing the Attic tragic fiction
that they were sprung from the incestuous marriage. The
preface closes with one of Pindar's majestic phrases concerning the mutability of fortune, an allusion—to be explained more clearly in the longer poem—to the chequered
history of the house of Kleonumos. And such a close is
evidence enough that the 'third' Isthmian was never intended to be an independent poem.

The first part of the 'fourth' Isthmian is devoted to a
warm and ample eulogy of the athlete's family, dwelling
on their long-continued prosperity and far-reaching reputation, but alluding also in words of mournful cadence to the
desolation brought upon their hearth by "a storm of battle"
in which four men of the house had fallen. We have reason
to believe that this was the great battle of Plataea and that
the loss was fairly recent. As Pindar was ashamed of the
part that Thebes had played in that great crisis, we may
understand why he passes over it here without further
comment. Then in a rich and lovely phrase he speaks of the
earth recovering from the wintry gloom and blossoming
with the flowers of spring; even so, the house of Kleonumos
has shaken off sorrow and its long slumber and is shining
with new glory like the morning-star. This is a polite and
poetic way of intimating that before the successes of
Melissos the house for a considerable period—since old

---

[1] *Ol.* ii. 43.

days when they won minor successes which former poets had celebrated—had won no distinction. They had entered their chariots, indeed, in some or all of the four great games, but had always lost. This delicately veiled fact alone could explain the moralising reflection that the worse man has often defeated the better man by guile and craft, a truth which he illustrates by the salient mythic example of the great Aias. He dwells impressively on his tragic end, which clouded the honour of the whole Achaean host, who were responsible for it; and then in a 'strophe' which rises to near the height of his greatest style he dilates on the noble tribute that Homer, in his immortal verse, has paid the hero, and thereby redeemed his honour. We observe that there is no outspoken reference here to the guile of the inferior man, the rival Odysseus, whom he unfairly vilifies in other odes. The mythic parallel only has real point if the Kleonumidai could be supposed to have lost their races, on some occasion at least, through the guile of a rival competitor, that is to say, through unfair driving, just as Menelaos in the funeral games of Patroklos in the *Iliad* complained that Antilochos had defeated him in the chariot-race through trickery. They may have actually put forward this usual excuse of the defeated, or Pindar suggests it for them. Doubtless they would be pleased with the poet and would easily pardon him for what may seem his unnecessary candour in alluding to their defeats at all, as he comments on them in so tactful and gratifying a manner.

But we cannot so defend his reputation for tact in regard to what he says of his athlete-patron Melissos. Nowhere else does he display such astonishing frankness, and that at the expense of the man who is paying him! We admire Pindar generally for his freedom from fawning and sycophancy. But to be frank it is not necessary to be rude; and Pindar's blunt candour almost amounts to rudeness. Evidently Melissos was a very unattractive-looking person and of mean physique, and Pindar might have been satisfied with saying of him, as he does, that he had not the beauty and stature of Orion—as we might say of a very ugly man that "he is no Adonis". But it was not necessary to proclaim the fact in a paid poem that he was of contemptible appearance ("blameable to look upon"); and one may wonder whether all the compliment and consolation that follow could quite atone for that easily remembered phrase. And the compliments also, when closely examined, are somewhat left-handed. Pindar praises him first as being an excellent soldier: that may well have been true—the hero Tudeus, according to Homer, was small but a first-rate fighting man. And for Melissos, being of poor physique, to have conquered at one of the greatest athletic competitions of Greece in so desperate a contest as the pankration—boxing, wrestling, and strangling—he must have possessed some remarkable gifts and qualities. He had learned all the arts and tricks that an excellent trainer, Orseas, could teach him. And Pindar intimates that it was by some clever trick that he had conquered; for he compares him to the fox, who, when attacked by the eagle, flings himself on his back. This seems to mean that Melissos was a master in all the tricks of 'ground-wrestling'. But Pindar allows us to suspect that there were some people who complained that Melissos had won by unfair means, though it is not easy to decide what was considered fair or unfair in that barbarous sport. At all events he defends him by the aphorism—"It is right to do everything to annihilate one's foe". A similar sentiment is put by Euripides into the mouth of one of his most unpleasant characters in the *Ion*. Nowhere else in his moralising does Pindar sink to this level; and it may be, as Wilamowitz suggests,[1] that he endeavours to correct the detrimental impression that these words might leave by the higher tone of religious ethic adopted in the 'third' Isthmian. He now characteristically seeks a mythic parallel for Melissos. He had given Aias as the counterpart to the noble but unsuccessful house of Kleonumos. And the rival of Aias was Odysseus, the inferior man who conquers by guile, as Pindar elsewhere describes him. And he is the most natural mythic parallel to Melissos, as Pindar presents him to us. Therefore, we may surmise, in his account of the tragic fate of Aias the name of his rival is not mentioned by him, lest the cap of Odysseus should seem to fit the head of his athlete-patron. A nobler parallel is at once found for him, the hero dearest to Pindar and Thebes, the great Herakles himself!

To compare the man of mean presence, a guileful 'foxy' man, even though he had also the lion's temperament, with the mightiest hero of Greece in whom there was no guile, seems mere effrontery of adulation. Pindar tries to justify

[1] *Pindaros*, p. 341.

it by the astonishing statement that Herakles, though the overthrower of giants, was short of stature. The statement is astonishing, because it contradicts all other literary and archaeologic record. Is it a mere audacious invention of Pindar's to suit the occasion, as we know that he can be audaciously free in dealing with myths? Or could there have been a dim memory preserved at Thebes of the personality of the real Herakles, that he was a short man though of immense strength, just as a similar memory seems to have been preserved in Homer's time of Tudeus? It is strange, then, that here alone does such a memory glimmer through. In any case we cannot but feel that Pindar is here putting force upon himself: the passage has a hollow ring, and his inspiration fails him. But he recovers it again in his glowing lines about the adventures of Herakles in distant seas and his blissful reward in heaven, which he lingers on as a theme of refuge from the athlete.

He then passes on to the description of the yearly Theban festival of Herakles, in which worship was also paid to the slaughtered children of Herakles and Megara, and which was followed by the athletic games named after his squire Iolaos. The detailed and fervent account of this ritual suggests that it was the occasion for which this Isthmian ode was composed. In reading this passage we are again startled by an eccentric trait in the mythology. The only tradition about the fate of the children of Megara known to us is that which Euripides follows in his *Hercules Furens*; namely, that they were young and helpless children slain by their own father in his fit of madness. But Pindar speaks of them as "mail-clad (warriors) dead". Mail-clad warriors are grown men, usually killed in battle. Pindar, therefore, has in his mind or invents for himself some entirely different tradition about their death, which he thinks more creditable to his hero; or he uses the epithet 'mail-clad' thoughtlessly and meaninglessly. Which of these two views we take depends on our general view of Pindar.

The last passage of the ode, containing praise of the athlete's trainer and further record of the athlete's successes, is only of mediocre interest, though the closing phrase is impressive and characteristic.

This ode does not show Pindar at the height of his inspiration; it may well have been that this Melissos was not an inspiring person; and Pindar exposes himself here to some charge of tactlessness and freakishness. Yet it has passages of bright graciousness and of solemn beauty; and the majestic verse shows the master of rhythm.

We have no clear indication of its date, but from internal evidence we may place it shortly after the composition of the ninth Pythian, that is, after 474 B.C. Pindar seems now sure of his position at Thebes, as a man of authority who can say what he wishes.

ISTHMIAN V (VI)

To Phulakidas of Aigina

"EVEN as when men (lift the bowl) at the high-tide of the
banquet,
So we mingle a second cup of the Muses' melodies,
In honour of Lampon's race of goodly athletes,
Having offered a first to thee, O Zeus, at Nemea,
When the flower of all crowns of victory came to our hands,
5 And now proffering another to the Lord of Isthmos and
to Nereus' fifty daughters,
For that the youngest of his sons, Phulakidas, is conqueror.
May it be ours (at a future time) to besprinkle Aigina with
a third libation
Profferèd to Zeus the Saviour, Lord of Olympia,
With the accompaniment of songs of honeyed voice!
10 For if a man, rejoicing in expenditure of wealth and toil,
achieveth high excellence founded on God's help,
And power divine causeth fair reputation to blossom for him,
He casteth anchor at last on the farthest shores of happiness,
honoured of God.
Even in such a spirit he, the son of Kleonikos, doth vow to
15 confront and welcome death and hoary age.
But I address myself to high-thronèd Klotho and her
Sister-Fates that they minister to a dear friend's
prayers for renown.[1]
And for you, ye heroes of the line of Aiakos,
20 I aver 'tis an ordinance right clear for me, when I fare to
this island, to shed upon you the dew of words of
praise.

---

[1] *I.e.* the prayer of the father Lampon that his son may conquer at Olympia.

There are a myriad broad highways, stretching endlessly,
  for the tale of your noble deeds to travel along, yea,
  beyond the sources of the Nile and through lands of
  the farthest North.

Nor is there any city of man so savage or perverse in
  speech

As not to be aware of the fame of the hero Peleus, the   25
  blessed son-in-law of Gods,

Nor of Aias and his father Telamon:

Whom, as fain battle-comrade, the son of Alkmana led away
  with his Tirynthian band in ships to brazen-shielded   30
  war against Troy—that toiling-ground for heroes—

In requital for the trespass of Laomedon.

And Herakles took Troy's citadel and with the help of
  Telamon slew the tribes of the Meropes,

And that giant-herdsman Alkuoneus, having found him
  in Phlegrai, in stature like a mountain,

Nor did his hands slacken in the loud twanging of his
  bow-string on that day.

But, when calling the son of Aiakos to fare with him to   35
  sea, he found him feasting with his people;

And as Amphitruon's son, the warrior of the mighty spear,
  stood there clad in the lion's hide,

The peerless Telamon bade him begin the libation-rite
  with the pouring out of fragrant wine,

And reached up to him a wine-receiving goblet roughened   40
  with gold:

He raising to heaven his unconquerable hands spake
  aloud such words as these—

'If ever thou, oh, Father Zeus, didst hearken to my prayers,
  fain in heart to grant them,

I pray thee with holy supplications—bring to ripe birth a   45
  valiant son, born to this man from Eriboia, fated one
  day to be my guest-friend:

Give him a body of such hardihood, even as the skin
  wherewith I am girt of that wild beast that I slew in
  Nemea, first of all my labours:

And let his spirit match his strength.'

50 Lo! to him thus speaking, God sent a great eagle, the
   king of birds.
Then sweet delight stung him to his inmost soul, and he
   spake out again prophet-wise:
'Verily, the son thou askest for shall be thine, oh, Telamon.
And after this bird that hath appeared call him by name
   "Aias", a man of far-prevailing might, inthepeoples'
   war-toils a wondrous man.'
55 Having thus spoken, thereupon he sat him down.
'Tis long for me to tell the full tale of their glorious deeds.
For I came hither, oh, Muse, to dispense triumph-songs
   to Phulakidas, Putheas, and Euthumenes.
With Argive brevity the story of them shall in some fashion
   be told even in scantiest speech:
60 For they bore off victories three from the pankration, one
   from Isthmos and those two from leafy Nemea,
The bright striplings and their mother's brother:
And how wondrous is their portion of poesy they have
   brought to birth!
Their own clan of the Psaluchidai they water with the
   sweetest dew-drops of the Graces;
65 And as the props of the house of Themistios they dwell in
   this God-belovèd city.
Lampon himself, 'bestowing pains on all he doeth',
   honoureth that saw of Hesiod full heedfully:
And by precept enjoineth it on his sons,
Thus bringing to his own city honour among men.
70 And for his kindly deeds to strangers he is well-belovèd,
Following in his heart the golden rule of moderation, and
   achieving it in act:
Nor doth his tongue stray from the thoughts of his heart.
And thou mightest say of him that for the men who train
   for contests he is as the Naxian whetstone—that
   subdueth iron—among the other stones.
I will pledge him and his kinsmen in a draught of Dirke's
75   holy water, that the deep-girdled daughters of golden-
   mantled Mnemosuné causèd to gush forth by the well-
   walled gates of Kadmos."

I have ventured once again to depart from the received order and to place the ode that usually appears as the sixth Isthmian prior to the so-called fifth, for it evidently preceded the latter in composition by some two or three years. Both may be read together with Nemean V., as forming a complex commemorating the exploits of the same family, the distinguished Aeginetan house of Themistios, whose eldest living representative was Lampon, the father of the two young athletes, Putheas and Phulakidas, and the brother-in-law of Euthumenes. All these three had won victories in the pankration, the severest and most dangerous of all the Greek contests, Euthumenes and Putheas (who is the hero of the fifth Nemean) at Nemea, Phulakidas the younger brother in the boys' contest at the Isthmian festival; and it is this victory which this ode commemorates. But by the time the so-called fifth Isthmian was composed Phulakidas had won two more such victories, one more in the Isthmian games, competing now among the men, and one at Nemea. Now it is clear from an allusion in it to the great naval battle of Salamis that the 'fifth' Isthmian was written not long after that event, perhaps in 479 B.C.: therefore the 'sixth' Isthmian must be dated at least three years earlier.

In all three odes, therefore, Pindar is dealing with the land that he loves for other reasons and because it supplies him with the great epic tradition on which he delights to expand himself, the glories of the Aiakidai; and it rarely happens that his poetry does not rise to the height of his theme.

The proem, with its vision of the gay banquet, has some measure of the lustre that Pindar loves to shed on the opening words of his odes. It bears a striking resemblance to the proem of the more famous poem, the seventh Olympian, when a similar thought is developed with more radiant imagery and phrase, while this has more of the solemnity proper to the ritual of libation. That the poet's effusion is as a cup of wine offered to the deity or to his patron is almost a commonplace of Pindar's imagination; but he turns it skilfully to varying effects. Here he works it out on the lines of the Greek banquet-ritual, where three cups were offered as libations, that is, a few drops were spilt from each before drinking, the first to Zeus Olympios, and the third to Zeus the Saviour. Pindar makes free with this ritual rule, and announces that, as he offered the first cup (that is, the fifth Nemean ode) to Zeus of Nemea and is now offering the second—the present ode—to Poseidon, Lord of the Isthmos, his hope is strong that the third will soon be consecrated to Zeus the Saviour, who is also Olympios as the God of the Olympian contest: and he means this as a prophecy that the young athlete will soon win the crowning glory of an Olympian victory. Such distinction, which can only be won by toil, outlay, and divine favour, is the high-water mark of earthly happiness, in Pindar's view; and he declares that Lampon also has these feelings. The sententious passages in this ode, though in clear and bright style, have not the nobility and profundity that mark his ethical poetry elsewhere; except for their pungency of phrase they have much of the sober tone of Hesiod, who has inspired the reflections at the end of the poem about the value of taking pains and the virtue of moderation.

He then passes to the most interesting and attractive theme of his ode, the eulogy of the mythic heroes combined with a mythic narrative. And he tells us frankly that, when-ever he comes to Aigina, he feels it to be a religious duty to glorify the Aiakidai: a statement which saves us from the temptation—to which some modern commentators have succumbed—to connect the Aeacid legend too closely with the individual athletes of the Aeginetan odes. The special myth that he then proceeds to give us, unfamiliar to the modern reader, is one of the most fascinating in the rich treasure-house of Greek mythology. It accords so well with the genial imagination of Pindar that we might have supposed that he invented it himself: only that we have clear testimony that he derived it from a poem of his old master, Hesiod. The motive of auspicious prophecy over a wonder-babe is familiar to us from other saga: it is always a useful motive for a poet, and Pindar had used it with great effect in the first Nemean in the prophecy over the heroic babe, Herakles. Here it is Herakles himself who utters the friendly prayer to his father Zeus and, reassured of its fulfilment by the mighty omen of the eagle, foretells the future greatness of the unborn child. We do not know whether Pindar borrowed from Hesiod the explanation of the name of 'Aias' as the 'Eagle-child' (from 'aietos'): a more plausible piece of 'folk-etymology' than the Sopho-clean explanation of it as "the child of sorrow". In the

actual prayer of Herakles there are two points that attract
attention. He prays that Telamon may have a son as tough
of fibre as his own lion's-skin: this idea is degraded by
later *littérateurs* of antiquity to a magical significance;
but Pindar, like Homer, keeps the high humanity of his
heroes aloof from magic. Again, he prays that the future
babe may grow up to be his own 'guest-friend'. Why should
Pindar make such a hero, the son of Zeus, pray for what was
never, and could not be, fulfilled? For naturally Herakles
and Aias could only be guest-friends if the former had
lived to an advanced age on earth, and the latter had come
back safe from Troy. Yet Pindar is not likely to have
written this carelessly and thoughtlessly in an impressive
prayer where there is no verbiage and every word is well
weighed. We may imagine that, in setting this strange
phrase into the prayer, he was moved by the desire
to give a mythical foundation to the friendship between
Thebes and Aigina. Herakles stands for Thebes, where his
spirit through cult and vivid folk-memory was still alive;
Telamon was his closest 'guest-friend', and he and his
family stand for Aigina. In praying that the unborn child
of Telamon might ever be his guest-friend, Herakles might
be understood to be praying that the friendship between
Thebes and Aigina, which had been proved by an alliance
towards the close of the sixth century, might continue for
ever; and at the time when this ode was composed Thebes
might well be regarded as needing the alliance of a powerful
state. For the same reason it may have been Pindar's cue
to dwell on the war-fellowship of Telamon with Herakles
here and elsewhere more than was profitable for mere
poetic-effect; thus both here and later, in the fourth
Nemean, he chronicles the legend, but leaves it colourless,
of the conquest of the Meropes, the aborigines of the island
Kos, by Herakles and Telamon; and in the third Nemean
he praises the help that the latter rendered to the great
hero against the Amazons, and both these exploits are set
in the same context with the capture of Troy; so also is
the slaying of the giant Alkuoneus, an adventure in which
Telamon plays his part and on which both in this ode and
in the fourth Nemean Pindar dwells more forcefully than
on the others. These various legends, then, having no
organic connection, are nevertheless welded together in
Pindar's memory; and it is natural to suppose that he found

them narrated together in some earlier epic poem on the deeds of Herakles. And this is confirmed by the fact that the early Attic vase-painters were familiar with them, at least with the stories of the Amazonian battle and the slaying of Alkuoneus; and in more than one representation of the former we see Telamon by the side of Herakles in the fray, and in one of the latter we can almost certainly recognise him.

Pindar, then, in glancing at these themes is dealing with living and popular mythology. But he reserves his full powers for his tale of the birth of Aias. The passage displays the high qualities of his best epic-lyric style with which we are familiar; and he presents us the scene in a vivid golden light—the hero in the lion's skin, standing before the feasters, holding the cup "bristling with gold", and raising his hands to the sky. It is this that raises the ode to one of the first order. And it closes more impressively than many others with a genial and inspiring greeting, pledged in the poetic water of Dirke.

ISTHMIAN VI (V)

To Phulakidas of Aigina

"Hail, Theia, mother of the Sun-God, thou Goddess of
    many a name,
'Tis through thy influence that men have ever deemèd gold
    a thing of power surpassing all other things:
Yea, for it is also through the boon wherewith thou blessest
    us that ships racing on the deep, and horses yoked to 5
    chariots in the swift-wheeling contests, become marvels
    to behold;
And in the athletes' strife he hath won the renown he
    yearnèd for,
Whose locks have been bound by garland upon garland
    of victory gained by strong hand or swiftness of feet. 10
The divine powers rule the judging of the prowess of men.
Two things there are alone that cherish with the full
    bloom of happiness the much longed-for flower of
    life,
To wit, fair fortune and a goodly report thereto.
Strive not to become as God: thou hast the fulness of life, 15
    if the lot of these noble gains falleth upon thee.
A mortal estate sorteth with our mortality.
For thee, Phulakidas, Isthmos guardeth the harvest of a
    double glory,
And at Nemea there is one for both brothers, thee and
    Putheas, gained from the pankration.
My soul is assaying melodies not unlinkèd with the 20
    Aiakidai;
And in company with the Graces have I come at the
    bidding of the sons of Lampon to this city of fair law.

But if it hath turned its face to fare along a fair and open
    high-road of deeds done by God's grace,
25 Then, Pindar, as fitting requital for their labours mingle
    in the cup of song proud words of praise ungrudgingly.
For also the goodly warriors among the heroes of old won
    for their meed the tongue of fame.
And through age upon age they are glorified on the lyre's
    strings and in the manifold voices of flutes.
Through God's benison these have thrown down a theme
    to the craftsmen of song—
30 The mighty sons of Oineus[1] are honoured in the bright
    ritual of the Aetolians;
And in Thebes Iolaos, lord of horses, hath worship, Perseus
    in Argos, the spear of Kastor and Poludeukes on the
    banks of the Eurotas:
But in the isle Oinone the great-hearted souls of Aiakos
    and his sons:
35 Even twice they ravagèd the city of Troy, helping their
    comrades of the war,
First following Herakles,
And after in the fellowship of the sons of Atreus. Oh,
    Muse, mount with me to the skies, spurning the earth!
Tell the tale, who were they who slew Kuknos, who
    Hektor,
40 Who the dauntless army-leader of the Aethiopians, the
    bronze-clad Memnon?
Who wounded good Telephos with his spear on the banks
    of the Kaïkos?
Those heroes to whom all men's lips assign Aigina as
    their fatherland, the island that shineth from afar.
45 Verily, long (in this land) hath a tower of fame been reared,
    only to be scalèd by high-soaring virtues.
My tongue hath many a shaft of song, to proclaim aloud
    their fame.
And now in these days, in the lists of the God of battles,
Aias' city of Salamis can bear witness that it was saved
    from sinking by the sailors [of Aigina],

---

[1] These are the heroes Meleagros and Tudeus.

In the deadly storm of God, in the hail of blood that 50
   whelmèd unnumbered hosts of men.
Nathless, quench vaunting in the soft rain of silence!
Zeus dispenseth now this now that, Zeus the Lord of all.
But also these honours (in the games) welcome the song
   of victory in honey-sweetened verse.
Let one learn the record of the house of Kleonikos, and 55
   then strive his manliest in the contests.
The long toil of the men was not blindly followed:
Nor did counting the cost fret away the pious faith of hope.
And I praise Putheas among champions (of the ring) as 60
   one most skilful of hand, to guide Phulakidas in a
   sure course for the right passage of his blows and as
   having the brain that matcheth hand.
Take with you a crown for him and bear him a garland
   woven with fair wool,
And therewith bring to his house this winged new-fledged
   hymn.''

In this ode, which may be assigned with some probability
to 479 B.C., there are many notable passages, but nothing
so notable as the proem with its invocation of the Goddess
Theia. Who was Theia, and what was her power and
function that Pindar should burst forth with this fervent
ecstasy over her? We know nothing about her—neither did
Pindar—except what Hesiod chose to say of her: and we
are practically sure that she was never worshipped, either
by Hesiod or Pindar or anyone else, and had no reality
in the Greek Pantheon. Later writers of the Greek decad-
ence tried hard to find a place for her, but only to justify
Pindar; and nothing of any value or help has been said
about her by them or by any modern commentator or
scholar except by Wilamowitz in his *Pindaros*:[1] and among
the commentators he appears to be the only one hitherto
who has understood aright the phrases expressing the
varied manifestations of her power: namely, Pindar intends
to say that the working of her influence is felt in certain things between which there is no real connection; for

[1] Pp. 201-202.

instance, in the magic lure of gold, and again in the strange fascination of a trireme-race or a chariot-race. There is something here to surprise the ordinary reader and the ordinary classical scholar. In the first place, Pindar's imagination is kindled by his feeling for gold, as something supernatural in its beauty and attraction, as something that shines in the dark and may lure men to their doom; such a character it possesses in some northern folklore and saga. Then he proceeds to mention trireme-races—the words properly admit of no other interpretation—and chariot-races as owing their fascination to her power. We are familiar with the fact that in all the great games the chariot-race was the contest *par excellence*, that the Greeks of the best period were utterly thrilled by it, though not to the same pitch of madness as the later Byzantines; and though we no longer race in chariots, we can imagine the splendour of the course, some forty teams of blood-horses flashing in the sun and straining towards the goal, and the glow of excitement on the faces of the charioteers such as appears on the face of the charioteer of the Mausoleum frieze. But few readers would expect to find trireme-racing mentioned in such a context; for few scholars were aware that the ancients had boat-races at all. But inscriptions prove that they were instituted at least at Athens. And we could understand this passage of Pindar best if we suppose—and the supposition is not at all hazardous—that the Greeks celebrated the victory of Salamis by trireme-races; for as a Greek army was wont to celebrate a victory by athletic sports, this form of contest would be the most natural where the rowing galleys of so many states were gathered together and rejoicing. Pindar could have been there, and for the first and last time in his life seen the glory of a great contest with oars. We are familiar with the thrill and beauty of the spectacle of a perfected racing-eight, such as may be seen at Henley. Wilamowitz himself saw it once in the May-races at Cambridge; and there he thought of Pindar and Theia, and had the same intuition. For the meagre lines of the racing-eight we substitute the long lines of the trireme with a hundred oars, and we can imagine the lift and the drive and the flash of the oars over the churned-up foam, as "like one strong chord of music their blades together sing", across the sparkling Aegean waters. We must suppose, then, that Pindar was at that moment inspired with an intuitive sense of a divine potency manifesting itself in all forms of light and brightness, in the glitter of gold, in the glory of the racing horse and the splendour of the racing ship. He could not find any of his anthropomorphic Gods and Goddesses that could satisfactorily embody this: his favourite 'Charites' might suffice for the glamour of the contests, but not for the magic of gold. He has recourse, then, to a vague name that he culls from Hesiod, who invented 'Theia' as the fictitious mother of the sun and luminaries of heaven. As her name means the "divine one" and she had no definite personality, she seemed to Pindar a useful term to express the vague intuition that was strong in him of a mysterious demoniac force, flowing out in the brightness and radiance of things.

Such an interpretation of the passage raises it to a striking utterance both of poetry and religion; and it reveals to us more than any other passage in the epinician odes that Pindar's enthusiasm for certain forms of athletic contests was not simulated or forced or bought, but genuine and deep, welling up from a mood that quickened poetry.

He then gives us in beautiful phrase his simple philosophy of life, the same that he afterwards gives in the first Pythian to Hieron: the flower of life is in prosperity conjoined with a good report: and he warns us here as elsewhere against "immortal longings".

But he cannot sing the praises of the sons of Lampon, Phulakidas and Putheas, without singing of the Aiakidai. As other lands have their local heroes, whose memories are preserved in local cult, so Aigina cherishes the memories of the sons of Aiakos. He then recounts with fervour and swiftness their exploits against Troy, specially the exploits of Achilles, his deeds of prowess recorded by Homer and the later epic poets. He had, indeed, more justification than usual for dwelling on them on this occasion, for Salamis, the city of Aias, was at this moment in every Greek's mind, and the Aiakidai, as Herodotus tells us, had rendered divine help at the great battle there to the Hellenic cause. He then allows himself a short and fiery outburst of exultation over that great event, which enhanced the glory of Aigina.

But suddenly he lowers his tone and utters a solemn warning against boasting; for we are all in the hands of

God, and He dispenses us fortune as He will. The passage is of striking solemnity. But it loses value if we date this poem and the Isthmia where the victory was won as late as 478 B.C., after the Persian terror had wholly departed and the Hellenic triumph was well won. If ever they had a right to boast a little, it was then, and the religious Aeschylus does so unrestrainedly. But the Theban only had no occasion to boast, for his state had played a vile part. Therefore, the moral warning of a Theban poet against boasting would lack dignity and authority.

It is otherwise if we may place the Isthmian and this congratulatory ode early in the summer of 479 B.C., after Salamis had been won, but before the equally momentous battle of Plataea had been fought. Such a time well accords with the solemn reticence of this passage: Salamis fight was indeed a great and terrible achievement, and blood was poured out there like hail: the Persian, however, is still a great power in the land, and who knows whether Greece is to remain free and Hellenic or to become a Persian province? Later, when the full victory was won, Pindar shows no reticence, and praises the Spartans for the victory at Plataea, the Athenians for the victory of Salamis, as he praises the dynasts of Syracuse for their triumph over the barbarian in the west.

If this theory is correct, the poem gains the further interest of being the only great literary work that has come down to us from that fateful period of suspense between the victory by sea and the victory by land.

For we may regard it as a great work in spite of a few defects, a certain obscurity in style here and there owing to an over-compressed syntax, and a slackening of inspiration towards the close. But it is memorable for the ecstatic enthusiasm that pervades the prelude and throbs in the golden diction of many passages: and the tense, rapt feeling is preserved in the swift review of the glories of the Aiakidai. We may feel too that the phrases about Salamis and the Tower of Fame reared in Aigina are masterpieces of the "grand style". The unity on the whole is well preserved, myth, religion, and moralising being easily blent with the athletic theme.

ISTHMIAN VII

To Strepsiadas of Thebes

"OH, Thebes of blessèd name!
What one of the many fair things in the past story of thy
    land gave most joy to thy soul?
Was it when thou broughtest Dionysos to the birth, the
    God of the tossing locks, the sharer of Demeter's
    throne for whom the cymbals ring?
Or was it the begetting of Herakles, when thou didst
    welcome the supreme God, descending at midnight 5
    in a golden snow-fall, at the hour when he stood in
    Amphitruon's portals and approachèd his wife?
Or didst thou most rejoice over the wise counsels of
    Teiresias,
Or over the skilled horseman Iolaos,
Or over thy progeny of the dragon's teeth, the warriors of 10
    tireless spear?
Or when thou didst send back Adrastos to the horse-
    feeding land of Argos, fleeing from thy mighty war-
    shout and bereft of unnumbered comrades?
Or because thou didst stablish in safety on its feet the
    Dorian colony of the men of Lakedaimon,
And thy offspring, the Aigeidai, captured Amuklai (for 15
    them) according to the oracle of the Pythian shrine?
Nay, but gratitude for ancient service slumbereth;
And men bear nought in memory, save that which, blent
    with the resounding tides of heroic verse, winneth to
    the perfect bloom of songcraft.
Therefore, now even for Strepsiadas join in the triumph- 20
    dance with the hymn's sweet melody!

275

For in the pankration at Isthmos he beareth away the
  victory:
And wondrous is he in strength and shapely to look upon;
And he beareth a soul of virtue that shameth not his form.
A light is shed on him by the Muses, weavers of violet-
  crowns,
Whereof he hath given a joint share in his garland to his
  mother's brother of his own name,
25 For whom the bronze-shielded War-God mingled the cup
  of doom:
But the prize of honour is set before brave men.
Let him know full well, whosoever in this cloud of war
  shieldeth his dear country against the bitter storm of
  blood,
Hurling back (?) death on the foemen's host,
That he increaseth fame in fullest measure for his genera-
30 tion of fellow-citizens, while living and when dead.
Thou, oh son of Diodotos, thou emulous of the warrior
  Meleagros, Hektor, and Amphiaraos,
Didst breathe forth thy youthful life in its rich-blossoming
  prime,
In the press of the foremost champions, where the bravest
35 bore the brunt of war's debate with forlorn hopes.
And I endurèd sorrow unutterable.
But now the God that girdeth the earth hath vouchsafèd
  me fair weather after storm.
I will bind my locks in crowns and sing.
40 Only, may the jealous eye of Heaven cast no shadow on the
  delight of the hour that day by day I chase, as I fare
  on tranquilly to old-age and the destined span of life:
For death cometh to all alike; but our life's portion is
  unequal.
And if a man casteth yearning glances on the things too far
  from his sphere, he is not of stature to win to the
  bronze-pavèd habitation of the Gods;
45 Since wingèd Pegasos flung his lord Bellerophon when
  fain to rise to the stalls of heaven to join the fellowship
  of Zeus.

A very grievous end awaiteth pleasure won unrighteously.
Thou God that bloometh with the golden locks, Apollo
    Loxias, grant us in thy contests at Putho a fair- 50
    flowering crown."

In the seventh Isthmian, one of the three odes in the
whole 'epinician' group dedicated to a Theban, Pindar
strikes a deep chord of personal and patriotic feeling. It is
in honour of the Theban Strepsiadas who had conquered
in the 'pankration': but it only devotes three lines to him
containing a short eulogy on his strength, beauty, and
virtue, and it concludes with a prayer that Apollo may
grant Thebes a victory in the coming Pythian festival, probably an allusion to Strepsiadas' intention of competing
there. Otherwise, the poem is preoccupied with the past
glories of Thebes and its present sorrows—in which the
house of Strepsiadas has part—and with the poet's present
philosophy of life.

To understand the underlying motives of the ode it is
necessary to know the condition of public affairs at Thebes.
In 458–457 B.C. the Athenians had been defeated at Tanagra on the Attic-Boeotian border by the combined forces
of Spartans and Boeotians in a bloody battle. The Spartans
thereupon returned home, and two months later the
Athenians marched again into Boeotia and defeated the
Boeotian force in a decisive battle at Oinophuta, a victory
which deprived Thebes of her predominance in Boeotia and
established an Athenian ascendancy. As the more intelligent
commentators have perceived, this ode must have been
composed not long after that disastrous Boeotian defeat,
which would well explain the striking battle-passage that
it contains, as well as the spirit of sorrow and resignation
that breathes in parts of it.

The prelude is unlike any other in the epinician odes of
Pindar. It is an outburst of pride over the great traditions
of Thebes, showing how deeply Pindar's soul was possessed
by the mythology of his mother-city, which for him is very
real. It reminds us vividly of a passage in the great hymn
that he had composed for the Thebans in his younger days,
of which a fragment has come down to us.[1] The form of
composition shaping this prelude is peculiar: it consists of

a series of rhetorical questions carried on at the risk of monotony. Rhetorical question and answer can have a strong poetic effect, as we feel often in the Book of Job and certain parts of the Apocrypha; but here for some twenty lines it is all question and no answer; they are, however, marked by many forcible and arresting phrases.

In this survey of her past glories he naturally omits mention of the house of Laios; for its tradition was not one of the things in which Thebes could "rejoice her soul": she might rejoice indeed in her repulse of the "Seven against Thebes", and that exploit is graphically celebrated here with lyrical brevity. But the two great myths on which she could most pride herself, and to which no other community ever seriously made a rival claim, were those concerning the birth of the God Dionysos and the hero Herakles. The faith that Thebes was the 'metropolis' of Dionysos was probably founded on the fact that this city was the first of any importance to adopt and then to propagate this immigrant cult: and the faith was probably fortified by a yearly ritual enacting the divine birth. In a few strong touches Pindar presents us the Theban God—as the early Attic vase-painters present him—mystically sharing in the Maenads' ecstatic dance with his hair "wildly flowing", and also as a partner in the mysteries of Demeter—an idea that he probably derives from the Attic Eleusinian mysteries, with which he was acquainted.

In his brief description of the birth of Herakles he makes a daring innovation, as the ancient commentators remarked. When Zeus entered Thebes for the purpose of begetting the hero, he heralded his approach by sending a snow-shower of gold: this had never appeared in previous literature and was never repeated in the later. Pindar freely adds new traits to old myths for the purpose of embellishment or to point a moral. He is here vaguely reminiscent of the shower of gold in the love-story of Zeus and Danaë, and of his own legend that Zeus celebrated the birth of Athena in Rhodes with a golden snow-shower.[2] This beautiful miracle may have been ultimately derived from some song concerning the Holy Marriage of Heaven and Earth in spring, when to the imaginative eye the showers, whether of snow or rain, may seem suffused with the light of gold.

---

[1] *Vide infra*, p. 293.　　　　　[2] *Vide Olymp.* vii. l. 34.

He then mentions, without dwelling on them, the personalities of the prophet Teiresias and the warrior Iolaos
as part of the proud tradition of Thebes. He next alludes
to the legend of the birth of the warriors from the dragon's
teeth, a legend of which to our regret he never gave a full
account, though only his lyric could have done it full justice.
And he alludes to it here merely because from them sprang
the four leading families of Thebes, possibly his own clan
the Aigeidai. Their name closes his catalogue of national
honours and serves him for a double purpose; it gratifies
his clan feeling and it gives him the opportunity of a skilful
transition to the present time. He dwells with pride on the
story of their exploit in aid of the Dorian conquest of the
Peloponnese, a story which may have had a historical
foundation. The Dorians found the conquest of Laconia
by no means easy, and the old stronghold of the Achaean
power, Amuklai, long resisted them, until they were advised
by their divine helper, the Pythian oracle, to apply for aid
"to the sons of Aigeus"; they found them at Thebes, and the
Aigeidai captured Amuklai for them. Then Pindar's verse
becomes pathetic in the noble style: gratitude for ancient
service has fallen asleep, that is to say, Sparta has abandoned us and exposed us unaided to the might of Athens.
But tactfully he only allows this thought to be half-uttered
beneath words of general import. Then follows a very brief
eulogy of the athlete, which immediately leads him on to
a theme that is nearer to his heart, namely, a panegyric on
the athlete's uncle of the same name, one perhaps of a
company like the famous "Sacred Band" of Thebes, who
fought a forlorn hope and died on the battle-field. The
whole passage describing him is strong and tingling with
battle-poetry and instinct with the war-morality of the city-
state: it appeals to us even in these changed times.

But in this encomium a phrase occurs that has puzzled
most readers and commentators. Pindar says that the elder
Strepsiadas died "praising Meleagros, Hektor, and Amphiaraos", which is only another way of saying that he took
them as his ideal, as warriors whose example he was to
imitate. Now, the first two names cause us no difficulty:
Meleagros, according to a version of his story that is perhaps the older, died in battle for his country valiantly and
victoriously, and not from the wasting of the firebrand—
the story that Swinburne follows: Hektor also died valiantly

for his country, though in a losing cause: both these were excellent examples for the athlete's uncle, and he may be compared with these. But as for Amphiaraos, his end was certainly marvellous, but not such as to inspire a patriot to fight to the last. For Pindar himself has told us in the ninth Nemean how he ended: having come with the Seven Champions to attack Thebes against his better judgment, he fled from the carnage of the field, and would have been pierced in the back by the spear of his pursuer, had not Zeus, to save him from this disgrace, opened the earth so as to swallow up him and his horses: he went down "quick into the pit" and never died at all, but remained a living underground hero in Boeotian soil, having a shrine near Thebes and a better known one near Oropos, both too far from the battle-fields of Tanagra and Oinophuta to have any connection with them or their story. The incongruity has been felt to be so strong that some commentators have been tempted to make a rash and impossible emendation of the text. There is no need, if we do not look at it too narrowly. In mentioning mythic warriors upon whom the elder Strepsiadas tried to model himself, Pindar was not bound to confine himself to those who had died in battle. In spite of his flight from the battle-field, the earlier epic poet and Pindar and Aeschylus had combined to present Amphiaraos as an ideal figure, the one righteous warrior in an unrighteous host, "the eye of the army", "good prophet and good spearman", the man "who determined to be good in very truth, not in mere seeming", a sort of mythical Aristeides. And Pindar apologises for his running away by inventing the naïve and audacious aphorism—"in supernatural terrors even the sons of the Gods will flee".[1] He had in fact become endeared to the Thebans, his spirit now being part of the Theban land. Pindar, therefore, can mention him in this context, especially as he is never too precisely logical in his mythologic parallels.

After expressing in pathetic lines the public sorrow felt for the bravest Thebans who fell in the forlorn hope, he speaks of the ray of light that has shone upon them from "the Isthmos", which justifies him in setting once more a crown on his head. But he turns his thoughts at once to his own approaching old age and the end of life; and there was much to justify the melancholy that marks the closing

[1] *Nem.* ix. 28.

portion of this ode; for not only was his own city humbled
and depressed, but the city that he loved next after her,
Aigina, had fallen before the power of Athens; and he felt
the shadow of old age gathering over him.

He will follow, therefore, the rule of a wise resignation,
not untempered with sweetness. And he prays that the
divine powers may not grudge it him, if he culls the joy
that the passing days may bring him as he "fares calmly
on to his end". This is higher than the mood of one who
says "let us eat and drink, for to-morrow we die"; for
Pindar's 'joy' included things of the spirit. But he does not
here feel inspired to preach any far-reaching vision of hope
that might lift us above our visible life. The story of
Bellerophon's punishment for attempting to scale Heaven
on Pegasos is a warning against "immortal longings" or
'other-worldly' ambitions.

Pindar appears to have been the first so to moralise the
story of Bellerophon's fall. It is likely that he hoped it
might also convey a foreboding of the possible fall of
Athens, whose projects might well appear to him as soaring
to superhuman heights; and we can hardly help detecting
an allusion to her in the aphorism that follows concerning
the bitter end that awaits unrighteous gains.

After this his force sinks slightly, and he ventures to pray
for nothing greater for his country than a victory in the
approaching Pythian games.

The poem belongs to Pindar's declining years, but it
shows no decline in power, warmth, and vitality, and it is
marked by his essential qualities. As was natural in the
circumstances of the time, it lacks the radiance and exultation that brighten most of his odes; its prevailing
emotion is pathos, tempered and heightened with nobility
of feeling.

ISTHMIAN VIII

To Kleandros of Aigina

"In honour of Kleandros and his youthful prowess,
Go, ye young men—one of you—to the fair fore-court of
his father Telesarchos' house,
And waken the revel-song, noble atonement for his toils,
And as requital for his Isthmian victory,
5 And for that he found out the way to triumph in contests
at Nemea.
Wherefore, I too, albeit sorrowing in my heart, am called
on to invoke the aid of the golden Muse.
But, being deliverèd at last from heavy woes,
Let us not be found in dearth of garlands,
Nor do thou (Pindar!) brood on thy private sorrows;
But turning our hearts away from inevitable evils,
We will bring forth before the people some sweet new
thing, albeit after storm and stress.
10 For now the stone as it were of Tantalos, poised above
our heads, a burden more than Hellas could brook,
Some God hath turned aside for us.
But the passing away of terror hath for me quelled heavy
tribulation:
And it is ever more gainful to fix one's mind on the matter
that lies nearest to one's hand.
For full of treachery is our span of days impending,
15 Making crooked the pathway of life.
But with Freedom for one's fellow, even for those troubles
there is healing.
'Tis meet for a man to take good hope to his heart:
And 'tis meet for a foster-son of seven-gated Thebes

To offer to Aigina first and foremost the garland of song
    woven by the Graces:
For that the twin-daughters,[1] the youngest-born of the
    sire Asopos, were pleasing to Zeus the King:
Who gave to one of them a home by the fair-flowing
    waters of Dirke, as chieftainess of the city that loveth 20
    the chariot;
But thee, Aigina, he bore to the isle Oinopia[2] and lay with
    thee there:
Where thou broughtest forth Aiakos, the god-like,
Of all men on the earth most near and dear to the Father,
    Lord of the deep-voiced thunder:
When the divine powers were at issue, it was even he who
    settled their matters of strife.
And his sons no worse than Gods, and the children of his 25
    sons beloved by Ares, were matchless in valour, to
    rule the roaring tumult of bronze-clad battle.
Temperate also and wise of soul they were.
These things were in the minds of the Blessèd Ones hold-
    ing council,
When Zeus and bright Poseidon were at issue concerning
    Thetis' marriage,
Either being fain that she should be his fair spouse, for
    desire of her possessèd them.
But the eternal wisdom of the Gods stayed them from
    accomplishing the union of the marriage-bed;   30
For they hearkened to the voice of Fate.
Themis, the Goddess of goodly counsel, spake in their
    midst how that it was destined
That Thetis the Sea-Goddess should give birth to a lordly
    son excelling his sire,
Who would wield in his hand another weapon mightier 35
    than the thunderbolt or the resistless trident,
If she mingled with Zeus or with the brethren of Zeus.
'But do ye put from you these desires,
And let her find her fortune in a mortal's couch,

---

[1] The nymphs Thebe and Aigina.
[2] Oinopia, like Oinone, was the old name of Aigina.

And behold her son fallen in battle,
One like to the War-God in might of hand and like to the
    lightning-flashes in speed of feet.
My counsel is that ye grant to Peleus, son of Aiakos, this
    marriage-boon of Heaven's awarding,
Whom report gives out for the holiest man of all nurtured
40   in Iolchos' plain.
Let tidings forthwith speed to the immortal cave of Cheiron,
And let not Nereus' daughter once more set in our hands
    sprays from the tree of strife.
But it were well if, at eventide of the full moon, in that
45   hero's embrace she loosenèd the lovely girdle that
    bridleth her maidenhood.'
So spake the Goddess in converse with the sons of Kronos:
And they moved their immortal brows in sign of assent:
And her words bore fruit that perished not.
For the King of Gods took counsel for the common weal
    as well as for Thetis' marriage.
And the lips of the wise revealèd to those who knew
    nought of it, the valour of the boy Achilles.
50 It was he who besprinkled the vine-clad Mysian plain
    with the dark blood of Telephos:
Who builded a bridge for the safe return of the Atreidai,
    and deliverèd Helen,
Having severed with his spear the sinews of Troy,
(The men) who at one time tried to hold him back,
When he was raising on the plain the crest of murderous
    battle,
55 Mighty Memnon of the great heart, Hektor, and other
    champions:
To all of whom Achilles, the warder of the house of Aiakos,
Shewèd the path to the dwelling of the Queen of the dead,
And shed lustre on Aigina and his own stock.
Even in death he was not left forlorn of song,
But the maids of Helikon came and stood around his
    pyre and grave-mound,
And poured forth a dirge in choir of many voices.
60 Forsooth the immortals deemèd it fitting to give to the

hymns of Goddesses so goodly a man for theme even
  when dead.
This beareth reason with it even now, and the car of the
  Muses fareth swiftly on to raise the hymn of praise
  in memory of the boxer Nikokles.
Oh, render due honour to him, to whom Fate gave the
  Dorian parsley-crown in the holy dell of Isthmos!
For that he also in this latter day conquered all the men
  of the countryside with the battering of his fatal hands. 65
Verily he suffereth no dishonour from the offspring of his
  father's noble brother:
Wherefore let one of his young comrades weave for
  Kleandros a sweet garland of myrtle for his prowess
  in the pankration.
For he had prosperous welcome from the contest of Alka-
  thoos, and earlier still from the youthful combatants at
  Epidauros.
'Tis meet and seasonable for a good man to praise him,
For he hath not quelled his youthful fire under a bushel, 70
  making no trial of noble things."

    The last in the collection of the epinician odes is one
of the many commemorating an Aeginetan victory, being
dedicated to a certain Kleandros who had conquered in the
pankration both at Isthmos and Nemea, and whose cousin
Nikokles, now dead, is mentioned at the end of the ode
as a distinguished boxer of his day. There is very little more
that is told us about the athlete and his family; and this
poem, like the last, lacks the brightness and festive enthusiasm usually found in Pindar's agonistic odes. But it
is deep-toned and of deep interest through its religious-
mythic content; also it contains an expression of personal
feeling which gives it a unique place in Greek poetry; for
it is composed just after the final triumph of Greece over
Persia, probably in 478 B.C. The poetry of Aeschylus and
Simonides reflect the joy and pride of free Greece in the
overthrow of the invader. A Theban writing at this time
could neither be joyful nor proud. Thebes had betrayed
Greece; she had been put to shame and received condign

punishment from the Greek army after the flight of the
Persian: several of her leading men had been put to death,
and the whole community might have feared the loss of
their autonomy.

This, surely, rather than the danger from Persia, is the
"stone of Tantalos" that had been impending over every
Theban's head; and it is for this that Pindar is still suffering
"anguish of heart", while the future is still dark with danger
for Thebes. Yet he encourages himself to hope as a brave
man should and not to brood over his private sorrows; he
declares they can remedy future evils, if only their city
remains free. We misunderstand the greater part of this
moving prologue if we think—as the ancient and many
of the modern commentators have thought—that it refers
mainly and chiefly to the Hellenic triumph over Persia.
Doubtless some of the language in it was intended with a
double reference, so as to appeal to Aigina as to Thebes;
but mainly it is too lugubrious to apply to any other than
the shame-faced and half-ruined Thebes, who was left
without friends in the Hellenic world.

Therefore at this juncture it was politic in Pindar, as
well as congenial to him through long intercourse and
natural sentiment, to strengthen the friendship between his
city and the powerful island-state by dwelling on their
ancient mythic relationship through the daughters of
Asopos, the heroines who gave their names to the two communities. These 'eponymous' fictions, that seem to us at
first sight the flimsiest in the fabric of Greek mythology,
were, as we have already seen, real and important for the
ordinary Greek mind; and the kinship of the nymphs Thebe
and Aigina had been appealed to for political purposes
already in the sixth century. Pindar is therefore quite in
earnest and sure of a sympathetic audience on both sides
in dwelling on it.

He escapes eagerly from the harshness of the real world
into the realm of myth. He begins with the legend—a well-
known folk-story—of the loves of Zeus and Aigina, which
he narrates with more warmth and colour in the later
eighth Nemean. Here it is touched on merely for the sake
of their offspring Aiakos, who receives a glowing panegyric
that resembles closely the eulogy on him in the Nemean
ode. But Aiakos in this lyric drama speedily gives place to
his illustrious descendants, Peleus and Achilles; and the

main inspiration of the ode is in the theologic setting of
the marriage of Peleus and Thetis and in the narrative of
the life and death of Achilles.

This version of the marriage—which should be compared
with the relevant passages in the fifth Nemean, an earlier
work, and the fourth Nemean, a later—belongs not to folklore but to what may be called epic theology; it is altogether
in the "grand style", and is a striking example of Pindar's
mythopoeic genius. The dignity of the High Gods is carefully maintained. The rivalry of Zeus and Poseidon for the
marriage of Thetis is silenced by the momentous com-
munication of Themis, whose rôle as counsellor of the Gods
was derived by Pindar from Homer. Both her personality
and her speech are presented here with great impressiveness
and solemnity; and Pindar may have been more devoted
to her and may have brooded more deeply on her nature
than other poets, as she was associated with the Delphic
oracle and he was specially the poet of Delphi. She speaks
saving words in golden diction. Only, towards the end of
the speech we are offended by the phrase "let not the
daughter of Nereus again put into our hands the leaves
of strife". The question of the explanation must be reserved
for the commentary, but to explain is not always to justify;
and as the physician Galen, who was a cultivated literary
man, complained of Pindar's affectation when he called
fountains and streams "the leaves of Ocean", he might have
commented with more severity on "the leaves of strife": it
would have certainly aroused Aristophanes, if he had heard
it: the metaphor probably arose, though more artificially,
on the same line of imagination as Pindar's "flowers of
law-abidingness";[1] in any case the explanation that the
ancient commentators supply us with, though it has been
tamely accepted by the moderns, is impossible. Nevertheless, the harangue of Themis is a masterpiece; and
when it is finished, Pindar clinches it by adapting one
of Homer's greatest phrases, expressing divine assent.

The question of greatest interest is—when and how did
this remarkable story arise, which has no clear parallel in
any other mythology or religion? It is no light or licentious
tale of the amours of the Gods. Folklore has nothing to say
in it. It is an earnest, far-looking narrative dealing with
events that deeply concern the world of Gods and men. The

[1] *Paean* i. 11.

two High Gods are rivals for the hand of the Sea-Goddess: a mysterious destiny has ruled that her offspring shall be stronger than the father: therefore, lest the Olympian dynasty should be overthrown, the Gods in council at the advice of Themis decide that Thetis shall marry a mortal, the most virtuous of men, Peleus. As he relieved them of the peril, it was natural that the Olympians should grace his wedding with their presence and bring noble gifts: and that his son Achilles, who fulfils the prophecy, should be their special favourite. Now one would naturally suppose that Homer was aware of this essential motive underlying the saga, for it would explain certain points in the framework of the *Iliad*, the remarkable influence of Thetis and the privileged position of Achilles: but there are stronger reasons for believing that he was ignorant of it.

Nor is there any trace in Hesiod, or any later epic poet known to us by tradition, of this momentous prophecy ruling the marriage of Thetis; and this poem of Pindar's is in fact our earliest authority for it. It is usually said that Pindar borrowed it from some unknown epic source; the same from which Aeschylus may have derived it for his Prometheus tragedy. This view may have been suggested by the difficulty of supposing that the Athenian poet had borrowed this leading motive from Pindar's poem. But we have convincing evidence that Aeschylus was familiar with the eighth Isthmian, for one passage in the *Prometheus Vinctus* was clearly drawn from it. Therefore Aeschylus had either heard or read the Pindaric poem and may have taken over from it what he chose. And Pindar is more likely than anyone to have been the father of such a myth: for we have seen from other examples that he was a bold and original myth-maker, and he seems to have specially delighted in expanding the legend of Peleus;[1] and it is well if we can put this one to his credit, for it is one pregnant of poetry and a great contribution to higher mythology. He may have constructed the story in its final form in his mind after he had composed the fifth Nemean, in which Poseidon does not appear as himself the wooer of Thetis, but as her brother-in-law who consents to her marriage.

In this Isthmian poem he omits description of the fateful marriage which he has brilliantly dealt with elsewhere; and he passes swiftly to the beginning of the heroic career of

---

[1] *Vide infra*, pp. 346, 350.

Achilles. The opening words have caused difficulty: but they become fairly clear if we see in them an allusion to the story that Thetis concealed the boy Achilles among the maidens of Skuros in order to keep him back from fame and death; but that he was revealed to the leaders of the Greek armament by the prophecy that Troy could not be taken without him, and he was discovered by a ruse. In the rapid lyrical narrative of his heroic career, Pindar draws as usual from the Homeric and the post-Homeric epic. He was evidently familiar with the story of Telephos, the adventure which first displayed the prowess of Achilles and Patroklos; and as he is the only writer of antiquity who calls Mysia 'vine-clad', we may suppose he had in mind the story that Telephos was wounded while stumbling over a vine-stock. His narrative of the events that follow reveals his art, being as usual rapid and untrammelled: he has no care for chronological sequence; he gives us at once the sum of the facts and then two striking illustrative details. Some of the diction here arrests us by its strangeness and power. "He cut out the sinews of Troy" by slaying her champions; even so Shakespeare's Talbot calls his soldiers his "strength and sinews". And there is a thrilling irony in the phrase which sums up Achilles' long career of homicide—"to whom he showed the way to the halls of Persephone".

The chronicle of the hero does not end with his death; for he was as marvellous in death as in life, and the Immortals grant him as a boon, which for Pindar is the highest pitch of felicity, that the Goddesses of Helikon sing around his pyre. The poet's imagination has been captured by the great passage in the last book of the *Odyssey*—the book condemned by "higher criticism"—telling how Thetis and the Nereids came wailing from the sea and joining with the Muses stood round the pyre and bewailed the godlike man, "singing in turn with sweet voices". Pindar can moralise a little on this: what the Goddesses did in time past they may do again for a brave man in the present; and this brings him back to the athlete and his predeceased cousin.

As is not unusual, the close of the ode is somewhat *piano* in tone, but not so as to injure the effect of the inspired work. It is unfortunate that the last line in Pindar's artificially arranged works should contain an obscure and doubtful phrase.

In spite of certain flaws we must rank the poem among

the highest, both for the glimpse that it gives us into Pindar's soul and for its striking and imaginative contribution to Greek mythology.

To this poem is appended in one of the MSS. a fragment, of which a translation is here given. It cannot have been composed to form part of the eighth Isthmian, but commemorates some Aeginetan victor, probably in the Isthmian games.

FRAGMENT I (4)

"Renownèd is the story of Aiakos; and Aigina, glorious for
   her war-ships, is a land of renown.
The Dorian host of Hullos and Aigimios came and estab-
   lished it under God's providence.
Under their rule of life they dwell, never transgressing
   Justice or violating the stranger's right.
For their prowess on the sea they are very dolphins,
And skilled stewards of the Muses' arts and of the contests
   where athletes strive."

The fragment is only of value as enhancing our sense of his enthusiasm for Aigina and of his love of Dorian institutions, about which he speaks here much as he had spoken in the first Pythian.

FRAGMENTS OF LOST WORKS[1]

[1] In this volume I have only dealt with those fragments of which enough is with certainty preserved to present some clear sequence of thought and literary impression. The numbering refers to Schroeder's edition, 1914.

FRAGMENT OF HYMN TO THEBES

(29, 30)

"OF whom shall we sing—
Of Ismenos or Melia, nymph of the golden spindle,
Of Kadmos or of the hallowed race of men sprung from
the dragon's teeth,
Or Thebe, Goddess of the dark-gleaming frontlet,
Of the all-daring might of Herakles,
Or of Dionysos' honour, wherein all men rejoice?
Or of the bridal of white-armed Harmonia?

. . . . .

In the earliest days, from the source of Ocean's streams,
Along the shining road to the holy slope of Olympos,
The Goddesses of Fate led Themis drawn by golden
steeds,
Themis of Heavenly birth, the Goddess of wise counsel,
To be the primal wife of Zeus, the saviour of men.
And she bore him the Hours, gold-frontleted and glad-
fruited, the Hours that keep true time."

This fragment of a hymn composed by Pindar in honour
of Thebes is brief and unsatisfying, yet it adds something
to our treasury of literature; for we can discern in it the
marks of Pindar's handiwork and feel the glow of the
Pindaric imagination. Later writers of antiquity contribute
much to our knowledge of the whole work and cause us
deep regret for our loss. It is associated with the well-
known anecdote concerning the elder Boeotian poetess
Korinna, who advised the youthful Pindar to draw on
mythology for his subject-matter, but to check his tend-

ency to exuberance.[1] We are thus assured that this was a youthful work, and we are astonished that at the beginning of his career he should have so impressed his fellow-citizens as to have received a public commission to compose this hymn for the state; possibly, there was some musical competition at Thebes, as there was at Delphi, at which anyone could offer a poem, but we know nothing of it.

Even if we doubt the anecdote, we detect a certain youthful crudity in the prelude, where Pindar seems indeed inclined to empty out his whole sack of mythology. He adopts again in a work of his later age, the seventh Isthmian, the same literary artifice of the 'questionnaire', but he uses it there more skilfully and avoids monotony.

The second part of the fragment is not lacking in grandeur and in a certain archaic solemnity of the older religious lyric. It deals with the holy marriage of Zeus and Themis, his first wife; and whatever else the poem included his must have been the main subject; for we learn from the late rhetorician Aristeides that the hymn was entitled "the marriage of Zeus".

But it included much more, of great value for our estimate of Pindar's originality. The writer just mentioned refers to a passage in it narrating how at the celestial marriage-feast the other deities, full of wonder at the recent works of creation and being asked by Zeus if they still had need of anything, replied with a petition that he would create new deities endowed with power worthily to celebrate "die unbegreiflich hohen Werke", as they themselves felt the theme too mighty for them. Zeus gratified their wish by begetting the Muses. Pindar has here invented a myth which, though he may have found the germ of it in Hesiod, is strikingly original and bold and on a level with some of Milton's celestial legends. As Goethe had studied Pindar, it may have suggested to him the theme of the wonderful angels' song, which is the prelude to his *Faust*.

We may suppose that it was partly the sublimity of its subject-matter that secured to this poem, in the ancient editions, its rank as the first in the collection of his hymns, also its long-continued reputation throughout antiquity. In a humorous narrative, Lucian describes an Olympian

[1] *Vide infra*, p. 358.

banquet at which the Muses sing a passage from Hesiod
and "the first hymn of Pindar". Like Goethe's angels, the
Muses were doubtless singing of the works of creation.
We have only this short fragment of their song, and perhaps
a few other faint echoes.

PAEANS

FRAGMENT OF PAEAN I

To the Thebans

"ERE the sorrows of old age draw nigh a man,
Let him shelter his spirit passion-free 'neath gladness,
Keeping still due measure, having heed to the resources
    stored within his house.
Cry aloud for joy:
For now hath the New Year, bringing all fulfilment,
And the Hours, the daughters of Themis, visited Thebes,
    city of charioteers,
Ushering in for Apollo the garland-loving festival.
May he long crown the generations of the folk with the
    flowers of well-tempered law-abidingness!"

This fragment is unquestionably of Pindar, and has been
preserved for us by a papyrus discovered more than twenty
years ago at Oxyrhynchos on the Nile, which contained
many other of his paeans, most, however, in a mutilated
condition and therefore not wholly available for the higher
purposes of literature.
This hymn is obviously addressed to Apollo and therefore may be classed among the paeans, which were specially

consecrated to him. But from the mention of the Year, the Hours, and the garlands, we may more immediately connect it with the great Boeotian-Theban festival called the Daphnephoria, to which all the Boeotian communities sent garlands and which commemorated the beginning of the year and the cycle of the seasons. It may then have been sung in the procession to the temple of Apollo.[1]

It certainly has charm, and marked Pindaric characteristics, the daring and unexpected phrase, the fusion of nature-poetry with ethical thought, which gives grace and solemnity to the last two lines.

The opening lines reveal that this is a work of Pindar's old age. But age has not banished his hopefulness and his temperate *joie de vivre*.

PAEAN II

To the Men of Abdera

"OH, son of the Nymph of Thronion and Poseidon,
    Abderos of the bronze cuirass,
Beginning with thy name will I follow this Paean's track
    for the sake of the Ionian folk,
5 As I fare along to the temples of Apollo of Derainos and
    Aphrodite.

.   .   .   .   .

25 I dwell in this Thracian land, a land of vines and blessèd
    with the fruits of the earth.
May mighty Time in the far future never weary
In marching forward with unfaltering step for me!
Young am I among cities; nathless I have seen [?] my
30   mother's mother stricken with the blast of the fire of
    the foe.

[1] *Vide infra*, p. 332.

But if a man, succouring his friends, sternly confronts the
    host of foemen,
His toil, challenging the battle at the hour of need,
Bringeth rest and peace at last.
Raise the glad cry! Hail, Paian!   35
May the God Paian never fail us in our need!

    .   .   .   .   .

That which cleaveth to good counsel and reverence for 50
    right
Is ever blessèd with soft days of tranquil weather:
And that happiness may God grant us!
But of those who have died before us long ago
Bitter-minded envy hath faded away;   55
And a man must bring to his sires the tribute and due of
    high renown.
For they it was who, having won by war a rich-dowered 60
    land,
Planted prosperity therein,
Having driven out the hosts of Paeonian spearmen beyond
    the mountain-range of Athos, their holy foster-
    mother.
But adverse fate befell them.
Yet they bided the storm, and thereafter the Gods brought 65
    their desire to pass.
He who hath wrought a fair deed is warmed with glowing
    words of praise.
And upon them fell light from the highest place,
When they stood before the foemen in front of the dark- 70
    leaved mount.
Cry aloud on Paian! May the God Paian never fail us in
    our need!
'But he shall pound him to dust when he draweth near the
    river, albeit with scant array against a mighty host.' 75
And lo! this befell on the first day of the month:
And Hekate, the kindly Maiden-Goddess of the ruddy feet,
Sent us this prophetic word that was fain of fulfilment.   80

    .   .   .   .   .

95 Hymns throughout his odorous shrine call upon his name,[1]
And around the high rocks of Parnassos the Delphian
    maids with the flashing eyes
Ofttimes set up the swift-footed dance and ring out the
100   sweet Apolline strain with trumpet-voice.
But for me, oh, Abderos, grant me a blessèd lot with fair
    fame;
And in thy might lead forth our host with their war-horses
    to their last of battles!"

This is one of the few newly recovered works of Pindar
that is more than a mere fragment, and in spite of much
mutilation and uncertainty has some literary value as an
organic poem.

We can discern something of the circumstances that
occasioned it and gave it shape. The citizens of Abdera,
on the Aegean shore of Thrace, have applied to Pindar to
compose for them a paean, a hymn invoking the aid of
Apollo. Evidently, they need his aid in peril threatening
them from their barbaric neighbours, the Thracians, with
whom they have had many conflicts, some victorious, some
adverse, and are preparing for another war, which they
hope may be the last. By the internal evidence of the poem
we may vaguely date it, as Wilamowitz has pointed out,[2]
as after the defeat of the Persians in Greece and the final
withdrawal of the Persian troops from Europe and before
the establishment of Athenian supremacy on the Thracian
coast; that is, somewhere between 478 and 468 B.C.

The Abderites must have instructed Pindar in some of
their previous history and local nomenclature. They would
have informed him of their local shrines of Apollo 'Derainos'
and Aphrodite, to which the chorus were proceding as they
chanted this poem; of the vicissitudes of their fathers since
the final planting of the colony from Teos, and of their
brilliant victory over the natives at the mountain with the
picturesque name 'Melamphullos', "the mountain of dark
foliage", mentioned also by Pliny. As an educated Greek,

---

[1] The God is not mentioned in the mutilated passage, but is obviously
Apollo.
[2] *Pindaros*, p. 320.

Pindar would himself be aware that Abdera had been finally colonised from Teos; and as Teos, being an Ionic city, was regarded as a colony from Athens, Pindar describes Athens, to whose recent sufferings in the Persian war he makes an interesting and sympathetic reference, as the grandmother of Abdera.

Pindar may also have been familiar with the foundation-legend of Abdera, which was in vogue in the fifth century, attaching to the 'eponymous' hero Abderos, the youth whom Herakles loved, and who followed him to Thrace in his expedition to capture the man-devouring horses of Diomed: left behind to guard the horses in Thrace, he was devoured by them, and the sorrowing Herakles instituted a cult and games in his honour on the site of Abdera. This is just such a myth as Pindar would have been tempted to engraft into a public hymn. The paean, as preserved, contains no allusion to it or to any mythic story, but many lines at the beginning, where he could naturally have dealt with it, are missing. There is merely a mythic touch in the genealogy which Pindar assigns to Abderos, and for which he seems to have had some authority, making him the son of Poseidon and the Nymph Thronia. This name points to Thronion in Lokris, and some possible reminiscence of early Locrian settlement on the Thracian coast.

The poem begins with an invocation, not of Apollo, but of Abderos, who is designated by the warlike epithet "he of the bronze-cuirass"; the epithet was not 'otiose', though Abderos was not famed for any martial exploit; but the buried hero is invoked to give battle-aid to his people, and therefore he must appear as a hoplite. The speaker is not Pindar, as might be supposed from the first few lines, but the leader of the chorus.

After the first long lacuna we find him praying in a striking phrase for the continued prosperity of his city. Then, after alluding to the destruction of Athens at the hands of the Persians, he reflects on the value of the stern patriotic effort that may win peace and safety in the end. The strong words would well apply to Athens, but may be also regarded as a martial encouragement to his citizens. After the liturgical call on Paian, the Saviour-God, the papyrus is again hopelessly mutilated. When we recover the text, we enjoy a characteristic Pindaric passage of ethical poetry on the value of wise counsel and reverence or respect for authority, which is part of Pindar's aristocratic political faith. The singer then descants on the praises due to their fathers, who have now passed beyond envy and malice, and whose feats and sufferings are outlined in the true style for historic-lyric. A critic of discernment has discovered the actual words of an oracle, prophesying a brilliant victory in time past, embedded in the text (ll. 73-75); this must have been the utterance of Hekate, whom the poet mentions immediately afterwards, "the word"—as he happily says —"which was fain to become deed".

Towards the end of the ode there is a fervent reminiscence of the Delphic worship of Apollo characteristic of the poet of Delphi: we cannot discern how it was harmonised with the preceding context, as there is a large gap in the papyrus just before the passage.

The ode closes as it began, with an appeal to Abderos and a prayer that he will grant fame and will lead their host to victory. The facts of hero-cult in earlier Greece show that the prayer could be sincerely meant; it reminds us of the legend of the Aiakidai at Salamis and of the Locrian practice of keeping a place for the lesser Aias in their battle array.

This poem may be called unique of its kind among the works of Pindar, as, keeping clear from mythology—so far as we can see—it renders so much contemporary history into lyrical form. And Pindar here assumes the rôle, to which he was by no means naturally inclined, of the preacher of patriotic war, as Turtaios was in former days for Sparta. The few phrases that here survive on this theme have a certain poetic quality, but not the fierce heat and thrill of the older war-poet.

Nowhere does the ode show marks of Pindar's greatest style and highest pitch; and there are some marks of carelessness. He speaks of the enemies of Abdera as the Paeonians; there is no historic reality in this, but he is under the spell of Homer; and if he really spoke of Athos as their frontier and their nursing mother, he was more ignorant of the geography of Northern Greece than he need have been.

Homer had bequeathed to later Greek poetry, epic and lyric, the use of the conventional, stereotyped epithet; and Bacchulides weakly revels in the use of this 'standardised' product. Neither is Pindar free from this convention; any

Goddess is for him "of the golden spindle" or "of the fair throne". When in the sixth Olympian we find him styling Demeter "the ruddy-footed Goddess", we might praise him for his real vision of the Goddess whose footstep was over the ruddy corn. But when as here we find Hekate called by this epithet, we feel it is becoming stereotyped, although it is a word of Pindar's own coining. In his use of epithets the strangest incongruity occurs in line 100, where he speaks of the 'brazen' voices of the Delphic maidens singing their hymns. Homer also calls the human voice 'brazen', but only the voice of the warrior on the battle-field, which might ring out like a trumpet. Hesiod with equal propriety applies the epithet to the barking of Cerberus. Did Pindar mean seriously that the voice of the Delphic girl was like a trumpet, or did he think that he need not take too much trouble for his distant clients of Abdera? We cannot give a final judgment on an ode of which so much has been lost; but we feel it is not one of his masterpieces.

PAEAN IV

To the Delian Apollo, composed for the island-state of Keos

"VERILY, though dwelling in a rocky home,   20
I[1] am known throughout the world for glorious achieve-
    ments in the games of Greece.
I am known, too, for furnishing the poet's handiwork in
    fair measure.
Verily also the tilth beareth something of Dionysos' life- 25
    giving fruitage, the healer of despair.
I have indeed no breed of horses and I have not the craft
    of the oxherd.
But Melampos was unwilling to leave his fatherland and
    rule as monarch over Argos,

[1] The leader of the chorus speaks as if representing the island.

30 Having establishèd his prerogative of divination.
    'Hail! Hail! Oh, God of Healing.'
    But one's home-city and kith and kin and comrades (?) are
        dear to a man, so as to bide contented. ·
    The love of things afar is a fool's longing.
35 I praise the utterance of Euxantios the king,
    Who, when the Cretans were yearning for him, refusèd to
        rule over them,
    And to take up his seventh share in the Hundred Cities
        with the sons of Pasiphae.
    And he told them the marvellous thing that had befallen
        him.
40 'I dread the feud of Zeus and the thunderous shock of the
        Earth-shaker.
    They in past time, with the thunder-bolt and trident,
    Hurlèd the land and the whole host of men into the depths
        of Hell,
45 But spared my mother and her fair-fencèd house entire.
    Am I then, in greedy quest for wealth and thrusting from
        me wholly into desolation the rites of the Blessed Ones
        established in the land,
    To take up a great heritage of land elsewhere?
    Too abiding would be the fear in my heart.
    Set far from thee, oh, my soul, the land of the cypress[1] and
50   the pastures round Mount Ida!
    A scanty strip of land hath been given to me,
    But I have no heritage of sorrow or domestic strife.'"

    This is the greater part, and all that is fairly well pre-
served, of the hymn which Pindar promised to send the
citizens of Keos, when he postponed fulfilling their request
in order that he might celebrate the Isthmian victory of his
fellow-citizen.[2] The mutilations of the papyrus have practically destroyed the first twenty lines, and some lines are
missing at the close; but enough has been preserved for our
judgment and enjoyment. The paean is unlike any other

---

[1] Crete, famous for cypresses.   [2] *Isth*. i. ll. 1-10.

of the surviving compositions of Pindar. The style is strikingly simple and straightforward, free from any strain and
tortuousness; and there is a certain naïveté and even archness in tone and expression that is rare in Pindar's work.

The speaker throughout is the leader of the chorus; and
the main burden of his song is the praise of Keos; and the
praise takes the form of an apology, which slightly reminds
us of Touchstone's apology for Audrey, "an ill-favoured
thing, sir, but my own".

Before we reach firm ground and consecutive lines, he
seems to have said that his island is a narrow ridge but
that he would not change it for Babylon. He then proceeds
to make the best of his native land: it may be only a rock,
but it has done well in athletic sports and made a sufficient
contribution to poetry: it has a fair vintage of wine, but no
pasture for horses or oxen: still, a man should be content
with his own home and kindred, as the examples of
Melampos and Euxantios show us. Pindar, one must believe, had visited Keos and evidently did not think very
much of it. Whether it deserved what he says of its athletic
prowess, we cannot test. Having produced Simonides and
Bacchulides, it deserved more than his rather cold admission
that it had done something for the Muses; but generosity
towards his rivals is not known to have been a trait of
Pindar. At any rate, a native of Keos may be allowed to
love his home and to refuse to leave it, being encouraged
by the examples of Melampos and Euxantios. These names
usher us into the realm of mythology, where Pindar feels
himself most at home. But in regard to Melampos, at least,
he deals strangely, perhaps recklessly, with tradition: for
he contradicts the prevailing tradition about him, as given
in Homer, Herodotos, and all later authorities, namely, that
he was a wandering prophet who came from Thessaly and
finally settled in Argos; and Pindar himself[1] was aware that
he was a Minyan, having associations both with Thessaly
and Messene; the story of the final settlement of his family
at Argos has probably some historic value. We cannot
suppose that Pindar found anywhere a rival version to this.
Either, then, he recklessly perverted the story, in order to
illustrate his text, being sure that the men of Keos would
know nothing against his way of telling it; or he innocently
perverted it through lack of memory. We can hardly accept

[1] *Pyth*. iv. 127.

the first alternative; for he must have known that there were many other Greeks who would know the truth and whose deep attention would be aroused by a paean of Pindar's publicly recited. The second is more likely and confirms our impression of a certain carelessness in the composition of these paeans.

As regards the story of Euxantios upon which Pindar expatiates with great effect, we had known nothing about him beyond that he was a son of Minos, who had some far-off connection with Miletos, until the discovery of Bacchulides' odes and Pindar's paean. The former confirms the latter to this extent that he calls Keos "the island of Euxantios"; and Pindar would not have ventured to present pure fiction as the tradition of their island to the singers of Keos; but he may have freely embroidered certain facts of legend and possibly of hero-cult. Pindar may have based his picturesque narrative on an antiquarian pretension of the island that they still possessed the family house of Euxantios, and on the tradition of an earthquake that destroyed the rest of the island but preserved that house: this would be a warning to Euxantios that he must cleave to Keos as his appointed home. At least we may be sure that Pindar is wholly original in the speech of Euxantios, in which our poet strikes a new chord of poetry. It has the charm of simplicity and directness, and the wistful homeliness of one who would be content to live and die in his own native isle; of one who was under the influence of the Hesiodic teaching and poetry and knew

"how much the half is better than the whole,
and how great blessing there is in mallow and asphodel."

It is sad that the closing words of his speech, when it was evidently approaching its highest point of effectiveness, are lost to us through the gap in the papyrus and the hopeless corruption of Plutarch's text, who quotes them to console a great man who has retired from the pomp of the world into a simple life. On the whole the men of Keos were well repaid, and could well forgive Pindar his somewhat tactless candour.

DELIAN PAEAN (V)

Composed for Athens

(Fragment)

"(The Ionians from Athens) took Euboia and made their
    habitation there:
And in the islands strewn on the main, rich in flocks of
    sheep,
They planted their homes;
When Apollo, the golden-haired, gave them to dwell on
    the rock, even the body of Asteria.
'Hail, all Hail, Delian Apollo.'
In this isle, oh children of Leto, I pray ye welcome me
    with kindly heart,
Me your minister approaching you with the ringing honey-
    sweetened utterance of the renownèd paean."

    The fragment does not present the characteristic and
impressive poetry of Pindar, but is not without literary
value. Like the former piece it has the charm of simplicity,
showing that he was capable of attaining this at times. The
metre, using merely the swaying dactylic movement, chimes
in with this simplicity of diction. We feel as a blemish the
phrase "the body of Asteria", a paraphrase for the rocky
island of Delos, once called Asteria, because this 'star-
maiden', refusing the amorous proffers of Zeus, was transformed into the rock afterwards called Delos. This allusive
style becomes an offence in the later learned poets of the
library; it is fortunately rare in Pindar.
    We cannot decide how far the content of this hymn was
directly religious, preoccupied with the celebration of Apollo
and Artemis, or how far it digressed into the narrative of
the Ionic settlements, an interesting theme of early history
and legend, of which no poetical chronicle has survived.
It seems that Pindar here attempted an outline of one. His

other paeans reveal how free he felt to wander away from the theme of religion in composing these hymns.

He was evidently interested in the story of the divine births in Delos; and he develops the legend of Asteria at some length in another passage of his paeans.[1] It has been suggested that, as the temple-poet of Delphi, he was cold to Apollo of Delos: the paeans alone are sufficient to refute this view.[2]

PAEAN VI

For the Delphians

"By the God of Olympus, oh, golden Putho, renownèd
    prophetess,
I implore thee to give me welcome in the fellowship of the
    Graces and Aphrodite,
5 At this holy time the spokesman of the songful maidens
    of Pieria.
For by the waters flowing through the lion-gate of bronze,
I heard Kastalia's voice,
Forlorn of the dance-step of the men:
Therefore I have come to help the need of thy clansmen
10   and for my own honour.
And obeying my own dear heart-promptings, as a child
    his trusty mother,
I have pilgrimaged to Apollo's holy grove,
Foster-mother of garlands and banquetings:
Where the maidens of Delphi, near the shadowy spot, the
    centre of the earth,
Full often beat the ground with nimble feet as they hymn
15   the son of Leto.

. . . . .

---

[1] vii. B (Schroeder).   [2] *Vide infra*, p. 326.

Whence sprang [the race] of the Immortals: 50
Such knowledge 'tis possible for the Gods to impart to the
    masters of song,
But 'tis hopeless for mortals to track it out themselves.
But oh! ye Muses, Maiden-Goddesses, for ye know all
    things,
Ye have this gift by divine ordinance, with the favour of
    Zeus, the Lord of the dark cloud, and of Mnamosunë.   55
Hearken then, ye Delphians. My tongue is yearning to
    distil sweet essence of honey,
As I have entered the broad lists of Loxias' poets-contest
    when the Gods are bidden to the feast.
For sacrifice is offered for all people of radiant Hellas,   60
For whom the Delphic tribe prayèd for deliverance from
    dearth . . .

.   .   .   .   .

(Twelve lines mutilated and unintelligible.)

(Achilles), whom our God, putting on the mortal form of   80
    Paris, lay low with an arrow,
And thus forthwith put off to a later day Troy's capture,
Having by a daring deed of blood stayèd the onset of the
    overmasterful son of Thetis, the dark-tressèd Sea-
    Goddess,
Him who was the Achaeans' trusty shield.   85
How heavy was the strife the God wagèd with white-
    armed Hera,
Clashing his unbending spirit against hers,
And his strife with Athena the City-Goddess!
Verily ere suffering grievous toils the Achaeans would   90
    have sackèd Dardania, had not Apollo guarded it.
But Zeus, who watcheth o'er the Gods, as he sits on the
    golden clouds and high places of Olympus,
Did not venture to unloose what Fate had bound.
It was destined belike that in the quarrel of high-tressèd
    Helen
The gleam of blazing fire should lay low the broad girth   95
    of Pergamon.

But when they had laid in the all-bewailèd tomb the valiant
    corse of the son of Peleus,
100 Messengers fared o'er the sea-wave and returnèd back
    bringing Neoptolemos the mighty;
Who sackèd Troy's city; but never henceforth saw his
    dear mother again
105 Nor the horses in his father's fields, as he gathered the host
    of the bronze-helmed Myrmidons.
110 But he reached the Molossian land near to Mount Tomaros,
And he escapèd not the ken of the tempests nor of the God
    of the wide quiver, the Far-darter.
For the God had sworn that he who had slain old Priam
115 After he had sprung to the altar of Zeus, the God of the
    garth,
Should never win to a welcoming home nor to the latter
    days of life.
But, as he was wrangling with the temple-ministers (of
    Delphi) concerning due apportionment of honours,
120 The God slew him in his own dear shrine by the broad-
    based centre of the earth.
Cry out, oh, youths, cry aloud in the measured verse of
    the paean.

．　　　．　　　．　　　．　　　．

Oh, isle Aigina of glorious name, at least thou art set in
    the Dorian sea as warder of the waters,
125 Bright star of Zeus, the God of the Hellenes.
Wherefore we will not let thee pass to thy rest to-night
    without late banquet of paean-hymns;
But as thou receivest the torrent-flow of our songs,
130 Thou shalt reveal from what place thou didst get thy
    destiny of sea-leadership,
And the excellence of thy righteous care for strangers.
Verily Zeus, the wide-seeing son of Kronos,
Who fashioneth all things, whether of good or ill,
Hath placed happiness in thy hands.
135 Of old time by the waters of Asopos, he snatched up the

deep-girdled maid Aigina from the vestibule of her
home;
Thereupon the golden tresses of the air veiled the shadowy
mountain-ridge of your land,
Where upon the immortal couch
(Aiakos was begotten)"

. . . . .

(Forty-three lines missing or unintelligible.)

This is the longest and most important of the newly
discovered paeans, and certainly the most perplexing of
all the poems that Pindar has bequeathed to us. It raises
literary problems that have not been adequately considered
by modern scholarship; and it supplies us with some striking
evidence as to the poet's religious insight and his attitude
towards the polytheism of his age.

As we have already observed, it is closely associated with
the seventh Nemean, which must have been composed soon
after this. There is no certain evidence, either external or
internal, as to the date of either poem; but the Nemean
ode, and therefore this also, was clearly composed when
Pindar was at the height of his fame and influence and
when Aigina was in full prosperity and a leading maritime
power.

The paean is composed to be chanted at a Delphic
spring festival called the 'Theoxenia', "the hospitable entertainment of the Gods".[1] The proem is warm and genial
and contains some impressive phrases. Pindar hears the
ripple of the fountain Kastalia, without any sound of the
dance by its brink; he therefore hastens to supply a hymn
that a chorus of men may learn. He can proudly speak of
himself as the recognised prophet of the Muses, and he
says charmingly that he obeys his natural impulse to speed
to Delphi as eagerly as a child comes at his mother's call.

We may specially regret the many lines that are missing
soon after the proem; for they may well have contained some
high religious poetry, of which an echo is still heard when
the text begins again. We may surmise that they bore some

---

[1] For an account of this festival, *vide* my *Cults*, iv. p. 292.

allusion to the traditional theme of the Muses' song, the
birth of the Gods; for we may thus restore a doubtful line,
and Pindar goes on to speak of a mystery that could only
be imparted by revelation. He then tells us somewhat of the
present religious occasion; for just enough is preserved of
the following fourteen lines to show that the Delphians are
sacrificing in behalf of "All-Greece"—Pan-Hellas—to avert
famine, and we have some evidence that this was part of
the annual ritual of the Theoxenia. It reminds us of the
Aeginetan tradition, regarding their Zeus Hellanios or
Pan-Hellanios, that Aiakos in a season of general dearth
offered sacrifice to him for all Hellas. Soon afterwards the
name 'Panthoos' occurs in a mutilated line, a mythic figure
which unites Delphi with Troy, and henceforth the paean is
occupied with the fate of Troy, Apollo's activities in its behalf, and the career of Neoptolemos. He speaks with great
emphasis and apparent admiration of the signal aid the
God lent to the doomed city, thereby deferring, though he
could not avert, its ultimate destruction. He directly attributes to the God, as no earlier writer had done, the slaying
of Achilles, Apollo assuming the guise of Paris for this
purpose: and he evidently thinks it a noble exploit that
exalts the God. It might have been noble for a Paris; but
that he should regard it as noble for a divinity shows Pindar
at a low level of religious imagination. Again, he thinks to
enhance the dignity of the God by dwelling on his boldness
in opposing Hera and Athena. These myths of quarrels
between divinities are frequent in the various polytheisms
and lower their value for higher religion, and Pindar high-
mindedly rejects them elsewhere as unworthy of the divine
nature.[1] Here he uses them for his Apolline panegyric. This
is one of the many perplexing features of the paean.

Then continuing his narrative for the glory of the Delphic
God, he comes to the story of Neoptolemos and gives us a
short lyric sketch of his life and death, which forms the
leading motive of the whole paean. And it is this that
troubles us most of all in this strange poem. We notice that
he accepts the version of the death of Priam most dis-
creditable to the young hero: Neoptolemos slays the aged
king at the very altar, an act of sacrilege repugnant to the
Hellenes of all periods. Therefore, we can understand that
Pindar, following his usual bent, should moralise sternly

[1] *Ol.* ix. 41.

on this incident; and, representing the death of Neoptolemos
at Delphi as a divine judgment on such a sin, should impute
to the high God of Delphi the function of executing the
moral law. It is interesting to note this sensitiveness of the
Hellenic conscience: and long before Pindar it was awake
to the fact that the conquerors of Troy committed certain
sins against the conquered. But we may ask—why does
Pindar adopt the darker version, when he must have been
aware that one of the old epic poets who described the
taking of Troy, and whose work was in great vogue in antiquity, declared that Neoptolemos did not slay Priam at
the altar but before the vestibule of his house, a circum-
stance which essentially alters the character of the act? And
the hero was the last great scion of the Aiakidai, the renowned family to whom Pindar and Aigina were most
devoted. Can we explain matters by supposing that the
Delphians hated him as an enemy of their temple and that
our poet was gratifying their feelings by blackening his
memory? If we had any proof of this, we should still think
ill of Pindar; but the supposition is inconsistent with what
he himself tells us in the seventh Nemean, namely, that
the Delphians mourned for Neoptolemos and gave him a
privileged position at the Theoxenia. This was a general
Pan-Hellenic feast, and it is inexplicable why Pindar should
have thought to gratify them by this severe condemnation
of the buried hero who was one of the presidents of the
festival.[1]

Again, Apollo was a great Pan-Hellenic God, and on this
occasion sacrifice is being offered "for all Hellas". Why then
does Pindar choose to glorify the God in his paean by representing him as passionately pro-Trojan, as a deity who did
all in his power to injure the Achaean cause before Troy,
defying greater deities than himself? We can understand
why Homer did this; but we shall never find due cause
why Pindar should have done so on just this occasion. The
whole theme seems flagrantly irrelevant.

There is a reverential attitude, a self-imposed humility
in the commentator, which refuses to blame because we
modern readers do not know all the facts; we should feel
Pindar is right—it may plead—if we only knew something
behind the scene. This attitude makes all criticism of the

[1] For a discussion of the Neoptolemos tradition, *vide* my *Greek Hero-
Cults*, pp. 310-321.

plot of his poems impossible; and the scholars of antiquity, who often knew more of the facts than we do, did not adopt it; but occasionally charged Pindar bluntly with sheer irrelevance.

Long practice in the difficult task of interpreting Pindar may give one the impression of a singular waywardness in him, a self-will that led him to defy the laws of relevance on any occasion. Something may have given to Pindar's reflections at this time a pro-Trojan bias. Let us suppose that it was the action of his state in setting up the cult of Hektor and importing his bones;[1] he might then feel obliged to give vent to these thoughts in the next poem that he composed—no matter for whom or for what. But the danger of such hypotheses is in their abuse, and "that way madness lies", and to explain is not to justify.

But the crowning irrelevance of the paean is its last strophe, the praise of Aigina. This theme has no proper place in a Delphic paean, for the island had no close connection with Delphi or the Delphic God.[2] And no suggestion has been made explaining or explaining away this final incongruity. And yet here, as elsewhere, we may be grateful to Pindar for his irrelevancies, for this one has given us what is by far the finest part of the whole poem. His heart goes out with fervent warmth to the praise of Aigina, which generally evokes his best style. The preceding parts of the paean that have been preserved are in some degree mediocre. This strophe shows the true Pindaric style in its full mastery and originality of phrase. His beautiful figure, "the golden tresses of air", has no parallel in Greek poetry, but recalls Shelley's "blind with thine hair the eyes of day" in his ode to Night. He devised various phrases in eulogy of Athens that remained tingling in the Athenian memory, but none perhaps so thrilling as this that he uses of this beautiful and gifted island-state, calling it "the radiant star of Zeus Hellenios". We regret that the strophe breaks off abruptly at the height of its inspiration, but the theme to which it appears to be leading up, the begetting of Aiakos, is dealt with in the proem of the eighth Nemean.

---

[1] For the facts and question about this astonishing cult, *vide* my *Greek Hero-Cults*, pp. 328-329.

[2] It had indeed, as Delphi had, the cult of Apollo Delphinios, the dolphin-God; but so had other communities.

Now, we have seen that the Aeginetans were highly displeased with Pindar for traducing their Aeacid hero, and
that he composed the seventh Nemean to reconcile himself
with them. One must regard them as over-sensitive and
ungrateful, if this magnificent panegyric on their state had
been originally composed for the paean as sung at Delphi
which displeased them; one might suppose that it would
more than atone for the unpleasantness of the Neoptolemos-
story. Therefore the suspicion arises that this eulogy of
Aigina was an after-thought, composed by Pindar as a
peace-offering to soothe the Aeginetans and attached as a
postscript to the paean some time after the Delphic
festival. And the suspicion is confirmed by the evidence
already noted that the paean had been revised and altered
by Pindar himself after its first performance, when he was
aware of the anger that it had produced in Aigina. We are
almost driven to this explanation in despair of any other;
for we cannot suppose that the Aeginetan passage was a
fragment from some independant Pindaric work, accident-
ally or foolishly 'contaminated' with the sixth paean by
some later editor; it was composed, as the opening lines
show, to fit into this place where it appears in the papyrus.

Whatever the explanation, the sense of incongruity,
which pervades the whole poem, remains strongest at the
close. It troubles us more than it troubled Pindar.

FRAGMENT OF PAEAN

Composed for Thebes

VIIB

"I PRAY to the fair-robed daughter of Heaven, Mnamosunë,
And to the Muses, her maiden-children, to grant me the
craftsman's happy gift.
For blinded is the mind of man,
Who by human wisdom dareth to explore deep-buried tracks

Without the aid of the Goddesses of Helikon.
To me they have given this toil that never endeth.''

This and other examples show that when Pindar prays
in verse, he prays well and with deep poetic effect; as in
the eighth Nemean for a guileless simplicity of life, here
for poetic skill and inspiration. Among no other people
beside the Greeks has 'memory' been incarnate as a real
Goddess 'Mnemosunë', and a real cult established. Pindar
derives his genealogy here from the theology of the poet
Hesiod, and Mnemosunë seems a product of theologic reflection. As her function is to preserve the record of the
earliest days of the Kosmos, she must belong to the oldest
stratum of divinities; as the Muses' primary theme was
heroic-religious tradition, Memory must be their mother.

The last few lines of the fragment present in a strong
and melodious expression Pindar's favourite dogma that
no artificial 'wisdom', bought or taught, but only divine
inspiration enables one to scale the heights or to fathom
the depths. The loss of one important word mars the perfection of the phrase.

FRAGMENT OF PAEAN

(*The Prophecy of Kassandra*)

VIII

"SEEING Paris speeding on his journey, Kassandra's holy
      heart,
Filled with God's power, rang out in deadly lamentation:
And the sum of the speech she revealèd was on this wise:
'Ah, all-seeing son of Kronos, God of boundless might,
Thou fulfillest the predestined woe that Hekuba saw com-
      ing on the sons of Dardanos,
When she was bearing this man in her womb:

It seemed to her that she brought forth a demon brandish-
    ing flame,
Hundred-handed, and that with a heavy [stroke], he
    batterèd the whole of Ilion to the ground.' "

This is a short fragment of a paean which, if preserved
in full, would have been of exceptional interest. The
papyrus gives us no indication of the occasion for which
it was composed. The theme of this surviving piece is evidently the prophecy of Kassandra concerning the evils that
would befall Troy from the voyage of Paris to Greece;
Pindar gives the summary of the prophecy very briefly:
"Now the dream of Hekuba is being fulfilled". Though he
may have had forerunners whom we cannot trace, he has
started a new theme for European literature, the dream of
Hekuba, which echoes down through the ages, so that
Shakespeare can use it in *Troilus and Cressida*—"Our
firebrand brother Paris burns us all". For in all the other
versions Hekuba dreams that she is delivered of a firebrand which destroys Troy, the firebrand being obviously
Paris. But though a slight corruption in the papyrus at this
point in the paean makes it uncertain what precisely
Hekuba's vision was, it was clearly not a firebrand, but a
hundred-handed monster brandishing fire, possibly a Fury,
that Hekuba dreamed that she had brought to birth. But
this is more probably the dream-symbol of Paris than of
any other agent in the drama of destruction.

Also Pindar is the first author in surviving literature
who has used this thrilling motive of epic-lyric poetry, the
doleful prophecies of Kassandra. Homer is altogether silent
about this tragic gift of hers; but a rambling epic-writer
of the eighth century, who composed a metrical chronicle
of all the events leading up to the *Iliad*, was beforehand
with Pindar in making Kassandra prophesy the future
when Paris set forth on his fatal journey to Greece; but
the author of that epic, sometimes called Stasinos of Cyprus,
was rather the cause of poetry in others than a poet himself.
This Kassandra-passage in Pindar's paean is not fully inspired, but it has in it the germs of poetry, and may have
suggested to others, such as Aeschylus, Euripides, and
through a long succession ultimately to Shakespeare, the

great poetic opportunities offered by the personality of the futile prophetess of evil.

The special forms of Greek religious lyric often originated in a particular cult, and derived a characteristic quality and a subject-matter from the particular divinity or the occasion for whom or for which they were intended. But in its progress Greek poetry refused to remain hieratic or fettered by religious trammels. Thus the paean arose in the Apolline ritual; but it came to be used in the service of other divinities. As he was a bright and radiant God, the paean was naturally associated with bright occasions; but as Apollo was often invoked as Saviour in time of danger and trouble, the paean, though never used in time of disaster or mourning, could admit graver and even semi-tragic themes. Thus Pindar, whose paeans—so far as we know—were always Apolline, felt free to deal with such a subject as the sad prophecies of Kassandra. Any Apolline myth could be treated, and Apollo was closely linked with the story of Kassandra.

PAEAN FOR THEBES

On Eclipse of the Sun

IX

"Oh, Sunbeam, searcher of the world, thou that engenderest
    sight in men,
What purpose hadst thou, that the peerless star of the
    firmament should be robbed of light in day-time?
Forthwith hast thou brought to nought for men both their
    strength and the path of wisdom,
Speeding along a darkened track.
Art thou bringing on us some strange fate unknown of
    aforetime?
But, oh, Goddess, that urgest on the steeds of the Sun, I
    implore thee in the name of Zeus—

Turn to some scatheless happiness for Thebes this image
    of terror for all mankind!

       .   .   .   .

          (Three lines missing.)
Bearest thou token of some war,
Or withering of crops,
Or unheard-of mass of snow, or deadly domestic strife,
Or the emptying on the plains of the depths of the sea,
Or the frost that bindeth the earth,
Or the fierce heat of the south wind wet with wild rain—
Or wilt thou bring a flood upon the earth and refashion
    the race of men anew?
Nought shall I bewail that I may suffer in fellowship with
    others.

       .   .   .   .

        (Fourteen lines missing.)
By some power divine have I been marked out
For your sakes to wed the swelling sound of voices to the
    flute and the meditations of my heart,
As we draw near Melia's immortal bridal-bed.
Oh, Apollo, the Far-Darter, I proffer my prayer to thee,
As I consecrate thy chamber of divination to the Muses'
    craft:
Wherein, oh God of Putho, Melia, daughter of Ocean,
    mingled with thee,
And bare mighty Teneros, peerless spokesman of Fate's
    decrees.
Him for his courage and wisdom's sake
Thou didst make guardian of the host of Kadmos and city
    of Zeathos;
For also he was honourèd beyond all men by the God of
    the Sea, the Brandisher of the trident."

       .   .   .   .

    The first part of this paean describes an eclipse of the
sun that is calculated to have occurred in 463 B.C., and was

almost total at Thebes: the second deals mainly with the personality of Teneros, a local hero of Mount Ptoön in Boeotia, and prophetic ministrant of an oracular shrine of Apollo in that neighbourhood. Pindar is our chief authority for his personality and the legend of his birth in Apollo's temple at Thebes called the Ismenion, from the union of the God and the fountain-nymph Melia who was specially worshipped in that shrine. This paean was evidently sung there, and one passage speaking of them as "drawing near the immortal couch of Melia" indicates that a "sacred marriage" was periodically enacted there, a ritual-drama of which we have other examples in Hellenic cult. The organic connection between the two parts of the poem can be easily shown: we may suppose that the Thebans, terrified by the portent of the eclipse, have arranged for a service to Apollo in the Ismenion as the Averter of evil; and that Pindar, perhaps self-prompted, has composed a paean for the occasion: it would be natural that he should first set down his own emotions evoked by the phenomenon; and it would be quite in keeping with his own method and with Greek convention that he should accompany his prayer to the God by a narrative of the shrine's legend concerning the love of Apollo and the Nymph and the birth of the hero. But when he goes on to represent Teneros as one of the early rulers of Thebes, "the city of Zeathos" (whom we know as Zethos the brother of Amphion), we suspect that Pindar was drawing, as he occasionally does, on his myth-making imagination.

It is the first part of the paean that interests us most and gives to this poem a unique place in Greek, even in European, literature; for it is the only poem by a great poet that we possess on that most terrifying portent in nature, a total eclipse of the sun. Our own experience may help us to understand the awe that it evokes in him: but his treatment of the theme is strange and characteristic. He gives us no naturalistic description of it at all, as he gave of the eruption of Etna in the first Pythian. He is born before the age of enlightenment, and has no inkling of the physical science that was dawning in Ionia and that was to relieve the human mind from many of the terrors that the physical world inspired. An eclipse stimulates poetry, in so far as it evokes in the natural man primeval feelings of awe and thrill: and this is the feeling tingling in Pindar's verse.

He is at once conscious that when the sunbeam turns
down "a darkened path", human strength and human wisdom are brought to nought and that some terrific doom is
impending. What is most strange is that he invokes, not
Helios the personal Sun-God, not Apollo immediately, so
often connected with Helios and the recognised averter of
ill, but "the sunbeam" which he personifies for the first
time, and even anthropomorphically as a charioteer. It is
difficult to see what he gains by this. But Pindar has a bias
towards the unexpected.

Then he questions what special peril was impending; and
his poetic imagination here works simply and deeply: and
this strophe ends with a really great utterance of ethical
poetry, a domain in which Pindar is unsurpassed: the
common danger of mankind raises him above cowardly
fears or thought of self. Nobility of sentiment is one of the
sources of great literary achievement.

The bad and defective preservation of the paean pre-
cludes a final judgment; but enough is given to allow us to
rank it high among Pindar's works.

FRAGMENT OF DITHYRAMB (61)

(*Weakness of Human Wisdom*)

"WHAT hopest thou of wisdom in very truth,
Wherein one man availeth little above another man?
For it is not possible that with human mind it should
    search out the purposes of the Gods:
For it was born of mortal mother."

The sense of the impotence of man before the divine
power, which was part of the emotion evoked in Pindar
by the eclipse, is reflected again in these poetic sentences.
They agree with his general doctrine of the cleavage between man and God, and with his dogma—expressed more

than once—that the human mind, unaided or uninspired, avails little. The fragment is quoted as from one of his dithyrambs. Originally a hymn to Dionysos, the dithyramb always retained some Dionysiac association. But succeeding poets handled it with ever-increasing freedom: and Pindar would feel as free in its composition as in his epinicians for sententious moralising and for mythic narrative.[1]

These few simple phrases are sufficient to infuse a sense of solemnity and suggest deep poetic meditation.

DITHYRAMB (75, 76, 83)

For the Attic Dionysiac Festival

"HASTE ye to the dancing-place, oh, Gods of Olympus,
And send down on us your glorious benison!
Ye who haunt in holy Athens the city's heart, trodden of
   many feet, fragrant with incense, and the all-adornèd
   market-place of fair fame,
Win your meed of violet-woven garlands and blossom of
   songs cullèd in the springtime.
And look down on me, wafted by God, mid the joyance of
   songs, speeding a second time to the presence of the
   ivy-crownèd God,
Bacchos whom we mortals call the Lord of the wild tumult,
   the Loud-shouter,
That I may glorify in verse the offspring of the Lords of
   Heaven and the women of Kadmos' line![2]

．　　　．　　　．　　　．　　　．

When the chamber of the Hours is openèd,
And the fragrance-breathing spring ushereth in the nec-
   tarous fruitage:

---

[1] Other fragments (61, 80) suggest that he handled in them such stories as the myths of Geruon and Orion.

[2] He means Zeus and Semele: he chooses to use the generalising plural.

Then, then, there is scattering to the ground of the lovely
tresses of violets,
Then our locks are blent with roses;
And the voices of our strains re-echo in fellowship with
the flutes,
And our choruses re-echo the name of diadem-crownèd
Semele."

FRAGMENTS FROM DITHYRAMB

In Praise of Athens

FRAGMENT 76

(*a*) "HAIL, renownèd Athens, city of shining streets and
violet crowns, great theme for the singers,
Bulwark of Hellas, city fillèd with spirit divine."

FRAGMENT 77

(*b*) *On the Battle of Artemision* (480 B.C.)

"WHERE the sons of the Athenians cast down the bright
foundation-stone of Freedom."

FRAGMENT 78

(*c*) "HEARKEN, Spirit of the War-Shout, Alala,[1] daughter
of War,
Thou prelude of the clashing of spears,
Whose beasts of sacrifice are men who die the hallowed
death for their fatherland."

Of these four fragments of dithyrambs, preserved for us
by later Greek writers or commentators, the first three belong to poems obviously composed for the Athenians, and
they thus acquire a special interest for us from the light they
throw upon Pindar's relations with the greatest Hellenic
state. But the first is the only one of sufficient length to

---

[1] 'Ălălā' was the actual war-cry of the Greeks.

make the impression of a substantive poem; and it has the further unique interest of being the only surviving dithyramb in the original sense of the word, a poem wholly in honour of Dionysos.[1] We gather that it was composed for the great spring festival in honour of the God of wine and vegetation at Athens, to be sung before the altar of the Twelve Gods in the market-place, which is here called the "fragrant heart (lit. 'navel') of the city". The very corrupt text which preserves it leaves us uncertain in regard to some important phrases; but enough that is clear and certain emerges to make critical appreciation possible. Accompanied by wind-music, the proper music for Dionysos, and using free and tumultuous rhythms, it expresses in some measure the ecstatic emotion evoked by the Dionysiac worship and the resurrection of the earth in spring; and there is a certain lusciousness, almost an exuberance, of phrase not usual in Pindar's style: the last lines suggest a carnival of flowers. It is likely that all that we have is the proem of a longer hymn, and that the chorus having mentioned Semele went on to describe the birth of Dionysos, the proper subject of a dithyramb according to Plato.

This piece, then, has the higher quality of religious lyric; but it does not reach the height of the inspiration fervent in some of the choral odes of the *Bacchai* of Euripides or the Dionysiac hymn in the *Antigone* of Sophokles.

As Pindar proceeded further with his hymn he might free himself from the trammels of the Dionysiac ritual and wander into other themes; and the praise of Athens would be quite relevant enough both for the Athenians and himself. Therefore it is quite possible that fragments (*a*) and (*b*) translated above belong to this dithyramb; for though the rhythms of the two fragments do not accord with the prevailing rhythms of the longer piece, being statelier to suit the high theme, we may suppose that a variety of rhythms was natural to the dithyramb. Or if they belonged to some other dithyramb, it must have been dedicated, not directly to the glory of Athens, but to Dionysos or some heroic subject, the praise of Athens being worked in as a by-motive.

[1] It may well have included the praise of Athens as a subsidiary topic. The other recently discovered dithyramb fragment, dealt with below, is also wholly Dionysiac so far as it is preserved, but its special theme was the adventure of Herakles with Cerberus.

In any case they are both striking and memorable utterances. Fragment (*b*) that celebrates the naval fight at Artemision—which the Greeks were hardly justified in calling a victory—is one of the few passages in Pindar's preserved works that touch on the Hellenic triumphs in the war with Persia,[1] and this passage is more impressive and exulting than the others and has the true Pindaric strength. He conceives of the Athenian prowess at Artemision as laying the foundation-stone of the temple of Hellenic Freedom: a beautiful phrase made all the easier as Freedom was a natural personification for the Greek and was sometimes worshipped. It was Simonides who was the chief poet-singer of the glories of Athens and Sparta in the struggle with Persia; here Pindar seems to be challenging him in his own field.

Certainly neither Simonides nor any other poet ever so gratified the ears and souls of the Athenians or any other people as Pindar with his inspired words of praise in fragment (*a*). Nor has anything that he ever uttered rung so far through the world as these. They intoxicated Athens; and their beauty and their music still appeal to us, to our senses, to our imagination, and to our spirit. They have quickened modern poetry and poetic sentiment about ancient Athens, and have taught us to attach to it the loveliest of all epithets ever linked to a city of man—"the city of the violet-crown", giving us a dream-vision of some transfigured place. But they have not taught us the exact meaning of that epithet. Did it allude — as the modern traveller has believed—to the violet-purple light that at sunset often encircles the ridges of Humettos and the Akropolis? Or did it allude merely to the many violet-crowns that made the streets of Athens gay in the springtime, the violets that give fragrance to his Dionysiac hymn? One might wish that Pindar intended the former meaning; but he probably intended the latter, and the choice of the epithet would be no less praiseworthy.

When Pindar was in Athens and under its spell, in the day of its unsullied greatness, he might idealise the city and forget that he was a Theban. But the Thebans did not forget or forgive their greatest poet for so magnifying the city which they hated deeply; and an interesting biographic story has been handed down about these dithy-

[1] Cf. *Pyth.* i. 76.

rambic phrases, that the Thebans fined him a heavy fine
and that the grateful Athenians paid it for him and raised
a statue to him.

We may believe the first part of this story without believing that a statue of Pindar was erected in Athens near to
the date when these poems were composed. They must have
been composed when Athens could still be regarded as the
champion of Hellas and not yet as its oppressor, that is
not much later than 470 B.C. And that would agree with
the date of the ninth Pythian, in which—according to the
theory I have put forth—Pindar defends himself against
accusations of lack of patriotism and tries to raise the
Thebans to a more generous sentiment concerning Athens.

Ten years later, when Athenian hegemony had become
a tyranny and she was planning the overthrow of Aigina,
the city to which he was devoted, he could not have written
these dithyrambic verses, and in no later passage does he
clearly refer to her empire or fame. If, as some have supposed,
there is a veiled allusion to her in the first part of the eighth
Pythian, he would imply that she has become a power of
evil. But, as we have seen, such an interpretation of that
passage is hazardous; and he nowhere clearly speaks out
his later mind about the democratic tyrant-state.

The last dithyrambic fragment, the invocation of the
battle-shout (frag. (c)), is the strangest of all the morsels
snatched from Pindar's rich table. It is quoted by a scholiast
as from a dithyramb; there is no evidence that it comes
from any poem composed for the Athenians. Plutarch gives
us to understand that Epaminondas quoted these words of
his native poet at some great crisis: he well might, for they
are an astonishing outburst of the poetic spirit of battle, of
which, without this evidence, we should not have thought
Pindar capable. One would suppose that war had no
glamour for him who steadily preached peace to his
countrymen and who uttered the wise reflection, "War is
sweet only to those who have not tried it". But here for a
moment he outdistances Turtaios, the war-poet of older
Greece; and the first verse is a musical trumpet-shout. It
contains one of the most daring ventures in Greek poetry,
the personification of the battle-cry; which is found nowhere
else in Greek literature, though Homer comes near to it in

personifying other phenomena of the battle-field. A still bolder imagination works out the idea: if 'Alala' is a Goddess, the men who die for their country are her sacrificial victims, which she gathers to herself, so that the patriot's death on the battle-field becomes in some sort a sacramental communion. The glimmering of such an idea appears also in a figurative phrase of Aeschylus[1] describing the first clash of the spears when the front ranks meet as "a preliminary sacrifice". By one of those coincidences not infrequent in the comparative study of literature, a strikingly similar passage occurs in Shakespeare, who makes the genial braggart Hotspur, one of his favourites, speak thus of the approaching royal forces before Shrewsbury:

> "They come like sacrifices in their trim,
> And to the fire-eyed maid of smoky war
> All hot and bleeding will we offer them."[2]

But the Pindaric passage is more earnest and masterful.

We may be sure that it was Pindar who composed it, though the evidence of authorship is only indirect. For whom, and in reference to what, he composed it, must remain unknown until some happy papyrus-find enlightens us.

OTHER HYMNS

Hymn Composed for Procession to Altar in Delos

(87, 88)

"HAIL, oh, isle of God's fashioning,
Daughter of the sea, most lovely blossom born for the children of bright-tressèd Leto,
The broad earth's marvel steadfast and unmovèd,
Whom mortals call Delos, but the Blessèd Ones in heaven,
'far-gleaming star in the dark-blue (firmament) of Earth'."

.   .   .   .   .

(Some lines missing.)

---

[1] *Agamemnon*, l. 65.   [2] *King Henry IV.*, Pt. I. Act iii. Sc. 5.

For in days of old it was borne to and fro adrift by the
  waves and the blasts of all manner of winds;
But when Koios' offspring,[1] wild with the pangs that herald
  birth, set foot on it,
Then at last four upright columns sprang up from earth's
  nether foundations,
And shod in adamant held up the rock on their capitals:
Where she was delivered, and her eyes beheld the blessèd
  birth."

The hymn of which these verses are a part was of that
type known as 'processional', being composed to be sung
by the worshippers moving in procession to the altar. The
metres proper to it would be stately and regular, suited to
the marching pace. And these verses of Pindar's have the
beauty and firmness that belong to a genial combination
of dactyls and trochees.

The poetry is adequate to the measure. He writes as
if Delos inspired him with no less enthusiasm than his
beloved Delphi. It has been supposed,[2] indeed, that he
cared less for the Delian than for the Delphic Apollo, as
though the two separate shrines implied two separate Gods:
this idea rests on a false view of Greek religion; we know
that Delos reverenced Delphi[3] and that for the Greeks the
personality of each shrine was the same. And the short
poem just translated attests the truth of what he told us in
the second Isthmian ode, that "his heart was poured forth
for Delos". In his invocation of her his imagination rises
to the height, and he glorifies and transfigures her in rap-
turous phrases.

Pindar is our first authority for the story—which we need
not suppose he invented—that Delos was a moving and
floating island[4] until it was fixed firm for Leto's travail and
the birth of Apollo and Artemis: he alludes to it again in
the paean fragment VIIB. It explains those words in the

---

[1] Leto.
[2] Wilamowitz, *Pindaros*, p. 330.
[3] *Vide* my *Cults of the Greek States*, vol. iv. p. 109.
[4] The legend of floating islands in the Mediterranean is based on geological
fact.

description of Delos which have caused doubt and difficulty, "the steadfast marvel of the broad earth"—the marvel being that the island which once was drifting about should now be unmoved.

Of the words that follow we are indebted to Wilamowitz[1] for a full appreciation: the uplift of Pindar's imagination is such that he can see our earth as the Gods in heaven may be supposed to see it: as we see the sky as a blue firmament above us, so they see our earth spread below them as a blue firmament with Delos as its most radiant star. Some sunny vision seen from his ship of Delos glittering like a jewel on the blue sea may have inspired him with this beautiful thought and these happy words, which he then thinks worthy of the divine language of Olympus. For Homer had taught him that the Gods have often different names for things from ourselves; only, Homer's examples do not show that the divine vocabulary is superior to our own. But those who listened to Pindar on this occasion might well feel that it was and that Pindar might teach it to them.

The concluding stanza, combining simplicity with majesty in the description of the submarine architecture of Delos, maintains the high level of the opening. We cannot discern how far the poem proceeded, and whether it contained a picture of the divine birth or admitted some subject not specially Delian. So far as we have it, it is more relevant to the religious occasion than were most of Pindar's religious lyrics. And if ever mythology in its highest poetic expression could quicken religion, this ode might have quickened it.

DITHYRAMB WRITTEN FOR THEBES ENTITLED "HERAKLES THE BOLD" OR "KERBEROS"

"IN days of old the song of the dithyrambs crawlèd along
     in a straight-drawn marching-line,
And the sibilant letter issuèd in spurious sound to human
     ears from the singer's lips.

[1] *Op. cit.* p. 328.

But now new gates of song are opened to the chorus standing in circle (round the altar?)

. . . . .

(Let us praise the God?), knowing well the fashion of
Bacchos' holy rites,
That the Heavenly Ones array in the halls of Zeus hard
by his sceptre.
The thunder of drums leadeth off the service in the presence
of the Great Mother of the Gods revered,
And withal there is the rattling of castanets and the
burning torch with the ruddy flare of pinewood.
Then are awakened the ringing outcries of the Naïdes,
Mad ecstasies, shoutings as of battle, tumult of dancers
with back-thrown necks.
And therewithal are stirrèd up the almighty Thunder with
its fiery breath,
And the spear of the War-God,
While the battle-aegis of Pallas giveth voice with the
clangorous sound of myriads of serpents.
And lightly fareth Artemis in her chariot alone,
Having yokèd thereto the lion-tribe in the Bacchic orgies.
But the God is soothed by the troops even of the beasts of
the wild joining in the dance.
Me the Muse hath raisèd up to be the chosen messenger
to fair Hellas of wise song-speech,
Praying for blessings on Thebes (?),
Where it is said that Kadmos by his high-soaring wisdom
won Harmonia:
And she heard the voice of God,
And brought forth offspring of fair fame among men.

. . . . .

Hail, Dionysos!"

This fragment of a dithyramb is one of the treasures
revealed to us by the find of papyri at Oxyrhynchos; and
in many ways it is an original contribution to our knowledge of Pindar. Its contents repay careful study, for they

are of equal interest for literature, scholarship, and Greek religion.

A few verses of it were known to us before the discovery through ancient quotations: notably, the three opening lines, which are *vieux jeu* for scholars, and will be specially discussed in the commentary on the text.

Certainly no religious lyric poem ever began so strangely. He calls attention to the higher development in the art of dithyrambic composition, and indirectly to the more cultured pronunciation of his chorus in regard to the letter 's'. A lacuna prevents us seeing exactly how this is joined with what immediately follows, the most singular religious passage in Greek literature; by prophetic knowledge or intuition he knows and proclaims the true ritual of the Bacchic orgy as it is performed by the deities themselves in the house of Zeus.

The High God does not seem to take part in the ecstatic revel himself, but the uproar surges round his throne. The violent music of the Phrygian Goddess, the Great Mother Kubele, opens the service; and we are reminded of the fact, of which Pindar himself informs us,[1] that he had set up a chapel in her honour by his own house, and thus contributed indirectly to that fusion of her worship with Dionysiac cult and myth which seems to have been complete by the time when Euripides composed his *Bacchai*. Of this blending of two streams of kindred religions we have ample testimony in later literature and art. But the introduction of the Naïdes into the celestial orgy is due to Pindar's self-will, and no one followed him in this: they are the substitutes for the Maenads, the proper ministrants of Dionusos, who as mortals could not be translated up into Olympus.

In the description that follows a resemblance has been discerned[2] to the famous passage in the beginning of the first Pythian concerning the soothing effects of Apollo's music in heaven. There the thunderbolt of Zeus and the fury of the War-God are lulled by its spell. The Bacchic orgy has the contrary effect; it rouses the thunder and the spear of Ares; and—strangest of all—the snakes in the aegis of Athena are excited and give voice.

His account of this wild ritual is incomplete, and ends abruptly. There are certain details which appear in no

---

[1] *Pyth*. iii. 78.
[2] By Wilamowitz, *Pindaros*, p. 344.

other Bacchic scene; but it seems likely that the poet, after mentioning the marriage of Kadmos and Harmonia, went on to narrate the birth of Dionusos, a proper theme for the dithyramb.[1] But what is most singular is Pindar's daring in transferring the scene from earth to heaven and imagining the deities as performing a Dionysiac service on their own account. For this I can remember no parallel in Greek religious literature. Olympus is not usually a place of divine worship, and the Hellenic deities do not offer sacrifice to each other, as the Gods occasionally do in the Vedic Sacred Books.

Considered as literature, this short Pindaric ode has some striking quality; it makes an impression from a certain rugged force and fierce vehemence. But we miss the nature-magic and the *abandon* which are the charm of Euripides' *Bacchai* and make the appeal of his Dionysiac poetry. We feel that Pindar's genius was more in accord with the tranquil grace of the Olympian religion, and that he was not called to be the spokesman of a new creed, of which a leading tenet was the fusion of the mortal in the Immortal. And the metres that he here employs are more stately and have not the rush and fire with which Euripides kindles his in the most inspired lyrics of his drama. We do not feel that Pindar, to use Euripides' own phrase, "has the Bacchic communion in his soul".

MAIDENS' HYMN

104D

(*Partheneion*) *for Thebes*

"APOLLO LOXIAS hath come with heart inclinèd to us,
To shed on Thebes blessing that dieth not.
But with all speed girding myself in my gown,
And bearing in tender hands a gleaming spray of laurel,
I will praise in my hymn the all-glorious homestead of
    Aioladas and his son Pagondas,

[1] *Vide supra*, p. 322.

Enriching my virgin head with garlands.
In singing to my reed-fashionèd flutes,
I will imitate the shrill-resounding Siren-voice (?),
Which lulleth the gusty breath of Zephyr,
And, when the North Wind swoopeth down shuddering
 with the tempest's might,
Sootheth the swift-hurtling waves of the sea (?).
Many a story of past days I might tell, with the embroidery
 of verse;
And much else there is that Zeus alone knoweth:
But me it beseemeth to think thoughts meet for maidens,
 and to speak such things with my tongue.
I must not miss to find a fitting strain of praise
For any man or woman, whose scions are dear to me.
I have come to join the dance as faithful witness
To the fame of Agasikles and his noble parents,
Honourèd in ancient days as now among the neighbouring
 peoples,
(?) As the guest-friends of their states,
And for the far-renowned victories of their swift steeds,
That crowned their locks with garlands on Onchestos' far-
 famèd sandy plains,
And near the renownèd shrine of Athena Itonia.
These men's wise quest of honour brought them into a bitter
 feud fraught with relentless speech; (?)
But it gave fair pledges and turnèd to love at the last.
Oh, son of Damaina, be thou my leader, moving on with
 stately step;
Thee the daughter in the first rank of the moving line will
 be fain to follow,
Marching with sandalled feet near the fair-leavèd laurel,
She whom Andaisistrota hath trainèd in manifold devices."

In the varied mass of ancient religious poetry one species
was distinguished as *Partheneia*, or songs sung by maidens
moving in procession to an altar or temple. We knew from
the ancient scholars that Pindar composed hymns for this

purpose. His predecessor in this line of composition had
been Alkman of the seventh century. And a single *partheneion* both of Alkman and Pindar has been partly recovered by papyrus-finds. But though a substantive portion
of the Pindaric maiden-ode is presented to us, a large part
has been lost; and it is difficult to arrive at a final and
satisfying judgment upon it.

Our interpretation of the poem may be helped by what
we know of the religious occasion.

The festival was the Daphnephoria, "the bearing of the
laurel": by a combination of two separate ancient accounts
the following picture of it may with probability be presented:
a heavy log of olive wood, like a maypole, hung with laurel
and other branches and flowers, was borne to the temple
of Apollo Ismenios by a troop, of which the leader was a
beautiful boy, having both parents alive and therefore a
lucky boy; solemnly attired, crowned with gold and bearing
a laurel branch, and probably regarded as a human double
of the God. He is accompanied by an elder man who carries
the maypole, a near relative or intimate friend; immediately
behind him march the chorus of singing maidens, also
bearing laurel. We can feel the beauty of the ritual, a
shadow of which still survives in some Mediterranean
villages. It was a spring festival, and its first intention
may well have been the consecration of the fresh and unsullied laurel to the young God, while the vegetation-magic
usual at such seasons would naturally gather round the
rite, which both signalises and evokes the fertilising divine
power: at one of the shrines, which the procession may have
visited, his presence was marked by an abundance of milk
in the flocks.

Such an occasion might have aroused in Pindar his most
genial power of creation. But so far as the preserved and
intelligible fragments of this poem are true tests of the
whole, we cannot say that it did. Nor does the poem just
translated bear out the dictum of one ancient literary critic,
that Pindar in composing his Parthenia abandoned his
characteristic austere and severe style, and wrote in a more
simple mode suitable for girls. We may doubt if Pindar
ever could write *virginibus puerisque*. Certainly, this poem
shows a harsh style and strained diction: the phrases are
forced and twisted, and at times we can barely understand
and cannot justify them. There is a certain strength and

vigorous resonance in the verses, but not the radiance or warmth of imagination natural to his best poetry, no brilliant achievement in the discovery of bold words to fit bold fancies.

Nor is the poem, so far as we have it, in any way religious, after the opening phrase about the presence of Apollo. The chorus appear to have taken up their stand outside the house of Aioladas and Pagondas, to whose family Agasikles, the laurel-bearer boy, belongs. Through the voice of one maiden representative of the group, they sing the praises of this family and their victories in the games, so that the poem has the character of an 'epinician' encomium, comparatively tame in expression.

Its chief interest is for the history of Greek religious lyric, showing how secular in tone it could be. We discern this also in Alkman's *partheneion*, composed for the Spartan maidens marching in procession in the ritual of Artemis. Nearly all that poem consists of a flirtation between the poet and the pretty girls of his chorus, naïve enough but carried on with much lyric beauty, so that we are charmed without being moved to worship. Pindar cannot charm us in this way, and his style has not the easy *abandon* and gaiety of Alkman's.

HIS DIRGES AND FUNEREAL POETRY

FRAGMENT 129

(*a*) "FOR them in the world below the sun gleameth brightly
    in his strength, while 'tis night with us.
And in meadows ruddy with roses the forecourts of their
    city are shaded with trees of frankincense,
And heavily laden with fruits of gold.

      .   .   .   .   .

Some there delight themselves with feats of horsemanship
    and the athlete's practisings,
Some with the draught-play, others with the music of lyres:

And among them the fair flowers of happiness bloom in
full measure.
And a lovely odour is wafted throughout the land unceasingly,
As they mingle all manner of sacrificial spices with far-
gleaming fire on the altars of the Gods."

"From the other region sluggish rivers of murky night
belch forth gloom that hath no ending."

(? Pindar's.)

FRAGMENT 131

(*b*) "BY a happy dispensation they won to an ending that
releaseth them from toil.
The body indeed of all of us followeth the call of death
the overstrong:
But there yet surviveth death the shadow of our living
self.
For that alone of us is of origin divine:
It sleepeth when our limbs are in busy motion,
But to us in slumber it revealeth in many a dream
Fate's coming decision concerning our weal or woe."

FRAGMENT 133

(*c*) "AND from whomsoever the Queen of the Dead shall
have receivèd satisfaction for ancient guilt,
Of them she sendeth back the souls once more in the ninth
year to the upper sunlight;
And they grow into kings reverèd,
Men mighty in strength and surpassing in wisdom.
And for all future time they are called of men by the name
of holy heroes."

FRAGMENT 137

(*d*) "HAPPY he who hath seen those mysteries ere he pass
    beneath the earth:
He knoweth the truth about life's ending,
And he knoweth that its first seeds were of God's giving."

FRAGMENT 104C

(*e*) "THE succession of man's days upon earth perisheth
    not, though his body perisheth.
But if a man's house is not wholly overthrown, subduèd
    by a violent doom, and be not left desolate of children,
Then having escapèd toil and distress, he liveth yet (in
    some sort):
As for the time before his birth (I have nought to tell you?)."

   .   .   .   .   .

   Most of these passages are of great poetic beauty and
are striking specimens of Greek religious lyric; and while
not all belonging to the same class of composition, called
'threnoi' or dirges to be sung at funerals or funeral feasts,
they all contribute some evidence of Pindar's view concerning the human soul and his belief in immortality. They
should be considered together with the famous eschatologic
passage already discussed in the second Olympian and with
the proem of the sixth Nemean.
   In regard to this burning question of the lower and
higher religions, Pindar seems to speak with a double voice
and to be double-minded. Some passages reveal a hesitating
belief in some existence of the soul after death, but one
shadowy and dimly conceived; he thinks it certain that the
buried ancestors still delight in their young descendants'
triumphs.[1] This on the whole might stand for Pindar's
average belief, and accords with the trend of his temperament. He is no theosophist or mystagogue; and he is neither
exigeant nor dogmatic in regard to the world behind the

   [1] *Vide Ol.* viii. 77 (102) and *Nem.* iv. 86 (139).

veil. The last passage of those just translated, though very obscure, suggests an even more exiguous belief than any of Pindar's other utterances concerning the posthumous life: the childless man may perish utterly, but those who leave children behind them may enjoy some sort of continuous life in their descendants: we may surmise from certain broken words in the text that he was going on to mention and to reject the Pythagorean doctrine of a pre-natal existence of the soul. On the whole his morality and view of life are not 'other-worldly'. Yet he was conscious of the divine affinity, if not the divine origin, of the soul of man: and this would make for the belief that it has power to survive death.

Only, such belief may be vaguely held without being forceful or constructive: and Pindar never prays for post-humous happiness, but for a good reputation after death that may be a glad heritage for his children. Such is the outlook on life of a brave and strong man, who does not give way to a too clamant self.

But Pindar is aware of another outlook, that of the Eleusinian and of the Orphic-Dionysiac mysteries: and to the teaching of these he has given in these fragmentary passages and in the second Olympian ode a lovelier utter-ance than any other Greek poet. The promise of posthumous happiness which both these mystic services proclaimed would be an appropriate theme for his 'dirges', to which most of these fragments belong, for the consolation of the kinsmen of the dead; and in this they resemble our own burial-service, while far excelling it in their visions of brightness and delight. We may assume that Pindar only handled such themes when the deceased had been initiated.

But was Pindar himself an initiate, so that he could speak with full knowledge and conviction? In the second Olym-pian he is certainly promulgating the general tenets and aspirations of the Orphic system, as was pointed out in the comment on that ode. Also the doctrines clearly proclaimed in fragment (c), the doctrines of Purgatory and the re-incarnation of souls, were specially the tenets of the Orphic sect. The latter doctrine was proclaimed also by Pytha-goreanism, which has close affinities with Orphism: but the belief in Purgatory, a state and period of penance and purification after death, came into the Mediterranean religious world both Pagan and Christian from Orphism only. And Pindar gives voice to this belief both in the Olympian ode and in fragment (*c*).

So far, then, we discern that Pindar is familiar with two of the leading tenets of Orphism. Another idea, pregnant for philosophy and religion, is that of the divine origin of the human soul: this dogma, implicit only in the proem of the sixth Nemean, becomes explicit in fragment (*b*)—"some part of ourself is of divine origin"—and in fragment (*d*), which has a high solemn tone of finality proper to revelation —"the initiate knows that life came originally from God". Where was this new truth proclaimed, and by whom, a truth which could not emerge from ordinary Greek mythology? According to Plutarch, who quotes the passage, Pindar is speaking "about the Eleusinian mysteries". We must not lightly disbelieve Plutarch's accuracy on this point; for he had, presumably, the whole 'threnos' before him, and, as the poet speaks of "these mysteries", he must have indicated in the context what mysteries he meant. The passage is of great importance, for if we accept it exactly as Plutarch gives it, and if we suppose that Pindar is speaking from inner knowledge, the poet becomes our sole authority for the fact that Eleusis proclaimed this high theory of the soul as an esoteric doctrine: and he evidently regards it as one of the precious gifts conveyed as a privilege to the initiate, a secret which nevertheless he reveals.

Now it is strange that all the other ancient authorities concerning the Eleusinian mysteries, including even Plato to whom such a doctrine would have been most useful and attractive, are silent about it. Nor is there anything in Eleusinian mythology that could have evolved it. But the divine origin of man was a leading tenet of Orphism and was propounded in the strange Orphic mythology. Therefore, if it were not for Plutarch, we should rank fragment (*d*) among Orphic and not among Eleusinian texts.

As Hellenes from all parts were initiated at Eleusis and Pindar was much in Athens, he might easily have been admitted to the rites. But we have no reason for supposing that he ever was. And what he says of Eleusinian hopes and promises may be only amplification of vague reports that had reached him.[1] On the other hand, we cannot believe

---

[1] A general doctrine of posthumous rewards and punishments, common both to the Eleusinian and Orphic systems and reflected in the second Olympian and fragment (*a*), was diffused beyond the circle of the initiated.

that Pindar was ever a member of the Orphic brotherhood: for Orphism grew out of the Dionysiac religion, which seems to have had much less attraction for Pindar than the rest of Greek polytheism; and the Orphic temperament as revealed in the Orphic texts seems utterly alien to the soul of Pindar as he shows it us in his poems.

We may only suppose, then, that he knew enough of Orphic doctrines and Eleusinian faith to sympathise with his friends and patrons who were attracted into these mysteries, so that on their decease he could compose appropriate 'dirges' in harmony with their "religious experience", for the consolation of their families.

Pindar may be said to be the father of eschatologic poetry. The passage in the second Olympian is not only a great poetic achievement, but is a landmark in the history of religion; for he there proclaims—apparently with conviction —a new theory concerning the moral government of the world, that had not yet emerged even in Israel: namely, that a blessed state of happiness can be secured in the next world by righteousness alone, not by sacrament or ritual or special theologic faith; he may have appropriated certain ideas current in Orphism, but he does not speak as an Eleusinian or Orphic mystery-preacher, nor as a sacerdotalist, but as a great prophet-poet.

The two descriptions of Paradise that Pindar has left us—that in the fragment (*a*) may be based on the Olympian ode—are so genially bright and glowing, and of such golden diction, that we might expect to find echoes of them in later literature. Aristophanes and Vergil may have caught from him the idea that Paradise possesses its own specially blissful sun; and Vergil is obliged by Pindar to admit athletic sports into his Elysium. The puritan Milton could not admit them into his Heaven; but he allows the rebel-angels so to disport themselves as some alleviation of the miseries of Hell. As Pindar is supersensitive to all the simple joys of life, he enriches Paradise with the scent of odorous spices; and the closing lines of his fragment are beautifully imitated by Tennyson at the close of his 'Teiresias'.

We may smile at the Blessed Ones playing draughts; and we may think of the wise Egyptian's phrase—"The Hellenes are always children". We may also remember that the Norse Gods played with dice in Valhalla.

FRAGMENTS OF HIS 'DANCE-SONGS'

(*Hyporchemata*)

FRAGMENT 108A

(*a*) "AT the beginning of each action, when God is the
    leader,
Forthwith the way becometh straight to the achievement
    of renown,
And fairer are its fruits at the end "

108B

(*b*) "IT is possible for God from the blackness of night to
    awaken unsullied light:
And again with a cloud of darkness to veil the bright gleam
    of day."

These snatches of Greek religious lyric are worth preserving both for their form and content: for they convey
grave thought with solemn music. And they deepen the
impression which we gather from the epinician odes that
Pindar was a great master in religious poetry. The two
latter are quoted as from his *hyporchemata*, a name given
to a species of song of which Pindar was said to be the
chief master or inventor, a song which was specially composed for a dance. As all Greek songs had been im-
memorially composed for some kind of dancing-step, one
may suppose that in these the song and the dance were so
blent as to form one creation. All the fragments of this class
that have been preserved from Pindar's lost works show
great stateliness and some uniformity of metre; and Greek
dancing was more religious than secular. So far as we can
judge from the specimens, their themes might be either
secular or religious; also mythology might be treated, and

the dancing-step was quite consistent, in Greek taste, with grave didactic utterance. The following specimen from his *hyporchemata* may show how Pindar could clothe the political sententiousness of Solon with the beauty of his own lyric art:

FRAGMENT 109

"WHEN a man striveth to set the commonweal of his
    citizens in a summer calm,
Let him seek out and find the shining face of deep-souled
    Peace:
Let him uproot from his own breast the wrathful faction-
    spirit,
The dispenser of poverty, a bitter fosterer of the young."

In the history of the old Greek States the wise poet is sometimes found to have been a teacher of saving counsel; and this poetic message from Pindar has a very modern appeal.

A FEAST SONG

FRAGMENT 124A-B

"OH, Thrasuboulos, I send thee this casket of lovely songs
To grace thy evening banquet:
Haply in the fellowship they may prove a sweet spur to
    thy boon-comrades,
To the flow of Dionysos' fruitage,
And to (the draughts from) Athenian wine-cups:
At the hour when the carking cares of men are gone from
    their breasts,
And we all, floating on a sea of deep golden wealth,
Fare onward in the same ship to some shore of the dream-
    mirage.

The needy man at that time becometh rich,
And those who have abundance are exalted still higher in
    their imaginations,
As the shafts from the vineyard overmaster them."

LOVE-POETRY

FRAGMENT 123

(*a*) "'TIS meet indeed, oh, my soul, to pluck the flowers of
    love in their due season, while youth is still one's
    comrade.
But if a man once seeth the light-rays flashing from the
    eyes of Theoxenos,
And is not tempest-tossed with yearning,
His dark heart hath been forgèd of adamant or iron in a
    flame grown cold:
And, held in contempt by the Love-Goddess of the quick-
    darting eye-glance,
Either he toileth constrainedly in the quest of wealth,
Or, with woman's shamelessness,
He fareth with soul adrift courting [love down] every
    path (?).
But as for me, through the Goddess' power I melt away,
Like the wax of holy (?) bees piercèd by the warm glow,
When I gaze at the young-limbed beauty of striplings in
    their first prime.
Meseemeth, then, that in Tenedos withal the Goddesses
    of Persuasion and of Grace have their habitation,
Even in the son of Hagesilas."

FRAGMENT 127

(*b*) "LET it be our law to love and be generous with
    Love's favours according to life's season:
Pursue not, oh, my soul, Love's task to an age past the
    right measure of years."

SONG IN HONOUR OF THE TEMPLE-COURTESANS AT CORINTH

To Xenophon of Corinth

FRAGMENT 122

(*c*) "OH, girls so kindly to all comers,
Ministrants of the Love-Goddess Persuasion in rich Corinth,
Ye who kindle on the altars the amber tears of the fresh
    frankincense-tree,
With your thoughts ofttimes fluttering upward to Aphro-
    dite of the Heavens, Mother of the Loves,
To you, young damsels, she hath given the boon
To cull the flower of tender beauty on lovely couches
    blamelessly:
For where necessity is, all things are fair.

    .   .   .   .   .

But I wonder what the lords of the Corinthian Isthmos
    will say of me,
That in the company of common women
I have fashionèd so sweet a prelude of a drinking-song.

    .   .   .   .   .

We have approved the nature of gold by the pure touch-
    stone.

    .   .   .   .   .

Goddess of Cyprus, hither to thy holy grove
Xenophon, warmed at heart by the fulfilment of his prayers,
Hath brought a drove of a hundred head of herded girls."

    These three short poems, dealing with the themes of love and wine, are of value for our full appreciation of Pindar. For, though we have other snatches of his songs proving that he exercised his genius in this field, these are the only surviving pieces of sufficient length for a literary judgment.

And there is no evidence that the first poem is a fragment merely; it may well be a complete short poem of sufficient compass to be sung over the cups. Its own words make clear that that was its intention, and that it was composed for that Thrasuboulos of Akragas, son of the dynast Theron, and a dear friend of Pindar's, with whom the sixth Pythian and the second Isthmian have already made us acquainted. We have no clue as to its date; it may well have been composed for a banquet given by Thrasuboulos in commemoration of his Isthmian victory.

We might doubt, *a priori*, whether Pindar could so far change his nature and his style, could lay aside his thunder, his magniloquence, his tense and hard-forged phrases, so as to produce masterpieces in this lighter field of poetry; for this demands *abandon*, ecstasy, the devil-may-care recklessness of the reveller, the spirit that could possess Anakreon, Burns, and Shakespeare, but apparently—so far as we can judge from these three poems—not Pindar. His drinking-poem shows his masterful style, of which he cannot lose control—whether he is writing for processional girls, or feasters, or courtesans. It is a strong, original work, and contains a grave thought which the more easy-tempered Bacchulides expands into simpler phrases. The Greek would enjoy reading Pindar's poem in the morning, but would probably prefer for a midnight catch a song with more of the Bacchic *joie de vivre*.

The other two poems, which are of the amatory class, are strikingly original. The first proclaims his ardent passion for Theoxenos of Tenedos, the younger brother of the Aristagoras for whom he composed the eleventh Nemean. At once a prejudice against such a subject arises in the healthy-minded Northerner. The unisexual sentiment which inspires this poem—as in a different form it inspires the famous love-poems of Sappho—is repugnant to us; and we cannot be won over by the magic or beauty of the diction.

But we know that the old Mediterranean world—except the Jewish part of it—was inferior to our own in this respect; and that Pindar's contemporaries tolerated and his fellow-citizens even encouraged these morbid emotions.

If, then, we try to judge the poem by the standard of his day, we should not suppose that it would be regarded as a masterpiece of its type. It lacks spontaneity and the throbbing ardour of Sappho's verse. This is no lover's song of hope or lament. In fact, Pindar half apologises for himself as an elderly lover, and then moralises (*more suo*), in stately verse of beautiful rhythm, on the causes of indifference, as again he moralises in the shorter fragment (*b*), of striking and partly obscure diction, which may have belonged to a similar poem, on the wisdom of regulating passion according to age.

The third poem on "the ministrants of Persuasion in wealthy Corinth", is more surprising still and is entirely unique. These young women are temple-prostitutes, slaves attached to the service and temple of Aphrodite Ourania at Corinth, a title designating the Oriental Goddess, out of which—by the irony of fate and through Plato's misunderstanding of it—has grown our phrase "Platonic affection". The institution of temple-prostitution was found at many centres of worship of the Goddess in Asia Minor. Greek ritual, on the other hand, was generally pure and austere; and it is only at Corinth—always a city of low morality— where the worship appears to have caught the contagion from the East.

Pindar's poem is explained by his association with the Corinthian Xenophon, whose victory at Olympia he had commemorated by the thirteenth Olympian, and who had vowed that if he won the victory he would consecrate a hundred of these young women to the Goddess. He fulfilled his vow, and gave a commemorative banquet, where Pindar himself was present, and some of the girls were performing as dancers.

As he calls his poem by the special name 'Skolion' or 'drinking-song', we must believe that he composed it for that banquet. And these "hospitable young women" were never so glorified in any other verse; for his style rises almost into splendour; he brings them under the shadow of religion and invents for them the tolerant aphorism "under necessity all things are honourable". The last stanza, in which he speaks of Xenophon's girls as a herd of sacred cattle presented to the Goddess, is remarkable for the choice irony of its diction; and his pretended fear that "the Lords of Isthmos" might be shocked at him is agreeable, for he knew that they, the Corinthians, were not puritanical in morals. Even in such company he is markedly the aristocrat, with a certain arch delicacy of expression.

But if to these short pieces we add the few snatches of
amorous poetry that may be found in his existing works,
such as in the ninth Pythian, we shall not feel that Pindar's
genius was specially endowed to shine in this domain
of poetry. He does not sing as a bird in the thicket. His
verse bears the impress of the hammer on the hot anvil.
Radiant sunlight and rolling thunder do not give the
atmosphere for the love-lay or the drinking-song. He was
more at home with Gods and heroes, and women evidently
did not count much for him or for the aristocratic world
that he loved.

'ENCOMIUM' ON THERON OF AKRAGAS AND HIS LINE

FRAGMENT 119

(*a*) "THEY dwelt in Rhodes, whence they farèd forth
And now inhabit the circle of a city set on a height;
Offering many a gift on high to the Immortals:
And a cloud of ever-flowing richness followeth their ways "

ON ALEXANDER, SON OF AMUNTAS, OF MACEDON

FRAGMENT 120

(*b*) "HAIL, namesake of the wealthy sons of Dardanos,[1]
son of Amuntas of daring counsel,

.   .   .   .   .

It is seemly for the noble to be besung with the fairest
songs:
For nought else but that hath hold on immortal honours:
The fair deed shrouded in silence passeth away and is lost."

---

[1] An allusion to 'Alexandros', the other name of Paris.

FRAGMENTS OF UNCERTAIN ORIGIN

FRAGMENT 172

(*a*) "THE youthful days of Peleus were lit with the lustre
of deeds unnumbered;
First he went with Alkmena's son up through the plains
of Troy.
Then on the quest of the girdle of the Amazonian queen,
And thereafter having accomplishèd Jason's glorious
voyage,
He won Medeia in the midst of the Colchians' homes."

PRAISE OF THEBES

FRAGMENT 194

(*b*) "A GOLDEN basement hath been welded for sacred
songs:
Up! and let us fashion thereupon fair structure of words,
cunningly devised and vocal,
And to Thebes, albeit far-famèd already, this will add the
coping-stone of honour down the highways of Gods
and men."

FRAGMENT 195

"GODDESS of Thebes, thou of the fair chariot and golden
robe, our most holy pride."

FRAGMENT 198

"FAR-FAMED Thebes hath rearèd me
As no alien to her nor as one unlearnèd in the Muses' craft."

PRAISE OF SPARTA

FRAGMENT 199

(c) "THE city peerless for the counsels of the elders,
For the spears of its young men, for the choral-dance,
The Muse and the Goddess of festal gladness."

RELIGIOUS FRAGMENTS

FRAGMENT 155

(d) "OH, God, the son of Kronos, mighty in the thunder,
I ask of thee that thing, the doing whereof may make me
    dear to thee,
Dear to the Muses and cherishèd by the bright-souled
    Goddess of the Feast."

FRAGMENT 140D

(e) "WHAT thing is God? He is the sum of things."

FRAGMENT 141

"GOD it is that fashioneth all things for men,   ·
And for song begetteth he beauty"
(or "begetteth our joy in song").

ETHICAL AND SENTENTIOUS FRAGMENTS

FRAGMENT 213

(f) "WHETHER by justice or by crooked wiles
The race of men on earth mounteth to a higher point of
    vantage,
My mind is divided as to the truth to tell."

FRAGMENT 214

(g) "(IF a man liveth righteously)
Sweet Hope is his fellow-comrade, cherishing his heart
    and comforting his age,
Hope that more than ought else pilots the changeful mind
    of men."

FRAGMENT 205

(h) "QUEEN Goddess Truth, Fount of (all) high excellence,
Let not my plighted honour stumble against harsh false-
    hood."

FRAGMENT 215

(i) "DIFFERENT men have different laws,
And each man commendeth his own rule of right."

FRAGMENT 169

(k) "CUSTOM, monarch of mortal men and the Immortals,
Leads on violence with a high hand, dressing it as justice.
The deeds of Herakles give me proof,
For he drave the oxen of Geruon, with no asking for them
    and no price paid, on towards the Cyclopian fore-
    courts of Eurustheus' palace."

Cf. fragment from Herculaneum papyrus:

FRAGMENT 80

(l) "I PRAISE thee, Geruon, set beside Herakles:
But on all that pleaseth not Zeus, let me keep silence
    utterly."

Advice of prophet to his son:

FRAGMENT 42

(*m*) "REVEAL not to alien men, what affliction is approach-
ing us.
Verily, this rede will I give thee:
Things fair and joyful 'tis meet to bring into the midst
and share with all the people;
But if some mischance insufferable, of the Gods' giving,
befalleth men,
'Tis seemly to veil this in darkness."

FRAGMENT 43

(*n*) "MINGLE with all cities of men, being in thy mind most
like the colour of the sea-beast that clingeth to the rock;
Willingly praise him in whose company thou art;
And let thy mood change with the changeful times."

FRAGMENT 212

(*o*) "ENVY is the fellow-comrade of hollow-hearted men."

FRAGMENT 159

(*p*) "TIME is the best redeemer of righteous men."

FRAGMENT 160

(*q*) "EVEN their friends are betrayers of the dead "

GENERAL REMARKS ON THE FRAGMENTS

We may deeply regret the lost works of Pindar; neverthe-less, the discoveries of recent years tend to give us the im-pression that it was the epinician odes on which he spent greatest power; and it was perhaps for this reason that they alone have been preserved. The paeans are interest-ing and bear the original impress of Pindar's handiwork; but so far as they have been revealed to us, we should not place them on the level of any one of the four collections of poems that have been handed down; it is only the poem on the eclipse and the concluding portion of Paean VI. that rise to the summit of poetry.

We have, then, a fairly large collection of fragments, nearly all preserved to us by ancient authors quoting Pindar; they are often quoted without any reference to their context or any indication of the kind of poem from which they were drawn. Modern papyrology has contributed a little more, but in so mutilated a state that it does not increase our literary treasure. A selection has been pre-sented in the translations above of all those that possess some literary value or that throw some light on the mind or the soul of Pindar.

We gain something from a survey of the fragments deal-ing with mythologic subjects; which deepen in us the im-pression of his creative mythopoetic brain. He certainly flung his net widely, and he must have handled all the leading Greek myths in some form or other. The fragment on Peleus[1] may come from a lost epinician ode on an Aeginetan victory; he is tireless in exalting the Aiakidai and in expanding their legend; and while he was almost certainly the first to attribute to Peleus all these various adventures, he becomes himself an authority and wins acceptance of them with Euripides and later writers. We also discern that there was no form of composition that he set his hand to which precluded him from indulging his passion for narrating and shaping myths.

Looking at the few fragments of his 'encomia' or eulogies on distinguished men, we may gather that they need not have differed much in content from the epinicians, many of which might be so designated. Though properly their subject belonged to present history, they would often allow

---

[1] P. 346, Fr. 172.

him to escape to the remote past, in so far as the person addressed, a Theron or an Alexander, drew his ancestry from the mythic period. They show a lighter and easier style, and while many of these personal fragments have little value as poetry, they prove that Pindar could sometimes unstring his bow.

If we may judge by the small fragments of the wreckage, none of these private poems to individuals equalled in splendour and richness of diction his hymn of praise on Thebes; the fragment[1] translated above is almost certainly the proem, and it "shines from afar", as he says in his epinicians that a proem should. A genuine and passionate devotion rings in the verses, and evokes his full strength, and he has a radiant vision of Thebe as a Goddess, all clad in gold. We are reminded of the inspired passage in the ninth Pythian, and the motive of both may have been the same, to rehabilitate himself in the opinion of his fellow-citizens who had charged him with want of patriotism. Henceforth they could hardly vex him on that ground.

The fragment[2] from the poem in praise of Sparta is of all the more value because in all his surviving works he brings us rarely into contact with the greatest military state in Greece: of which one reason probably was that Sparta thought she had something more important to do than to produce prize-athletes. These verses are stately and beautiful in rhythm, and noticeable for the picture they present of the city that we were sometimes taught to regard as a mere barracks. It is praised for the wisdom of its council of elders—Pindar would put all city-government into the hands of wise elders—for the matchless prowess of its young men, for its devotion to the arts of music and dancing, and for the festal cheerfulness of its life; in respect of the last point, Pindar is probably thinking of the common meals. We are not sure that he was well acquainted by personal intercourse with Sparta of the fifth century, though a portion of his clan may in old times have settled there. And his eulogy loses some of its value as an authority when we discern that it is almost a *verbatim* reproduction of the eulogy on Sparta composed by Terpander of Lesbos nearly two hundred years earlier. Nevertheless, even in the fourth century Sparta was in some repute for her cultivation of a certain type of music; and we have sufficient

[1] P. 346, Fr. 194.   [2] P. 347, Fr. 199.

indication from other parts of his works that Pindar had a genuine admiration for her and would have sided with her against Athens in the great struggle, as indeed he preferred Dorians generally to Ionians.

Of the other homeless fragments, a few are of deep religious colour and contribute material to our study of the religion of Pindar, which will be dealt with in a later volume. The translation of those selected above may attest their poetic value. Pindar's words become poetry always when he was in earnest, and he was in earnest about religion.

Finally, we have many fragments that are of a didactic, sententious, or ethical character, utterances in which he moralises on human action or life. We know that Pindar never—like Hesiod or Wordsworth—composed a poem of wholly didactic content. But we know also that he had a strong didactic vein which he inherited from the old Boeotian school; and that he hardly ever failed to moralise on the action that he is describing in his lyric verse. And again and again we have felt in reading his preserved works that if ever a man could kindle morality with poetry, it was Pindar, though he was occasionally betrayed by his didactic trend. In fact, later philosophic writers, especially Plato, only quote Pindar to illustrate some moral point or to introduce some ethical question for debate, as if he were a recognised moral authority.

These fragments mainly confirm our impressions. None of them have the dullness and flatness of ordinary didactic verse, and some are deeply instinct with poetry. What may surprise us at the first glance is that, while Pindar is usually the champion of high morality and later writers specially praised him for his piety, some of these utterances suggest an enlightened and sceptical man of the world, who was not always on the side of the angels. What he says about 'custom' in fragments 215 and 169 might have been said by a sophist at Athens preaching revolutionary doctrines and the relativity of all morality. Yet Pindar's scepticism or free-thinking does not here go very far; he criticises the story of Geruon[1] from the point of view of the higher morality and intimates that Herakles, his ideal hero, was wrong in carrying off his cattle, and that Geruon was right in defending them; but he then retreats in alarm from his own casuistry, feeling that to censure Herakles, the son of Zeus, might be

[1] P. 348, Fr. 80.

displeasing to the High God. There is more naïveté than enlightenment in this. Had he played the moralising censor on Greek mythology generally, his career as epic-lyric poet would have closed.

The fragment (43) in which he recommends us to imitate the polypus, to be versatile, to adapt ourselves to our surroundings, "to be all things to all men", is more poetical, but neither more nor less moral, than St. Paul's aphorism. He has derived his strange comparison from some older epic poem; and his utterance probably is drawn from an ode in which he was describing the setting forth of the prophet Amphiaraos as one of the "Seven against Thebes". The other fragment (42), which belongs probably to the same context, is of deeper tone and higher in the scale of ethical poetry: the departing father here gives his son noble counsel: let him share his joy and his good tidings with his neighbours, but let him veil his sorrows in silence. Pindar has followed his own advice, for nowhere in his poetry appears the egoism of self-pity.

Fragment 213 is one of the best known of his sententious utterances: for it is quoted first by Plato in a prominent place in his *Republic*, where it helps to start the main discussion of that treatise. The passage at first sight suggests the 'antinomian' spirit, and a Platonic philosopher of a later age censured the poet for it. But a very severe moralist may be allowed to doubt whether virtue really pays best in this world. And Pindar in another place—fragment 159 —in a phrase that is one of those that "sparkle on the finger of old Time", proclaims his deep conviction that the righteous are justified in the end.

His text on envy—fragment 212—is an echo of the same high style and high thinking. But the last fragment (160) selected for translation above is the most striking of all, if only we could be sure of the exact phrasing. The words are weighty with a tragic and solemn sadness: they arrest and startle us, and one would give much to know their context and the bitter experience of Pindar's that evoked them. The disillusion of this post-war age may have driven deep into the souls of some of us this sentiment of Pindar; but no modern has uttered it so tensely and so movingly.

All the great Greek poets were didactic, and no other didactic poetry reaches to the level of the Greek; and in this department as in others Pindar has supremacy.

PINDAR'S LIFE AND WORK

PINDAR'S LIFE AND WORK

BORN in 518 B.C. at a little village near Thebes, Pindar
was fortunate in the time of his nativity; for it fell on the
threshold of the greatest period in the history of human
culture and of the most momentous epoch in the world-
struggle between East and West: he was also not unfortunate
in its place, for the immediate neighbourhood of Thebes is
even now full of charm, and the mountain of the Muses,
Helikon, is still a beautiful feature of the landscape; while
the countryside and the city in Pindar's time were richer
in mythologic and religious lore than any other Greek community; and from this source Pindar's genius was to derive
its deepest impress and to draw its most congenial nutri-
ment. The heroic traditions of Thebes that had fertilised
the early epic poetry of Greece, and were to enrich the Attic
stage, were Pindar's birthright; and those traditions were
still a living force and articles of faith in the time of the
poet and even later; for the great families of Thebes still
traced their descent back to the house of Laios and to the
warriors who sprang from the dragon's teeth. There is
strong reason for believing that Pindar himself belonged
to a noble house, the clan of the Aigeidai, who had offshoots
of themselves in Sparta, Thera, and perhaps in Cyrene; for
this is the natural interpretation of the passage in the fifth
Pythian;[1] and this might partly explain his attachment
to Sparta and his warm interest in Cyrene. And even
apart from this record we might have divined that he was
of high descent; so clear is the impress of the aristocratic
temper on his style, his theory of life, and on his personal
bearing towards the great ones of the earth.

In the days of Kadmos, Thebes may have been a centre
of advanced culture. It certainly was not that in the days
when Pindar was born. There may have been lingering
there a tradition of Hesiod and the old Boeotian school

[1] L.. 73.

named after him; and Pindar owed to them a not inconsiderable debt. But they were writers in a sober and *bourgeois* style, and could in no way claim Pindar as their brilliant offspring. And nothing that we know of the national temperament of Thebes and its relation to the world of art and letters explains Pindar. He is the one man of genius that his city throughout the whole course of her history produced in either of these spheres. Boeotia also produced the poetess Korinna, his contemporary and adviser. But the few fragments of her works that have been preserved explain why nearly all of them have perished; for she composed in the broadest Boeotian dialect, and therefore could only appeal to her own countrymen. And she only concerns the story of the youthful Pindar because of the literary anecdote, which we need not reject as valueless, that she advised him in the beginning of his career to draw upon Greek mythology for his poetic material; and when she found his youthful ardour too exuberant in obeying her, she checked it by the pithy remark, "We must sow with the hand, not with the whole sack", a rustic proverb that forms the golden rule of all style. But all that Boeotia could teach him of use for his future craft was flute-playing; for Boeotia was fond of the flute, and good reeds grew by the river and lake. The position that his community held in the ideal world was sufficiently indicated by the taunting phrase, to which he jestingly refers and which he thinks he may have silenced—"the Boeotian hog".

Therefore his parents sent him to Athens, as a place where his genius, that must have already announced itself in boyhood, could receive the highest training in the musical and poetic craft of choral composition. For, thanks to the devotion of the Peisistratidai to the higher culture, thanks also to the great expansion of the Attic spirit consequent on their expulsion, Athens towards the close of the sixth century had taken for the first time a leading place in the world of Greek civilisation. But she had not yet begun, and did not begin until after the Persian sack, to reach forward to her height of pre-eminence. And the youthful Pindar during his apprenticeship would see nothing great in her art, unless he had the discernment to see the nascent greatness of her vase-painting.[1] She was develop-

---

[1] He took note of Attic vases—vide *Nem*. x. 35 and *Frag*. 124 *a·b*.

ing indeed a native style of sculpture, aided by Ionian
talent, that attracts us by a certain archaic sweetness and
grace; but neither her sculpture nor her architecture were
as yet deeply impressive. But the city even then would
doubtless seem brilliant as compared with his native
Thebes; and his imagination might well have been warmly
stirred by the natural beauty of the Akropolis and of the
surrounding mountains with their strange light upon them.

It was also an inestimable advantage for the impression-
able youth that he should thus early come into familiar
contact with a far nobler and more refined society than he
could meet at Thebes, a society that was on the threshold
of the most marvellous cycle in the world's history. And it
would not repel him by any extreme manifestation of the
democratic temper; for the old aristocracy was still influen-
tial and of high prestige. Among the greatest were the
Alkmaionidai, a clan that produced more than one man
of genius. Pindar's early association with Delphi would
attract him to them, the great benefactors of the Pythian
shrine; and it may have been in his student days that he
began that friendship with them that glows in the seventh
Pythian, a work of his early prime. Of the names of the
Athenians with whom he is recorded in one of the traditional 'Lives' as having associated during his first residence
there, two are obscure names of his teachers of choral
technique: another is the name of Aeschylus. This record,
though it stands in a 'Life' of doubtful value, is of the
highest interest, and may be accepted as certain. For,
though a few years his senior, Aeschylus would have
been training himself at Athens, at the time when Pindar
arrived, in the technique of choral composition, and in the
other arts necessary for the future Founder of Tragedy.
And it is justified by the internal evidence. Nowhere else
in the history of literature do we find poets so alike in
style and spirit; such rare qualities as daring, sublimity,
nobleness of mind, reserved force, austere pathos, are
common to both. Of course there are marked differences;
Aeschylus is the deeper thinker, and lacks Pindar's impetuous swiftness, the eagle's swoop; he had also the nobler
profession, one that left no room for the expression of egoism. But the differences are in no way so marked as the
kinship; and the reader who loves Aeschylus will love
Pindar. The numerous echoes noted above in their respect-

ive works, echoes that sometimes leave us in doubt which of the two is the borrower and which the lender, are proofs of a close intercourse and interchange of poetic work, each having opportunity to read or to hear the works of the other.[1] And they may have often met when each was in the zenith of his fame; for Aeschylus was at the court of Hieron simultaneously with Pindar in 476 B.C.; and even when relations between Athens and Thebes were strained, we may suppose that Pindar, like many another foreigner, was often attracted to Athens at the time of the City Dionysia, when Aeschylus in the theatre was astonishing the world by his new dramatic art. How long Pindar could continue to enjoy this inspiring intercourse with the society of the greatest city of Greece is a doubtful question. He may have ceased to visit her as she advanced down the path of democracy, and after she had destroyed the power of Aigina, the community he loved next to his own. But being as happy in the date of his death as he was of his birth, he died before she committed her worst crimes. It is probable that he never lost his warm admiration for her; and he never openly spoke against her in his poems, though he must have grieved with the rest of his countrymen when she gained the ascendancy over Thebes and Boeotia in 456 B.C., and must have rejoiced when Boeotia shook it off in 447. His splendid panegyrics of Athens must be ascribed to the earlier period when she could be regarded as the champion of Hellenic freedom against Persia. His eulogies reveal his deep impression of her as a city of wonder; but they were composed before she reached that zenith of glory and beauty to which Perikles and Pheidias brought her. He never saw the architecture of Iktinos or the sculpture of the Parthenon. But he could have enjoyed there in his later visits the art of the transitional period before Pheidias, when her vase-painters were revealing themselves in the fulness of their powers and the transitional sculpture was showing the promise of coming grandeur, but was not yet at the height of its mastery.

As regards the countryside of Attica, with its wealth of local legend and cult, this is not reflected in his poems. Attic legend for the most part lay outside the old heroic epic, upon which his imagination brooded. In some of his

---

[1] We have noted above, pp. 148-149, the strange resemblance between the eleventh Pythian and the *Agamemnon* of Aeschylus.

lost poems he seems to have touched on the story of Theseus
at certain points; but the only Attic legend recorded in his
surviving works—very briefly—is the legend of Iolaos, who
rose from the earth to slay Eurustheus in the battle waged
by the Athenians for the children of Herakles. Whether
Eleusis with its solemn mystery-cult and its lovely myth of
the Madre Dolorosa had any fascination for him in his
youthful or maturer years, there is no evidence to show. It
is doubtful if he really knew the mysteries and their teaching.[1] And there is some point in that remarkable tale that
he was visited in a dream by Persephone a few weeks before
his death, who complained that he had never written a
poem on her, but promised him that he should soon have
the opportunity.

It is very important, then, for our full appreciation of the
influences that shaped his genius that he learned his poet's
craft in Athens and was intimate with Aeschylus. Nevertheless, for all that this means, we still have to admit that
his poetic inspiration drew more from Aigina, its atmosphere and traditions, than it drew from Attica: and through
all his life he was pro-Dorian rather than pro-Ionian.

And whatever else he may have derived from Athens he
imbibed little or nothing of Ionic science or enlightenment.
In fact, he frequented the city before she became the
'Schoolmistress' of Greece, before Protagoras the sophist
and Anaxagoras the scientist had arrived there to break up
the old traditional order of thought and to lay the foundations of 'modernism'. We need not suppose that either in
Athens or on his travels to the west his ears and mind were
wholly closed against the new views; and we have noted his
poetic fragment on 'Custom', as the ruling principle of the
life of men and Gods, which might well be an echo of
sophistic theory. And he must have heard about Ionic physical science, and especially, when he was in Sicily, of Em-
pedokles; and he may have been thinking of this when he
wrote his moving verse on the futility of the human in-
tellect,[2] and when he speaks scornfully of those who "cull
the unripe fruit of Wisdom", inventing a phrase that Plato
approved. Therefore it is not as the scientist but as the
inspired poet that he reacts to such exciting stimuli as the
eruption of Etna and the total eclipse of the sun. And he

[1] *Vide supra*, pp. 336-337.
[2] Cf. *supra*, p. 319.

would have agreed with Keats about the "awful rainbow". Only having by no means a vague imagination, but clear Greek eyes, he describes the phenomena of Etna—apart from the mythic monster buried below the crater—with more realism and fidelity to fact than does Vergil who borrows from him.

It may well have been that to Pindar the highest type of Athenian would seem to be incarnate in Aeschylus, who was not only the mighty poet but "the man of Marathon".

The ancient biographies of Pindar do not indicate how long his apprenticeship at Athens lasted; but they preserve one anecdote illustrating the precocity of his youthful genius and the swiftness with which his powers developed and won public recognition. Before he was fully mature, his fame must have spread from Thebes and Athens, for in 498 B.C., when he was twenty years old, he received an important commission from the great Thessalian family of the Aleuadai to compose an ode in honour of the victory in the boys' double footrace at Delphi.[1] It has been pointed out in the commentary on this poem that, although it reveals some crudities and uncertainty of purpose, it approves the young poet as already fully trained in the technique of choral lyric, and as the master of an individual and arresting style of diction which he maintained throughout his long literary career. This first 'epinician' also exhibits the method of composition that he afterwards followed, almost as a conventional rule, in this species of poem; namely, as natural themes for the subject-matter, the praise of the victor, his family and state, moralising on the joys of success and on the laws of human life and our relations to the higher powers, the introduction of some mythic theme relevant to the occasion or to the family or to the community. It is well to remember that Pindar was not the pioneer in this field. His elder contemporary Simonides was the first to develop the epinician ode, and to fix its features and structural outlines, which the younger poet took over from him.

For his next dateable work we must wait till 490 B.C., and can only fill up this gap in his biography with surmises. At some early time in his career he became intimately attached to Delphi, and this attachment grew to such a point that he comes to speak and to feel like the specially

[1] *Pyth.* x.

appointed prophet-poet of Apollo. We do not know when
it began or the causes that led to it. Neither his family nor
his city had any special connection with Delphi, or any
prerogative that might have commended him to the priesthood. We must suppose it was his own genius and self-
devotion to the temple; it is of course possible also that in
his early years he won the prize in some musical competition
there by the composition of some paean. We have seen
how in the sixth Paean he speaks almost as if he were
Delphi's 'retained' poet and as if Apollo's shrine were his
spiritual mother: and this intimate relation of the poet to
the God lasted all his life and even long after his death. It
is likely that it was already established by the time he
received his first commission; for not only is the tenth
Pythian markedly Apolline in its colour, but the Hyperborean myth, its leading theme, was rooted in Delphi as
in Thessaly.[1] The region and the temple of Delphi gave
Pindar his deepest religious experience: we may be sure
also that the scenery struck the deepest impress upon his
poetic imagination; for it is the most haunting in Europe;
and anyone who has slept for a night on the mountain-
terrace above the gorge will feel what Pindar felt when he
called it "the loud-roaring land", "the land of many
voices". It has not yet become wholly common and secular
ground.

We again find sure footing in the chronology in the
year 490 B.C. He then composed two Pythian odes, the
one gratuitously offered to Xenokrates, the other composed
in honour of the flute-player Midas, both of Akragas, works
which, though neither of the highest order, might help to
swell Pindar's fame in Sicily. (We may note in passing
that this is the year of the battle of Marathon, a momentous
event about which later Athens was sufficiently vocal, but
which was not noticed by Pindar nor by any contemporary
poet till Aeschylus alludes to it in his *Persae* and in his self-
composed epitaph.)

This decade before the Persian invasion is only meagrely
and doubtfully represented by a few poems in our surviving
collection. That he kept in close touch with Athens and with
the great house of the Alkmaionidai is proved by his short
ode on Megakles, the seventh Pythian, the only composition of this period that can be dated with some certainty.

[1] *Vide* my *Cults,* vol. iv. pp. 100, 105.

Coming now to the crucial epoch of Pindar's life, the years of the Persian invasion (480–479 B.C.), we naturally wish to consider what part Pindar played in the struggle and discover if possible what his movements were. We can see at once that circumstances deprived him of the privilege of striking a blow for the cause of Greece. His contemporary and friend, Aeschylus, belonging to a higher-minded community, enjoyed this privilege, and probably owed to it the battle-spirit that inspired the great poetry of his "Seven against Thebes" and his "Persians". It is good for a poet to face death in the field; but there is no indication that Pindar ever served in any of his city's campaigns, although like any other citizen he must have been liable for military service. Of course the pro-Persian policy that his country adopted prevented him joining the patriot-army. But we would like to discover, if possible, what were his inner thoughts about that policy. The modern historian finds some excuse for Thebes, in that, after the allied forces had mismanaged the defence of Thermopylae and the selfish timidity of Sparta had abandoned all Greece north of the Isthmus, Thebes had no choice save submission or extinction or withdrawal from Boeotia with women and children. And if there was any Theban at that time to preach the policy of heroic despair, it certainly was not Pindar. He was not of that temperament; and in any case, being so devoted to Delphi, he would have been influenced by the cautious opportunist policy of the oracle sitting on the fence. But we need not believe the later historian Polybius when he declares that Pindar definitely advised his countrymen to 'medise'.[1] At any rate, Thebes at the time was in the hands of some wholly unscrupulous oligarchs, who thought to make capital out of the Persian triumph, which they regarded as certain. Hence Thebes became the centre of the great Persian host under Mardonios, and a large Theban force fought on its side against the allies at Plataea. Was Pindar living then at Thebes, exposed—himself and his family—to the usual violence of an Oriental army, and was he conscripted for military service in the ranks? We can be certain, at all events, that he did not fight at Plataea;

[1] Polyb. iv. 31. 5, who quotes as proof fragment 109, translated, p. 340; there is no reason to think that the poem from which those lines were taken was composed on the "Persian question", *vide* Macan, *Herodotus*, vol. ii. p. 59 and pp. 11-12.

so untoward an action on his part, so detrimental to his future career as Pan-Hellenic poet, would have been certainly recorded. And there are reasons for believing that he was not residing at Thebes at all during the Persian occupation. If the arguments put forward above[1] for placing the so-called 'fifth' Isthmian between the battle of Salamis and Plataea are valid, we discern from that ode that Pindar was then in Aigina; and it is inconceivable that during the Persian occupation of Thebes a Theban citizen would have been free to pass to and fro between Thebes and the Allied lines. Pindar might well have retreated from the storm and found safe quarters at Delphi.

Therefore, he had not earned, like Aeschylus, the right to the rôle of the warrior-poet, nor is there any hint or sign in his poems that he had ever fought on any stricken field. Nevertheless, this did not debar him, being of such creative imagination, from rousing himself to a few great utterances of war-poetry, such as have been gathered and noticed above, or eulogising in a later ode the great achievements of Athens, thus competing in this *métier* with the successful Simonides, who was probably more unwarlike than himself. A poet does not always need the experience of facts, though it will help him; he can quicken an imagined emotion in himself and others. One of the greatest war-poets was said to be a lame schoolmaster.

Inactive as he was in the great struggle, he felt deeply the shame and the danger that his city incurred. The victory of Plataea was a dark hour for Thebes; and Pindar could not freely express his joy at the deliverance of Greece. The rolling away of the stone of Tantalos meant something different for him from what it meant for the patriot-Greeks, and the eighth Isthmian, written a year after the deliverance, is full of depression and tribulation of spirit.

Probably not long afterwards appeared the poems which we call the third and the fourth Isthmian odes. His reputation must by this time have risen high, although none of the few surviving works of this earlier period are of the first rank.

For near to the date of 476 B.C. he received an invitation from the great Hieron of Syracuse to visit him and to commemorate the Olympian victory of his famous horse. The invitation and the commission must have been welcome to

[1] Pp. 273-274.

Pindar for more than merely material reasons. The change of scene offered him a requickening of spirit and great new experiences. His imagination was deeply stirred by such a physical phenomenon as the eruption of Etna, by the splendour of the Hellenic cities of the west, especially Akragas, also by the glorious triumphs of Hellenism over barbarian powers under such leaders as Gelon and Hieron. Stimulated by these influences he produced such masterpieces of the world's lyric poetry as the poems on Hieron and Theron; and he stands forth now as a true Pan-Hellenic poet, with a patriotic afflatus, which there is no reason to regard as simulated. The achievements of Gelon and Hieron at Himera and Kumai would have been known to us only through the arid and brief record of the historians, had it not been for Pindar's poetry which makes them shine for us.

Hieron, like Peisistratos, was desirous of attracting distinguished men of letters to his court. And Pindar <u>had the opportunity there of meeting Aeschylus</u>, a privilege which he would have valued, for the great Athenian dramatist was in no way his rival; and their intercourse there might account for some of the mutual interflow of poetic influences that we note in their works. He could also have met Simonides and Bacchulides and with them his relations were not likely to be cordial. In the first place, they were his rivals, and successful rivals: for, after some experience of this strange Theban poet, Hieron gave to Bacchulides the commission to celebrate the greatest of his Olympian victories, the victory with the four-horsed chariot, perhaps because he did not appreciate Pindar's free moralising or because he found Bacchulides' poetry easier to construe. Now the scholiasts preserve the tradition of the early commentators that the epinician odes of Pindar are full of spiteful and depreciatory allusions to his two rivals. In most cases we may consider their discernment at fault, and that the poetry of the odes is not so frequently disfigured: but in regard to the well-known passage in the second Olympian[1] there is something to be said for their interpretation. As regards Simonides, we should grieve if Pindar's professional jealousy blinded him to his genius; and certainly when Pindar in his hymn composed for the men of Keos is praising the island of Simonides and Bacchulides for its contribution

impossible: A was there between 472 + 468, see my HighL., p. 148.

---

[1] *Vide supra*, p. 16.

to the Muses, he might have been rather warmer.[1] But we can understand that the former poet, who could compose such an ode of fawning low-toned morality as that one of which has come down to us in honour of a scoundrel of a ruling Thessalian house, would be temperamentally un-congenial to Pindar. For Pindar has the free pride of the true aristocrat: and he knows how to speak frankly but tactfully to kings and dynasts. As regards Bacchulides, such a man as Pindar might be pardoned if he came to regard him as a negligible minor poet. And generosity towards successful rivals was not a common trait in the Greek character. In spite of the annoyance they may have caused him, Pindar retained to the end his friendship with Hieron, and it was more than the friendship of the bought hireling. He gives to him and to his son some good advice as to government, and between the lines we may read proof that he was aware of some of his patron's defects.

Doubtless, he formed acquaintance with other leading men in Sicily, some of whose names are associated with his odes. And as he stayed nearly two years in Sicily he no doubt visited its chief cities—besides Syracuse, Kamarina and Akragas, and probably the city of the Lokroi in Magna Graecia. From the internal evidence of his Cyrenaean odes, we should gather that he also visited Cyrene, which was not difficult to reach from Syracuse; for he shows curiously minute knowledge of its topography and legends, also a remarkable acquaintance with Egyptian origins of the Ammon-cult, which it is difficult to imagine how he could acquire except through conversation with the priesthood on the spot. And it was probably the enthusiasm inspired by personal travel that induced him to set up the cult of Zeus Ammon at home.

It was not natural that a man of his imperious and in-dependent temper should be content to reside permanently at a despot's court. And he was probably not sorry to return to his home in 474 B.C., with a great and Pan-Hellenic reputation and leaving many admirers in Sicily. Some time after returning to Thebes he must have sent out to a Syracusan noble his sixth Olympian which ranks with his masterpieces; and he remained on friendly—even affectionate—terms with Hieron and other of his Sicilian friends. On the other hand, it is clear that he was regarded

[1] *Vide supra*, p. 303.

with some suspicion and disapproval by his fellow-country-
men; his enemies charging him with disloyalty to Thebes
and with his devoting his genius to the exaltation of other
cities, even to Athens their most hated foe. A long digression
in the ninth Pythian is framed to defend himself against
these accusations, according to the interpretation I have
offered of it.[1] And it is possible that the splendid hymn
composed in honour of Thebes was partly inspired by the
same motive.[2] Also, if we were convinced that the enigmatic
poem, the eleventh Pythian, was composed about the time
of his return to Thebes, we could confidently explain the
passage in it which expresses his disapproval of tyrants as
intended to persuade his countrymen that he had not been
corrupted by the atmosphere of Hieron's court. His efforts
to recover the good opinion of his native city must have
been successful: for he seems to have resided there more or
less for the rest of his life in peace and prosperity, and the
fragments of his poem on the eclipse indicate that his
position there was one of admitted authority, and the
seventh Isthmian ode breathes the spirit of whole-hearted
patriotism.

Though after 474 B.C. he does not appear to have
travelled far afield, we may suppose that he made not infrequent visits to Delphi, Athens, and Aigina, and to the
centres of the great games. And his reputation, now at its
zenith, traversed the whole of the Greek-speaking world:
he receives commissions from the Ionians of Abdera as
from the Dorians of Corinth, Argos, and Rhodes; and he
was chosen by the Locrians and the Molossians to be their
public representative at Thebes, a social honour much
valued by the Greeks.

For the rest of his life we have no external evidence, only
the tradition that he lived till the age of eighty, and that
he died in the theatre at Argos reclining at the feet of a
beautiful youth whom he loved. The works that may be
ascribed to his latest years show that his poetic powers
abided with him unimpaired; as in so many of the illustrious
Greeks the creative spirit was strong up to the end.

His life was doubtless full of interest and colour, and
rich in opportunities for the exercise of his professional
craft. Yet we must call it uneventful, in view of the fact
that he was contemporary with some of the momentous

---

[1] *Vide supra*, pp. 138-139.   [2] *Vide* p. 346.

events that have shaped the history of the world. In some measure like Goethe, he lived detached from them. But there is nothing to suggest that he cultivated a temper of philosophic detachment and aloofness. On the contrary, he gives the impression of a bold and energetic character, of one who could play a strong part in the struggle if called upon. However, circumstances did not call upon him, but allowed him to watch the victorious world-contest of his race without participating. Fortunately, also, he died before witnessing the racial energy turning to self-destruction.

But in recommending Pindar to the modern reader as a poet of high significance and value, one must face the question whether the world that his poetry reflects is of present interest or importance. No one doubts but that the struggle between Greece and Persia, the birth of Ionic science and of Attic philosophy and art, the development of Athenian democracy and maritime power, are events that must interest man as long as he remains a rational being with a memory. But, as we have seen, the poetry of Pindar only faintly reflects the world-struggle and not at all the intellectual forces that were turning the human spirit down new ways of thought. It reflects the Greece that insisted on keeping up its athletic sports when the host of Xerxes was darkening the land; a Greece that still regarded an eclipse as a sign of the wrath of God; and his social ideal is the small independent community under a well-tempered constitution administered by 'moderate' aristocrats of genial hospitality who kept race-horses, loved music and glory, and who were proud of their hero-ancestors in the past and of their athletes in the present. Now, to some moderns, this world of Pindar's—representing the pre-Persian period of Greece—may not appear of sufficient worth and interest to make poetic appeal. It does not appear so to Wilamowitz, most original of our modern commentators on Pindar; at the close of his treatise he pays him a noble tribute of personal devotion, but prefaces it by such words as these: "His world is wholly alien to us; its habits, mode of thought and fashions are without attraction for us where they are not shocking".[1] And in an earlier part of that chapter he suggested that the Pindar-problem is similar to the Dante-problem: to explain how poetry can maintain its greatness, coming from a world that repels us.

---

[1] *Pindaros*, p. 463.

But an imagination that can penetrate more deeply into the past might enable us to say that the first fallacy in this statement is that it unduly depreciates the world of Pindar's youth. Hellas at the close of the sixth century was endowed by nature with more beauty than any part of Europe;[1] though not so replete as it became in the days of Pheidias and Polukleitos with works of beauty by the hands of man, there was a rising art sufficient to quicken the *joie de vivre*; the aristocratic societies were at least as genial and attractive as the later democratic; these aristocratic families cherished an ancestral mythology that is the most beautiful that comparative mythology presents to us, and it did not belong wholly to the past, for many contemporary people believed in it, and it affected men's actions; the inhabitants of the land were not yet debased by malaria and exhausting wars, but were probably the finest physical stock that has yet existed; there was less cruelty and hatred rife in the cities and the land than in the later periods; finally, the figures of the polytheism were full of grace and charm. A great poet who can transmute such a world into his verse can produce work that may well abide through the changes of time.

There is another fallacy latent in the criticism mentioned above that might prejudice the modern world against Pindar: the implication that his want of 'enlightenment' impairs his poetic value. But 'modernism' is not essential to the highest poetry; it sometimes raised Euripides to greatness, it sometimes betrayed him into ugliness and discord. That an 'enlightened', wholly free-minded Pindar would have written better poetry, and therefore been more helpful to us, is a bold assumption. The intensive spirit is as strongly creative as the extensive. The poet with cosmopolitan sympathies who ranges through the world does not necessarily count more for us than one who writes "great verse unto a little clan". Given the keen vision, the priceless jewel may be found in a very narrow plot. Pindar's 'narrowness', therefore, need not trouble us; and some of his best moralising poetry is wide-viewed enough.

But what may well surprise the modern man is that a great poet should have been moved to write lyric verse of surpassing merit on the subject of athletic sports. It is

---

[1] That is almost true to say of modern Greece in spite of its defacement by man.

rash to say of any subject, even a prize-fight of the early nineteenth century, that it is incapable of being treated poetically; for we cannot set limits to the possible creativeness of a possible poet. All that we can say is that our modern games have not evoked poetry of the highest order; but that the ancient games of Greece were able to attract two of the greatest Greek poets to sing of them. And yet the games-spirit, the passionate admiration of the athlete's prowess, is as tempestuous in modern England as it was in Pindar's Greece, and violent emotion is one of the stimuli of poetry. But anyone familiar with the striking difference in respect of circumstances and conditions between ancient and modern games will understand why the latter in England have never called for a Pindar or a Simonides. If our successful athletes had heroic ancestors or came from localities that rejoiced in great heroic legend, if they contended in the precincts of Westminster Abbey, consecrated with memories and legends of Edward the Confessor, King Arthur, Brutus of Troy, if they paid the best poet to celebrate their victories and encouraged him to interweave these heroic legends or the glories of their ancestors into his verse, and the poem was to be sung before a festal gathering of the kinsmen or on a procession as they marched to lay their cups or their trophies in St. Paul's, then such conditions might have evolved great poetry, nominally dealing with games, but virtually with things of deeper and more permanent value. Such are not the conditions prevailing in modern England; but such or something similar were the conditions under which Pindar worked. The odes themselves, with such commentaries as have been attached above, are sufficient to show this.

All the regular athletic contests of Greece, greater and lesser, were associated with religion, with the shrines of Gods and heroes, and many sacred or heroic legends clustered round the place of contest; and the surrounding scenery was often such as stimulated poetic imagination. The "truce of God" prevailed during the contests, suppressing all private feuds or public enmities, so that we never hear of dangerous outbreaks of passion or vulgar uproar or cursing of judges or umpires; the athletes themselves were for the most part of the old aristocratic houses, some of them cherishing great epic traditions about their ancestors. Also, the athlete's triumph did not concern himself alone,

though his honour and profit were immense and lifelong—
sometimes continuing after death—but deeply concerned his
kin, the whole city and the men of past ages as well. Pindar
can say of his Rhodian boxer—"with the glad fortunes of
the Eratidai the whole city holds high festival"; and the
city welcomed with fervour his lyric version of the birth of
Athena.[1] The victory of a young boy of Orchomenos
gives the occasion to Pindar for a masterful hymn on the
Graces.[2]

Therefore, the task of writing 'epinicians' was not really
cramping; the public and the patrons were tolerant in the
matter of relevance; and if a poet used his freedom tactfully,
he had almost free scope to range through the glittering
past of Greece, and this would satisfy most poets, as it
satisfied Pindar. Such freedom had its danger; it might
tempt a poet to the sin of irrelevance, which in poetry is
like chattering in ordinary conversation; and once at least
we have found Pindar committing this sin.

Also, the athlete-triumph gave the poet scope in another
direction. The exultation it caused was overpowering; and
the Greeks knew that all excess was dangerous; a jealous
eye, the divine Nemesis, an ironical Power, is watching us;
therefore it is right for the poet to warn the victor—king
or commoner, man or boy—that he has attained the height
of mortal felicity, but that he must not aspire to become a
God; he must think mortal thoughts; he must remember that
the limbs he adorns are one day to be covered in the earth.
These are the saws of old morality appropriate on transcen-
dent occasions, and they give the cue to Pindar to indulge
his didactic vein; and we have gathered enough testimony
of Pindar's peculiar power in this line. From this starting-
point he can moralise on the great issues of life.

The 'epinician' theme, then, handled in this manner was
stimulating enough. And there is no reason to suppose
that his interest in watching athletic contests was simulated.
The scene and the occasion might easily inspire him with
enthusiasm; the solemn beauty of the Delphic gorge, the
sunlit field, hill, and river at Olympia, which were beginning to be ennobled with forms of architecture and sculpture,
were congenial with the poetic mood; and such features
that might chill inspiration at our modern spectacles,

[1] *Ol.* vii. l. 93; *vide supra*, p. 37.
[2] *Ol.* xiv.

the lowering sky, the drab surroundings, the "submerged tenth" and the betting-ring, were absent from the ancient. Also, the Greek contests were not team-games of highly complicated technique which not everyone can understand, such as cricket and football, but individual feats of strength, swiftness, and skill, such as running, jumping, wrestling, and boxing; these are primeval exercises to which man has been devoted since his arboreal days, and they would appeal instantly to every Greek, whether poet or plain man. Probably such sports gave a more obvious display, especially as the competitors were naked, of symmetry, beauty, and strength than any of our team-games; and probably none of our horse-races, not even the Grand National, can compete in respect of brilliance and the thrilling sense of danger with the racing of the four-horsed chariots at Olympia and Delphi. Pindar himself confesses to his ardent susceptibility to the beauty of young limbs displayed in manly contests. And his inspired passage concerning Theia, the goddess of radiance, shows the strange rapture into which he could be lifted by the sight of racing trireme or car.[1]

We may believe, then, that he took up the epinician theme *con amore*, though Voltaire, who could not read him, mocks at him for it; and he enjoyed the opportunities it offered for high poetry to the full, and infects us with his enjoyment.

But the *métier* had its drawbacks; and Pindar, bold, original, and defiant as he is, does not wholly escape them. When the athlete or his family had piled up victories, they might demand their "pound of flesh", and require of their hired poet that he should chronicle them all. And Pindar knew well how hard it is to turn a long catalogue of athletic events into poetry. When it was demanded of him, we observe with what extraordinary skill he generally solves the problem; for he is a master-inventor of the strange, far-fetched, pithy phrase that makes common things impressive and unfamiliar. "Nemea withstandeth him not." "Eleusis pleads the cause of his renown." "The altar of Zeus, the Light-God, will rise up and bear him witness." "The stone-tablet at Megara hath no other story"—these are poetic devices that drive away dullness. But the strain might become too great if the victor or his family were

---

[1] *Vide supra*, pp. 272-273.

too professional and too *exigeant*. And in his Corinthian
ode, the thirteenth Olympian, Pindar droops under the
burden and frankly confesses his exhaustion; and the poetic
composition is injured.

The epinician odes, though probably the compositions
on which he spent most pains and art, were only a portion
of his output. As a writer of hymns for various religious
services he was in great demand and favour; and the fragments of these that survive, together with the many passages
in the odes containing religious thought or sentiment, com-
pel us to rank him with Aeschylus as a great master of
religious lyric. His austere and high-toned style and temper
fitted him to shine in this great field of poetry. Religious
conviction is also essential to success, and the question of
Pindar's religion will be considered in a later chapter.

All his various compositions, athletic odes, hymns to
Gods or heroes, *encomia* or odes in praise of cities or
individuals, dirges, banquet-songs, belong to what is called
'occasional' poetry. And here we strike a salient difference
between Greek lyric and our own; the Greek lyric muse,
and Pindar's, was social, not solitary. He composes for
crowds or groups of men meeting in the sunlight or in the
feasting-hall, for singers proceeding to a temple or standing round an altar; and all these are meeting for some
special purpose that shapes the poetic composition. Such
social, occasional lyric would seem to offer little scope to
free self-expression, and will probably be lacking in depth.
But what surprises us most in Pindar is that while appearing
to observe the laws of the occasion he claims and uses the
freest licence of self-expression, and that he can prelude a
Nemean ode with thoughts that go as deep as any that are
found in Wordsworth's *Intimations*. And he has the magic
art of turning the passing occasion to eternal value, and can
conjure up all the strong and bright powers and elements
in the world to exalt the solemnity of an athletic triumph.

The translations and criticisms of the odes may have
revealed sufficiently the various riches in the treasure-house
of Pindar's poetry, as well as certain flaws in his workmanship and taste. But it may be helpful by way of conclusion
to recall some salient features and to try to formulate the
essential qualities of his style.

As he was a great master of narrative poetry, a great
portion of his work, both of his epinicians and his other

compositions, is what has been called epic-lyric, the re-
telling of epic legends in a lyric style, swift, passionate, and
thrilling. His greatest achievement is generally judged to
be in this *genre*; and the passages in his odes that recount
the story of the Argonauts, the death of Kastor, the birth
of Athena, the birth of Iamos, are among the world's
masterpieces. He drew deeply on ancient literature for his
materials, the poems of Homer, the post-Homeric epic,
Hesiod and Stesichoros (who was the first to retell the epic
legends lyrically); but he felt free to reshape the stories,
and claimed to be himself a master-inventor of saga. His
handling of myths will be considered again in a later
chapter, in connection with his religious beliefs. The mythic
element in the composition of these epinician odes had been
received by him as a tradition. It exposed the poet to certain
dangers, the danger of diffuseness; and the danger of
irrelevance. Now Pindar is well aware that diffuseness or
garrulity is a literary sin (a sin with which Euripides was
charged, and Homer might be); he frequently expresses his
fear of wearying the audience and therefore sometimes stops
short in the middle of a narrative; while the style natural
to him, swift, abrupt, condensed, is at the opposite pole to
the style of the garrulous; nevertheless, he is not impeccable
in this respect, and having launched himself in a long story,
he sometimes carries it on beyond the point of vantage;
his narrative of Ixion in the second Pythian is a salient
example.

As regards relevance, a principle necessary to the unity
of any composition, Pindar certainly pays it respect, but
by no means the respect of a bond-slave. He and his audience
interpreted it in a freer and easier fashion than we might;
and if a myth was in some—even far-off—way relevant to
the athlete or his family or state or the locality of the games,
or if it merely illustrated some moral reflection natural to the
occasion, it was relevant enough for Pindar and his public.
Bacchulides is consistently irrelevant through weakness of
mind. But there is only one hopeless case of inexplicable
irrelevance in Pindar, the Agamemnon story; for which
even the ancient scholars condemned him. In fact, the
modern commentators have sinned more than the poet, as
Wilamowitz has well pointed out, in forcing the 'relevance'
of a mythic story into far too narrow bounds; of supposing
that there must always have been something in the athlete's

life or his family's history to explain it, and by inventing bogus and sometimes scandalous incidents.[1]

The other domain, in which many brilliant examples have been given of Pindar's mastery, is the domain of ethical poetry. It is one, as we are painfully aware, in which it is most difficult for a poet to shine. For when we are being preached at or instructed, we are at once on our guard, and our mood becomes naturally unpoetic. Therefore it requires a poet of high genius to cast the spell on us then, one who can so "criticise life" as to make it glow and throb in us or for us. Pindar received from his old Boeotian master Hesiod the tradition that preaching was part of the poet's mission, and unlike Hesiod he fulfilled his mission poetically. Sometimes, like Aeschylus, he moves us with the impression of grandeur—"the shadow of a magnitude"—in his grave, deep moralisings; sometimes he excites us by the tingling, pungent aphorism in a brief melodious phrase, and in this he is specially a master. But he is never impeccable in any line of work, and occasionally, though rarely, we may find his moralising vein betraying him into banality.[2] Such lapses, even if more frequent, would count as nothing against his triumphs: the eschatologic passage in the second Olympian shows us the perfect flower of ethical poetry, and the moral and political counsels that he gives in the first Pythian to Hieron and in the fourth Pythian to Arkesilas reveal him as the great poet, if not as the profound moralist and statesman. Perhaps his greatest achievement in this line is Jason's exhortation to Pelias: the awe-inspiring young hero, with the golden locks "flaming down his back", can preach to the old king without any injury to his heroic character and with enhancement of the dramatic thrill.

Pindar's moral thought about human life cannot well be considered apart from his religious views. For this summary account it is enough to emphasise the fact that it is entirely suffused with his poetry, to which as a tonic influence it adds strength and uplift. His judgment of life represents a golden mean between optimism and pessimism; and he gives us the counsel of a strong and brave man in bidding us "turn to view the fairer side of things", to conceal our own sorrows and share only our gladness with our friends: we may be only creatures of a day, dream-shadows, but at

---

[1] *Vide supra*, p. 149. [2] *Vide supra*, p. 162.

any moment "a gleam of heaven-born radiance" may lighten our lives:[1] this inspired passage in his Pythian ode suggests a view, to which much of his poetry may assist us to rise, that the temporary may have eternal value.

Temperamentally, his genius has a natural bias towards the greater and nobler forms and functions of life, and shows no power of expressing the humble and lowly things. The style that he made his own brought with it this limitation. It is a style very difficult to characterise, and it can only be apprehended and appreciated by those who are penetrated with Greek. Part of his diction is conventional form, common to the poets of choral lyric: it merely gave him a number of stereotyped phrases, dead epithets that have a sort of surface-glitter, like "deep-girdled Muses", "Aphrodite of the flashing-eyes": upon this he superimposes a style that can only be called 'Pindaric', which is unlike any other, so that small fragments broken from his work can always be detected as the master's. It is strained, audacious, fantastically high-pitched, yet fiery and swift—"hot with speed" —like work done with intense force on a glowing anvil. The forms produced are often like nobly carved gold, rich and mellow, but sometimes are gnarled and strange. His prayer for boundless power was certainly granted. And at times his severe stateliness is tempered and sweetened with a lusciousness all the more attractive as it is rare in him, notably in the passage describing the birth of Iamos in the sixth Olympian. This style often reminds the sympathetic reader of Shakespeare's. But, unlike our poet, Pindar could not change it, and therefore he could not express the plain man: when he appears to be trying to do so, as in the fourth Pythian, where the townsmen are commenting on the mysterious young hero, the phrasing is more than usually 'Pindaric'. We have seen also that such a style was not well adapted for the *abandon* of the lover's song or the gay recklessness of the drinking-song; nor, in more serious themes, for the expression of tender and gentle pathos.

But it was masterfully framed for all forms of sublimity and nobility, either in the world of nature or in the soul of man, and therefore for such high 'Dorian' pathos as ennobles the dying scene of Kastor.[2] He was well-advised, then, in choosing for his themes subjects and individuals on a high plane; and he is happiest "with eagles in the air".

[1] *Pyth*. viii. 98.   [2] *Vide supra*, p. 230.

Yet he never becomes giddy or morbid, for he had more than most Greeks the Greek qualities of balance and sanity. His favourite God, Apollo, seems to have breathed something of his spirit into him.

In speaking of the formal side of his work, his diction and style, it is impossible to avoid, even in the most general review of him, the question that arises about the musical setting of his odes. For us they are merely written poetry intended for reading or at most for recitation: for Pindar and his audience they were songs intended for music and dancing, and only by the help of these accompaniments could the antistrophal system, according to which nearly all of them are composed, win its true effect. But Pindar's musical notation is utterly lost; and as it seems that the scholars of Alexandria who collected and edited his works did not trouble to preserve it, we cannot hope that any papyrus-find will restore it to us.

According to the natural and traditional view, Greek metres are quantitative systems arranging the syllables according to the time-values, long and short, that they had in the spoken and written language. Anyone with a metrical ear and some knowledge of Greek metrical laws can discover and appreciate the metrical systems of most of Pindar's odes; especially those of the more solemn and stately mode, sometimes called 'Dorian', of which the rhythm lifts us and takes possession like melodious thunder; others are more complex and difficult to fix, and yet make an aesthetic impression on the modern ear as far from any prose-rhythms as the dipping, undulating flight of a bird is from mere walking-gait. And we believe that these metrical impressions help us to a full appreciation of Pindar's poetry.

But some scholars have been warning us that we may be deceived, and that lacking the music we cannot get any certain perception of Pindar's metres at all.[1] We are familiar with the misfortune to which our modern song-speech, even the most sacred, is liable, when it is taken charge of by a musician—most gifted perhaps in his technique, but illiterate in the sense that he has no reverence for words: he will often degrade the word by falsifying the natural length of the syllables, often severing by a long interval

---

[1] *Vide* article by Prof. Mountford, "Greek Music in the Papyri", in *New Chapters in Greek Literature*, by Powell and Barber, second series, p. 157.

one syllable from another, with which in our true speech it
is inseparably connected. This degradation—against which
there are now healthy signs of reaction in the modern
musical world—arose when the musician who was no
longer a poet was allowed to tyrannise over the poet's words.
And recent discovery has shown that Greek music as early
as or before the second century B.C. had fallen into this
vice, artificially changing the time-value of syllables for
its own purposes. Now we have even some reason for believing that Euripides was the first sinner in this matter,[1]
and we have every reason for believing that the trouble had
not yet arisen when Pindar was composing. He masterfully
expresses what he believes to be the true relation between
his words and the music, by his phrase at the opening of
the second Olympian, "Ye songs that rule the lyre": that
is to say, the music is the servant, not the master, of the song,
and must carefully follow the metres of the spoken speech,
giving to each syllable its proper value. Therefore our
metrical enjoyment in reading Pindar's verse is not illusory,
but real; only, without the melody we have not the full
reality.

It may be helpful to our modern appreciation of him to
know something of the ancient criticism and judgment of him.

The high fame that he acquired in his lifetime became
permanent and dominant soon after his death. Certain
echoes from his works that we may find in Aeschylus may
be due to direct literary fellowship. But as we find a parody
in Aristophanes of one of his poems to Hieron, we may
conclude that some of his odes at least were in circulation
at Athens before the end of the fifth century: whether
Pindar or his executors published a collection of his odes
we have no record, but can only conjecture. But it is obvious
that they were generally known to the literary world early
in the fourth century B.C. Evidently Plato had read him
freely, for he quotes him as a moral authority, and he
speaks reverently of Pindar's views about life after death,
which he illustrates by the striking verses of "the Dirge"
that has been translated and discussed above.[2]

We may surmise that our poet was more congenial to
Plato than to Aristotle; who in his treatise on "The Art of
Poetry"—so far as it has been preserved—nowhere mentions

---

[1] He is ridiculed for it by Aristophanes in his *Frogs*, 1314.

[2] *Vide supra*, p. 334, Fr. 133.

him; although he must have read some of his works at
least, for twice elsewhere he quotes him without any comment. We may here suspect a certain dullness of sense in
the great scientist; for he seems to have been equally in-
different to Pindar's brother-poet, Aeschylus. If the stories
of later *littérateurs* can be trusted, his warmest admirer in
the fourth century was Alexander the Great, whose only
poets were said to be Homer and Pindar, the latter "because
of the magnificence of his nature", and who when he cruelly
sacked Thebes took special care to spare Pindar's house.[1]

But the final and complete collection of all his works and
the arrangement of them that has handed down to us the
epinician odes was first made after Alexander's death, by
the scholars who were attracted to Alexandria by Ptolemy's
great library. They were probably helped by some pre-
existing literary publication of part at least of the poems;
for others they may have had to make sporadic and extensive search through the cities and temples of the Greek-
speaking world, that may have been the sole depositaries
of certain odes. It is these scholars who have preserved to
us all that we have of Pindar; and although the legacy that
they wished to hand down has been woefully diminished,
our debt to them is immense; and we are further indebted
to them from some useful commentaries on his text. It is
they also who assigned to him his place of supremacy in
the galaxy of Greek lyric poets.

Looking through the last period of Greek literature before
the Roman domination, we find some evidence of the literary
appreciation of him in three epigrams of the Greek An-
thology: two of them lay the stress on his trumpet-tones,
"As the trumpet rings out above the flutes, so does thy lyre
above all others"; and the other speaks of "the great voice
that rang out from Thebes", contrasting it with "the sweet-
breathing muse of the honey-voiced Simonides" and with
"the babbling siren"—their apt *sobriquet* for Bacchulides.
More subtle appreciation of his strange style is shown by
a phrase in one of them, "the heavy forger of holy hymns",
describing him as a heavy-handed Smith-God working
molten metal on a hot anvil: the phrase might have been
suggested by the style of such a passage as the volcanic
eruption in the first Pythian.

[1] These legends are of some value as suggesting a sense of the affinity in
their different spheres between the daring poet and the world-conqueror.

The references to him in the later grammarians, rhetoricians, and men of letters are not infrequent, but only a few are helpful. An industrious but uninspired writer of the beginning of our era, Dionysius of Halikarnassos, classes him with Aeschylus as an ideal example of the austere style, and speaks of his archaic roughness in the setting of his words as a source of power in him; in another passage he well contrasts the majestic pathos of Pindar with the soft emotional pathos of Simonides: to appreciate the truth of this one need only compare Pindar's "dying Kastor" in the tenth Nemean with Simonides' beautiful fragment on Danaë and her babe floating in the chest.

More important is an appreciation which we find in a treatise "concerning the Sublime", of uncertain authorship and date, though we generally call the author 'Longinus', in some ways the most striking work on style that classic antiquity has left us: "in the impetuous rush of his verse at times Pindar lights up all about him as with a fire; but he is often strangely extinguished and fails most unhappily". He does not indicate to what his censure refers; he may have been thinking of some of Pindar's strained phrases and metaphors, on which the critical Galen is also severe. (Ancient critics were more intolerant than the modern in respect of metaphors, and would have severely censured Shakespeare.) But 'Longinus' redeems himself at once by asking: "Nevertheless would you rather be Bacchulides or Pindar?"—that is to say, it is better to sin with the great than to be faultless with the mediocre. And elsewhere, to prove that we are more moved by grandeur and Titanic power than by faultlessness, he contrasts the conflagration of Etna with the neat glitter of a domestic fire, using language vaguely reminiscent of Pindar's.

It is interesting, also, to find a warm appreciation of Pindar in Rome's greatest master of prose-style and in one of Rome's greatest poets, Cicero and Horace. In two passages Cicero sets Pindar on the heights with other luminaries of the world; and one contains an assertion, that might be helpful for a modern philosophy of art, that the great poets, Homer, Archilochos, Pindar, Sophokles, like the great sculptors Pheidias and Polukleitos, aimed at something higher in their works than merely to give pleasure.[1] But antiquity has left us no judgment so memorable as that

[1] *De Finibus* ii. 34.

contained in the well-known verses of Horace; and the
verdict of one great poet on another has always a special
value: Pindar is inimitable, he is the tempestuous flood
rolling down the mountain-side bearing all before it: he is
the daring inventor of new diction, and is carried along
in metres that are under no restraint of law: he is the swan
that soars safely through the highest tract of clouds.[1] Some
part of the real Pindar appears in these lines, but not all;
Horace had evidently read his various works, but was not
able to understand the subtle laws of his versification; and
one does not see why among bird-types he selected the
swan; for the true Pindaric bird was the eagle, as Pindar
was aware himself; and Gray, in his famous lines on the

> "Ample pinion
> That the Theban eagle bare,
>   Sailing with supreme dominion
> Through the azure deep of air",

is reminiscent both of Pindar and of Horace.

The later rhetoricians of the Empire quote him and speak
of him with the conventional phrases of the school-book;
but the last writer of genius in classical antiquity, Lucian,
mentions him frequently and always with enthusiasm.

It is probable that all through antiquity he was deeply
studied and revered only by the *élite*: both his themes and
his diction became more and more alien to the general
public.

The four books of our odes were preserved in obscurity
through the dark ages, and were brought to light and made
accessible to Western Europe after the fall of Constanti-
nople. But it was long before the Western scholars could
rise to the true appreciation and interpretation of them.
In the learned world of the Elizabethan period, even in
such a scholar as Buchanan of Scotland, I am not aware
of any evidence that Pindar was read; nor have I found
any clear trace of his influence on Milton, learned as he
was in Greek literature.[2] The first voice in England that
speaks from genuine experience of his greatness is the poet
Gray's, in the lines quoted above, showing that he knew

---

[1] Odes iv. 2.

[2] In *Paradise Lost*, Book viii. l. 173, "be lowly wise", etc., there may
seem to be an echo of a thought expressed by Pindar; but it will be an
unconscious coincidence.

and concurred in Pindar's own judgment of himself. They are in pleasant contrast with some verses quoted by Wilamowitz[1] from Voltaire, which throw an unfortunate light on contemporary knowledge of the classics in France: they form the beginning of a 'Pindaric' ode to Catherine of Russia:

> Sors du tombeau, divin Pindare,
> Toi qui célébras autrefois
> Les chevaux de quelques bourgeois
> Ou de Corinthe ou de Mégare:
> Toi qui possèdes le talent
> De parler beaucoup sans rien dire,
> Toi qui modulas savamment
> Des vers que personne n'entend
> Et qu'il faut toujours qu'on admire.

That such foolish slander of greatness is not possible anywhere now is greatly due to the praiseworthy efforts of German scholarship at the end of the eighteenth and beginning of the nineteenth century. The scholars of other countries have played their part; but it is still a German scholar, Wilamowitz von Moellendorff, the most brilliant Hellenist of his nation, who has written best in recent times on Pindar's life and work; and he closes his treatise with an eloquent tribute, declaring that the poet constrains first our admiration, then our love, and that the longer we live with him the greater is his hold upon us.[2]

Having had the same experience in long years of study, I will pay the same tribute and testify that it is good to have lived long with Pindar: one's soul is brightened and strengthened by the intercourse. To help others to this privilege, if one can, is sufficient reward for much toil.

---

[1] *Pindaros*, p. 5. [2] *Pindaros*, p. 463.

END OF VOL. I

LIST OF COINS

Printed in Great Britain by R. & R. CLARK, LIMITED, *Edinburgh.*

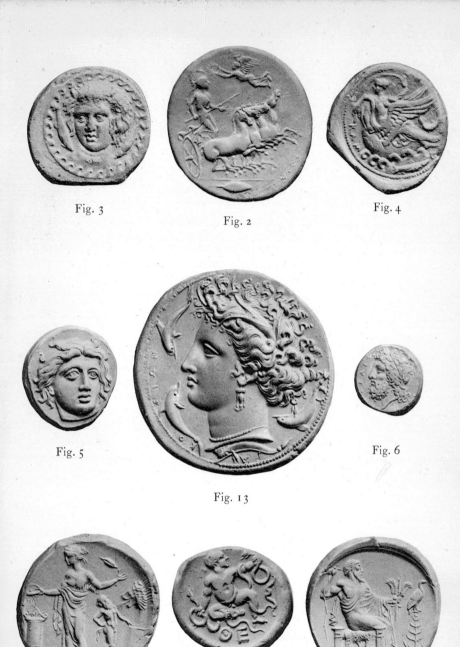

Fig. 3

Fig. 2

Fig. 4

Fig. 5

Fig. 13

Fig. 6

Fig. 7

Fig. 14

Fig. 8

Enlarged by one-half